Internet Programming with Visual Basic

BUDI KURNIAWAN

```
Internet Programming with Visual Basic
Copyright © 2000 by Budi Kurniawan
```

ISBN (pbk): 1-893115-75-5

Printed and bound in the United States of America 12345678910

Technical Reviewer: Don Kiely
Editors: Anne Marie Walker, Nancy Delfavero
Production Services and Page Composition: Impressions Book and Journal Services, Inc.
Cover and Interior Design: Derek Yee Design

Distributed to the book trade in the United States by Springer-Verlag New York, Inc., 175 Fifth Avenue, New York, New York, 10010
and outside the United States by Springer-Verlag GmbH & Co. KG, Tiergartenstr. 17, 69112 Heidelberg, Germany

In the United States, phone 1-800-SPRINGER; orders@springer-ny.com; www.springer-ny.com
Outside the United States, contact orders@springer.de; www.springer.de; fax +49 6221 345229

For information on translations, please contact Apress directly at 901 Grayson Street, Suite 204, Berkeley, California, 94710
Phone: 510-549-5930; Fax: 510-549-5939; info@apress.com; www.apress.com

Dedication

To my parents

Hans Kurniawan and Lily Kurniawaty

Acknowledgments

My name may be the only one that appears on the cover of this book. However, credits are owed to so many people who contributed to the design, production, and completion of this book. My thanks go to these people:

Daniel Appleman and Gary Cornell from Apress who gave me the opportunity to write this book. Thanks also for making me feel as if Apress really is the author's publisher.

Don Kiely, who did the technical review, for his expertise and for pointing out what could be better with more and more research. Don made this a much better book than it would have been, by giving me what is known in politics as "constructive criticism."

Copy editors Anne Marie Walker and Nancy Delfavero for a wonderful job correcting tons and tons of grammatical mistakes. Thanks to them, this book is indeed more readable and enjoyable. All mistakes left are mine.

Impressions Book and Journal Services, Inc., for the polishing touch with the layout and the focus on detail.

And of course, Grace Wong, the project manager, for putting every single piece together. Indeed, without Grace, this book would have never happened. Thank you for saying that one day all the chapters would stop coming back. You've kept your promise.

Budi

Contents at a Glance

Contents

Introduction

VISUAL BASIC (VB) 6 INTRODUCED A NEW WAY of creating robust and scalable Internet applications. With a new technology called the Internet Information Server (IIS) application (also known as the WebClass technology), millions of developers can now use the world's easiest and most popular programming language for writing WebClasses that glue together all the elements of an Internet application.

Creating Internet applications with VB is not much different from developing other types of projects. If you are a VB developer with no experience in building an Internet application, you'll be surprised by the similarity between IIS applications and traditional form-based VB applications. Not only can you use the sophisticated debugging tools that come with the VB Integrated Development Environment, you will also find the familiar error handling and the usual wizards that can help you create the skeletons of your projects and save you a lot of coding time. In short, you will feel comfortably at home.

If you are familiar with Microsoft scripting technology Active Server Pages (ASP), you will find the IIS application a nice enhancement that is easier to write. IIS applications utilize all the ASP objects that ship with IIS, but all your business rules are now located in compiled objects. As a result, IIS applications are much faster and more scalable than interpreted ASP applications.

This book is an easy-to-understand guide to building a browser-independent Internet application using Visual Basic. Examples are abundant to help make learning as quick as possible. Nevertheless, the coverage is of sufficient depth to make you, the reader, an expert in IIS applications.

Following is an overview of each chapter:

Chapter 1, The Internet Information Server (IIS) Application: This chapter reviews the major technologies for Internet development using Microsoft products. It presents performance comparisons among the existing Microsoft Internet technologies and highlights why the IIS application is the optimum choice.

Chapter 2, The WebClass and the WebItem: This chapter introduces you to the concept of IIS applications and shows you how to build your first IIS application. WebClasses, the WebItem, and virtual directories are among the topics discussed. More important, in this chapter you can also discover how to create your first browser-independent dynamic content.

Chapter 3, Working with ASP Objects: IIS applications are based on the ASP objects that come with IIS. Understanding the role of each ASP object is of utmost importance. This chapter covers each ASP object and demonstrates how to use them in your code.

Chapter 4, Accessing Databases: This chapter discusses how to connect to the database to manipulate data. It starts with introducing ODBC and how to set up a Data Source Name connection with the database server of your choice. In this chapter, you can also learn about Microsoft's Universal Data Access strategy for managing a database.

Chapter 5, Database Access Optimization: This is where you can find various database optimization techniques. Because database manipulation plays an important role in the scalability of an Internet application, you have compelling reasons to manipulate your data in the most efficient way. Speed is not the only factor that matters, however. You sometimes need to compromise speed for other factors such as user friendliness and code maintainability. This chapter gives you all the options to make the best application that suits your need.

Chapter 6, Client-side Processing: This chapter covers client-side processing, an important topic because moving some of the processing from the server to the client browser will reduce the server workload and result in faster response to your Internet clients. If your IIS application targets a large audience with various browsers, then your best choice is to use JavaScript for client-side processing. This chapter introduces the basics of JavaScript and presents useful JavaScript functions that are ready to use in your code.

Chapter 7, State Management: HTTP is a stateless protocol, which means Internet applications cannot remember previous user requests. For example, there is no way to determine whether a client is visiting your Web site for the first time or the same user has requested pages for the tenth time in five minutes. This chapter introduces you the concept of sessions and how to manage state using the URLData property, Session object, database, cookies, and hidden fields.

Chapter 8, File Uploading: This chapter covers file uploading, that is, how to upload binary and text files from the browser to the Web server. File uploading is especially useful when building a Web-based e-mail application or any other application that requires you to provide file uploading through HTTP. Once received by the server, a file that is uploaded can then be stored in the database or as a normal file. This chapter also provides a reference on the HTTP request, a key element that a VB developer needs to understand in order to do file uploading.

Chapter 9, Working with E-mail: This chapter demonstrates how to send and receive e-mails with just a few lines of code, and also provides code for handling attachments. Combined with the instruction on file uploading in Chapter 8, you can build a full-blown Web-based e-mail system such as Hotmail or Yahoo Mail.

Chapter 10, Securing Your Server: Security is an important topic and every programmer should always be aware of security issues. While a discussion of computer security could fill a book of its own, this chapter covers the topics most important to IIS applications, such as how to use NT and IIS security and as how to install certificates to enable SSL for secure transactions.

Chapter 11, Installable Components: The ASP team at Microsoft has written quite a few COM components to be used in ASP applications. Known as *installable* components, these ready-to-use components can be useful in IIS applications and save you hours of coding. This chapter lists all the installable components plus all the properties and methods of each component. This chapter also discusses when to use installable components and when to create your own components.

Chapter 12, Deploying Your IIS Application: Deployment is not an easy business. With their jungle of DLL files that need to be included in each installation, Windows applications often confuse even the most seasoned programmers. When deploying an IIS application, you must know for sure which files must be included in the deployment package and which files must be registered on the server. This chapter shows you how to use the Package and Deployment Wizard that can assist you with the deployment and installation process.

NOTE *To try out the examples in this book, you can download the code listings from the publisher's Web site at* www.apress.com.

CHAPTER 1

The Internet Information Server (IIS) Application

THE RATE AT WHICH COMPUTER SCIENCE IS GROWING IS probably tiring for computer programmers who must stay on top of cutting-edge technology. Keeping up with changes in this field is more than a full-time job. Usually, you purchase a book on a new programming topic and immediately hear that another new technology has surfaced. This is especially true concerning the Internet. Technologies emerge faster than anyone can truly master.

If you are an Internet programmer or are learning to become one, you have to choose the technology you want to specialize in, but never stop watching for the new ones. When a new technology starts to become the dominant player and the one you are specializing in is in infirmity, you should be ready to climb on the new bandwagon. For example, at one time, Common Gateway Interface (CGI) was the main technology of the Internet. It is still being used, but better technologies have been invented and CGI is no longer everyone's favorite.

However, while the entire Internet industry becomes more dynamic every day, the basics remain static, so it is not too difficult to adapt to a new technology regardless of how loud the propaganda is. HTTP (currently at version 1.1) is still the protocol used and HTML (at version 4) is still the language used for content presentation on Web pages.

How Does the Internet Work?

When you surf the Internet, you basically ask for certain files located in a particular computer in a given location where those files are stored. In a typical Web site, the computer where the files are stored is expected to be up and running all the time, and its main job is to serve anyone who requests a file. Not surprisingly, this computer is called a server, more precisely: a Web server. The file returned by the Web server is displayed in the user's Web browser. Note that the term Web server can be used to refer to the computer or to the software package that is used in the Web server computer.

For this whole process of requesting a file and sending a file to happen, both the server and the user (called the client) must have a valid Internet address. The server address is something like `http://www.apress.com` or another type of Internet address. The client address depends on where the user accesses the Internet. When you connect to the Internet through an Internet Service Provider (ISP), for example, you are given a temporary Internet address, so the server knows where to send the requested file. When you are connected through your corporate LAN, you could have a fixed IP address or you could be given a temporary IP address also.

When you click or type in a URL, the following process happens:

- The browser connects to the server.

- The browser requests a file.

- The server responds by sending the requested page to the browser, and then closes the connection.

Of course, a connection to the server can only be established if the server is running and is not too busy serving other requests.

What happens after the server sends the requested file depends on the user. The user can just close the browser and walk away or request another file from the server. However, when the server is connected for the second time, it cannot tell whether it is the second request from the same user or a first request from some other user.

The fact that the server cannot remember users who have previously requested pages has a deep impact on how an Internet application is developed. Programmers who are used to the conventional client/server programming might find it confusing at first to figure out how an Internet application works. For now, just keep this information in mind. Further discussion on this issue will be found in Chapter 7.

The architecture of an Internet application is shown in Figure 1-1.

Also keep in mind that the server does not serve only one user. For an Internet application, anyone connected to the Internet can request a page from the server. At times, in popular Web sites, thousands of requests come in simultaneously. And, if you are running a corporate intranet application, everyone with access can request a page. Therefore, it is very important for the Web application to be as efficient as possible.

The Available Technologies

In the software industry, including Web technology, Microsoft products seem to be more and more dominant. As far as Web technology is concerned, Microsoft

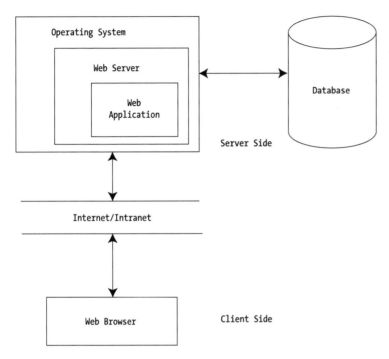

Figure 1-1. Web application architecture

provides a total solution. You can use Microsoft products exclusively to deliver a scalable Web solution. If you decide to do so, choosing each component in the system is easy because Microsoft products don't compete with each other. It is almost certain that you will choose Windows NT or Windows 2000 Server for your operating system, IIS as your Web server, SQL Server for your database server, and Component Object Model (COM) technology as your developing framework. The good news is, if you have been using a Microsoft compiler, you won't need to change the programming language.

On the other hand, if you are more inclined toward other products and vendors, your choice is more varied. Getting the right combination of products is often a political issue, not to mention that there is always a risk of incompatibility between products from different manufacturers. A typical Web solution without Microsoft presence could include a Unix or Linux operating system; an Apache (still the most popular today) or a Java Web server; a MySQL, Oracle, Informix, Sybase, or other database; and PERL or PHP or Java as your language of choice.

However, because you have chosen this book from the shelf, chances are you are using Microsoft products. If you are new to Microsoft's Internet technologies, please read the next section. It describes the existing technologies and the position of each.

The Facts about Microsoft Internet Technologies

Before the arrival of the IIS applications technology in Visual Basic, there were and still are three types of Web applications in use that can run using IIS. They are Common Gateway Interface (CGI), Internet Server Application Programming Interface (ISAPI), and Active Server Pages (ASP).

CGI is easy to program and is the slowest Web technology available on the Windows platform. In Windows operating systems, the Web server creates a separate process for each HTTP request and communicates with the process through environment variables and standard input (`stdin`) and standard output (`stdout`) streams. If 1,000 clients access a CGI application at the same time, the server creates 1,000 instances of the CGI application to handle the requests. Each instance requires its own memory space and system resources.

Because process creation and interprocess communication are time and resource consuming operations, it's not surprising that a CGI application is the slowest compared with other available technologies. CGI applications are usually implemented as a C/C++ executable or with a scripting language like PERL. The output of a CGI application is generated using the basic output functions of the language, for example, `printf` in C. CGI programs are not as bad in Unix, which is designed to handle multiple processes with very little overhead.

ISAPI is the fastest among the three applications and was developed specifically for IIS as a high-performance Windows alternative to CGI. ISAPI is an API for developing extensions to the IIS server and other HTTP servers that support the ISAPI interface. Compiled as a runtime dynamic link library (DLL) file, the ISAPI model reduces the overhead required by multiple requests because only one DLL is needed for multiple requests.

The first time an ISAPI DLL is requested, the server loads it into memory. Unless the Web server is shut down, the DLL stays in memory waiting for another request. Therefore, there is no overhead for process creation after the first request. Furthermore, ISAPI applications run in the same address space as the Web server and have access to all the same resources. There is no need for interprocess communication. However, ISAPI applications development is also the hardest, requiring implementation using C++/MFC. This factor alone deters many from selecting this solution.

There is also a maintenance problem with ISAPI. Even a minor change requires a recompile and relink of the ISAPI application. Also, an ISAPI DLL can cause the Web server to crash if it is not thoroughly tested before being deployed and run in the Web server process. Fortunately, with IIS 4.0 and later, you can select to run ISAPI DLLs in separate processes, with performance being sacrificed of course. Note that ISAPI applications are not the same as ISAPI filters, which are DLLs that allow preprocessing of requests and postprocessing of responses for site-specific handling of HTTP requests and responses.

ASP is certainly the current star. Introduced as part of IIS 3.0, its benefits are in the simplicity of the available scripting languages, and you get performance that is much more superior than that of a CGI application.

When IIS receives a request for a file with an .asp extension, IIS passes it to ASP.DLL, the scripting engine that is an ISAPI application. Because ASP must interpret and compile scripts before executing them, complex scripts can be four times slower than plain HTML and two to three times slower than ISAPI *on the first request*. Afterward, the compiled version of the page is cached in server memory, making subsequent requests substantially faster.

ASP is not limited to a particular programming language. VBScript and JScript are the two most commonly used languages to create ASP scripts. However, any language for which a third-party ActiveX scripting engine is available can also be used. This includes PerlScript, REXX, and Python. You can even use more than one scripting language on a single ASP page, even though this is not a recommended practice because doing so will make processing slower. ASP applications often include custom ActiveX components that are called from ASP pages to enhance scalability.

To get a feel of how each type of application rates as compared with another, Table 1-1 summarizes a test result of the three types of applications in three types of operations: DataGrab, GetObject, and ServerVars.

In the DataGrab operation, the applications pull data from a database using a database-access COM component written in Visual Basic. The component object provides a method that can be used to connect to a small Access database, send an SQL query string, and return the query result. Unfortunately, there is no result for CGI for this category.

The GetObject operation includes instantiating a simple COM component, calling a method provided by that COM component, and sending the result of the call to the client.

In the third operation, the ServerVars, each application accesses 18 server variables and sends the result to the client.

The test was undertaken using the Microsoft Web Capacity Analysis Tool (WCAT) that can be found on the IIS Resource Kit CD. This tool runs simulated workloads on client/server configurations to allow you to test how IIS and your network configuration respond to a variety of different client requests.

The tests whose results are given in Table 1-1 were run with five clients, each running 20 threads for a total of 100 virtual clients. The virtual clients fired requests at the server and recorded how many of the requests were served, in other words, how many pages per second the server was able to serve. The CGI application was PERL scripts run by PERL for Win32. The numbers in the table are relative figures, where higher figures reflect better performance. For example, the ISAPI application is nearly three times faster than ASP in the ServerVars operation.

Table 1-1. Relative Performance of Dynamic Pages in Different Technologies*

	ISAPI	ASP	CGI
DataGrab	69.37	57.19	N/A
GetObject	209.14	169.64	1
ServerVars	560.07	195.97	33.16

*From *Microsoft Internet Information Server Resource Kit*, Microsoft Press, pages 59–61, 1998, Chapter 3. A dozen writers contributed to this work; the contributing writer for Chapter 3 was Jon Singer.

Where Does the IIS Application Stand?

The IIS application is the most recent Internet technology from Microsoft that ships with Visual Basic 6 and later. When you create an IIS application with VB, you create classes that resemble classes in other VB projects. These classes in IIS applications are called WebClasses. The technology that the IIS application is based on is also known as the WebClass technology.

An IIS application is a Visual Basic application that resides on a Web server and responds to requests from Web browsers. An IIS application sends plain text to the client-side to present its user interface, therefore you have a great deal of flexibility. You can send standard HTML tags to make your IIS application browser independent, or, if the project requirement says so, you can send output to cater to a specific browser.

To the user, an IIS application appears to be made up of a series of HTML pages. To the developer, an IIS application is made up of a special type of object called a WebClass. This WebClass in turn contains a series of resources called WebItems. The WebClass acts as the central functional unit of the application, processing data from the browser and sending information to the users.

At a glance, an IIS application looks very similar to ASP. However, the IIS application was conceived after the delivery of ASP. Therefore, it was designed to overcome the disadvantages that are inherent to ASP. Despite its popularity, ASP has the following disadvantages:

1. You use VBScript, JScript, or other scripting languages. All are interpreted languages, and interpreted languages are slower than compiled languages. Scripts are also less likely to scale well to large numbers of users.

2. With ASP, people can see your code once they get access to the server. In most cases this is not a big deal, unless of course you have invented a new algorithm for generating random numbers. Even though code encryption is supported in the new version of ASP, version 3, the method used is still very weak and can be easily cracked.

3. For long pages, it's very hard to differentiate code from HTML tags. Undifferentiated script scatters business logic throughout the application, making it hard to find bugs and increasing the cost of maintenance.

4. Scripts are not as reusable as classes.

5. Some Windows functionality is beyond ASP's reach without the help of COM components. This includes accessing the Registry, issuing a shell command, and so on.

ASP developers usually try to overcome these weaknesses by using components. If you are an expert ASP developer, you must be familiar with the motto: the less script, the better, to create a scalable ASP application. It is therefore understandable that IIS applications, which can be regarded as 100 percent component-based solutions, are considered better ASP. An IIS application overcomes the disadvantages of ASP by possessing the following characteristics:

1. It is a compiled application created using Visual Basic 6 or later. Thus, it is faster.

2. Only you can see the source code, so privacy and copyright are relatively secure.

3. There is a separation between the code and the presentation layer.

4. WebClasses are reusable.

5. An IIS application is a VB application, therefore it enjoys all the benefits that a VB application has.

The only advantage of ASP over IIS applications is the fact that simple ASP applications that consist only of pages can be hosted in an external ISP. ISPs normally do not allow you to install custom components on their server for security and other reasons. They can't afford to have their server down simply because one of the users' components crashes, bringing down other people's innocent applications.

How Fast Is an IIS Application Compared with ASP?

After having stated that IIS applications are better than ASP, let me present further performance results. I tested three types of operations: Server Variables 1, Server Variables 2, and Database Access. For each type, an ASP application and an IIS application were written, and the code for the ASP page and the WebClass was basically the same.

In all of the ASP pages, no COM component was used. Each category of operation was performed five times for each application, and the results were averaged. VB's Timer function was used to measure performance. The Timer function returns a number representing the number of seconds elapsed since midnight. The precision is to a hundredth of a second.

The function was invoked twice, once at the beginning of the process and once at the end of it. By subtracting the first number from the second one, the result of how long (in hundredths of a second) it takes the Web server to complete the process is obtained. The results are summarized in Tables 1-2a and 1-2b. The code for each application and the complete testing procedure are given in Appendix F.

In Server Variables 1, both applications read 16 server variables and sent them to the browser. Server Variables 2 was similar to Server Variables 1, but the process was repeated 100 times. Server Variables 2 was conducted because Server Variables 1 was too easy for the IIS application. As a result, the two Timer function invocations resulted in the same number, which provides assurance that the process took less than 10 milliseconds. I then had two options: go to the museum to borrow a much slower machine or give my CPU some extra work doing the same function in a loop. I chose the latter, which was more practical. This was implemented as Server Variables 2.

Why didn't I drop Server Variables 1? At first I was tempted to do so, but then I realized that it might also be useful to compare performance for very simple operations, such as Server Variables 1. This, at least, wiped out the suspicion that ASP applications might be more superior in small applications.

Table 1-2a. Test Results for ASP Applications

	TEST 1	TEST 2	TEST 3	TEST 4	TEST 5	AVERAGE
Server Variables 1	0.06s	0.06s	0.06s	0.00s	0.05s	**0.046s**
Server Variables 2	5.05s	4.28s	3.85s	4.01s	4.07s	**4.252s**
Database Access	4.33s	4.45s	4.77s	4.72s	4.78s	**4.61s**

Table 1-2b. Test Results for IIS Applications

	TEST 1	TEST 2	TEST 3	TEST 4	TEST 5	AVERAGE
Server Variables 1	0.00s	0.00s	0.00s	0.00s	0.00s	**0.00s**
Server Variables 2	0.16s	0.16s	0.16s	0.16s	0.16s	**0.16s**
Database Access	4.01s	3.57s	3.35s	3.39s	3.68s	**3.60s**

The third test, Database Access, performed three database operations: Insert, Select, and Delete. It first inserted 300 records into an empty Access database table, and then selected all the records and displayed them in an HTML page before deleting all the records.

The results show that for Server Variables 2, on average, it took 4.252 seconds for the ASP application and 0.16 seconds for the IIS application. The IIS application is about 27 times faster than the ASP application in this category. In Database Access, however, the performance difference is not that obvious. This is understandable because most of its time was spent on opening and establishing the connection, and then waiting for the database engine to perform the database operations.

Please note that the results of this experiment have no relation to the results presented in Table 1-1 because the tools used and the environment were different.

Comparison with Form-based VB Applications

IIS applications are also different from traditional form-based Visual Basic applications. In an IIS application, the user interface consists of a series of HTML pages rather than traditional Visual Basic forms. An HTML page is like a form in that it contains all the visual elements that make up the application's user interface.

An HTML page referenced in an IIS application is saved to an .htm file, which is analogous to a .frm file in that it is used to render and display the page to the end user. Also, in an IIS application, you don't use VB to create the HTML pages that makes up the application's user interface. A Web graphic designer creates the

Table 1-3. A Comparison between IIS Applications and Form-based VB Applications

	FORM-BASED VB APPLICATIONS	IIS APPLICATIONS
User interface	VB forms	HTML pages
User interface elements	Controls	HTML elements*
File format	.frm files	.htm or .html files
Creator	Developer	Developer with artistic skill or Web graphic designer
Run time	VB runtime on both the client- and the server-sides	Web browser on the client-side and IIS, ASP engine and WebClass runtime on the server-side

*You could embed Java applets or ActiveX controls in your HTML pages, but they are beyond the scope of this book.

pages using an HTML authoring program. Table 1-3 summarizes the difference between form-based applications and IIS applications.

The Structure of IIS Applications

An IIS application consists of the following parts:

- One or more WebClasses that are generated automatically when the IIS application project is created.

- Zero or more HTML templates and their events.

- Zero or more custom WebItems and their events.

- An .asp file used to host the WebClass in IIS. This file is generated automatically when you compile or run a WebClass project.

- A WebClass runtime component, MSWCRUN.DLL, that helps process requests.

- A project DLL that contains your VB code and is accessed by the runtime component.

The structure is best illustrated by Figure 1-2.

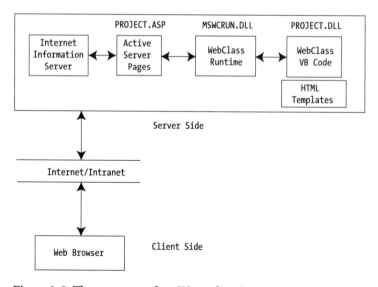

Figure 1-2. The structure of an IIS application

Software Requirements for the Development Computer

To create and test an IIS application, you need to have a Web browser and a Web server installed on your development computer. You can use any of the combinations in Table 1-4 for development purposes only.

IIS 5.0 is installed on Windows 2000 Server by default. The Web servers for Windows NT Server 4.0 and Windows NT Workstation 4.0 can be found in the Option Pack 4.0 CD. If you are using Windows 98, you must install the Virtual Private Network (VPN) to install Personal Web Server.

Web Server Administration

If you are using the Personal Web Server, you use the Personal Web Manager to administer your site. What you can do as an administrator is quite limited compared to the functions available when using IIS. To display the Personal Web Manager, select Start ➔ Programs ➔ Internet Explorer ➔ Personal Web Server ➔ Personal Web Manager. Your screen should look like Figure 1-3.

If you are using Window NT 4.0, there are two tools you can use to administer IIS. The first is Internet Service Manager, which is hosted in the Microsoft Management Console (MMC) and can be administered within a local area network (LAN). The second tool, Internet Service Manager (HTML), can be accessed remotely using a Web browser from an intranet or the Internet.

Internet Service Manager uses a Web site listed as Administration Web Site to access IIS properties. When IIS is installed, a port number between 2,000 and 9,999 is randomly selected and assigned to this Web site for security reasons. On another machine, other than the machine that hosts IIS, you can only access this site if you know the port number and append it to the URL.

Configuration options for both tools are the same with exceptions in some logging and security features.

To start Internet Service Manager, select Start ➔ Programs ➔ Windows NT 4.0 Option Pack ➔ Microsoft Internet Information Server ➔ Internet Service Manager.

Table 1-4. Software Requirements for Developing IIS Applications

OPERATING SYSTEM	WEB SERVER
Windows 2000 Server	Internet Information Server 3.0 or later with ASP
Windows NT Server 4.0	Internet Information Server 3.0 or later with ASP
Windows NT Workstation 4.0	Peer Web Services 3.0 or later with ASP
Windows 95 or Windows 98 or later	Personal Web Server 3.0 or later with ASP

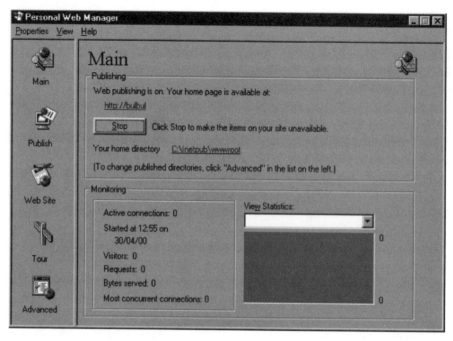

Figure 1-3. Personal Web Manager

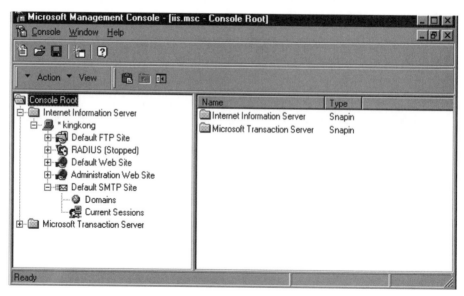

Figure 1-4. Microsoft Management Console in Windows NT 4.0

To start Internet Service Manager (HTML), select Start → Programs → Windows NT 4.0 Option Pack → Microsoft Internet Information Server → Internet Service Manager (HTML). To use it remotely, you need to type the domain name and the assigned port number for the Administration Web Site, for example, `http://www.apress.com:9869`.

When using the Internet Service Manager (non-HTML version), the MMC is invoked and looks similar to Figure 1-4.

In Windows 2000 Server, Internet Service Manager is called Internet Information Services snap-in. Hosted in the MMC, the IIS snap-in has been integrated with other administrative functions of Windows 2000. Internet Information Server is now called Internet Information Service, and Default SMTP Site has become Default SMTP Virtual Server.

The Internet Service Manager (HTML version) is still available in Windows 2000 Server, however, you can no longer access it from the Start menu.

Where to Go from Here?

HTML is at the basis of every Web application. An understanding of HTML is therefore a mandatory preparation for anyone trying to build a Web application. This book provides a crash course and complete reference on HTML in Appendix A. Those unfamiliar with HTML should take a few minutes to look at Appendix A. Those who have been working with HTML should continue to Chapter 2 and refer to Appendix A when necessary for helpful reference.

The WebClass and the WebItem

THIS CHAPTER INTRODUCES YOU TO YOUR FIRST Internet Information Server (IIS) application and the concept behind WebClasses. Those who claim to be ASP (Active Server Pages) developers will recognize that WebClasses are more than ASP pages plus COM objects. Those familiar with traditional form-based Visual Basic (VB) applications will probably be struck by the similarities between the type of applications they are used to working with and this new genre. Both are heavily event-driven. Developers who are not in these two categories will find that an IIS application is very easy to develop. In fact, I would say that IIS applications are the easiest and fastest Web applications to build.

This chapter starts with a description of how to create an IIS application using the wizard in VB 6. The WebClass will naturally be the subsequent topic. It then digs deeper by discussing WebItems and events. A few sample applications will be created to demonstrate these topics. The chapter concludes with a brief note explaining which Web browsers to use in the development phase.

Creating Your First IIS Application

Visual Basic 6 provides a wizard that helps you create an IIS Application in three easy steps:

1. Double-click the VB icon on your desktop. If not previously disabled, the New Project window is displayed. If the window doesn't appear, select File ➔ New Project.

2. Scroll down until you see the IIS Application icon and click on it, as shown in the Figure 2-1.

3. Click the Open button.

That's all it takes to create an IIS application.

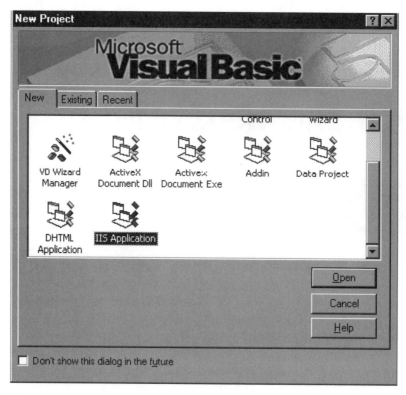

Figure 2-1. The IIS Application icon

By clicking the Open button, you actually start a wizard in VB, which tells VB to perform some magic. This wizard creates an IIS application of the simplest form. VB then displays a window similar to Figure 2-2.

Instead of a form, as in the traditional VB application, VB creates a WebClass. In the Project Explorer, which you can display at any time by pressing Ctrl+R, the WebClass is wrapped inside the Designers folder. In most cases, you only need one WebClass for each IIS application. However, there are times when your application requires more modularity and code reusability, in which case, the use of multiple WebClasses is more than justifiable. With multiple WebClasses in the same application, navigation between WebClasses is the main issue. This topic will be addressed in Chapter 3.

You can now run the new application. However, before you run the application, it is a good idea to save the project. When you save the project, there are two files you need to save: a .dsr file and a .vbp file. The .dsr file is the designer file that holds your code and other information contained in your WebClass. The .vbp file is the project file. You should save them both in the same directory. This directory will become your project directory, and you should only store files related to your project in this directory.

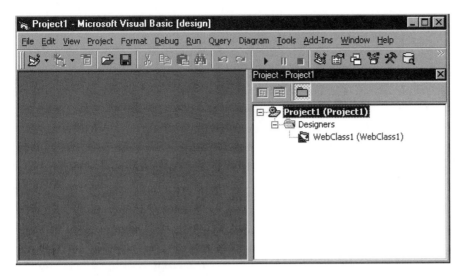

Figure 2-2. The Project Explorer for an IIS application

VB will also automatically create several files in the same directory. The .asp file is the one you should be most interested in. When end users want to access your IIS application, they will use a Web browser to call this .asp file. The Web browser, through the HTTP protocol, will tell the Web server that it wants the .asp file. The Web server then runs the .asp file, which in turn creates an instance of your WebClass.

Virtual Directories

If you are the type of person who is not satisfied with short explanations, you are probably wondering how the Web server finds the .asp file. Read on to find the answer.

When you install a Web server (in this case, IIS or its little brothers Personal Web Server and Peer Web Services), the wwwroot directory under the inetpub directory is the Web server home directory. If, let's say, the computer that hosts the Web server is called BigMomma and you put an HTML file called CompanySecrets.html in the wwwroot directory, you can use a Web browser to request the HTML file by typing **http://BigMomma/CompanySecrets.html** in the Web browser URL box.

Or if you are browsing from the same computer, you can just type **http://localhost/CompanySecrets.html** (or **localhost/CompanySecrets.html** as a shorter version). Accessed from the Internet, the URL will look something like **http://www.yourdomain.com/CompanySecrets.html**.

Like other home directories, a Web server home directory can also have sub-directories. In fact, a Web application (all sorts of Web applications including CGI, PERL, and ASP) will reside in one of the subdirectories, separating the application and all its components from other Web applications.

Therefore, if you have a Web application called DailyNews, you need to store all files that are part of your application in the DailyNews subdirectories under the wwwroot directory. This way, the Web server knows how to find your files when the user types a URL such as `http://www.yourdomain.com/DailyNews/MainPage.html` to access a file from the Internet, or `http://MachineName/DailyNews/MainPage.html` to access the file from an intranet.

Does this mean that you must create your IIS application project directory under the wwwroot directory? The answer is no and here's why. You can store your project files in any directory as long as you let the Web server know where they are. The directory containing your Web application files is often called a *virtual directory* or *virtual root*. A virtual directory, or virtual root, is a directory outside the Web server's home directory, which browsers identify as a subdirectory of the Web server home directory.

For each Web application, you can either store the application files in a subdirectory under the wwwroot directory or in a virtual directory. The latter is what VB chooses to use for an IIS application. With the creation of every IIS application, VB handles the details of creating a virtual directory for that application and reports the location of the new virtual directory to the Web server.

Running the Application

Similar to other VB applications, the quickest way to run an IIS application is by pressing F5. The first time you run the application, VB will prompt you to decide how the application will start (see Figure 2-3). Let the default settings stand and click OK.

If this is the first time the application is run, it will not yet have a virtual root. VB can take the initiative to create one and map it as a virtual directory. Nevertheless, VB requires that you type in the name of the virtual directory in the Create Virtual Directory dialog box that appears (see Figure 2-4).

Most people use the project name as the name of the virtual directory. However, there is no such rule that states you can't use another name. Because the virtual directory becomes part of the URL that your users have to type to get to your application, there is a compelling reason to use a name that's short, easy to remember, and not necessarily the project name.

After typing in an appropriate name for the virtual directory, click OK. An appropriate name means a name that consists of one word and doesn't contain punctuation marks that may wreak havoc with Web servers, such as "or !.

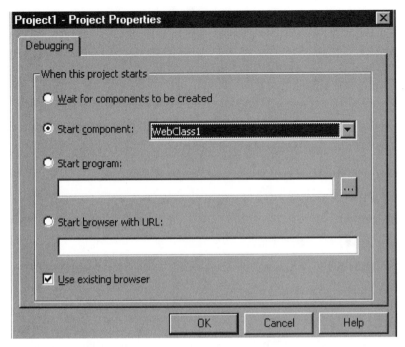

Figure 2-3. When the IIS Application is first run, you must decide how the application should start.

If you haven't saved the project, this new virtual root will be associated with the system's temporary directory, usually the C:\Temp directory. Therefore, you should always save your project before you run it for the first time.

Once you click the OK button, VB will do all the donkey work to bring the application into existence. It launches the default browser on your computer and displays your starting page (see Figure 2-5).

Take a look at the URL http://localhost/Bulbul/WebClass1.ASP. Because VB is running the application on the same computer where the Web server resides,

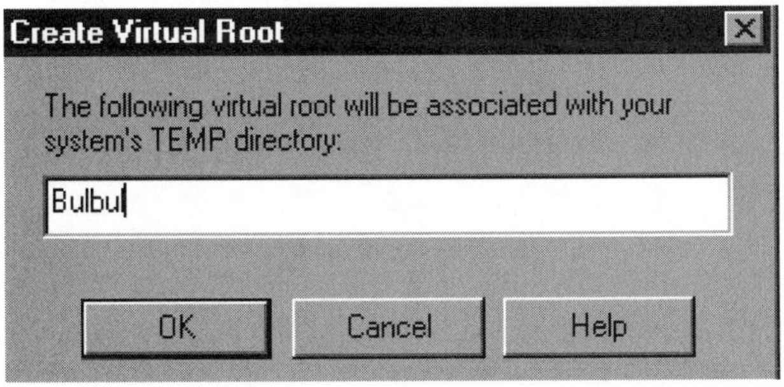

Figure 2-4. When first run, an IIS Application requires the name of the virtual directory.

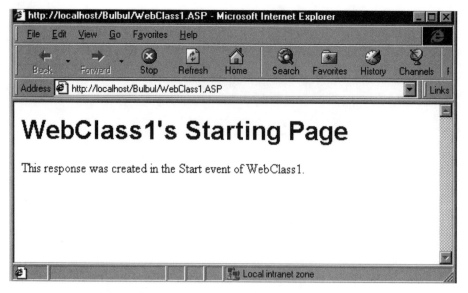

Figure 2-5. The starting page of a default IIS Application

the word localhost is associated with the computer name. Bulbul (named after my brown dog) is the Web application name, and WebClass1.ASP is the .asp file VB automatically created for this new project.

Every time you run your IIS application from the VB IDE the following events occur:

1. VB creates the global.asa and one .asp file for each WebClass in the project. Information about the global.asa file can be found in subsequent chapters, and the .asp file will be explained in the next section of this chapter.

2. VB compiles the WebClass and registers it to the Registry.

3. VB starts the Web browser and directs the Web browser to the .asp file that hosts the WebClass.

4. The .asp file creates an instance of the WebClass and passes the HTTP request to it.

5. The WebClass processes the request and sends the response back to the Web browser via the Web server.

When you stop your application, VB will also unregister your WebClass from the Registry and delete the global.asa and .asp files. Unless your operating system crashes when the IIS application is running, you probably wouldn't even realize that one global.asa file and at least one .asp file exists. However, you *can* see these files from Windows Explorer when the IIS application is running.

To better understand what happens behind the scenes, let's take a look at the Personal Web Manager.

1. Click the Advanced applet on the left side of the screen. Personal Web Server displays all applications inside the home directory (see Figure 2-6). If you cannot see your application, don't panic. Just scroll the window in the Virtual Directories frame.

2. Click the application directory, and then click Edit Properties.

The dialog box that appears shows the association between the physical directory where the project resides and the alias known to the Web server (see Figure 2-7). When the Web server receives a request for a page in a particular application, the Web server always searches for this association to determine the physical location of the file. Note that in this example the project directory is not under the wwwroot directory.

If you are using IIS, open the Internet Services Manager Microsoft Management Console (MMC), and you should see your virtual directory under Default

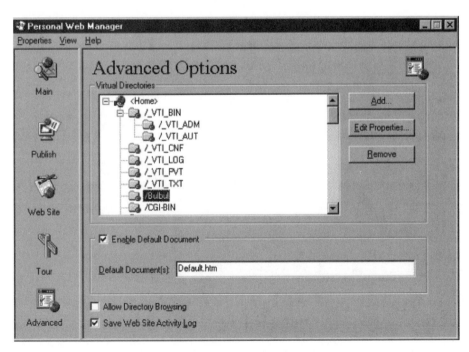

Figure 2-6. The virtual directories in the Personal Web Manager

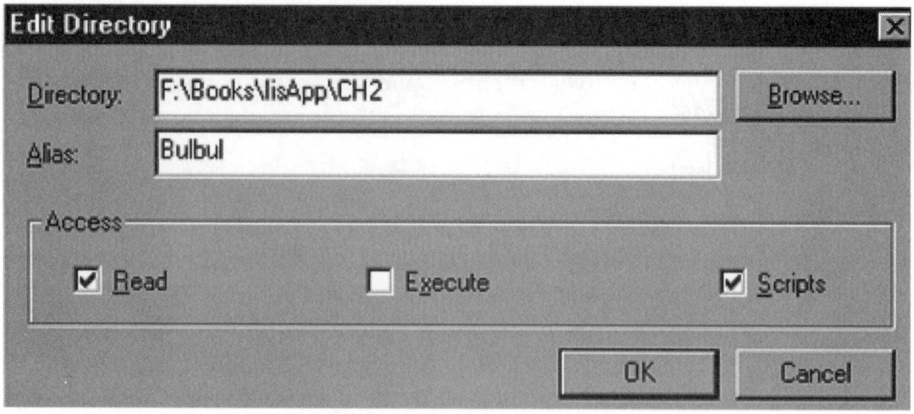

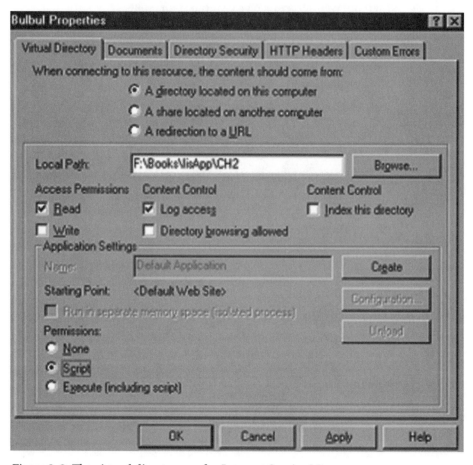

Figure 2-7. The Edit Directory dialog in Personal Web Manager

Figure 2-8. The virtual directory under Internet Service Manager

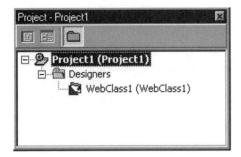

Figure 2-9. The WebClass icon in the Project Explorer

Web Site. Right-click the icon and click Properties. The dialog box similar to Figure 2-8 is displayed.

The physical directory is displayed on the Local Path box.

Looking at the Code

Return to the VB IDE, and press CTRL+R to display the Project Explorer as shown in Figure 2-9.

In the Project Explorer, right-click the WebClass1 icon, and select View Code to bring up the code window.

You should examine the code in Listing 2-1.

Listing 2-1

```
Option Explicit
Option Compare Text

Private Sub WebClass_Start()

  'Write a reply to the user
  With Response
    .Write "<html>"
    .Write "<body>"
    .Write "<h1><font face=""Arial"">WebClass1's Starting Page" & _
      "</font></h1>"
    .Write "<p>This response was created in the Start event of " & _
      "WebClass1.</p>"
    .Write "</body>"
    .Write "</html>"
  End With

End Sub
```

It is a bit surprising that an Internet application can run with a snippet as small as this, isn't it?

At the core of this code is the `WebClass_Start()` subroutine, which is the event procedure for the Start event of the WebClass object. The code simply uses the `Write` method of the Response object (this object will be explained in detail in Chapter 3) to output the following string in one long line:

```
<html><body><h1><font face="Arial">WebClass1's Starting Page</font></h1><p>This
response was created in the Start event of WebClass1.</p></body></html>
```

This string is the HTML code for the Web page displayed in the Web browser. Switch to the Web browser to view this source code. To view the source code in Internet Explorer, click Source from the View menu. In Netscape, click Page Source from the View menu, or press `Ctrl+U`.

It's as simple as that to create a Web page in IIS Applications. Once you become a serious IIS application developer, you'll use the `Write` method very frequently. This method is definitely very important.

Even though there is nothing wrong with the code in Listing 2-1, the HTML code produced is an eyesore when viewed from a browser's source page. This is especially true when the page is more complex. Why do you need to be concerned about this code? At times, the HTML code you generate will not work as intended, and you'll need to view it from a Web browser. At those times, you'll realize that more readable HTML code is preferable.

The code in Listing 2-1 can be modified a bit. The modified version is displayed in Listing 2-2.

Listing 2-2

```
Option Explicit
Option Compare Text

Private Sub WebClass_Start()

  'Write a reply to the user
  With Response
    .Write "<html>" & vbCr
    .Write "<body>" & vbCr
    .Write "<h1><font face=""Arial"">WebClass1's Starting Page" & _
      "</font></h1>" & vbCr
    .Write "<p>This response was created in the Start event of " & _
        "WebClass1.</p>" & vbCr
    .Write "</body>" & vbCr
    .Write "</html>"
  End With

End Sub
```

The modified version produces the following HTML code, which is apparently easier to read and understand.

```
<html>
<body>
<h1><font face="Arial">WebClass1's Starting Page</font></h1>
<p>This response was created in the Start event of WebClass1.</p>
</body>
</html>
```

You'll thank yourself when you have to debug this page.

For those of you who value efficiency, the code in Listing 2-2 can also be rewritten to increase its speed, as given in Listing 2-3.

Listing 2-3

```
Option Explicit
Option Compare Text

Private Sub WebClass_Start()

  'Write a reply to the user
  With Response
    .Write "<html>" & vbCr & _
      "<body>" & vbCr & _
      "<h1><font face=""Arial"">WebClass1's Starting Page</font>" & _
        "</h1>" & vbCr & _
      "<p>This response was created in the Start event of " & _
        "WebClass1.</p>" & vbCr & _
      "</body>" & vbCr & _
      "</html>"
  End With

End Sub
```

Note that the vbCr and not the vbCrLf is used because vbCr translates into one character instead of two. Because bandwidth is still expensive, a savings of one byte is definitely an increase in performance. Moreover, this savings comes at no cost.

The use of the vbCr character only affects the appearance of the HTML tags when viewed in the Source window. It does not affect the rendering of the HTML page in the Web browser.

Because the HTML page is generated by sending a string or strings of HTML code, you can also include other files, such as graphics or sound files. For example, the following code is valid:

```
Response.Write "<img src=""images/logo.gif""></img>"
```

It will pass the string `<img src="images/logo.gif"></img>` to the Web browser. Upon receiving the image tags, the browser will then try to fetch the logo.gif in the images subdirectory under the application virtual root.

Remember, all files included in the HTML code must be placed in the same directory as the project directory or in a subdirectory under it. Directories outside the virtual root are not visible to the Web browser. If you store a file, such as an image file, in a subdirectory under the virtual directory, you must include the subdirectory in your code, as shown in the previous example.

As your IIS application grows, it is imperative to structure your files so different types of files are organized in their own subdirectory by type. One good approach is to create an images subdirectory for all image files, a sounds subdirectory for all sound files, and so forth.

Renaming Your WebClass

Even though the name WebClass1 provided by VB seems fine and you know exactly what it does, to other people the name probably wouldn't make any sense. Therefore, you should always name your WebClasses and all their items in an indicative way, so they can be easily identified.

Meaningful names make a programmer's life more convenient. For example, let's say that two years after successfully deploying your application and making yourself famous in your company (well, two years is a very long time in Internet terms, let's make it two months), you decide to make a comeback and enhance your application. Wouldn't it be nice if you could just refresh your memory about the application simply by reciting its objects' names?

Or, if you are currently working in a team environment, wouldn't it be easier on your teammates if you used meaningful names rather than the cryptic WebClass1, WebItem23, Template24, and so forth?

Indeed, you can rename your WebClass by following these steps:

1. Right-click the WebClass icon that you want to rename in the Project Explorer.

2. Click Properties.

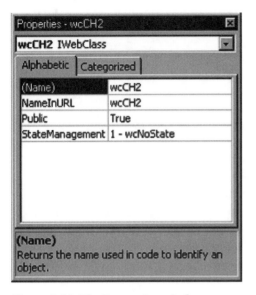

Figure 2-10. The Properties window

3. Change the name of the class and the NameInURL property. The NameInURL property is how the WebClass will be referenced in an HTML or an .asp page. The Properties window is shown in Figure 2-10. Note also that the .asp file created for the WebClass will be the same as the value in the NameInURL property.

To display the Properties window, the Project Explorer must have been previously displayed. If you try to display the Properties window when the Project Explorer is hidden, the Properties window will appear blank.

The ASP File

An IIS application only has one .asp page for each WebClass, and in most cases, an IIS application only has one WebClass. Unlike the ASP files in an ASP application that you often edit extensively, an .asp file in IIS applications is born immaculate and not meant to be edited. Its function is to create the WebClass it is associated with. However, you can view the contents of a typical .asp file in an IIS application.

Remember that your playing field is the WebClass not the .asp page, so don't try to change anything on the .asp page. The code in Listing 2-4 shows the contents of an .asp file.

Listing 2-4

```
<%
Server.ScriptTimeout=600
Response.Buffer=True
Response.Expires=0

If (VarType(Application("~WC~WebClassManager")) = 0) Then
  Application.Lock
  If (VarType(Application("~WC~WebClassManager")) = 0) Then
    Set Application("~WC~WebClassManager") = _
      Server.CreateObject("WebClassRuntime.WebClassManager")
  End If
  Application.UnLock
End If

Application("~WC~WebClassManager").ProcessNoStateWebClass _
  "Project1.wcCH2", _
  Server, _
  Application, _
  Session, _
  Request, _
  Response
%>
```

If you are or once were an ASP developer, and have not been hypnotized into forgetting the past, the code in Listing 2-4 should look familiar to you. If you have not done any ASP development, the following explanation will probably not make sense to you. You should return to this section after you finish reading Chapter 3.

To begin, the <% . . . %> pair is used to enclose your code.

The code first sets the ScriptTimeout property of the Server object:

```
Server.ScriptTimeout=600
```

The ScriptTimeout property specifies the maximum amount of time in seconds a script (an .asp page) can run before it is terminated. By setting this property to 600, the Web server is forced to wait up to 10 minutes for the .asp file to be processed.

It then sets the Buffer property of the Response object:

```
Response.Buffer=True
```

By setting the `Buffer` property to `True`, response to the Web browser will be buffered and sent at once when the whole page has been processed or when the Response is explicitly flushed from a location inside the WebClass.

It then tells the Web browser not to cache the page:

```
Response.Expires=0
```

The following line uses the `VarType` function to check if the Application object's variable `~WC~WebClassManager` has been initialized:

```
If (VarType(Application("~WC~WebClassManager")) = 0) Then
```

The `VarType` function returns a value indicating the subtype of a variable. The Application object is one of ASP's built-in objects. The `VarType` function returns zero if the variable is empty or uninitialized.

If the variable has not been initialized, the code then locks the Application object so other users can't change its internals:

```
Application.Lock
```

It then sets the `Application("~WC~WebClassManager")` variable to `WebClassRuntime.WebClassManager` (MSWCRUN.DLL) if the variable is still uninitialized:

```
If (VarType(Application("~WC~WebClassManager")) = 0) Then
    Set Application("~WC~WebClassManager") = _
      Server.CreateObject("WebClassRuntime.WebClassManager")
  End If
```

Remember that because the WebClass runtime is an ISAPI application, it will load into memory at the first call and stay there as long as the IIS is running. Therefore, the `CreateObject` method of the Server object will only be called once and subsequent requests to your WebClass will be much faster.

After unlocking the Application object, the code concludes by calling the `ProcessNoStateWebClass` method, passing six arguments.

```
Application("~WC~WebClassManager").ProcessNoStateWebClass _
  "Project1.wcCH2", _
  Server, _
  Application, _
  Session, _
  Request, _
  Response
```

The first argument is your project DLL, and the last five arguments are the five IIS objects.

If you don't understand the description of each line, it's okay; there is no need to suspect your IQ. This briefing is meaningful only to those who understand ASP. Don't worry, everything will start to make sense once you finish Chapter 3. Now, let's get back to the easy stuff.

The WebClass Designer

When developing an IIS Application, you'll continually switch from the Code window to the WebClass Designer and vice versa. The WebClass Designer, also called the Designer window, graphically lists all items in your WebClass. There are two types of items in a WebClass: the HTML Template WebItem and the Custom WebItem. Both are optional and will be explained shortly.

The WebClass Designer is a very useful window that comes equipped with a series of tools in its toolbar. The two rightmost tools are for stopping and restarting the Web server. When you are developing your application, you sometimes need to stop and restart when updating the global.asa file or when the server goes awry. You can display the WebClass Designer by pressing Shift+F7 or by clicking Objects from the View menu. Figure 2-11 shows the WebClass Designer.

The WebClass Designer displays all the elements that are in your WebClass. Before we leave the WebClass and discuss WebClass elements in more detail, let's discuss another important topic that you need to know: the lifecycle of a WebClass.

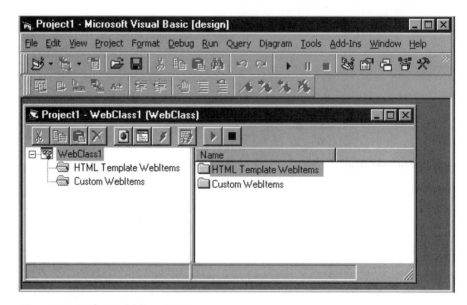

Figure 2-11. The WebClass Designer

The Lifecycle of a WebClass

Like a butterfly, the life of a WebClass goes through several phases. It starts when it is created using the CreateObject method of the Server object in an .asp page. It ends by being destroyed when the object variable assigned to it is set to Nothing or the .asp page loses its scope. The following list contains the key events in the life of a WebClass.

1. The Initialize event occurs when the WebClass is created as an object, that is, when the Web server reaches the line that calls the CreateObject method of the Server object. This is always the first event in the WebClass's lifetime.

2. The BeginRequest event is the next event called after the Initialize event. This event marks the beginning of processing for an HTTP request. In a form-based VB application, this is equivalent to the Load event of a form. However, every HTTP request is a new request in an Internet application. This event is fired *each* time the user clicks the hyperlink to your WebClass.

3. The Start event may or may not be fired after the BeginRequest event, depending whether or not the URL contains a reference to a WebItem (see the "WebItem" section). In the absence of a reference to a WebItem, this event is fired. You use this event to send an initial response to the browser or to shift the processing to a WebItem.

4. The EndRequest event occurs when the WebClass has finished processing an HTTP request and has returned a response to the client. The processing of an event might require the WebClass to process several templates or WebItems and their associated event procedures before a response is returned to the client. In a form-based VB application, this is equivalent to the UnLoad event of a form.

5. The Terminate event tells the runtime DLL to destroy the instance of the WebClass. The WebClass fires the Terminate event each time it sends a response to the browser if the StateManagement property for the WebClass is set to wcNoState, that is, the project DLL is destroyed each time it finishes processing the HTTP request. If the StateManagement property for the WebClass is set to wcRetainInstance, the WebClass fires the Terminate event only after it calls the ReleaseInstance method and the project DLL is retained in memory. More information on this topic can be found in Chapter 7.

To illustrate the sequence more clearly, let's look at a demonstration with all the events. A Debug.Print statement is put in each event that outputs a string to the Immediate window when the event is fired. The code is listed in Listing 2-5.

Listing 2-5

```
Option Explicit
Option Compare Text

Private Sub WebClass_BeginRequest()

  Debug.Print "BeginRequest event ... "

End Sub

Private Sub WebClass_EndRequest()

  Debug.Print "EndRequest event ... "

End Sub

Private Sub WebClass_Initialize()

  Debug.Print "Initialize event ... "

End Sub

Private Sub WebClass_Start()

  Debug.Print "Start event ... "

End Sub

Private Sub WebClass_Terminate()

  Debug.Print "Terminate event ... "

End Sub
```

When you press F5, VB launches the Web browser, which calls the .asp file, which in turn creates the WebClass, which then fires the events in it. The Web browser doesn't receive anything from the Web server, but you can view the VB Immediate window, which illustrates the sequence of a WebClass.

```
Initialize event ...
BeginRequest event ...
Start event ...
EndRequest event ...
Terminate event ...
```

You might be wondering if it is possible to use the `Response.Write` method, which sends strings from all five events to make the demonstration more vivid. No, it is not. Although it is all right to send a string to the browser without sending the <html> or <body> tags, the Response object cannot be accessed from the `Initialize` event and the `Terminate` event.

Creating Dynamic Content

The attraction of IIS applications, among other factors, is the ability to produce dynamic contents, which simple HTML pages cannot do. In the next basic sample application, you'll see how the WebClass responds to a user request based on the server time. You already know that the `Start` event is fired when you run the application. Therefore, you simply need to put the code in Listing 2-6 in the `WebClass_Start` event procedure.

Listing 2-6

```vb
Private Sub WebClass_Start()

  Dim strGreeting As String
  If Hour(Now) > 5 And Hour(Now) < 12 Then
    strGreeting = "Good Morning."
  Else
    strGreeting = "Hello."
  End If

  'Write a greeting
  With Response
    .Write "<html>" & vbCr & _
      "<body>" & vbCr & _
      strGreeting & vbCr & _
      "<br>Welcome to the Most Fun Web Site." & vbCr & _
      "</body>" & vbCr & _
      "</html>"
  End With

End Sub
```

If the user happens to visit your site between 6 A.M. and 12 A.M., the greeting will be

```
Good Morning.
Welcome to the Most Fun Web Site.
```

At any other time, the string sent to the browser will be

```
Hello.
Welcome to the Most Fun Web Site.
```

Hopefully, this simple example is sufficient to illustrate how to create an ever changing HTML page based on certain conditions. For the time being, you need to bear in mind that using the `Write` method of the Response object is not the only way to send HTML code to the Web browser. Your WebClass can also send an existing HTML page to the browser. The exciting part is, you can change a certain part of the HTML page programmatically. This topic is discussed in the following sections.

WebItems

A WebClass can have elements or items called WebItems. There are two types of WebItems: HTML template WebItems and Custom WebItems.

An HTML template WebItem is an HTML page that you associate with your WebClass. Templates are very similar to regular HTML pages. The only difference is templates often contain replacement areas the WebClass can process before sending the page to the browser, making it possible to customize your response programmatically.

A custom WebItem is a collection of event procedures that are logically grouped together to help organize your Web application. The event handlers are triggered by the URL passed by the HTTP request to the WebClass. This information will become clear when we discuss the custom WebItems in the next few sections.

HTML Template WebItems

Sending HTML tags is easy with the Response object's `Write` method. However, there is an even easier way to output HTML tags to the Web browser, which is by sending the content of an existing HTML file. This way, if you want to change the content of an HTML file, you just need to change the file without having to change your code.

When you use the Response object's `Write` method, the string of HTML tags to be sent to the Web browser is hard-coded in your WebClass. If you want to edit the HTML tags, for example, change the name of an image file, you have to change the code and recompile your WebClass. When you use an HTML template, the HTML tags are in an HTML file, and your WebClass processes and sends the content of this HTML file to the browser.

Editing the tags is the same as editing a text file. However, using the HTML template is slower because the WebClass scans the content of the HTML template and processes it accordingly before it is sent to the browser. Nevertheless, HTML templates are handy and often created by Web graphic designers using sophisticated HTML authoring tools. Translating the tags in the file into a string that gets passed as a parameter to the Write template is definitely a tedious task.

The better news when using an HTML template is that you can launch your text editor from VB IDE. You can have as many HTML templates as you like in a project. You can even choose which one to send to the Web browser.

Before you can add a template to a WebClass, you must first save your project. If you don't, VB will prompt you to do so. To add an HTML template WebItem, click the Add HTML Template WebItem button on the WebClass Designer toolbar, and browse to select an existing HTML file. If the template file you choose references any additional files, such as .gif or .jpg files, copy those files to the project directory or a subdirectory beneath it. If the template file contains absolute references to the previous locations of those files on the development computer, you need to make changes to the .htm file to reflect the location the files will have when deployed to the server.

After you add the template, VB performs one of the following functions:

- If the .htm file you choose for the template is located outside the project directory, VB makes a copy of the template file and places it in the project directory.

- If the .htm file you choose for the template comes from the project directory or if there is another .htm file there with the same name, the system creates a copy of the .htm file but appends a number to its name. For example, a file called Login.htm would be changed to Login1.htm. Please note, even though the extension .htm and .html are the same to the Web browser, VB only recognizes .htm.

The action of copying the .htm file occurs when you save or debug the project, or when you use the Edit HTML Template menu command.

After being added to the project directory, the .htm file acts as the source file for your project. If you want to make changes to the HTML page's appearance, do so in this copy of the HTML page.

If your HTML template file references any additional files, such as images, you must copy those files into the project directory or a subdirectory of it. You can do this before you add the template to the WebClass or after, but you must do it before debugging or running the project.

In addition, if you import an HTML page for which a similarly named .htm file already exists in the project directory, VB appends a number to the .htm file it creates for the new file. This prevents VB from overwriting an existing .htm file if you reuse a template in more than one WebClass. For example, suppose you have an HTML page called Login.htm. The first time you add this to a WebClass, VB generates a file in the project directory with the name Login.htm.

If you add this same file to another WebClass in the application, the new .htm file VB creates is named Login1.htm. After you import an HTML Template WebItem, the WebItem will be displayed in the WebClass Designer, as shown in Figure 2-12.

After you add an HTML template to your WebClass, VB will treat this template like other objects. The template has three standard events: Respond, ProcessTag, and UserEvent. We will return to these events later in this chapter under "WebItems's Standard Events."

An HTML template also has one method, namely the WriteTemplate method. This is actually the method you use to send an HTML template WebItem to the

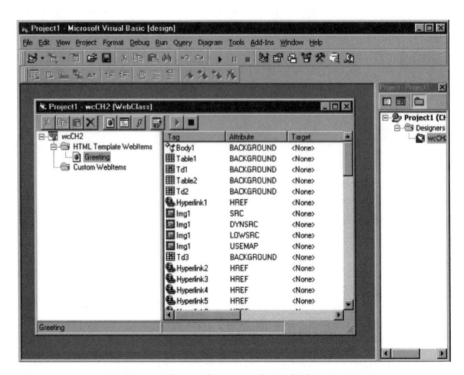

Figure 2-12. An HTML template WebItem in the WebClass Designer

Web browser. For instance, you can put the line of code in the WebClass_Start event procedure, as shown in Listing 2-7.

Listing 2-7
```
Private Sub WebClass_Start()

 'Write the template Greeting
 Greeting.WriteTemplate

End Sub
```

Greeting is the name of an HTML template WebItem added to the WebClass. It will send the content of the HTML template when the user calls your application.

Before it is sent, VB scans that file and looks for HTML tags that are capable of launching a request to the server. Such tags include form elements, image tags, hyperlinks, and most other tags that contain a URL reference. Note that each HTML template WebItem can only represent one HTML page.

You can remove a template from a WebClass if you no longer want to send that template file to the browser in response to requests. You cannot replace one template with another; instead you must remove the first template file and add a link to a new file. If the template files have the same name, any event procedures written for the former template will be available to the new template.

To remove a template from the WebClass, right-click the template WebItem, and click Delete.

Editing the HTML for a Template

After you have inserted an HTML template file, you can use the HTML editor of your choice to make changes to the page's content and layout. By default, VB launches either your default HTML editor or Notepad when you edit your template. VB automatically detects your default HTML editor by looking at the system Registry, but you can choose the text editor you want by using the following procedure.

1. Click Options from the Tools menu.

2. Click the Advanced tab (see Figure 2-13).

3. Click the button to the right of the text box in the External HTML Editor frame and browse until you find your favorite text editor. Personally I like

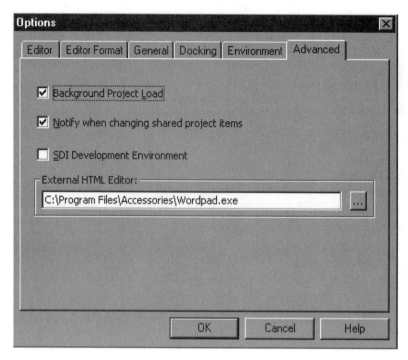

Figure 2-13. Selecting an HTML editor

Wordpad because the program is not too big yet has plenty of tools for basic text editing.

4. Click OK.

You can then edit your HTML template WebItem. The beauty of IIS applications is that you can edit your HTML template without leaving the VB environment. When you edit an HTML template, you edit the copy that is placed in the project directory, not the original file. To edit an HTML template, follow these steps:

1. In the left panel of the Designer window, right-click the HTML template you want to edit, then select Edit HTML Template.

2. Make your changes to the .htm file, save, and return to VB.

3. If you have made any changes to the event tags in the file, right-click the WebItem and select Refresh HTML Template, or respond to the prompt to refresh as shown in Figure 2-14.

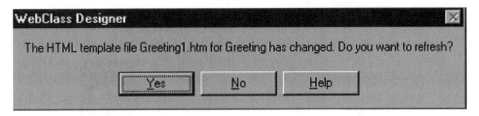

Figure 2-14. You need to refresh the HTML Template WebItem after editing it.

If you don't immediately save the changes you made, you can also update the WebClass by refreshing the link between your template and its external file. When you refresh the template, VB checks to see whether the events currently listed for the template still exist and whether any new attributes should be added. The program adds any new attributes and processes any changes for existing events.

If an event for the template no longer exists in the .htm file, VB removes it from the WebClass. Any procedures written for the event are not removed—you must clean up the event procedures yourself.

If another user makes changes to an .htm file used in your WebClass, you receive a prompt asking whether you want to refresh the template. This message appears each time a user saves the .htm file in an editor.

To save changes to the .htm file you've referenced in a later stage, right-click the template for which you want to refresh your import in the left panel of the WebClass designer, then select Refresh HTML Template.

Now that you have the HTML template in your project, you can send it to the browser by using the WriteTemplate method of the template. The code in Listing 2-8 will send the HTML template named Greeting to the browser.

Listing 2-8

```
Private Sub WebClass_Start()

  'Write the template Greeting
  Greeting.WriteTemplate

End Sub
```

Yes, all it takes is one line of code.

You can also insert custom tags into the HTML page and replace the tags with text on the fly. Let's use the same example as we did previously. Suppose you added an HTML template called Greeting, which contains the HTML code as in Listing 2-9:

Listing 2-9

```
<html>
<body>
Hello.
Welcome to the Most Fun Web Site.
</body>
</html>
```

Now you could change the greeting according to the Web server time. What you need to do is insert a replacement indicator in the HTML template file, then add some code to process the replacement indicator. This is possible because when you issue the WriteTemplate method, VB scans the template file for special indicator tags and replaces them or their contents with custom content. After all replacements are finished, the WriteTemplate method sends the contents of the HTML template file to the browser.

The replacement indicators, also called custom tags, contain the following three parts:

1. A tag prefix. In IIS applications, the default tag prefix in every template is WC@.

2. A tag name. This is a descriptive name to identify the replacement area.

3. Tag contents. These represent the current contents of the tag before replacement.

The previous HTML code should be edited into the code in Listing 2-10.

Listing 2-10

```
<html>
<body>
  <WC@GREETING>Text to be replaced</WC@GREETING>
  <br>Welcome to the Most Fun Web Site.
</body>
</html>
```

<WC@> is the tag prefix and GREETING is the tag name, whereas Text to be replaced is, not surprisingly, the text to be replaced.

The replacement can take place because when you call the WriteTemplate method, the ProcessTag event of the HTML template WebItem is fired and the code in the event procedure runs. The ProcessTag event is triggered *every time VB encounters a tag prefix.* This being said, you should now realize the consequence of having too many <WC@> tag prefixes. They will decrease the speed of your code.

To make a replacement, insert the code in Listing 2-11 in the Greeting_ProcessTag event procedure.

Listing 2-11

```
Private Sub Greeting_ProcessTag(ByVal TagName As String, _
  TagContents As String, SendTags As Boolean)

  If Hour(Now) > 5 And Hour(Now) < 12 Then
    TagContents = "Good Morning."
  Else
    TagContents = "Hello."
  End If

End Sub
```

Then call the WriteTemplate method of the Greeting HTML template WebItem in the WebClass_Start event procedure. The code is given in Listing 2-12.

Listing 2-12

```
Private Sub WebClass_Start()

  Greeting.WriteTemplate

End Sub
```

When you run the code, your Web browser will open and display one of the following greetings depending on the Web server time:

```
Good Morning.
Welcome to the Most Fun Web Site
```

or

```
Hello.
Welcome to the Most Fun Web Site
```

If there are several WC@Greeting tags in the page, all tags will be replaced when the Process_Tag event procedure is processed.

An HTML template can have more than one tag name. For example, the previous page could have two types of tags as shown in Listing 2-13.

41

Listing 2-13

```
<html>
<head>
  <title><WC@PageTitle>Custom Title</WC@PageTitle></title>
</head>

<body>
  <WC@GREETING>Text to be replaced</WC@GREETING>
  <br>Welcome to the Most Fun Web Site
</body>
</html>
```

If you don't perform some filtering, all tags will have the same replacement text. For the previous HTML template, you need to modify the ProcessTag event procedure of the Greeting object. The modified version is given in Listing 2-14.

Listing 2-14

```
Private Sub Greeting_ProcessTag(ByVal TagName As String, _
  TagContents As _String, SendTags As Boolean)

  If TagName = "WC@PageTitle" Then
    TagContents = "Welcome"
  Else
    If Hour(Now) > 5 And Hour(Now) < 12 Then
      TagContents = "Good Morning."
    Else
      TagContents = "Hello."
    End If
  End If

End Sub
```

This code processes each tag according to the tag name. If you have more than two types of tag names in your HTML template, you can use the Select . . . Case statement. Note that the tag name argument includes the tag prefix as well, that is, WC@PageTitle, not just PageTitle. If you don't include the prefix, the code in Listing 2-14 will not work.

Also note that sometimes when debugging the code, the content passed to the Web browser refuses to change even after editing your HTML template. In this case, you need to click the Refresh button (in Internet Explorer) or the Reload button (in Netscape).

Notice that the ProcessTag event procedure has three arguments. The last one, SendTags, tells VB whether or not to send the tags to the browser. By default the value is False, but if you set it to True, all the tags will be sent together with the replacement. Therefore, if you insert the following line in the Greeting_ProcessTag event procedure, as shown in the code in Listing 2-15, the tags will also be sent to the browser (see Figure 2-15).

```
SendTags = True
```

Listing 2-15
```
Private Sub Greeting_ProcessTag(ByVal TagName As String, _
  TagContents As String, SendTags As Boolean)

  If TagName = "WC@PageTitle" Then
    TagContents = "Welcome"
  Else
    If Hour(Now) > 5 And Hour(Now) < 12 Then
      TagContents = "Good Morning."
    Else
      TagContents = "Hello."
    End If
  End If

  SendTags = True

End Sub
```

You can actually change the tag prefix for an HTML template by editing the TagPrefix property of the HTML template in the Properties window (see Figure 2-16). To display the Properties window of the HTML template, click the HTML template in the WebClass Designer, and then press F4.

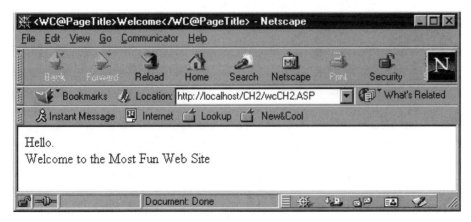

Figure 2-15. The tags are sent to the browser and displayed in the Title bar.

*Figure 2-16. You can change the
TagPrefix in the Properties window.*

However, using different tag prefixes is not recommended because it only increases the items you need to remember when building your application. In most cases, using the default tag is good enough.

Connecting Your Template Element to an Event

In traditional VB applications, you work with forms and controls. In IIS applications, you have neither. Instead, you have HTML pages, which are IIS applications' equivalents of forms. You can't have controls in your HTML pages if you want your application to remain browser independent. However, you can have elements in an HTML page. These elements can be hyperlinks, images, forms, tables, and so forth.

In a form-based VB application, forms and controls have a number of events associated with them. For example, a command button control has `Click` and `LostFocus` events. When you click a command button control, you trigger its `Click` event, and VB runs whatever code you have put in the button's `OnClick` event procedure.

In an IIS application, elements in an HTML page can be associated with certain events too, just like controls in a form. Elements are represented by tags. For example, an image element in an HTML page is represented by its `<IMG>` tag. Elements and tags are really two faces of the same coin. As an IIS application programmer, you don't work with elements, you work with tags that represent the elements.

Tags are an IIS application's equivalent of controls. But remember that in an HTML page you see the elements: images, hyperlinks, or tables. Only when you view the code of the HTML page do you see the tags.

Tags within an HTML template WebItem can act as event sources if the browser calls the server when the user selects their corresponding elements. Elements are the only objects in an HTML template that can raise events. Elements call the server if their tags have attributes that contain a URL. When the user clicks a hyperlink, for example, the browser sends a URL request to the Web server to request the page in the hyperlink. Upon receiving the request, your WebClass fires an event that is associated with the HREF attribute of the `<a>` ... `</a>` tags of the hyperlink.

A tag normally has one attribute, but some tags, such as `<IMG>`, can have several. Each attribute can be associated with a different event procedure. However, unlike controls in a form-based VB application that has events associated with them by default, tags know nothing about their events. Even after you add an HTML template WebItem to your WebClass, tags in the HTML template do not have any event, they only have attributes. It is your job as an IIS application developer to associate attributes with events.

The process of enabling a tag to fire a certain event consists of two steps:

1. Associate a tag's attribute with an event. When you do this, it is said that you connect the attribute to the event.

2. Write code in for the connected event.

Connecting a tag's attribute simply means that you are activating it, enabling the attribute to be treated as an event. Until an attribute is connected, it does not appear in the Code Editor window for the WebClass, and you cannot write procedures for it. After the tag's attribute is connected, it appears in the Procedure drop-down list in the Code Editor window with the three standard events: `ProcessTag`, `Respond`, and `UserEvent`.

Associating an Event with a Tag's Attribute

The first of the two steps to connect a tag's attribute to an event is to select an event. You can select an existing event or, if necessary, create a new event.

A tag's attribute in an HTML template WebItem can be associated with:

1. One of the HTML template WebItem standard events.

2. A custom event (created when you select Connect to Custom Event after right-clicking the element).

3. A standard event of another HTML template WebItem.

4. A custom WebItem's standard event.

5. A custom WebItem's custom event.

Custom WebItems are discussed in the next section.

Even though, in theory, you can connect a tag's attribute to one of these five options, the easiest is to connect it to a custom event. You can do this by following these steps:

1. Click the HTML template in the WebClass Designer. VB displays the list of tags that can be associated with events in the right panel of the WebClass Designer (see Figure 2-17).

2. Right-click the tag, and select Connect to custom event.

VB creates an event and gives it a name. If the tag has only one attribute, the event name is the same as the name of the tag. If the tag has more than one attribute, the name is a combination of the tag name and the attribute name.

The tag itself gets its name from the name given to each element in the HTML page. If a name has not been given to the tag, VB will name it according to the type of element it is plus a number. For example, the first unnamed form element will be referred to as Form1.

Writing Code for Event Procedure

After you connect a tag's attribute to an event and a user tries to trigger the event, nothing will happen if there is no code in the particular event procedure. You need to provide the code that will be run when an event is fired.

Let's practice the material learned so far in one simple application. First, you need to add an HTML template WebItem and rename it SubmitDetails.htm. The HTML template must contain the code in Listing 2-16.

Listing 2-16

```
<html>
<body>
  <form method=post>
    <input Name=UserName>
    <input type=submit>
  </form>
</body>
</html>
```

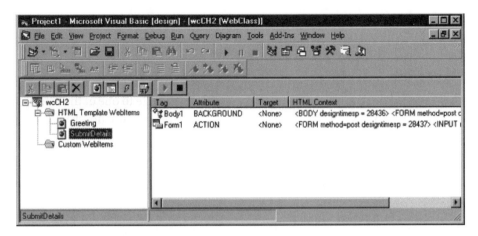

Figure 2-17. The connectable attributes of an HTML Template WebItem

When you add the template, VB scans the template for the tag's attributes that can be associated with an event and displays them in the right panel of the WebClass Designer as shown in Figure 2-17. Remember that VB only displays attributes that can contain URLs. For example, a form (an HTML element, not related to forms in a traditional VB application) can have attributes such as METHOD and ACTION, but only the latter is shown in the WebClass Designer's right panel, because the first does not contain a URL.

In this example, VB found two tags: Body1 and Form1. <None> under the Target column indicates that the tag's attribute is not associated with any event.

1. Right-click the Form1 tag, and select Connect to Custom Event. When you select it, VB creates the event represented by the Event icon under the SubmitDetails template in the left panel of the WebClass Designer (see Figure 2-18).

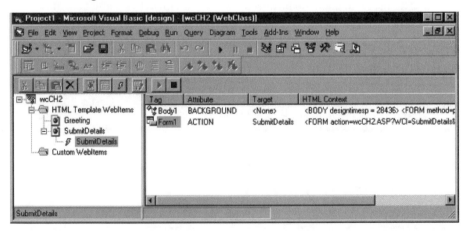

Figure 2-18. The ACTION attribute of Form1 is connected to the SubmitDetails event of the SubmitDetails custom WebItem.

The Event is initially named Form1, but you can change it to SubmitDetails by selecting Rename after right-clicking the Event icon. The Target value for the Form1 element is now the `SubmitDetails` event, the name you just gave the event. The Form1 tag is then associated with the `SubmitDetails` event. For a form tag, there is only one action the user can execute to fire the event. That action is submit form. The user normally submits a form by clicking a button of type Submit inside the form.

2. Double-click the SubmitDetails event icon to display its Code window.

3. Type the following code:

```
Private Sub SubmitDetails_SubmitDetails()

    Response.Write "Thank you for submitting your details."

End Sub
```

4. In the `WebClass_Start()` event procedure, type this code:

```
Private Sub WebClass_Start()

    SubmitDetails.WriteTemplate

End Sub
```

When you press F5 to run the application, the .asp file calls the `WebClass_Start` and displays the content of the SubmitDetails.htm.

The form has two elements, a Text (which looks like a TextBox control in a form-based VB application) and a Submit (a special type of button). The user can click the button to submit the form (see Figure 2-19).

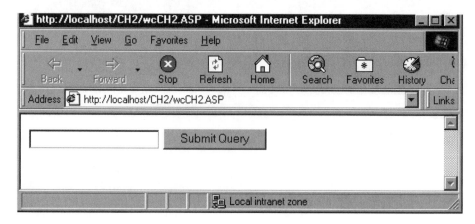

Figure 2-19. The Form element in the Web browser

5. Type something in the text box, but don't submit it yet. You'll see how the Web browser tells the WebClass to fire the event associated with it if you view the source code of the HTML page, which should look similar to the following snippet:

```html
<html>
<body>
  <form method=post action=wcCH2.ASP?WCI=SubmitDetails&amp;
    WCE=SubmitDetails&amp;WCU>
    <input Name=UserName >
    <input type=submit value="Submit Query">
  </form>
</body>
</html>
```

VB has updated the content of the HTML template and added the action attribute to the form. This attribute contains the destination URL. It is still going to the wcCH2.asp, but it now has three other attributes, WCI, WCE, and WCU. Remember that & in HTML simply means the character &. WCI indicates the WebItem name, and WCE indicates the custom event name. It is clear that the URL is referring to the SubmitDetails event in the SubmitDetails WebItem.

6. Click the button to submit the form. The WebClass fires the event and sends the string to the Web browser as shown in Figure 2-20.

Hold on. What happens to the text the user typed in? How does the WebClass capture it? The answer to these questions can be found in Chapter 3 where the Request object is discussed.

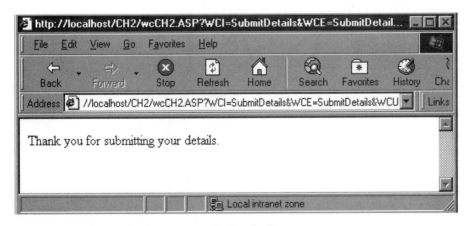

Figure 2-20. The result after a user submits the form

Connecting to a WebItem

You may recall that when you selected the Connect to Custom Event from the popup menu after you right-clicked the Form1 tag, there was another option to select: Connect to WebItem. You could have selected this too. Why could you have done this? Isn't a WebItem an object and not an event? Yes, but when VB says Connect to WebItem, it actually means Connect to WebItem's Respond standard event.

If you choose to connect an element to a WebItem, the dialog box in Figure 2-21 is displayed for you to select a WebItem. You can then click a WebItem, and click OK.

If you have chosen to connect to a WebItem and have associated it with the SubmitDetails HTML template, the result is the following HTML template code after some editing by VB:

```
<html>
<body>
  <form method=post action=wcCH2.ASP?WCI=SubmitDetails&amp;WCU>
    <input Name=UserName>
    <input type=submit value="Submit Query">
  </form>
</body>
</html>
```

As you can see, the action attribute is still very similar. The WCI argument is still there, but the WCE is missing. Without the WCE, the WebClass leaves it to the WebItem to fire an event. The WebItem fires its default event: the Respond event.

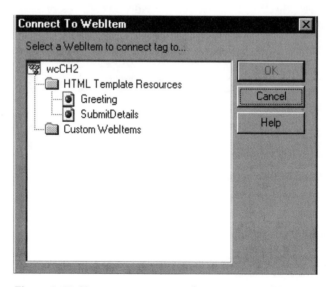

Figure 2-21. You can connect an element to a WebItem.

Instead of typing your code in a custom event procedure, you should put it in the SubmitDetails_Respond() event procedure.

In addition to the Respond event, an HTML template WebItem has two other standard events: ProcessTag and UserEvent. These three events are displayed in the Procedure drop-down list box of the Code Editor window. When you add a custom event, the custom event is also displayed. Once created, a custom event appears in the WebClass Designer. A standard event is always present, but doesn't appear in the WebClass Designer.

Custom WebItem

When you program event procedures for events you have connected to HTML tags, you'll find the flexibility to choose whether to connect the tag to a WebItem or to a custom event. VB even allows you to connect a tag to an event of another HTML template WebItem. This flexibility can easily lead to hard-to-manage applications.

To avoid disasters from happening, keep in mind that you should never connect a tag to another HTML template WebItem. However, there may be times when you need to make a generic event that is fired by several tags from different HTML templates. This is where the custom WebItem comes into play.

Custom WebItems can help you produce more modular, structured code. Unlike HTML template WebItems, which are linked to and manipulate HTML pages, custom WebItems are containers that generally group a set of code procedures. You want the WebClass to be able to access the procedures from multiple places in the application, including from elements of different HTML template WebItems.

Custom WebItems allow you to send a response to the browser at times when a template file is not a good solution or not available.

You can create a custom WebItem by clicking the Add Custom WebItem button from the WebClass Designer's toolbar. When you add a new custom WebItem, the new custom WebItem will contain three standard events, the same events that accompany an HTML template WebItem: ProcessTag, Respond, and UserEvent. These three events are discussed in more detail in the "WebItem's Standard Events" section later in this chapter.

Note that a custom WebItem also has the WriteTemplate method. However, if you try to call this method by writing something like the following line, VB will raise the runtime error "9006: Invalid path to HTML template":

```
MyCustomWebitem.WriteTemplate
```

Clearly this method is only for HTML template WebItems. Because you can't call the WriteTemplate method, the ProcessTag event of a custom WebItem is also never fired.

The URLFor Method

With the HTML template WebItem, you can connect an HTML element to an event. By doing this, the hyperlink to the event is sent to the browser. However, what if you don't have an HTML template and you want to send HTML tags using the Write method of the Response object? How do you connect an HTML element to an event then? The answer is simple: Send the hyperlink to the browser. The easiest way to do this is by using the URLFor method of the WebClass.

The URLFor method has the following syntax, where Item is a WebItem and Event is the WebItem's event:

```
URLFor(Item, [Event])
```

In the absence of the Event parameter, the method returns the hyperlink to the Respond standard event of the WebItem.

For example, the following lines of code send a hyperlink to the SayHello custom event of the Members WebItem:

```
Response.Write "<a href=""" & URLFor(Members, "SayHello") & _
   """>Click here</a>"
```

Note that the event name must be enclosed with double quotes, but the WebItem must not.

Connecting an HTML Element to a Custom Event of a Custom WebItem

You can easily connect an element in an HTML Template WebItem with an HTML Template or the default event of a custom WebItem by right-clicking the HTML element in the WebClass Designer and selecting Connect To WebItem. However, you cannot use this procedure to connect an HTML element to a custom event of a custom WebItem. To do this, you can either use the URLFor method or edit the HTML template and type in the URL to the custom WebItem's custom event yourself.

The following example demonstrates how to use the URLFor method to achieve the goal. In the next chapters, however, you'll see how you can edit the HTML template to achieve the same result. To use this example, you need to create an HTML Template WebItem called Login and a custom WebItem called Members. You also need to create a custom event called Authorize for the Members custom WebItem.

This example demonstrates how to connect an element in the Login HTML Template to the Authorize custom event. The code for the HTML template is given in Listing 2-17 and the VB code that you need to paste into your WebClass is given in Listing 2-18.

Listing 2-17

```
<html>
<head>
  <title>Login Page</title>
</head>

<body>
<center>

Please enter your password
<br>

<form method=POST action=<WC@Action></WC@Action>

<input type=password Name=UserPassword>
<br><input type=submit>
</form>

</center>
</body>
</html>
```

Listing 2-18

```
Private Sub Login_ProcessTag(ByVal TagName As String, _
  TagContents As String, SendTags As Boolean)

    TagContents = URLFor(Members, "Authorize")

End Sub


Private Sub WebClass_Start()

    Login.WriteTemplate

End Sub
```

The HTML code in Listing 2-17 contains a form whose ACTION attribute will be connected to the Authorize custom event of the Members custom WebItem. The Login_ProcessTag event procedure uses the URLFor method to replace the

`<WC@Action>`/`WC@Action` tags in the HTML template with the URL of the Authorize custom event in the Members custom WebItem.

WebItem's Standard Events

As previously mentioned, every WebItem has three standard events: `Respond`, `ProcessTag`, and `UserEvent`. The `ProcessTag` of an HTML template WebItem is fired when you call the `WriteTemplate` method of that HTML template WebItem. The use of this event was explained when we discussed HTML template WebItems in the previous section.

The `Respond` event occurs when a WebItem object is activated by a user request and no event is found that directly corresponds to the selected element. In other words, this is the default event of a WebItem that is fired when the WCE argument is not present in the URL. This is also the event that is fired when you use the `NextItem` property of the WebClass. The `NextItem` property is explained in the following section.

The `UserEvent` event is fired when a WebItem object is activated and there is a reference to an event, but the event cannot be found. Of course, if the event can be found, the corresponding custom event is fired.

You'll find examples that use these events in the upcoming chapters.

The NextItem Property

The WebClass's `NextItem` property is used to shift processing to a specific WebItem in the current WebClass during a single request. The `Respond` event of the WebItem is fired. For example, the following line of code hands over control to the code in the `Respond` event procedure of the Product WebItem:

```
Set NextItem = Product
```

Custom WebItems are not a complex matter, but programmers new to Internet applications may find this hard to digest all at once. That's the reason I chose to end this discussion and revisit WebItems in the upcoming chapters rather than going into more depth now. You don't just plunge into the deepest water when you learn to swim, do you?

Which Browser to Use?

Before you dive into the next chapter, you probably want to know which browser is best to use. Both Netscape and Microsoft browsers still dominate the Internet and work equally well. It is really up to your users to choose because IIS applications are browser independent.

When creating a browser independent Internet application, you should test your application with every browser your users will be using. However, strictly following this advice could mean that you would have to test every change in your code at least twice, once with Netscape and once with Internet Explorer. If you want to be more practical, however, it is recommended that you use a Netscape browser because its rules are more stringent, whereas Internet Explorer is more tolerant. Consider the code in Listing 2-19.

Listing 2-19

```
<html>
<body>
<table>
  <tr>
    <td>
      Please enter a value
    </td>
  </tr>
</body>
</html>
```

This code displays well in Internet Explorer, but won't display anything in Netscape. If you watch carefully, the snippet is not perfect because the closing `</table>` tag is missing. If you use Internet Explorer, this bug will probably go undetected. On the other hand, if you use a Netscape browser, you'll immediately spot that there is something wrong with the HTML code generated.

It's better to find the bug when you are still coding than get an email from your users complaining that they can't use Netscape browsers to run your application. So, use Netscape when you are still in the development stage, and use other browsers as well for the final testing.

CHAPTER 3

Working with ASP Objects

IN CHAPTER 2, YOU LEARNED THAT YOU CAN EASILY send a string of HTML tags to Web browsers using the Write method of the Response object. All you need to do to send a string is enter the following code line in the `Webclass_Start()` event procedure or other routines:

```
Response.Write "<b>Click here if you like this site.</b>"
```

What has not been mentioned is that the Response object is only one of the few built-in ASP objects that come with Visual Basic's IIS Application projects. The IIS application is an enhancement of ASP. Therefore, it's not surprising that ASP objects are still used in IIS applications. In fact, understanding ASP objects is imperative in developing an IIS application.

> **NOTE:** *If you have IIS 4.0 installed on your machine, you have ASP version 2.0. If you are using IIS 5.0, however, you have ASP 3.0. This chapter lists the ASP 2.0 objects' methods and properties. For a reference on methods and properties of ASP 3.0 objects, see Appendix B.*

Other built-in ASP objects that you can use in your projects are `Request`, `Server`, `Application`, `Session`, `BrowserType`, and `ObjectContext` objects. You inevitably will use all or some of these objects in your application. The last object, `ObjectContext`, which actually belongs to the Microsoft Transaction Server (MTS), is not built-in and must be explicitly added to your project if you want to use it. Include it in your project only if you want to use the MTS. It will therefore not be discussed in this book.

There is also a new object in ASP 3.0: the `ASPError` object. This object allows you to retrieve the error properties to display and/or log meaningful error information. This object is of little or no use in an IIS application, however, because you don't put your error handling code in the asp file. Instead, you must put all your code in the WebClass and then use the `Error` object in Visual Basic to achieve the same goals.

This chapter will discuss the rest of these objects, but not all details will be covered. A complete reference on ASP objects is given in Appendix B. I will revisit some of these objects for more advanced details in the chapters that follow. The advanced topics include cookies and state management.

This chapter will present important items an Internet developer should know including how data transfer between a Web server and a Web browser works. It is logical to begin the discussion with the object that takes care of requests from the Web browser: the Request object.

The Request Object

When Internet users type in a URL like **http://www.labsale.com/index.html** in their browser URL or Location box, they make a request, in this case, for the index.html file to the Web server that hosts www.labsale.com. The Web server receives the request and handles it accordingly. If the URL doesn't have a file name, the Web server interprets this as a request for the default page, which is normally index.html, default.html, default.asp, or whatever is set in the Web server configuration page.

If the page requested happens to have an .asp extension, such as myWebClass.asp, the Web server hands the request over to the ASP engine. If the ASP page in turn happens to host a WebClass, the request is submitted to the WebClass. All request information from the Web browser is contained in the Request object. It's then up to the programmer to respond accordingly from inside the WebClass. The Request object is summarized in Table 3-1.

Table 3-1. Request Object Summary

PROPERTIES
TotalBytes

COLLECTIONS
ClientCertificate
Cookies
Form
QueryString
ServerVariables

METHODS
BinaryRead

EVENTS
None

The Request object has one property, one method, and five collections. The only property in this object is the read-only TotalBytes property, which specifies the total number of bytes the Web browser sends in the body of the request. Of the five collections, the Form and QueryString collections are the most frequently used.

The Form collection has three properties: Key, Item, and Count. Key represents the name of a specific element in the Form collection. You can retrieve the name of the first element on an HTML form by using

```
strKeyName = Request.Form.Key(1)
```

Please note that the numbering begins with 1. Therefore, in the code in Listing 3-1, the first element is "LastName" and the fourth is "B1."

Listing 3-1

```
<form method=post>
Last Name: <input type=text name=LastName>
<br>First Name: <input type=text name=FirstName>
<br>Title:<select name=Title>
    <option Value=1>Mr</option>
    <option Value=2>Ms</option>
    <option Value=3>Miss</option>
    <option Value=4>Mrs</option>
    </select>
<br><input type=submit Name=B1>
</form>
```

The Name attribute must be present in the element you want to send to the server. If you drop the Name=B1 part of the fourth element, for example, the element won't appear in the Form collection of the Request object, and then the Form collection will have only three elements. If the name of the element in the form consists of two words, for instance, Last Name, you must enclose it with double quotes. You should avoid giving your element a two-word name.

The Item property represents the value of a particular element in the Form collection. To specify an item, you can use an index number or a key. The index number specifies the number of the element on the HTML form.

The following statement assigns "LastName" to the strKeyName variable and assigns the value of the LastName variable input by the user into the form element to the strKeyValue variable:

```
strKeyName = Request.Form.Key(1)
strKeyValue = Request.Form.Item(1)
```

The last property, Count, simply returns the number of elements in the collection. As previously mentioned, an element only counts if it has a name. So, if your HTML form has four elements as in the code in Listing 3-2, the Count property of the Form collection will return 3.

Listing 3-2

```
<form method=post>
Last Name: <input type=text name=LastName>
<br>First Name: <input type=text name=FirstName>
<br>Title:<select name=Title>
    <option Value=1>Mr</option>
    <option Value=2>Ms</option>
    <option Value=3>Miss</option>
    <option Value=4>Mrs</option>
    </select>
<br><input type=submit>
</form>
```

The fourth element in your HTML file, which is a submit button, won't even be recognized. If you try to retrieve its name or value, VB will return an "index out of range" runtime error.

To gain a better understanding of this, look at the example in Listing 3-3, which enables a user to log in to a Members Only area. In this example, there are three HTML pages. The first page (see Figure 3-1) is a welcome page and contains a link to enter the second page. In the second page (see Figure 3-2), there is a form with one TEXT element, one PASSWORD element, and one SUBMIT element. The user must type in a login name and a password. Once the submit button is clicked, the server will send the third page which is the confirmation page that tells the user whether the supplied login name and password are successful (see Figure 3-3) or if the login has failed (see Figure 3-4).

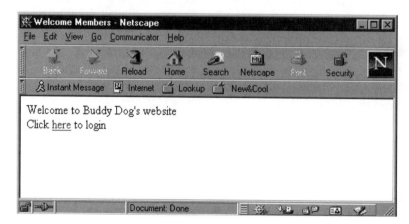

Figure 3-1: The first page, the Welcome page

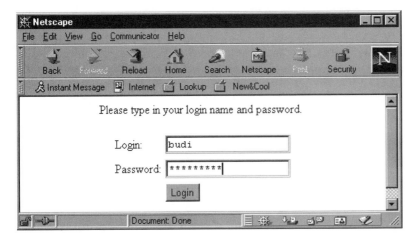

Figure 3-2: The second page, the Login page

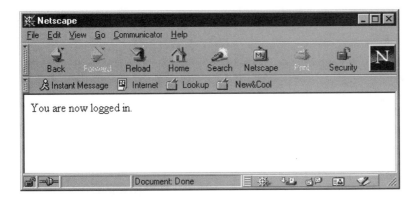

Figure 3-3: The successful login page

Figure 3-4. The failed login page

There are a few approaches to the previous scenario. In this next case, an HTML Template WebItem is used for the second page and the Response object is used to output HTML tags for the first and third pages.

The HTML Template WebItem is named LoginPage and contains the HTML code in Listing 3-3.

Listing 3-3

```
<html>
<head>
</head>

<body>
<center>
Please type in your login name and password.
<form method=post>
<table>
  <tr>
    <td>Login:</td>
    <td><input type=text name=Login></td>
  </tr>
  <tr>
    <td>Password:</td>
    <td><input type=password name=UserPassword></td>
  </tr>
  <tr>
    <td> </td>
    <td><input type=submit value=Login></td>
  </tr>
</table>
</form>
</center>
</body>
</html>
```

For the first page, place the code in Listing 3-4 in the Webclass_Start() event procedure.

Listing 3-4

```
Private Sub WebClass_Start()

  With Response
    .Write "<html>" & vbCr & _
      "<head>" & vbCr & _
      "<title>Welcome Members</title>" & vbCr & _
```

```
      "</head>" & vbCr & _
      "<body>" & vbCr & _
      "Welcome to Buddy Dog's website" & vbCr & _
      "<br>Click <a href=" & URLFor(LoginPage) & _
        ">here</a> to login" & vbCr & _
      "</body>" & vbCr & _
      "</html>"
  End With

End Sub
```

Pay special attention to the line printed in bold. The URLFor method of the WebClass object is used. The method returns a hyperlink that is associated with an event in an item in the WebClass.

In the preceding example, this method returns the URL for the LoginPage HTML Template WebItem. Because the URLFor method is used without the Event parameter, the Respond event is implied. Next, you need to place the code in Listing 3-5 in the Respond event procedure.

Listing 3-5

```
Private Sub LoginPage_Respond()

  LoginPage.WriteTemplate

End Sub
```

It sends the content of the LoginPage HTML Template WebItem to the Web browser.

The statement URLFor(LoginPage) returns wcCH3.ASP?WCI=LoginPage. Note that when you want to connect this hyperlink to the Respond standard event, you must not use "Respond" as the argument, such as in the following line.

```
URLFor(LoginPage, "Respond")
```

This will return wcCH3.ASP?WCI=LoginPage&WCE=Respond, and your WebClass will think that it is associated with a custom event called Respond.

The WebClass Designer should look similar to Figure 3-5.

Now you need to add a custom WebItem by following these steps:

1. Right-click the Custom WebItem folder.

2. Select Add Custom WebItem.

3. Type **Members** as the name of the new custom WebItem.

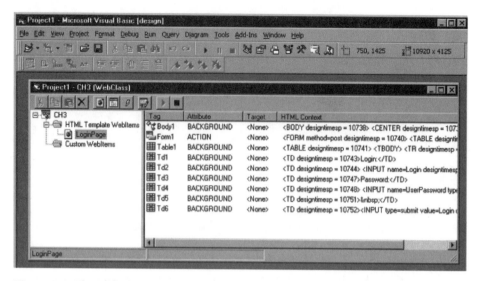

Figure 3-5. The WebClass Designer with the LoginPage WebItem highlighted

4. Right-click the Members WebItem icon, and select Add Custom Event.

5. Type **VerifyLogin** as the name of the event.

The WebClass Designer should now look like Figure 3-6.

Now you need to connect form1 in the LoginPage HTML Template WebItem to the VerifyLogin custom event of the Members custom WebItem. However, you cannot automatically connect to a custom event of a custom WebItem. You can only connect automatically to the standard events of a custom WebItem.

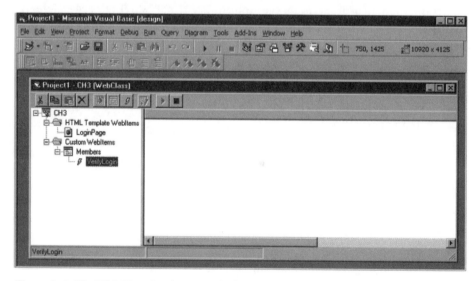

Figure 3-6: The WebClass Designer with the Members WebItem highlighted

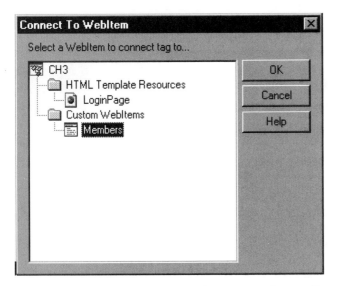

Figure 3-7. Connecting an HTML element to a Custom Event requires editing the HTML Template WebItem

In Chapter 2, I explained how you you could do this by either using the URLFor method or editing the link manually, and provided an example of using the URLFor method. The following example will show how to edit the link in the HTML Template WebItem.

1. Click the LoginPage template.

2. Right-click form1, and select **Connect to WebItem**. A dialog box, which is shown in Figure 3-7 appears.

3. Click the Members WebItem icon, and then click OK.

The form Action attribute is now associated with the Respond standard event of the Members WebItem. Save the WebClass by pressing Ctrl+S<\ss> to apply changes to the LoginPage HTML Template WebItem. The template should look like the code in Listing 3-6.

Listing 3-6

```
<html>
<head>
</head>

<body>
<center>
```

```
Please type in your login name and password.
<form method=post action=CH3.ASP?WCI=Members&amp;WCU>
<table>
  <tr>
    <td>Login:</td>
    <td><input name=Login ></td>
  </tr>
  <tr>
    <td>Password:</td>
    <td><input type=password name=UserPassword></td>
  </tr>
  <tr>
    <td> </td>
    <td><input type=submit value=Login></td>
  </tr>
</table>
</form>
</center>
</body>
</html>
```

Visual Basic has edited the line shown in bold. The characters & represent the ampersand character (&) in HTML. Now add WCE=VerifyLogin& to that boldface line so that it becomes

```
<form method=post action=CH3.ASP?WCI=Members&amp;WCE=VerifyLogin&amp;WCU>
```

If your custom WebItem has only one event that needs to be triggered, you can comfortably use the Respond standard event. Using this event does not require you to connect to the event manually. However, when your WebItem has many custom events that can be fired by different HTML elements, you need to use the URLFor method or manually edit the link to connect an HTML element to a custom event.

From the WebClass Designer, double-click the VerifyLogin event to open its Code window. Insert the code shown in Listing 3-7.

Listing 3-7

```
Private Sub Members_VerifyLogin()

  If Request.Form.Item("Login") = "budi" And _
    Request.Form.Item("UserPassword") = "SeeNoEvil" Then
    Response.Write "You are now logged in."
  Else
```

```
     Response.Write "Login failed."
  End If

End Sub
```

The `Request` object's `Form` collection is used to retrieve user input.

The `Request.Form.Item(`*itemname*`)` can simply be written `Request.Form`
(*itemname*) or even `Request(`*itemname*`)`. With the latter, extra caution must be
taken because if another collection of the Request object has an element with
the same name, VB will not be able to tell which item you are referring to.

In theory, writing `Request.Form(`*itemname*`)` should produce faster code than
`Request(`*itemname*`)`. The reason for this is that without the collection name, all of
the collections must be searched until *itemname* is found. The order of the search
will be QueryString, Form, Cookies, ClientCertificate, and ServerVariables.

If a variable with the same name exists in more than one collection, the
Request object returns the first instance that the object encounters. Therefore,
it is strongly recommended that when referring to members of a collection, the
full name be used, especially if there is a possibility that the same name is used
in two or more collections. For example, rather than `Request.("TheID")` use
`Request.Form("TheID")`.

If you are familiar with HTTP, you probably know that there are two methods
for submitting a form. The first is POST and the second is GET. If the form is missing the method attribute, the GET method is used. With the GET method, the elements' names and values are appended to the URL in the following format:

```
www.myCorp.com/myPage.asp?name1=value1&name2=value2 . . .
```

However, there is a limit on the length of a URL string—typically 2,000 characters. Therefore, the Web browser will truncate a string that contains more than
2,000 characters.

When submitted using the POST method, the content of the form is hidden in
the HTTP request body.

Microsoft has issued a warning against the use of the GET method to submit
a form in IIS applications because the URL is used to pass the destination
WebItem information. If you use the GET method or the method attribute is missing, VB will display the dialog box shown in Figure 3-8 when you try to save the
HTML file you just edited.

If you insist on using the GET method by sending the HTML page containing
a form element using the `Response` object, as in the code in Listing 3-8, you will
get the results shown in Figure 3-9, which look normal. However, when you click
the submit button, the form won't be processed. Therefore, you should stick with
the POST method.

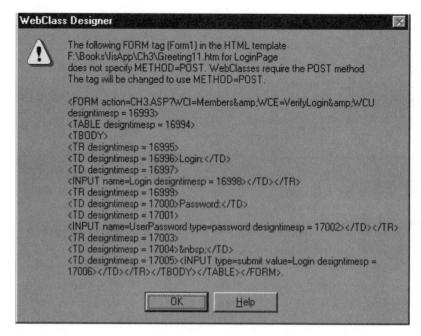

Figure 3-8. You must use the POST method when submitting a form

Listing 3-8

```
Private Sub WebClass_Start()

   With Response
    .Write "<html>" & vbCr & _
      "<head>" & vbCr & _
      "<title>Login Page</title>" & vbCr & _
      "</head>" & vbCr & _
      "<body>" & vbCr & _
      "<form method=get action=" & URLFor(Members, "VerifyLogin") & _
        ">" & vbCr & _
      "What's the password?" & _
      "<br><input type=password name=UserPassword>" & _
      "<br><input type=submit value=""Try Get Method""></form>" & _
      "</body>" & vbCr & _
      "</html>"
   End With

End Sub
```

Figure 3-9: The form using the GET method looks normal, but will fail to submit.

Retrieving Values from Other Types of HTML Elements

So far the examples shown have used the Text element in an HTML form. Retrieving values from other types of HTML elements is no different. As long as you
know the name of the HTML element in a form, you can retrieve the value using
the Request.Form.Item(ElementName) or Request.Form(ElementName) syntax. Use
the following sections as a guide for retrieving values from various types of HTML
elements.

Text

The value will be whatever is typed into the Text element.

Password

The value will be whatever is typed into the Password element, even though the
characters are displayed as asterisks.

Hidden

The value will be whatever is passed from the Web server when the Web server
returns the HTML page where the Hidden element resides.

Select

If the Value attribute is present in the selected option, as in the following code, the value will be the value of the Value attribute of the selected option.

```
<Select Name=Title>
<Option Value=1>Mr</Option>
<Option Value=2>Miss</Option>
<Option Value=3>Ms</Option>
<Option Value=4>Mrs</Option>
</Select>
```

For example, if Miss is selected, Request.Form("Title") will be 2. If the Value attribute is not present, the value will be the text of the selected option, i.e. Miss.

For Select elements that include the Multiple attributes, users can select more than one option. The value will be the combination of all selected options separated by commas. Consider the following example:

```
<Select Name="JobType" Size=5 Multiple>
<Option Value=0>Full time</option>
<Option Value=1>Part time</option>
</Select>
```

If the user selects both Full time and Part time, the value will be 0, 1.

If the Value attribute is not present, as in the following code, the value will be the actual text Full time, Part time, if the user selected both.

```
<Select Name="JobType" Size=5 Multiple>
<Option>Full time</option>
<Option>Part time</option>
</Select>
```

Radio

The value is that of the Value attribute of the selected radio button. For example, the following code will return 4 if the user selects the fourth radio button:

```
<Input type=radio name=Title Value=1>Mr<br>
<Input type=radio name=Title Value=2>Miss<br>
<Input type=radio name=Title Value=3>Ms<br>
<Input type=radio name=Title Value=4>Mrs<br>
```

Checkbox

The value is "on" if the checkbox is selected. If the checkbox is not selected, the element will not even be a member of the Form collection or the Request object.

QueryString

In ASP applications, the QueryString collection allows you to retrieve the information sent by the client using the HTTP GET method with an HTML form and data appended to the URL when the page is requested. Like the Form collection, the QueryString has three properties: Item, Key, and Count.

The syntax is also very similar to the Form collection. To retrieve the value of an item in the QueryString collections, use the following syntax, where *n* is the number of the element in the HTML form.

```
strKeyName = Request.QueryString.Key(n)
strKeyValue = Request.QueryString.Item(n)
```

The Count property returns the number of elements in the collection.

You can use this collection to pass values to the subsequent HTML page. The following example consists of two HTML pages. The first page simply displays a hyperlink. The code to display the first HTML page is written in the WebClass_Start event procedure and is given in Listing 3-9.

Listing 3-9
```
Private Sub WebClass_Start()

  Dim strName As String
  Dim intApplicationID As Integer

  strName = "Laylian"
  intApplicationID = 27
  Response.Write "<a href=" & URLFor(Members, "SayHello") & _
  "&Name=" & strName & "&ApplicationID=" & intApplicationID & _
  ">Continue</a>"

End Sub
```

The code in Listing 3-9 simply displays a hyperlink that connects to the SayHello custom event of the Members custom WebItem. However, appended to the URL are two pairs of variables: Name and ApplicationID. The values of these variables are strName and intApplicationID, respectively. Each variable name and value pair is separated from each other by the ampersand (&) character. Note that the WebClass has at least one such variable that indicates the WebItem and event to connect to; therefore, the first variable Name is also prefixed with an ampersand. Also notice that the variable names and values are appended to the URL:

```
http://localhost/CH3/CH3.ASP?WCI=Members&WCE=SayHello&Name=Laylian&ApplicationID=27
```

These variables are contained by the QueryString collection of the Request object. To retrieve the values, you need to create the Members custom WebItem and the SayHello custom event. You also need to use the code in Listing 3-10.

Listing 3-10

```
Private Sub Members_SayHello()

  Response.Write "Your name is " & Request.QueryString.Item("Name") & _
    "<br>" & "Your application ID is " & _
    Request.QueryString.Item("ApplicationID")

End Sub
```

When the previous code is run, the Web browser will display a hyperlink. When you click the hyperlink, the following result appears on your Web browser.

```
Your name is Laylian
Your application ID is 27
```

Remember, your QueryString's item key must not be WCI, WCE, or WCU because VB uses these three keywords for its event processing. Consider the modified code in Listing 3-11.

Listing 3-11

```
Private Sub WebClass_Start()

  Dim strName As String
  Dim intApplicationID As Integer

  strName = "Laylian"
  intApplicationID = 27
  Response.Write "<a href=" & URLFor(Members, "SayHello") & _
    "&WCI=" & strName & "&ApplicationID=" & intApplicationID & _
    ">Continue</a>"
```

```
End Sub

Private Sub Members_SayHello()

  Response.Write "Your name is " & Request.QueryString.Item("WCI") & _
    "<br>" & "Your application ID is " & _
    Request.QueryString.Item("ApplicationID")

End Sub
```

Notice that the key name "Name" is replaced with "WCI". The following result appears when you click the hyperlink.

```
Your name is Members, Laylian
Your application ID is 27
```

VB doesn't complain and it looks legal, but now the value of WCI is the combination of values of both WCI variables, separated by a comma.

Although this is a very effective means of passing values to the next page, special caution must be taken when using this method. Bear in mind that Web browsers limit the length of a URL to about 2KB. Also, several special characters are used in the QueryString collection:

- &: The ampersand is used to delineate separate parameter/value pairs that have been added to the QueryString collection.

- ?: The question mark is used to define the beginning of the QueryString in the URL.

- %: The percentage symbol is used to encode other special characters.

- +: The plus sign represents a space.

If your QueryString happens to have any of these four characters, you must encode it using the URLEncode and HTMLEncode methods of the Server object. These two methods are very easy to use. Note that if you use the Response object's Write method to send the string to the browser, the Write method does this encoding for you.

Apart from appending variable/value pairs to the URL, you can also use the URLData property of the WebClass to pass a value to the subsequent HTML page. Take a close look at the following example shown in Listings 3.12 and 3.13. This example consists of two pages. The first page, in Listing 3-12, displays a hyperlink that connects to the SayHello event of the Members WebItem, like the previous example. The difference is the URLData property, which is used to pass the value 37. Like the QueryString collection, a value passed this way is part of the URL. However, VB has set aside a special variable name for the content of the URLData property. The variable is WCU.

Listing 3-12

```
Private Sub WebClass_Start()

  URLData = 37
  Response.Write "<a href=" & URLFor(Members, "SayHello") & ">Continue</a>"

End Sub
```

Use the code in Listing 3-13 to retrieve the URLData property and pass it back to the Web browser.

Listing 3-13

```
Private Sub Members_SayHello()

  Response.Write "The value from the previous page is " & URLData

End Sub
```

The result of the second page is

```
The value from the previous page is 37
```

And the URL is

```
http://localhost/CH3/CH3.ASP?WCI=Members&WCE=SayHello&WCU=37
```

When you use the URLData property and the value you want to pass contains one of the special characters, the Write method automatically encodes it for you. Suppose the value of the URLData property is ???. The three questions marks are automatically translated into %3f%3f%3f. This is then translated back into ??? on the subsequent HTML page by the Web browser.

ServerVariables

The ServerVariables collection contains items that hold useful environment information in the context of the client's specific HTTP request of the Web server.

Among other things, you can retrieve information about Windows user accounts and the client machine's TCP/IP. For example, you can use the REMOTE_ADDR element to limit access to certain users or to reject access from a particular machine that has been caught trying to hack into your organization.

To retrieve a value, simply type **Request.ServerVariables(*key*)**, where *key* is the element of the ServerVariables collection. A complete list of all the elements in the ServerVariables collection is given in Appendix B.

If a client sends a header other than those specified in Appendix B, you can retrieve the value of that header by prefixing the header name with HTTP_ in the call to Request.ServerVariables. For example, if the client sends the following header:

```
myHeader:myValue
```

you could retrieve myValue by using the following syntax:

```
Request.ServerVariables("HTTP_myHeader")
```

You can also use an iterator to loop through each server variable name, as in the code in Listing 3-14.

Listing 3-14

```
Private Sub WebClass_Start()

  Dim element

  For Each element In Request.ServerVariables
    Response.Write element & " : " & _
      Request.ServerVariables(element) & "<br>"
  Next

End Sub
```

Cookies

Cookies were created to overcome the problem of having a stateless protocol like HTTP. Cookies are small pieces of information passed from the Web server to the Web browser and vice versa to retain information from a previous HTML page. Cookies and the problems associated with a stateless protocol are discussed in Chapter 7.

ClientCertificate

The ClientCertificate collection provides access to the certification fields of the client's digital certificate. This topic is discussed in Chapter 10.

Response Object

In Chapter 2, you saw that you can use the Response object to send output to the Web browser. Actually, you can do much more with this object. Not only can you control what you send with the Response object, but when and how you send it. Table 3-2 provides a summary of the Response object.

There are many properties and methods that are useful to control how the Web server sends its output. For instance, using the Buffer property, you can

Table 3-2. Response Object Summary

PROPERTIES
Buffer
CacheControl
Charset
ContentType
Expires
ExpiresAbsolute
IsClientConnected
PICS
Status

COLLECTIONS
Cookies

METHODS
AddHeader
AppendToLog
BinaryWrite
Clear
End
Flush
Redirect
Write

EVENTS
None

defer sending output to the Web browser until the entire code is processed. Or, if you know that processing will take some time, you can force the Web server to send whatever is ready so users won't think their computer has crashed. The Buffer property is an important one. In fact, the ASP page that hosts your WebClass uses the following statement by default:

```
Response.Buffer = True
```

This, in effect, makes the WebClass buffer the output string in the Response object until the processing is finished. If the flow of a program goes the wrong way, perhaps because an error occurs, you can clear the buffer by using the Clear method. If you think that it's better to let the user know that the Web server is still working hard processing the request, you can force the Web server to send whatever is in the response buffer using the Flush method. To clear the response buffer if an error occurs, you can use the following code in the event handler.

```
ErrHandler:
    ' an error has occured and the buffer is holding
    ' some output prior to the error
    Response.Clear   ' clear the Response buffer
    Response.Write "An Error has occured. Please contact the Administrator."

    . . .
```

If you don't use the Flush method, the Response buffer automatically flushes when the WebClass is about to be terminated or when you call the End method as in:

```
Response.End
```

However, when you use the End method, the processing of your WebClass will be abruptly terminated and the code after the call won't be processed. You can only call the Clear, End, or Flush methods if the Buffer property has been set to True. If the Buffer property is set to False, any call to the Clear, End, or Flush methods results in a runtime error. If the Buffer property is set to False, the Web server sends information to the browser as your code is processed. Note that in ASP 2.0 the Buffer property has a default value of False, but in ASP 3.0 this property defaults to True.

Having access to the Response object means that you control all aspects of what you send to the browser. With the Response object, you can determine whether the proxy servers serving your pages can cache your page. You control this by using the CacheControl property, which accepts either the string value "Private" (the default) or "Public". If the value of this property is "Private", the page won't be cached by the proxy server. Conversely, if it is set to "Public", it will be cached by the proxy server if the proxy server has been configured to do so. Because WebClasses return output that changes all the time, depending on user requests, you may want to leave the CacheControl property setting with the default value and not let proxy servers cache your page.

Although the CacheControl property controls the caching at the proxy server, it has no control over the other level of caching: the browser caching. Nevertheless, you can use the Expires and ExpiresAbsolute properties to politely ask the Web browser to retain your HTML pages in its cache for a certain length of time.

The Expires property specifies the length of time in minutes that the Web browser must cache the current page. If you set this property to 60, as in the following code line, and the user comes back within an hour to the same page, the Web browser will not try to request the page from the Web server. Instead, it will just grab the cached page and present it to the user.

```
Response.Expires = 60
```

The ExpiresAbsolute property sets a date and time on which the current page will cease being cached on the client machine. The syntax of this property is

```
Response.ExpiresAbsolute [ = [Date] [Time]]
```

A valid example using this syntax is

```
Response.ExpiresAbsolute = #May 2, 2002 13:00:00#
```

Note that you must use the pound # character to designate the date and time with this property. If the time portion is missing, the time is assumed to be midnight on the date specified. The ExpiresAbsolute has one disadvantage: It only works as intended if the Web server time is the same as the client machine's. Understand that some people don't bother to set their computer time, and some purposely set it behind the real time, in some cases because they want to enjoy 30-day freeware a little longer.

At any rate, whether or not the Expires and ExpiresAbsolute work is at the discretion of the Web browser.

When programming with WebClasses, oftentimes you don't want your page to be cached at all, so that any time a user returns to the same page, the Web browser will make a new request for that page to the Web server. To do this, you can set the Expires property to 0, which will make your page expire right away.

```
Response.Expires = 0
```

Another important feature of the Response object is its ability to redirect users to another URL. Take a look at the following example.

```
Select Case Request.Form("OtherWebSite")
  Case "Microsoft"
    Response.Redirect "http://www.microsoft.com"
  Case "Oracle"
    Response.Redirect "http://www.oracle.com"
  Case "Symantec"
    Response.Redirect "http://www.symantec.com"
  Case Else
    Response.Redirect "AnotherLocalPage.asp"
End Select
```

Depending on the value the user entered into the form on the previous HTML page, the user will be redirected to another URL. Note that you must include the http: part of the URL to redirect the request to a page outside your application. If http: is not used, VB will think that it is supposed to redirect the user to one of its pages on the same application, such as the following, which of course doesn't exist:

http://localhost/ch3/ch3.asp/www.microsoft.com

> **NOTE:** *If you are using IIS 5.0 and you are redirecting a request to another URL in the same machine, you can use the* Transfer *method of the Server object to do the redirection. The* Transfer *method is faster than the* Redirect *method because with the* Redirect *method, the Web server actually sends a response to the browser that makes the browser request another page. With the* Transfer *method, however, the Web server does the redirection itself, therefore eliminating the round-trip to the client. Note that you can't transfer requests to a different machine using the* Transfer *method.*

Navigating between WebClasses

For modularity and code reusability, you may want to split your application into more than one WebClass. If your IIS application has more than one WebClass, a new issue that arises, which is how to navigate between WebClasses.

Each WebClass in an IIS application has a corresponding .asp file, and the only way to pass a request to another WebClass is through its .asp file. You do this by using the Redirect method of the Response object. When a redirect is called in an event procedure, the runtime DLL suspends processing on the current WebClass, shifts its focus to the indicated WebClass, and launches its BeginRequest event. Control can be returned to the original WebClass by using another redirect. For example, the following line of code redirects control to the Search custom event of the Products custom WebItem in the OtherWebClass WebClass:

```
Response.Redirect "OtherWebclass.asp?WCI=Products&WCE=Search"
```

If you are using IIS 5.0, you can also use the Server object's Transfer method, and the previous line can be rewritten as such:

```
Server.Transfer("OtherWebclass.asp?WCI=Products&WCE=Search")
```

Server Object

The Server object represents the Web server itself. Much of the functionality of the Server object is simply the functionality of the Web server. For example, the Server object's property ScriptTimeout specifies the maximum amount of time the Web server will continue processing your script before it eventually gives up and sends an error message to the Web browser.

The default value of this property is 90 seconds. When a user requests the ASP page that hosts your WebClass, the WebClass is given 90 seconds to process the request. You need to increase this time if your WebClass will be performing a time-consuming task. Change the default value by assigning a new value to this property as in

```
Server.ScriptTimeout = 300
```

Table 3-3 contains a complete summary of the Server object.

Table 3-3. Server Object Summary

PROPERTIES
ScriptTimeout

COLLECTIONS
None

METHODS
CreateObject
HTMLEncode
MapPath
URLEncode

EVENTS
None

The Server object doesn't have a collection or an event. Though not as frequently used as the Request or Response objects, its four methods are invaluable. The HTMLEncode method encodes certain characters that have special meanings to a Web browser. For example, if you want to send the less than character (<) to the browser, you need to use the HTMLEncode method because HTML pages use tags that are enclosed by the less than character (<) and the greater than character (>), as in <br>.

As an example, you might try this:

```
Response.Write "Use <br> to change line."
```

to display this string

```
Use <br> to change line.
```

However, in a Web browser, it will be displayed as

```
Use
to change line.
```

The < and > characters are considered sacred by the Web browser and should not be used as normal characters. If you want to display these characters, you must change them to < and > respectively. Thus, the following code line is accurate:

```
Response.Write "User &lt;br&gt; to change line."
```

Imagine how troublesome it is to deal with these special characters. The Server object's HTMLEncode method comes to the rescue. Using this method eliminates the need to translate special characters; for example:

```
Response.Write Server.HTMLEncode("Use <br> to change line.")
```

The MapPath method returns the physical path on the server given a virtual or relative path. For example, if you want to open an Access file called CompanySecret.mdb that resides in the ForYourBossOnly directory under the current directory you can use

```
Server.MapPath("/ForYourBossOnly/CompanySecret.mdb")
```

to refer to it, instead of writing the physical path
`C:\AcctApp\ForYourBossOnly\CompanySecret.mdb`.

By using the `MapPath` method, you don't have to change the code if your application is deployed to a different physical path than your development machine. This method is similar to the App.Path in VB. You must remember two things when using this method. First, it does not support the standard MS-DOS relative directory notation (. or ..). Second, it is your responsibility to make sure that the given physical directory exists.

Another example of this method's usage is given in Chapter 5.

Similar to the `HTMLEncode` method is the `URLEncode` method. The latter, as mentioned earlier in this chapter, encodes a string to be appended to a URL. You can use this method if your string contains the space character, ampersand, or equals sign to save you from having to convert it into hard to remember alternatives.

So, instead of writing &name=budi, you can now use

```
Server.URLEncode("&name=budi")
```

The final method, `CreateObject`, instantiates an object on the server. This method is explained in Chapter 11.

Application Object

The `Request` and `Response` objects are exclusive to one user request. Having the `Application` object is like having access to global variables. For each IIS application running on the Web server, there is one `Application` object no matter how many users are accessing the application. In other words, all users share the same Application object.

Table 3-4 Application Object Summary

PROPERTIES
None

COLLECTIONS
Contents
StaticObjects

METHODS
Lock
Unlock

EVENTS
OnStart
OnEnd

For example, you can have a counter that gets incremented each time a user requests the main page. Because they are accessible to all users, variables in the `Application` object are said to have application scope. Table 3-4 summarizes the features of the `Application` object.

The `Application` object is created the first time a user requests any ASP page in the virtual root. Because you normally only have one ASP page in your IIS application, it is the ASP page that is created by VB when you first start your project. When is the `Application` object destroyed? Never. After it is created, it lives as long as the Web server is running or until the IIS application is unloaded from the Web server (using the MMC).

Like global variables in traditional form-based VB applications, application-level variables in IIS applications should be handled with care. Use them only if they are irreplaceable. Every variable takes some space in memory and once created, the variables also live as long as the `Application` object exists. Put another way, you can never reclaim the memory used by this type of variable.

The `Application` object has two collections: `Contents` and `StaticObjects`. You can use the `Contents` collection to store your application variables and use the `StaticObjects` to store all objects that you want to be accessed by all users. More information about the second collection is offered in Chapter 7. For now, let's discuss the `Contents` collection in more detail.

The `Contents` collection has three properties: `Key`, `Item`, and `Count`. `Key` represents the name of a specific element in the `Contents` collection. If you want to know the *name* of your application variable, use this property. The `Item` property, on the other hand, allows you to access the value of the application variable.

You don't dimension an application variable to use it. The moment VB reaches the line of code that assigns a value to the `Contents` collection's item, similar to the following line:

```
Application.Contents.Item("VisitorCount") = 9
```

one of two things can happen:

1. If the variable of the same name (in this case `VisitorCount`) does not exist, one with that name will be created and assigned a value (in this case 9). Variable names are not case sensitive, therefore `VisitorCount` and `VISITORCOUNT` are the same.

2. If the variable of the same name can be found, the old value will be overwritten by the new value.

The third property, `Count`, represents the total number of elements in the Contents collection.

If you don't know the name of a particular element, you can use its index number to obtain it. The indexing starts with 1 not 0. The following line assigns the name of the fourth member of the Contents collection:

```
strKeyName = Application.Contents(4)
```

To obtain its value, use the Item property, as follows:

```
strKeyValue = Application.Contents.Item(4)
```

However, other than for enumerating the collection, this technique should be avoided. In fact, there is ample flexibility in how to access an element in the Contents collection. Suppose the fourth element is called VisitorCount. You can get its value by using one of the following lines:

```
strKeyValue = Application.Contents.Item(4)
strKeyValue = Application.Contents (4)
strKeyValue = Application (4)
strKeyValue = Application.Contents.Item("VisitorCount")
strKeyValue = Application.Contents ("VisitorCount")
strKeyValue = Application ("VisitorCount")
```

Because application-level variables are shared among all users, you may wonder if there is a possibility that two users can try to change a variable value at the same time? Yes, there is. That is the reason the Application object comes equipped with two important methods: Lock and Unlock.

The Lock method prevents other users from changing the value of any application-level variable. Normally, you call this method before you update an application-level variable value. After the change, you unlock the Application object by calling the Unlock method.

If you don't unlock the Application object after you've locked it, it will be unlocked automatically when the .asp file that created the WebClass finishes processing. As good programming practice, you should call the UnLock method as soon as it is possible to do so.

The Application object has two events: OnStart and OnEnd. The OnStart event is triggered when the first client request is received. This only happens once during the life of the IIS application. The OnEnd is triggered when the IIS application is unloaded from the Web server.

The question you may want to ask is, how do you write event procedures for these two events? You don't write these event procedures in your WebClass. You write them in a special file called global.asa. In Chapter 2, I noted that this file is created when you run your IIS application from inside VB, and it will be deleted automatically when you end the application. If you want a permanent global.asa file, you must create it yourself. If VB senses the presence of a global.asa file in the virtual directory, it won't create a new one and it won't delete it when you end the application.

The global.asa is also the place where you dimension and initialize all your application-level variables. Even though you can do this from your WebClass, it is not recommended to do so because if you do, the variables will scatter all over the code and will be more difficult to manage.

What kind of information needs to be global? Not much, but you can record information that can help you analyze how successful your Web site is. For example, you can monitor when your application is first active by writing code to record the time when it is first accessed. You can also store a variable to count the number of hits the main page gets, and so on.

> **WARNING:** *Use application-level variables with caution.*

Session Object

One serious fact: Web servers are forgetful. After the server sends the response to the user who requests a page, the Web server will not remember whether or not the user has been to that page. After sending the page to the user, it just closes the connection (and does not expect the user to come back for another page). This means that if a Web site requires you to type in a login name and password for each page, you would then have to type in this information every time you move to another page.

But this doesn't happen, thanks to those smart guys who invented the HTTP protocol. They found ways to get around this problem by somehow retaining user information. The topic of how to retain user information is of paramount importance and has been given a lengthy chapter of its own in this book in Chapter 7.

The information retained by the server for each individual client is stored in the Session object. Because the Web server can have multiple connections, it will create one Session object for each client. The Session object is created when a client requests a page. Any information, such as login name and password, can be stored in the Session object. In addition to the page requested, the server also sends a unique number, a Session ID, to the Web browser, which is invisible to the user and stored in the user's machine. The Session ID is the unique identifier that distinguishes one Session object from another.

When the user requests another page, the Web browser passes back the Session ID. Upon receiving this request and the Session ID, the Web server finds the Session object created for that particular user and uses the information stored previously. These hidden bytes of information passed back and forth between the Web server and the browser are called cookies.

Unfortunately, not all browsers are modern enough to accept cookies from Web servers. For the sake of security, some people turn off the cookies' accepting feature of their browsers because they don't want strangers to be able to write a file to their disk. Therefore, it must not be taken for granted that the use of the Session object is always acceptable. Also, because a Session object consumes server memory, you must not use it excessively. Table 3-5 summarizes the Session object.

The SessionID property is a random number generated by the Web server. It is a 32-bit signature that is guaranteed unique from the minute the Web server is restarted to the time it is sent to sleep. But, how random is a random Session ID? Unfortunately, it seems that the randomness only applies to the first Session ID issued by the server. The subsequent Session ID properties are simply numbers that are incremented by one.

The Timeout property determines how many minutes the Session object for a user is retained from the last time the user accessed a page in the application. The default is 20 minutes, but you can change this value.

The OnStart and OnEnd events of the Session object are very similar to those in the Application object. The difference is the events of the Session object are of session scope. The Session object's OnStart event is triggered the first time a user accesses a page on the Web server. How does the web server know that it is someone's first time? Because the request does not come with a Session ID that is recognized by the server. The implication is, a request without a Session ID triggered this event. This happens when a user turns off the Web browser support for cook-

Table 3-5. Session Object Summary

PROPERTIES
CodePage
LCID
SessionID
Timeout

COLLECTIONS
Contents
StaticObjects

METHODS
Abandon

EVENTS
OnEnd
OnStart

ies. The request from the user triggers the OnStart event for any requests follow-ing the first.

What can you put in the OnStart event procedure? You can use the OnStart event, among other things, to increase a counter stored in the Application object or a file to get statistics on how many *different* users have visited your Web site.

The OnEnd event is triggered when a session times out, that is, the Web server has waited 20 minutes (or whatever period set for the Timeout property) and the user has not returned. If the same user returns 30 minutes after his or her last ac-cess, the request still carries the Session ID from the previous session, but it is too late to retrieve the previous information. So, the rule says that any request with-out a Session ID must be redirected to the Login page, therefore, the user will have to log in again.

The OnEnd event can also triggered when the code deliberately terminates a session by calling the Abandon method. This is normally used when users want to log out, so if they leave their Web browser open, no one can use the Session ID assigned to them to access pages without first identifying themselves.

You use the OnStart and the OnEnd event procedures in the global.asa file.

More details about the Session object are included in Chapter 7.

The BrowserType Object

You can use the BrowserType object to determine the capabilities of the user's browser and make processing decisions based on that information. For example, depending on whether or not the user's browser can handle JavaScript, you can either send an HTML form that includes JavaScript client-side input validation functions, or send the same form without JavaScript scripts. To detect whether the user's browser can handle JavaScript, use the following lines of code.

```
If BroswerType.javascript Then
' Send HTML page containing JavaScript scripts
    .
    .
    .
Else
    ' Send HTML page without JavaScript scripts
    .
    .
    .
End If
```

Or, you can use BrowserType.tables to find out if the user's browser can ren-der HTML tables.

However, when using the BrowserType object to detect whether the user's browser supports JavaScript, your Web server won't know whether the JavaScript capability is turned on or off. The user's browser could support JavaScript, but if this feature is turned off, the browser can't process the JavaScript scripts. Chapter 6 explains how you can detect whether or not the JavaScript capability is turned on.

How does the Web server know what type of browser the user has? Remember that one of the variables in the Request object's ServerVariables collection is HTTP_USER_AGENT. This variable returns a string, such as:

```
Mozilla/4.5 [en] (Win98; I)
```

or

```
Mozilla/4.0 (compatible; MSIE 4.01; Windows 98)
```

which the BrowserType object can use to detect the user's browser type. However, how does the BrowserType know what features are supported by that browser? The HTTP headers sent from the browser to the Web server don't include this information. The answer lies in an .ini file called browscap.ini that resides on the Inetsvr directory under the Windows System directory. This file contains the information about most current and older browsers. There is also a default section that's used when a browser's user agent string does not match any of the ones specified in the file. The browscap.ini has the following syntax.

```
[; comments]
```

```
[HTTPUserAgentHeader]
```

```
[parent = browserDefinition]
```

```
[property1 = value1]
```

```
. . .
```

```
 [propertyN = valueN]
```

```
[Default Browser Capability Settings]
```

```
[defaultProperty1 = defaultValue1]
```

```
. . .
```

```
[defaultPropertyN = defaultValueN]
```

The parameters are described in the next few sections.

Comments

A comment consists of any line that starts with a semicolon (;). Comments, which are ignored by the BrowserType object, can occur anywhere in the browscap.ini file.

HTTPUserAgentHeader

This parameter specifies the HTTP User Agent header to associate with the browser property value statements specified in *propertyN*. The browscap.ini file may contain multiple browser definitions, each one starting with a unique *HTTPUserAgentHeader* value.

You can use the asterisk * character as a wild card character in the *HTTPUser AgentHeader* to replace zero or more characters.

For example, if you specified the following string for *HTTPUserAgentHeader*:

```
[Mozilla/2.0 (compatible; MSIE 3.0;* Windows 95)]
```

it would match all of the following User Agent headers:

```
[Mozilla/2.0 (compatible; MSIE 3.0; Windows 95)]
[Mozilla/2.0 (compatible; MSIE 3.0; AK; Windows 95)]
[Mozilla/2.0 (compatible; MSIE 3.0; SK; Windows 95)]
[Mozilla/2.0 (compatible; MSIE 3.0; AOL; Windows 95)]
```

> **NOTE:** *The BrowserType object first attempts to exactly match the User Agent header to a value of HTTPUserAgentHeader. If that fails, it attempts to make a match that uses wild card characters.*

If more than one browser definition containing wildcard characters matches the User Agent header, the BrowserType object returns the properties of the first matching definition.

browserDefinition

The *browserDefinition* is an optional parameter specifying the HTTP User Agent header string of a browser to use as the parent browser. The current browser's definition will inherit all of the property values declared in the parent browser's definition. This helps define properties for a new version of a browser because new versions usually retain most of the properties of the previous release. These inherited property values can be overwritten by explicitly setting a new value for the property by using the syntax *propertyN = valueN*.

propertyN

An optional parameter, *propertyN* specifies the name of the browser property to set. It must start with an alphabetical character and cannot be longer than 255 characters. Each browser definition in the browscap.ini file can contain as many statements of property values as needed.

For example, if your application only needs to know whether or not a user's browser supports VBScript, you would only need one property statement for each browser definition. Table 3-6 lists some possible properties.

valueN

An optional parameter, *valueN* specifies the value of *propertyN.* This value is a string by default. To specify an integer, prefix the value with a number sign (#). To specify a Boolean value, use TRUE or FALSE.

Table 3-6: Possible Browser Properties

PROPERTY	DESCRIPTION
ActiveXControls	Specifies whether the browser supports ActiveX controls.
Backgroundsounds	Specifies whether the browser supports background sounds.
Beta	Specifies whether the browser is beta software.
Browser	Specifies the name of the browser.
Cdf	Specifies whether the browser supports the Channel Definition Format for webcasting.
Cookies	Specifies whether the browser supports cookies.
Frames	Specifies whether the browser supports frames.
Javaapplets	Specifies whether the browser supports Java applets.
Javascript	Specifies whether the browser supports JScript™.
Platform	Specifies the platform that the browser runs on.
Tables	Specifies whether the browser supports tables.
Vbscript	Specifies whether the browser supports VBScript.
Version	Specifies the version number of the browser.

defaultPropertyN

An optional parameter, *defaultPropertyN* specifies the name of the browser property to which to assign a default value if none of the defined *HTTPUserAgentHeader* values match the HTTP User Agent header sent by the browser.

defaultValueN

An optional parameter, *defaultValueN* specifies the value of *defaultPropertyN*. This value is a string by default. To specify an integer, prefix the value with a number sign (#). To specify a Boolean value, use TRUE or FALSE.

In the following example, the parent tag allows the second browser definition to inherit from the first, so that the Microsoft Internet Explorer 3.01 definition inherits all the properties of the Microsoft Internet Explorer 3.0 definition (for example, frames=TRUE, tables=TRUE, and cookies=TRUE). It adds platform-specific information by adding the line, platform=Win95, and overwrites the version information in the following lines:

```
version=3.01.
;;ie 3.01
 [IE 3.0]
browser=IE
Version=3.0
majorver=#3
minorver=#0
frames=TRUE
tables=TRUE
cookies=TRUE
backgroundsounds=TRUE
vbscript=TRUE
javascript=TRUE
javaapplets=True
ActiveXControls=TRUE
Win16=False
beta=False
AK=False
SK=False
AOL=False
```

```
;;ie 3.01
 [Mozilla/2.0 (compatible; MSIE 3.01*; Windows 95)]
parent=IE 3.0
version=3.01
minorver=01
platform=Win95

; Default Browser
[Default Browser Capability Settings]
browser=Default
frames=FALSE
tables=TRUE
cookies=FALSE
backgroundsounds=FALSE
vbscript=FALSE
javascript=FALSE
```

Because new versions of Web browsers are continuously released, it is very important to keep the browscap.ini up-to-date. Fortunately, you can download an updated version of this file from Microsoft's Web site and from some other companies' Web sites, such as CyScape, Inc. at `http://www.cyscape.com/browscap/`.

CHAPTER 4
Accessing Databases

WITHOUT THE ABILITY TO ACCESS A DATABASE, an Internet application is more than crippled. The World Wide Web would not be as popular as it is today if it did not have the capability to store and retrieve data. Your skills to create efficient Web applications are needed to access and manipulate data. Without exaggeration, data access is one of the most important parts of a successful Web application.

Because data access is such an important topic, two lengthy chapters in this book provide detailed information: this chapter and Chapter 5. In addition, there are also two appendixes related to database access at the end of this book. In this chapter, you will learn how to set up a connection to your database and do some simple manipulations, such as retrieving data, inserting a new record, and updating and deleting a record. In the next chapter, you will find discussions on how to optimize your data access to make your application run faster and consume fewer system resources.

Some Database Basics

Data must be stored in a database, either in a desktop database or in a server database. If the size of your data is reasonably small and the traffic that stores and retrieves data is relatively low, then a desktop database is appropriate for your application. With Internet Information Server (IIS) Applications, your choice of database is naturally Microsoft Access. On the other hand, if you expect to have heavy traffic and the size of your data is huge, you need to turn to a more powerful type of database: a server database. There are a variety of products to choose from. Microsoft SQL Server, Sybase SQL Server, and Oracle are examples of good products.

In theory, you can access any database from your WebClass as well as from other traditional VB applications. Also, the database does not have to be Windows-based. If you have an Informix database server sitting on a Unix platform, you can store your data and access it from your WebClass.

Your database does not have to be on the same machine as the Web server. In fact, if you are building a large Web site that gets a lot of hits, you may want to put your database server in a separate machine to provide a better and faster response to the user. You might ask, isn't putting it in a separate server slower because data has to travel through the network? Yes, data does have to travel through the network, but the time taken by the data transfer is relatively trivial compared to the database processing time.

Installing a database server on a separate machine means that the database server has a monopoly on the CPU time of that machine. It doesn't have to share the CPU power with the Web server and your IIS application.

A Universal Way of Accessing Data

Prior to OLE DB, Windows applications communicated with databases through programs called Open Database Connectivity (ODBC) drivers. The driver needed was specific to the database. A different driver was needed to access an Oracle database than the driver used to access a Microsoft SQL Server database.

ODBC works well and it still serves the software community. However, it falls short when you need access to non-database information, such as e-mails on your Exchange Server. To overcome this problem, Microsoft devised a new technology, which it expects will become a universal way of manipulating data and hence solve this problem.

Microsoft calls this new technology *Universal Data Access*. Introduced in 1996, the idea was to provide access to all types of data through a single data access model. This Universal Data Access paradigm utilizes OLE DB and ActiveX Data Objects (ADO). More information on Universal Data Access can be found at http://www.microsoft.com/data/.

OLE DB's architecture goes beyond Microsoft Jet and Indexed Sequential Access Method (ISAM) as well as relational databases. OLE DB is envisioned to interface with all sorts of data, regardless of its format or storage method. OLE DB is also an open standard that will replace ODBC in the future, though not the near future. However, OLE DB will also include ODBC, so wherever a native provider (which is equivalent to an ODBC driver) to a database is not yet available, an application can still access a database through ODBC. Figure 4-1 shows the architecture of OLE DB.

However, OLE DB is very complex, and you can't access it directly from Visual Basic. Fortunately, Microsoft created ADO, which hides the complexity from the programmer. Easy to understand, ADO takes over the difficulty of communicating with OLE DB providers.

When you install VB, ADO components will also be installed for you. As Microsoft keeps issuing new versions, you should continually update to the latest version from the Microsoft Web site. ADO is bundled in the Microsoft Data Access Components (MDAC), which you can download gratis from www.microsoft.com/data/download.htm. The MDAC typical redistribution installation contains the core components (ADO, OLE DB, and ODBC) and additional OLE DB providers and ODBC drivers for various data stores.

Let's take a look at the ADO object model.

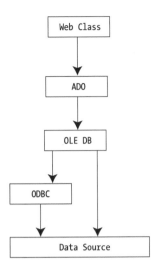

Figure 4-1. OLE DB architecture

The ADO Object Model

Even though you can use other object models, such as the aging Data Access Objects (DAO) and Remote Data Objects (RDO), ADO is really the way to go. If you are familiar with the two ADO predecessors, you will be relieved to find out that the new star is much slimmer and easier to deal with.

ADO enables programmers to access a broader variety of data sources through either OLE DB providers or existing ODBC drivers via the OLE DB to ODBC bridge. This bridge really made ADO more acceptable and helped it to gain the popularity it has today. By using this bridge, programmers can instantly access any database that has an ODBC driver while waiting for other databases to get OLE DB providers of their own.

ADO is believed (at least by Microsoft) to be the future of database technology and is Microsoft's current golden child. Using the older technology will probably deprive you of proper support in the future.

ADO 1.0 first appeared in the winter of 1996 with the introduction of Microsoft Transaction Server 1.0 and IIS 3.0. Less than a year later, in 1997, version 1.5 was born, bringing with it much of its desirable functionality. ADO 2.0 ships with Visual Studio 6.0 and Visual Basic 6.0, and not long after that, version 2.1 became available.

At the time of this writing, ADO is at version 2.5. Some new objects for handling unstructured data, such as the Record object and the Stream object, have been added to the new version. However, this book will concentrate on ADO version 2.0 and will not include discussion of the new objects.

The ADO object model is shown in Figure 4-2.

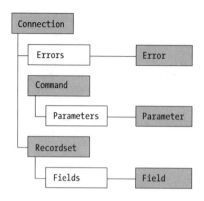

Figure 4-2. The ADO object model

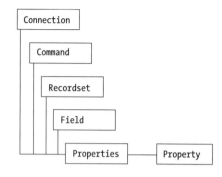

Figure 4-3. The Properties collection

There are six objects in the model: Connection, Command, Recordset, Error, Parameter, and Field. There are also three collections: Errors, Parameters, and Fields. Each of the Connection, Command, Recordset, and Field objects also has a Properties collection, as shown in Figure 4-3.

The Connection and Recordset objects, the two most commonly used objects in ADO, are discussed in this chapter. Discussions about other objects can be found in Chapter 5. A complete reference on all the objects is given in Appendix C.

The Connection Object

The Connection object plays a very important role in ADO. You need a Connection object to connect to a database. Just like a telephone conversation in which you need to dial a number to set up a telephone connection in order to "communicate" with the database server, your WebClass must have a connection, too.

An ADO object can be created in either of two ways: explicitly and implicitly. You create an ADO object explicitly when you specifically declare a Connection object variable and use the New keyword to instantiate the variable, as in the following code:

```
Dim cn as ADODB.Connection
Set cn = New ADODB.Connection
```

Note that you can combine the previous two lines into the following line:

```
Dim cn as New ADODB.Connection
```

However, the latter choice is not a good idea because using variables declared using the New keyword can slow your application. Every time Visual Basic encounters a variable declared using New, it must test whether or not an object reference has already been assigned to the variable.

Also, by separating the object variable declaration and instantiation, you can wait until you actually need to use the object variable before instantiating it; therefore, you can manage your object more tightly.

An ADO object is created implicitly when you create an object at the lower end of the hierarchy without first creating the parent object when you are actually implying in your code that you need the parent object—for instance, when you want to create a Recordset object to retrieve data in a table without passing an active connection parameter to the Recordset or assigning an active connection to the Recordset's ActiveConnection property. In this case, the Connection object will be created automatically.

The advantages are clear: You don't need to dimension and open the Connection object and there are fewer objects to maintain. Examples of how to use a Connection object without creating it explicitly are provided in the section on the Recordset object, later in this chapter.

Setting Up Connections

The Connection object maintains connection interface information about the data provider and manages transaction scope and the errors associated with the connection. With OLE DB, you can connect to a database in several different ways. For example, you can connect to an SQL Server database through its OLE DB native provider or through ODBC.

You can pass different connection strings to the Connection object to determine how you want to connect to the database. The Connection object then takes care of the communication with the driver or provider. You might find that sometimes building a connection string is the trickiest part in using ADO.

Before you can manipulate the data in a database, you need to establish a connection to the database by using the Open method. The syntax is

```
connection.Open ConnectionString, UserID, Password
```

The UserID and Password parameter are optional. For example, if you are using a Microsoft Access database, you may not need a user name and a password to access it, therefore you don't need to include them in the Open method. Also, you can embed the user ID and password in the ConnectionString. If the user ID and password are already present in the connection string, you should not pass the same user ID and password as the UserID and Password parameters. Doing so might cause an unpredictable error.

When opening a Connection object, you can pass the ConnectionString parameter into the ConnectionString property and call the Open method without this parameter. For example:

```
connection.ConnectionString = myConnectionString
connection.Open
```

Nevertheless, except in the event when you really have to, there is no reason to use two lines of code when you can make your code faster by calling one concise line.

Note that if you use the ConnectionString parameter of the Connection object's Open method and also set a value for the ConnectionString property before calling the Open method, the value passed to the Open method is the value that the ConnectionString property eventually receives.

Also note that when using ODBC to connect to a Microsoft SQL Server, you can make the ODBC data source pass the Windows NT Login name and password as the User ID and Password for the database. This will be demonstrated later in this section when a Data Source Name (DSN) is set up.

After the connection is open, you can use the Execute method to pass an SQL statement to the database server, or use the BeginTrans, CommitTrans, and RollbackTrans methods to manage your transaction. After you're finished with the Connection object, you use the Close method to tell ADO to disconnect from the database server. Using the Close method of the Connection object also closes any active Recordset objects associated with the connection.

As stated previously, you use a different data provider to connect to each database, but to you, the programmer, the difference is only in the connection string. There are a couple of ways to connect to a database. You can set up an ODBC data source and use the OLE DB Provider for ODBC, build your own connection string, or use a file to store information on the database connection.

The easiest way is to set up an ODBC data source. This option will be used for all examples in this chapter. However, other methods will also be explained in the Connection String section in this chapter. Again, whichever method you use, once you have the correct connection string, most of your code will remain the same. Some advanced features of ADO are not supported by all data providers. For example, the NextRecordset method of the Recordset object is available with Microsoft SQL Server, but not with Microsoft Access.

When you choose to use an ODBC data source with the OLE DB provider for ODBC, you need to first set up a DSN using the ODBC Data Source Administrator. Prior to Windows 2000, this program was opened by double-clicking the ODBC Data Source applet in the Control Panel in the computer where your Web server resided. If you are using Windows 2000, however, the ODBC Data Source Administrator is located under Administrative Tools, which is found by selecting Start ➜ Programs.

The setup process is very straightforward; you just need to follow the instructions in the dialog boxes that are displayed by the wizard. Make sure that you have permission to add a new ODBC data source. The series of dialog boxes are slightly different for different databases, but the principle is the same: You need to provide information, such as server name, user ID, and password for the ODBC driver to connect to the database.

You need to remember that each ODBC data source is specific for one database. If you have two Access databases as sources for your application, you need to create two ODBC data sources.

The following example describes how to set up a DSN for an Access database:

1. Go to the Control Panel and double-click the ODBC applet. Before you can proceed, you need to make sure that the computer you are working with has the ODBC driver for the database you will be using.

2. Click the Driver tab to see the list of ODBC drivers (see Figure 4-4). If you don't see the driver for your database, you will need to install it.

3. Click the System DSN tab (see Figure 4-5).

4. Click the Add button on the right side of the tab.

5. Select a driver. For an Access database, select Microsoft Access Driver (*.mdb).

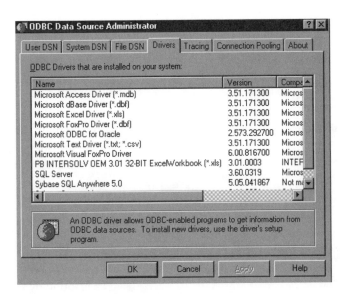

Figure 4-4. ODBC drivers

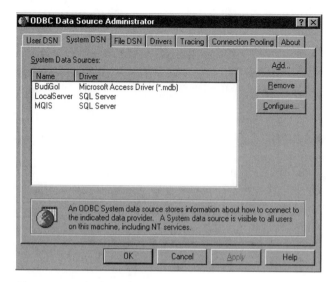

Figure 4-5. The list of system DSNs

6. Click Finish. The ODBC Microsoft Access 97 Setup dialog box will appear (see Figure 4-6).

7. Type in your DSN for your database. It can be different from the database name. Optionally, you can enter a description for it.

8. Click Select and browse to select the database file.

9. Click OK, and you will return to the previous window.

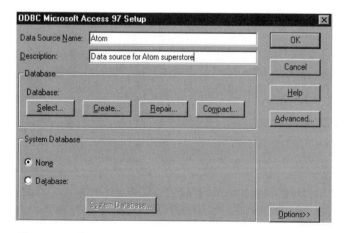

Figure 4-6. ODBC Microsoft Access 97 Setup

10. Click OK again, and your DSN will be listed in the System DSN tab.

The setup process for SQL Server or Oracle is a bit different. You need to type in the user name and password to get access to the database.

If you are working with a Microsoft SQL Server database, you need to follow these steps to set up a DSN:

1. From the System DSN in the ODBC applet, click Add.

2. Select SQL Server.

3. Type in the DSN name and the SQL Server to connect to. Optionally, you can enter a description for the data source (see Figure 4-7).

4. You need to supply the authentication details (see Figure 4-8). You can type in the Login ID and password, or you can use the same details as your Windows NT login name. If you choose to use your Windows NT login name and password, you should be aware that it is your application that needs access to the database, not you.

WARNING: *Because the instance of your WebClass will be created by the Web server, your application will inherit the Web server identity. You need to make sure that your Web server is in the list of users of the database server. The WebServer, in this case IIS, is given a name: IUSR_machinename. If you install the Web server on a Windows server called TORQUAY, the name will be IUSR_TORQUAY. This can sometimes be tricky, and it is advisable to use an SQL Server login ID.*

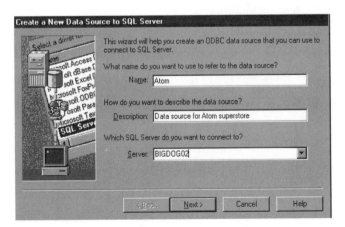

Figure 4-7: The new data source to Microsoft SQL Server

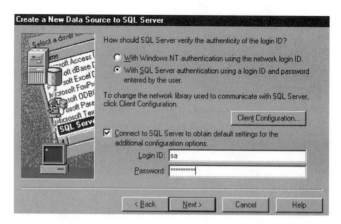

Figure 4-8. Connecting to the SQL Server using an SQL Server login ID

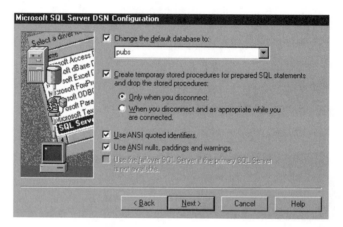

Figure 4-9. Microsoft SQL Server DSN configuration

5. Click Next. ODBC Data Source Administrator will try to connect to the database server. If you typed in the correct login ID and password, you will see the window shown in Figure 4-9.

6. Select a database from the "Change the Default Database to" box.

7. For the next three dialog boxes, click Next, Next, and Finish.

8. The window that lists the configuration setting of your data source will be displayed. Click the **Test Data Source** button to make sure the connection is set up properly.

9. Click OK.

That's it. It's that simple. You don't even have to restart your machine for the new DSN to take effect. Note that not all database servers can use Windows NT authentication. If you are using other databases, you may see a different set of dialog boxes. For example, for Sybase System 11, the process is completed through one dialog box as shown in Figure 4-10.

In the Sybase System 11 setup, you don't type the login name and password, so you need to supply them when you access the database, i.e in the connection string.

Once you have a DSN set up, you need to reference ADO in your Project, as follows:

1. Select References from the Project menu.

2. Scroll down the list box until you see Microsoft ActiveX Data Objects 2.0 Library or other versions of ADO.

3. Select the checkbox to the left of the item (see Figure 4-11).

The code in Listing 4-1 is used to instantiate the Connection object and open the connection. Remember that you have a DSN called Atom (shown in Figure

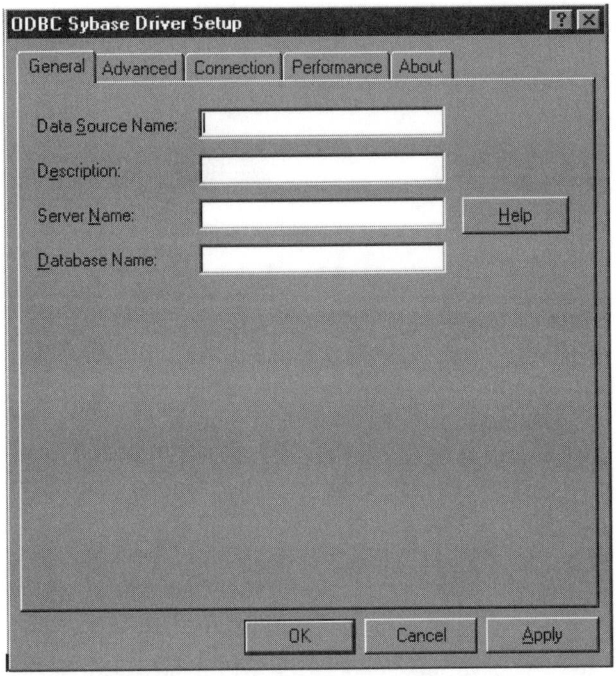

Figure 4-10. DSN registration for Sybase system 11

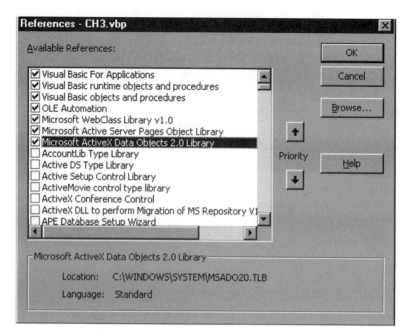

Figure 4-11. Referencing the ADO Library

4-7), which connects you to a Microsoft Access database. After the DSN is set up, you don't even need to know what type of database you are connecting to.

Listing 4-1

```
Dim cn As ADODB.Connection
Set cn = New ADODB.Connection

cn.Open "Atom"

' Do your database manipulation here

cn.Close
Set cn = Nothing
```

When programming with databases, it is important to make the life of the Connection object as short as possible to free the memory resource as soon as possible. Or when the connection pooling is enabled in the IIS, to make the connection usable by another object that needs access.

The previous code closes the Connection object as soon as it is no longer needed and sets the Connection object variable to Nothing to free the resource used by the Connection object.

The Recordset Object

Opening the connection is only the preliminary step to retrieving the data from the database. You need another ADO object called `Recordset` and some SQL skill. If you are unfamiliar with SQL, Appendix D provides a basic survival guide to SQL.

A *recordset* is a conceptual representation of an orderly arrangement of data into rows and columns. A recordset is also called a *resultset,* but Dr. Edgar F. Codd, who originated the relational approach to database management, used the term "relation" for recordsets when formulating the relational model.

You are correct in your assumption if you imagine a recordset is something like a table. However, a recordset is not a table and an in-depth discussion of the concept of recordsets is beyond the scope of this book. You can refer to Codd's "A Relational Model of Data for Large Shared Data Banks" in *Communications of the ACM*, Vol. 13, No. 6 (June 1970), which is a good reference if you are interested in learning more about the concept of relational databases. There are also many other books on relational databases and database design that explain a recordset more thoroughly.

Opening a Recordset Object

In this book, it is sufficient to know that you always need a recordset to retrieve data from a database. For the recordset to retrieve data from the database, it needs a `Connection` object that takes care of the process of connecting to the database server, such as identifying itself as an authorized user by presenting the user ID and password to the database server.

You use the `Recordset` object's `Open` method to retrieve the data. The `Open` method requires an active `Connection` object and an SQL statement as parameters. The latter is to let the database server know which data you want to retrieve.

The `Open` method of the `Recordset` object has the following syntax:

```
recordset.Open Source, ActiveConnection, CursorType, LockType, Options
```

Like the `Connection` object, the arguments that you pass to the `Open` method of the `Recordset` object are used to set the `Recordset` object's properties. If you wish, you can access these properties separately. For example, you can set the properties before you open the `Recordset` object. The following line of code:

```
rs.Open strSQL, cn, adOpenForwardOnly, adLockReadOnly
```

is equivalent to the next five lines:

```
rs.ActiveConnection = cn
rs.CursorType = adOpenForwardOnly
rs.LockType = adLockReadOnly
rs.Source = strSQL
rs.Open
```

Again, there is no reason why you should not simplify your code.

When you open a recordset, it is very important to know what type of cursor and lock type you need. Cursors and lock types are given in Table 4-1 and Table 4-2. By default, a recordset will be opened with options that take the least amount of resources. When the `CursorType` and/or the `LockType` parameters are not present as in the following code, adOpenForwardOnly and adLockReadOnly are implied for the CursorType and LockType parameters:

```
rs.Open strSQL, cn
```

Choosing the Right Recordset Cursors

Simply put, a cursor is the pointer to the current record in a recordset. When you first open a recordset, the current record is the first record, provided of course that the recordset is not empty. When you call the `MoveNext` method, the second record becomes the current record, and so on. In other words, it is the cursor that manages the set of records in a recordset.

When opening a recordset, you first want to make sure that you don't abuse the flexibility ADO gives you by demanding the type of recordset that is resource hungry if you don't really need it. Second, you need to make sure that you are using the right type of cursor for your recordset. Choosing the wrong cursor when you expect thousands of people a minute to visit your Web site can easily bring down your server.

A cursor is simply a mechanism used to address the individual rows of the recordset. You use different types of cursors when you need to update a record and when you need to display the field values once.

ADO provides for different types of cursors (see Table 4-1). You choose the cursor type by passing one of the constants when you open the recordset.

In addition to the `CursorType` property, a `Recordset` object also has a `CursorLocation` property, which can take one of two values: adUseClient and adUseServer (default). This property is used to indicate where the cursor is implemented. The ADO client-side cursor only supports a static cursor.

Table 4-1. The Cursor Types

CONSTANT	DESCRIPTION
adOpenForwardOnly	Default. This is the least resource hungry cursor and is the type you need most of the time when programming with your WebClass. With this type of cursor, you can only scroll forward through records. For example, you cannot use the MovePrevious method to scroll back one record. You can, however, call the MoveFirst method to bring you back to the first record in the recordset.
adOpenStatic	Using this type of cursor, you can scroll backwards and forwards. It's almost as resource friendly as the forward-only cursor. When you use this type of cursor, a static copy of a set of records is created for you to find data. Because it is static, changes, additions, or deletions by other users are not visible. This is the only option for client-side cursors.
adOpenKeyset	This is a resource hungry type of cursor, though not as much as the dynamic cursor. This cursor type is fully scrollable, and you can see data changes by other users, but deletions are still inaccessible. This cursor type is only available for server-side cursors.
adOpenDynamic	Dynamic cursors, the most resource hungry and slowest type of cursor. In addition to being fully scrollable, all updates and deletions by other users are visible.

Choosing LockType options

The LockType parameter is especially important in a multiuser environment, such as the Internet. It controls the locking type of the recordset when users update data. The main purpose of using a locking mechanism is to prevent other users from changing the records you're working on.

Four options are available when opening an ADO recordset: adLockReadOnly, adLockPessimistic, adLockOptimistic, and adLockBatchOptimistic (see Table 4-2).

How do you read individual values in a given column and row? You can only read the current record in the recordset. The value of each column can be retrieved using the one of following formats:

```
rs.Fields(n)
```

or

```
rs.Fields("ColumnName")
```

or

```
rs(n)
```

or

```
rs ("ColumnName")
```

where *n* is the position of the column in the order.

Note that accessing the column value using the column position is faster because ADO doesn't have to do name lookup.

To move to another record, you can use the MoveFirst, MovePrevious, MoveLast, and MoveNext methods of the Recordset object. Suppose you have a table called Users in your database, and you pass the following SQL statement to the Open method of your recordset.

```
SELECT LoginName, Password FROM Users WHERE Status='VIP'
```

Again, suppose that the recordset produces the results shown in Table 4-3.

Table 4-2. LockType Options

CONSTANT	DESCRIPTION
AdLockReadOnly	Default. It prevents the updating of data in the recordset opened. This lock type produces the lowest impact recordset.
AdLockPessimistic	Pessimistic locking. It locks rows or pages immediately upon opening and the lock remains in place as long as the cursor is open. This lock type is available only for server-side cursors.
adLockOptimistic	Optimistic locking. The database provider locks records only when the Update method is called. This is the lowest impact locking strategy.
adLockBatchOptimistic	Optimistic batch updates. This is required for batch update mode as opposed to immediate update mode.

Table 4-3. Recordset Results from the SQL Statement Example

LOGINNAME	PASSWORD
John	Jfk
Bigshark	Bgbg1990
Pascal	Tt66
Jill	Romeo
007	MyPassword

When it is first opened, the current record is the first record. Therefore the value of rs(0) or rs("LoginName") is "John", and rs(1) or rs("Password") is "Jfk".

Calling the MoveNext method will move the cursor one record forward and the values of rs(0) and rs(1) will respectively be "Bigshark" and "Bgbg1990". Calling the MoveLast method brings the cursor to the last record, calling the MoveFirst method will make the cursor point to the first record, and calling the MovePrevious method moves the cursor one record back.

Note that with the OpenForwardOnly cursor you can't scroll back to the previous records. This means that you can't call the MovePrevious method, you can only call the MoveFirst method when the cursor is at the first record, which makes the MoveFirst method virtually useless.

What happens if you call the MoveNext method when the cursor points to the last record? ADO will set the current record to the position after the last record in the recordset and the EOF (End Of File) property of the recordset will be set to True. An attempt to move forward when the EOF property is already True generates an error. That is why you must always test this property before calling the MoveNext method.

The same applies to the MovePrevious method. If you call the MovePrevious method when the cursor points to the first record, ADO will set the current record to the position before the first record in the recordset and the BOF (Beginning Of File) property of the recordset will be set to True. An attempt to move backward when the BOF property is already True generates an error. You must always test the BOF property before calling the MovePrevious method.

It is also possible that you can open an empty recordset, which occurs when no record matches the criteria in your SQL statement. Trying to read a column value will generate an error. The common practice is to make sure that your recordset is not empty before trying to manipulate a record in a recordset. The BOF and EOF properties of an empty recordset are both True, and both properties can only be true at the same time if the recordset is empty. Therefore, you can test these properties to find out if the recordset is empty.

The use of the Recordset object is best explained with an example. In this case, a login verification will be made before allowing access to another page. You have a login page HTML template with a form element on it. This form in turn has two elements in which users can enter their login name and password. Upon submission, this login information will be contained in the Request object. You then capture the two items and compare them against the list of user names and passwords in the Users table in the database.

The LoginPage HTML template contains the code in Listing 4-2. Notice that the form has been connected to the VerifyLogin event of the Members WebItem.

Listing 4-2

```
<html>
<head>
</head>

<body>
<center>
Please type in your login name and password.
<form action=CH3.ASP?WCI=Members&amp;WCE=VerifyLogin&amp;WCU method=post>
<table>
  <tr>
    <td>Login:</td>
    <td><input name=Login></td>
  </tr>
  <tr>
    <td>Password:</td>
    <td><input type=password name=UserPassword></td>
  </tr>
  <tr>
    <td> </td>
    <td><input type=submit value=Login></td>
  </tr>
</table>
</form>
</center>
</body>
</html>
```

And the code in Listing 4-3 needs to be pasted in your WebClass.

Listing 4-3

```
Private Sub WebClass_Start()

    LoginPage.WriteTemplate
```

```
End Sub


Private Sub Members_VerifyLogin()

  Dim cn As ADODB.Connection
  Dim rs As ADODB.Recordset
  Dim strSQL As String

  ' Compose the SQL statement that retrieves the record that
  ' with specific Login name and password.
  strSQL = "SELECT * FROM Users" & _
    " WHERE Login='" & Request.Form("Login") & "'" & _
    " AND Password='" & Request.Form("UserPassword") & "'"

  ' Assign the Connection to cn
  Set cn = New ADODB.Connection
  ' Assign the Recordset to rs
  Set rs = New ADODB.Recordset

  ' Open the connection and recordset
  cn.Open "Atom"
  rs.Open strSQL, cn, adOpenForwardOnly, adLockReadOnly

  ' Check if there is such a record
  If rs.BOF And rs.EOF Then
    ' recordset is empty, login failed
    Response.Redirect URLFor(LoginPage)
  Else
    ' login was successful
    Response.Write "Welcome Member."
  End If

  rs.Close
  Set rs = Nothing
  cn.Close
  Set cn = Nothing

End Sub
```

The application starts by writing the LoginPage HTML template to the Web browser, as shown in Figure 4-12.

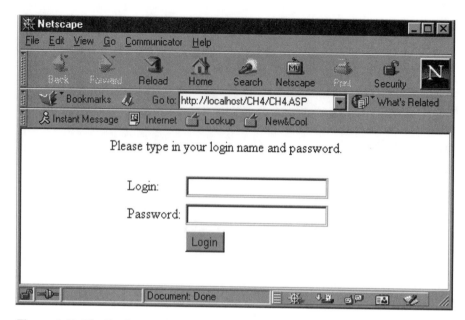

Figure 4-12: The Login page

The user then has to type in his or her login name and password. When the userclicks the Login button, the WebClass triggers the VerifyLogin event of the Members WebItem. It then forms the SQL statement on the fly:

```
strSQL = "SELECT * FROM Users" & _
   " WHERE Login='" & Request.Form("Login") & "'" & _
   " AND Password='" & Request.Form("UserPassword") & "'"
```

The asterisk indicates that the database is to return all fields from the Users table. However, in practice, you often don't need to use all the fields in a table. You should therefore retrieve only fields that you will use.

The following code lines assign a Connection object to cn and a Recordset object to rs and then opens them.

```
Set cn = New ADODB.Connection
Set rs = New ADODB.Recordset
cn.Open "Atom"
rs.Open strSQL, cn, adOpenForwardOnly, adLockReadOnly
```

The open Connection object is passed as an argument to the Recordset object's Open method to tell the Recordset object to use the Connection object to connect to the database.

You then use the BOF (Beginning Of File) and EOF (End Of File) properties to check if the recordset is empty. Both properties can only be true at the same time if the recordset is empty.

```
If rs.BOF And rs.EOF Then
   ' recordset is empty, login failed
   Response.Redirect URLFor(LoginPage)
Else
   ' login was successful
   Response.Write "Welcome Member."
End If
```

Getting an empty recordset means that the login name/password pair doesn't exist in the table. In other words, the user did not type in the correct login name and password. If the login fails, the WebClass redirects the same login page using the Redirect method of the Response object. If the login is successful, the WebClass displays the "Welcome Member." string.

The Recordset object also has the RecordCount property that you can use to inquire about the number of records in the recordset. Some programmers use this property to check whether the recordset is empty, as in the following code lines.

```
If rs.RecordCount = 0 Then
   . . .
End If
```

However, using the BOF and EOF properties is more efficient than using the RecordCount property. Also, the RecordCount property only works with certain cursor types.

The ADO object model has a loose hierarchy. Recall the times when you worked with DAO and RDO. With these two objects, you had to traverse the hierarchy to instantiate objects in the tree. ADO allows you to create objects independently of each other.

For example, you can create and open a Recordset object without explicitly creating and opening a Connection object. You still need a Connection object, but it is created automatically by ADO. This results in fewer ADO objects and thus a smaller working set.

You only need to create a Connection object explicitly if you need to use the Connection object's methods or properties, for instance, to execute an SQL statement or begin a transaction. You may want to create and open a Connection object explicitly if you need to open more than one recordset to guarantee that those recordsets use the same Connection object. Opening two Connection objects when one is sufficient is definitely a waste of resources.

However, if all you need to do is open a recordset to retrieve data, it is recommended that you not open the Connection object explicitly, but instead let ADO take care of it. These lines of code

```
Set cn = New ADODB.Connection
Set rs = New ADODB.Recordset
cn.Open "Atom"
rs.Open strSQL, cn, adOpenForwardOnly, adLockReadOnly
```

have the same effect as these lines of code:

```
Set rs = New ADODB.Recordset
rs.Open strSQL, "Atom", adOpenForwardOnly, adLockReadOnly
```

Notice how the connection string is included in the Open method, replacing the Connection object cn.

If you need to display the data, you can scroll through the open recordset and populate an HTML table. For example, the snippet in Listing 4-4 lists all users whose status is VIP.

Listing 4-4

```
Private Sub Members_ListVIP()

  Dim rs As ADODB.Recordset
  Dim strSQL As String

  ' Compose the SQL statement that retrieves the record
  ' with UserType = VIP.
  strSQL = "SELECT * FROM Users" & _
    " WHERE UserType = 'VIP'"

  ' Assign the Recordset to rs
  Set rs = New ADODB.Recordset

  ' Open the recordset
  rs.Open strSQL, "Atom", adOpenForwardOnly, adLockReadOnly

  ' Check if the Open method returns any record
  If Not (rs.BOF And rs.EOF) Then
    Response.Write "<b>VIP Members</b><br>" & _
      "<table>" & vbCr & _
      "<tr>" & vbCr & _
      "<td>Member ID</td>" & vbCr & _
      "<td>First Name</td>" & vbCr & _
```

```
        "<td>Last Name</td>" & vbCr & _
        "</tr>"

      ' List VIP members here
      While Not rs.EOF
        Response.Write "<tr>" & vbCr & _
          "<td>" & rs("ID") & "</td>" & vbCr & _
          "<td>" & rs("FirstName") & "</td>" & vbCr & _
          "<td>" & rs("LastName") & "</td>" & vbCr & _
          "</tr>"
        Rs.MoveNext
      Wend
      Response.Write "</table>"
    End If
    rs.Close
    Set rs = Nothing

End Sub
```

Or, if you want to display all the records and all the fields in a recordset, you can use a generic function similar to the code in Listing 4-5. You simply pass a connection string and the SQL statement to the function, and the function displays the content or the recordset returned in an HTML table.

Listing 4-5

```
Private Function ListAll(strConnectionString As String, _

  strSQL As String) As Boolean

  Dim rs As ADODB.Recordset

  On Error GoTo ErrHandler

  Set rs = New ADODB.Recordset
  rs.Open strSQL, strConnectionString, adOpenForwardOnly, adLockReadOnly

  If Not (rs.BOF And rs.EOF) Then
    Response.Write "<table>" & vbCr
    While Not rs.EOF
      Response.Write "<tr>" & vbCr
      Dim lngCounter As Long
      ' Loop through all fields
      For lngCounter = 0 To rs.Fields.Count - 1
        Response.Write "<td>" & rs(lngCounter) & "</td>"
```

```
      Next lngCounter
      Response.Write "</tr>" & vbCr
      rs.MoveNext
   Wend
   Response.Write "</table>" & vbCr
 End If
 ListAll = True


FunctionExit:
 On Error Resume Next
 rs.Close
 Set rs = Nothing
 Exit Function


ErrHandler:
 ' Do your error handling here
 GoTo FunctionExit


End Function
```

Populating a Select Element

Another task that you will frequently perform when developing a Web application is populating a Select element with values from a lookup table from which users can select an option. Examples include populating a Select element with product names, a list of countries, and so on.

On the browser, the user can select an option from the Select element and submit it as an HMTL form input value. Figure 4-13 shows a very simple HTML form with one Select element, where users can select the product they want to purchase.

The key to populating a Select element is to send options in the following format.

```
<select name=Product>
<option value=1>ProductName1</option>
<option value=2>ProductName2</option>


   .


   .


   .


<option value=n>ProductNamen</option>
</select>
```

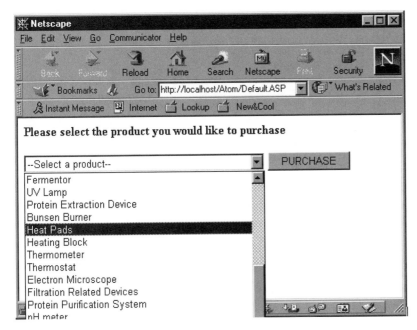

Figure 4-13. An example of a Select element

In this example, the options for the Select element are taken from the Products table. The ProductID field contains the unique identifier for each product and the Product field contains the description of each product. You can send the HTML tags using the Write method or an HTML template WebItem. Both approaches are given next.

To send the HTML tags in the previous example using the Write method, you need to have the code in Listing 4-6 in your WebClass.

Listing 4-6

```
Dim strConnectionString As String
Dim rs As ADODB.Recordset

strConnectionString = "atom"

Response.Write "<b>Please select the product you would like" & _
  " to purchase</b>" & vbCr & _
  "<form method=post action=" & URLFor(Products, "Purchase") & _
  ">" & vbCr & _
  "<select Name=Product>" & vbCr

Set rs = New ADODB.Recordset
rs.Open "SELECT ProductID, Product FROM Products", strConnectionString
```

```
Response.Write "<option value=0>--Select a product--</option>" & vbCr
'populate the Select element
Do Until rs.EOF
  Response.Write "<option value=" & rs(0) & ">" & rs(1) & _
    "</option>" & vbCr
  rs.MoveNext
Loop

rs.Close
Set rs = Nothing
Response.Write "</select>" & vbCr & _
  "<input type=submit value=PURCHASE>" & vbCr & _
  "</form>"
```

Alternatively, if you choose to use an HTML template WebItem, open the database and retrieve the lookup data from the ProcessTag event procedure. The HTML template code should look something like the one in Listing 4-7.

Listing 4-7

```
<b>Please select the product you would like to purchase</b>
<form method=post action=WebClass1.ASP?WCI=Products&WCE=Purchase>
<select Name=Product>
<option value=0>--Select a product--</option>
<WC@Options>Populate the select list here</WC@Options>
</select>
<input type=submit value=PURCHASE>
</form>
```

And, you need the code in Listing 4-8 for your ProcessTag event procedure.

Listing 4-8

```
Private Sub SelectProduct_ProcessTag(ByVal TagName As String, _

  TagContents As String, SendTags As Boolean)

  Dim strConnectionString As String
  Dim rs As ADODB.Recordset
  Dim str As String

  strConnectionString = "atom"

  Set rs = New ADODB.Recordset
  rs.Open "SELECT ProductID, Product FROM Products", strConnectionString

  Do Until rs.EOF
```

```
    str = str & "<option value=" & rs(0) & ">" & rs(1) & "</option>" & vbCr
    rs.MoveNext
Loop
rs.Close
Set rs = Nothing

TagContents = str

End Sub
```

Displaying a Record in Various HTML Elements

At times, you may need to retrieve a particular record from the database and display the field values of the record in an HTML page. For example, in an online job application, you may want to create an HTML page that allows users to update their applications. For users to update applications, you need to retrieve their records and display them in an HTML page. Depending on the type of the field, you might have to use a different type of HTML element than a Text element.

The following example displays a purchase order that has been placed by the user. The values need to be displayed in Text, Hidden, Select, Checkbox, and Radio elements. The data comes from an Orders table with the following fields:

- *OrderID*: The primary key, which is stored in a Hidden element.

- *ProductID:* The product ordered. The value is displayed in a Select element. For each value there must be a product description from the Products table.

- *Quantity:* The quantity ordered, which is displayed in a Text element.

- *Delivery*: The delivery method. This can have one of three values: 1, 2, or 3. 1 is for Airmail, 2 for Seamail, and 3 for Courier, and is displayed in a radio button.

- *ChargeOnDelivery*: This field is a boolean, can be True or False, and the value is displayed in a checkbox.

The HTML page is a simple order confirmation page, and each order can only have one product. The routine that displays the HTML page is written in the Order custom WebItem's Confirm event. It is assumed that this WebItem's event is triggered from a previous page that hosts an HTML form containing the OrderID value.

The HTML page is shown in Figure 4-14.

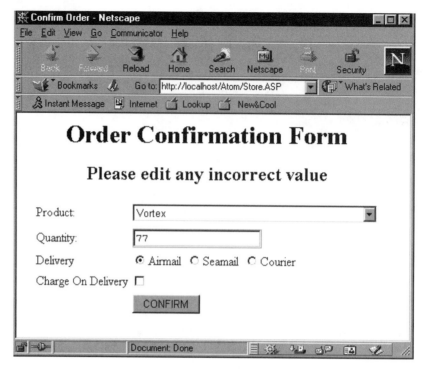

Figure 4-14. The order confirmation form

Listing 4-9 provides the code for the order confirmation form shown in Figure 4-14.

Listing 4-9

```
Private Sub Order_Confirm()
  Dim lngOrderID As Long
  Dim cn As ADODB.Connection
  Dim rs As ADODB.Recordset
  Dim strConnectionString As String
  Dim strSQL As String
  Dim lngProductID As Long
  Dim lngQuantity As Long
  Dim bytDelivery As Byte
  Dim blnChargeOnDelivery As Boolean

  strConnectionString = "atom"
  lngOrderID = Request.Form("OrderID")

  Set cn = New ADODB.Connection
  cn.Open strConnectionString
```

```
Set rs = New ADODB.Recordset

strSQL = "SELECT ProductID, Quantity, Delivery, ChargeOnDelivery" & _
  " FROM Orders WHERE OrderID=" & lngOrderID
rs.Open strSQL, cn
If Not (rs.BOF And rs.EOF) Then
  lngProductID = rs("ProductID")
  lngQuantity = rs("Quantity")
  bytDelivery = rs("Delivery")
  blnChargeOnDelivery = rs("ChargeOnDelivery")
End If
rs.Close

Response.Write "<html>" & vbCr & _
  "<head>" & vbCr & _
  "  <title>Confirm Order</title>" & vbCr & _
  "</head>" & vbCr & _
  "<body bgcolor=""#ffffff"" text=""#111100"">" & vbCr & _
  "<center>" & vbCr & _
  "<h1>Order Confirmation Form</h1>" & vbCr & _
  "<h2>Please edit any incorrect value</h2>" & vbCr & _
  "<form method=post action=" & URLFor(Order, "Delivery") & ">" & _
    vbCr & _
  "<input type=hidden Name=OrderID value=" & lngOrderID & ">" & _
    vbCr & _
  "<table>" & vbCr & _
  "  <tr>" & vbCr & _
  "    <td>Product:</td>" & _
  "    <td><select Name=Product>"

strSQL = "SELECT ProductID, Product FROM Products"
rs.Open strSQL
Do Until rs.EOF
  Response.Write "<option value=" & rs(0) & _
    IIf(rs(0) = lngProductID, " SELECTED>", ">") & _
    rs(1) & "</option>" & vbCr
  rs.MoveNext
Loop

rs.Close
Set rs = Nothing
cn.Close
Set cn = Nothing
```

```
        Response.Write "</select></td>" & vbCr & _
          "  </tr>" & vbCr & _
          "  <tr>" & vbCr & _
          "    <td>Quantity:</td>" & vbCr & _
          "    <td><input type=Text name=Quantity value=" & lngQuantity & _
          "></td>" & vbCr & _
          "  </tr>" & vbCr & _
          "  <tr>" & vbCr & _
          "    <td>Delivery</td>" & vbCr & _
          "    <td><input type=radio name=Delivery"
If bytDelivery = 1 Then Response.Write " CHECKED"
Response.Write ">Airmail " & vbCr & _
          "<input type=radio name=Delivery"
If bytDelivery = 2 Then Response.Write " CHECKED"
Response.Write ">Seamail " & vbCr & _
          "<input type=radio name=Delivery"
If bytDelivery = 3 Then Response.Write " CHECKED"
Response.Write ">Courier</td>" & vbCr & _
          "  </tr>" & vbCr & _
          "  <tr>" & vbCr & _
          "    <td>Charge On Delivery</td>" & vbCr & _
          "    <td><input type=checkbox Name=ChargeOnDelivery"
If blnChargeOnDelivery Then Response.Write " CHECKED"
Response.Write "></td>" & vbCr & _
          "  </tr>" & vbCr & _
          "  <tr>" & vbCr & _
          "    <td> </td>" & vbCr & _
          "    <td><input type=submit value=CONFIRM></td>" & vbCr & _
          "  </tr>" & vbCr & _
          "</table>" & vbCr & _
          "</form>" & vbCr & _
          "</center>" & vbCr & _
          "</body>" & vbCr & _
          "</html>"
End Sub
```

Although displaying a value in a Text element is straightforward, selecting a value in a Select element, radio button, or checkbox requires some extra work. The lines in bold in the code in Listing 4-9 is the extra processing needed to display values in those elements.

Populating a Select element and selecting the correct value is undertaken by the following lines:

```
strSQL = "SELECT ProductID, Product FROM Products"
  rs.Open strSQL
  Do Until rs.EOF
    Response.Write "<option value=" & rs(0) & _
      IIf(rs(0) = lngProductID, " SELECTED>", ">") & _
      rs(1) & "</option>" & vbCr
    rs.MoveNext
  Loop
```

Because the lookup values for the Select element come from the Products table, you need to open a recordset that retrieves the ProductID and Product fields from that table. Selecting the selected value is achieved by comparing the ProductID value of each record with lngProductID. When the selected value is found, the " SELECTED" attribute is added to the option.

As for the radio button, a similar comparison has to be done. This time the possible values are not from a lookup table, but are limited to three values: 1, 2, or 3. When a match is found, the attribute "CHECKED" is added to the radio element.

```
"     <td><input type=radio name=Delivery"
If bytDelivery = 1 Then Response.Write " CHECKED"
Response.Write ">Airmail " & vbCr & _
  "<input type=radio name=Delivery"
If bytDelivery = 2 Then Response.Write " CHECKED"
Response.Write ">Seamail " & vbCr & _
  "<input type=radio name=Delivery"
If bytDelivery = 3 Then Response.Write " CHECKED"
Response.Write ">Courier</td>" & vbCr & _
```

For the Checkbox, the following line does the job of checking the Checkbox if blnChargeOnDelivery is True.

```
If blnChargeOnDelivery Then Response.Write " CHECKED"
```

This example was implemented by sending HTML tags using the Response object's Write method. Why not use an HTML template? You could. You could have an HTML template similar to the one in Listing 4-10.

Listing 4-10
```
<html>
<head>
  <title>Confirm Order</title>
</head>
```

```
<body bgcolor="#ffffff" text="#000000" link="#0000ee" vlink="#551a8b">
<center>
<h1>Order Confirmation Form</h1>
<h2>Please edit any incorrect value</h2>
<form method=post>
<input type=hidden Name=OrderID value=<WC@OrderID></WC@OrderID>
<table>
  <tr>
    <td>Product:</td>
    <td><WC@Product></WC@Product></td>
  </tr>
  <tr>
    <td>Quantity:</td>
    <td><WC@Quantity></WC@Quantity></td>
  </tr>
  <tr>
    <td>Delivery</td>
    <td><WC@Delivery></WC@Delivery></td>
  </tr>
  <tr>
    <td>Charge On Delivery</td>
    <td><WC@ChargeOnDelivery></WC@ChargeOnDelivery></td>
  </tr>
  <tr>
    <td> </td>
    <td><input type=submit value=CONFIRM></td>
  </tr>
</table>
</form>
</center>
</body>
</html>
```

You could write code for the ProcessTag event procedure that retrieves the value of each field. However, can you see the problem here? The ProcessTag event is fired each time a custom tag is found. This means that if there are five custom tags, the event will be fired five times. Each time the ProcessTag event procedure is executed you will create a recordset to retrieve the respective field value. As the number of fields that need to be displayed grows, the time to process the code will become more and more unacceptable.

You could, of course, get around this by making all replacements take place at one time. However, this adds complexity to your code and makes the use of an HTML template impractical.

Inserting a New Record into the Database

It is natural to want to add a new record to a table in a database. This can easily be done using the Execute method of the Connection object. The SQL statement for this purpose is

INSERT INTO TableName (*field1, field2, ... fieldn*) VALUES (*value1, value2, ... valuen*)

where TableName is the name of the table to insert a new record into and field1 ... fieldn is the list of the fields where value1 ... valuen are to be stored. As an example:

INSERT INTO Users (Login, Password) VALUES ('budi', 'Proj170845')

In the following example, you have an HTML page with a form for users to fill in their details. There are three fields required: LastName, FirstName, and Email. The form on the HTML page is connected to the GetDetails custom event of the Members custom WebItem. To try this example, you need to create a WebItem called Members if it doesn't already exist as well as the corresponding GetDetails custom event.

You also need to have an HTML template WebItem called Register that contains the code in Listing 4-11.

Listing 4-11

```
<html>
<head>
<title>Discount Club Member Registration Page</title>
</head>

<body>
<form method=post>
<table>
  <tr>
    <td>Last Name:</td>
    <td><input name=LastName ></td>
  </tr>
  <tr>
    <td>First Name:</td>
    <td><input name=FirstName ></td>
  </tr>
  <tr>
    <td>Email:</td>
```

```
      <td><input name=Email ></td>
    </tr>
    <tr>
      <td><input type=reset value="Reset"></td>
      <td><input type=submit value="Register"></td>
    </tr>
  </table>
  </form>
  </body>
  </html>
```

Because you cannot connect an element directly to a custom event of a custom WebItem, you need to first connect the element to the custom WebItem, and then manually connect the element to the event.

After you connect the Form1 element to the Members custom WebItem, VB automatically edits the action attribute of the form element into this:

```
<form action=CH4.ASP?WCI=Members&amp;WCU method=post>
```

You then need to add the WCE attribute, so that the line looks similar to this:

```
<form action=CH4.ASP?WCI=Members&amp;WCE=GetDetails&amp;WCU method=post>
```

You need to add the text in bold. Don't forget to refresh your template after you edit it.

You then need to write the code in Listing 4-12 in your WebClass.

Listing 4-12

```
Private Sub WebClass_Start()

  Register.WriteTemplate

End Sub


Private Sub Members_GetDetails()

  Dim cn As New ADODB.Connection
  Dim strSQL As String

  strSQL = "INSERT INTO Members (LastName, FirstName, Email)" & _
    " VALUES ('" & Request.Form("LastName") & "'," & _
    " '" & Request.Form("FirstName") & "'," & _
    " '" & Request.Form("Email") & "')"
```

```
cn.Open "Atom"
cn.Execute strSQL
cn.Close
Set cn = Nothing
```

```
End Sub
```

The `WebClass_Start` event procedure simply sends the content of the Register HTML template WebItem. In your Web browser, it looks similar to Figure 4-15.

After the user clicks the Register button, the `GetDetails` event will be triggered.

It first builds the `strSQL` string.

```
strSQL = "INSERT INTO Members (LastName, FirstName, Email)" & _
    " VALUES ('" & Request.Form("LastName") & "'," & _
    " '" & Request.Form("FirstName") & "'," & _
    " '" & Request.Form("Email") & "')"
```

If you put a `Debug.Print strSQL` statement after the previous statement, the value of `strSQL` in the Immediate window will be similar to:

```
INSERT INTO Members (LastName, FirstName, Email) VALUES ('Kurniawan', 'Budi',
'budi@labsale.com')
```

Figure 4-15: The Registration page

The line after that:

```
cn.Open "Atom"
```

opens the connection to the database. If no error occurs, VB will execute the next line, which executes the strSQL.

```
cn.Execute strSQL
```

VB then closes and frees the cn object variable in the last two lines.

```
cn.Close
Set cn = Nothing
```

A Request object's element is never NULL, so there is no need to prefix a value with a blank string as in the following line in anticipation of having a NULL value for the element.

```
strMobilePhone = "" & Request.Form("MobilePhone")
```

If the user doesn't type anything for an HTML Text element or if that element doesn't exist, the Request object's element is a blank string. In the previous example, Request.Form("MobilePhone") returns a blank string if the user doesn't type anything in the MobilePhone text box or if there is no form element with the name MobilePhone. This also applies to Session-level and Application-level variables.

The Single Quote Factor

So far so good. However, did it occur to you that the previous code is not perfect? The flaw is in the line that composes the SQL statement on the fly:

```
strSQL = "INSERT INTO Members (LastName, FirstName, Email)" & _
    " VALUES ('" & Request.Form("LastName") & "'," & _
    " '" & Request.Form("FirstName") & "'," & _
    " '" & Request.Form("Email") & "')"
```

What if one of the input fields contains the single quote or an apostrophe (') character? For example, one of your users may have a last name that contains this character, such as O'Connor.

Try to enter this name in the LastName input box. The error message you'll receive is shown in Figure 4-16.

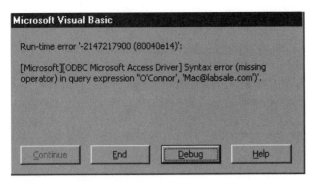

Figure 4-16: The result of the single-quote factor

It is best to catch this error at the development phase.

The following is the SQL statement built by the code.

```
INSERT INTO Members (LastName, FirstName, Email) VALUES ('Mac', 'O'Connor',
'Mac@labsale.com')
```

Notice that the single quote character between the O and C characters in O'Connor confuses the database engine. It thinks that the second field is O and expects to find a comma after it. Instead, it finds the C character and detects that the SQL statement is impossible to execute. It then communicates its concern to VB, which in turns raises an error.

Fortunately, this is a minor issue and can easily be fixed by adding an extra apostrophe for every apostrophe that is part of a field value. You then need to check if a field value contains this character and add an extra one if you find one. In VB6, you can use the Replace function like this:

```
Replace(str, "'", "''")
```

You can modify the line that builds the SQL statement., as follows:

```
strSQL = "INSERT INTO Members (LastName, FirstName, Email)" & _
    " VALUES ('" & Replace(Request.Form("LastName"), "'", "''") & "'," & _
    " '" & Replace(Request.Form("FirstName"), "'", "''") & "'," & _
    " '" & Request.Form("Email") & "')"
```

The Replace function was not used for the Email field because a single quote character is illegal in an e-mail address. This of course assumes that there is a strict input validation on the client- or server-side. Input validation is discussed in Chapter 6.

Adding a New Record with the Recordset Object

You can also use the AddNew method of the Recordset object to add a new record. Let's modify the previous example. There is no change in the HTML template, you just need to edit the Members_GetDetails event procedure. The modified version is given in Listing 4-13.

Listing 4-13

```
Private Sub WebClass_Start()

  Register.WriteTemplate

End Sub


Private Sub Members_GetDetails()

  Dim rs As New ADODB.Recordset
  Dim strSQL As String

  strSQL = "SELECT * FROM Members WHERE LastName=''"
  rs.Open strSQL, "Atom", adOpenForwardOnly, adLockOptimistic
  rs.AddNew
  rs.Fields("LastName") = Request.Form("LastName")
  rs.Fields("FirstName") = Request.Form("FirstName")
  rs.Fields("Email") = Request.Form("Email")
  rs.Update
  rs.Close
  Set rs = Nothing

End Sub
```

The key methods are AddNew and Update. Before assigning values to the fields, you call the AddNew method, as in:

```
rs.AddNew
```

You then assign a value to a field by using the Fields collection. Each field is the member of the Fields collection.

```
rs.Fields(strFieldName) = Value
```

The previous syntax can also be written in a shorter form:

```
rs(strFieldName) = Value        ' example: rs("LastName") = "Sawaki"
```

or

```
rs!Field = Value      ' example: rs!LastName = "Sawaki"
```

or even

```
rs(n) = Value         ' example: rs(2) = "Sawaki"
```

where *n* is the *n*th field in the recordset, starting from 0.

And finally you need to call the Update method to actually write to the recordset.

```
rs.Update
```

You cannot use adReadOnly for the LockType argument because this value doesn't allow you to write to the recordset. Also, notice that the single-quote problem does not arise here.

Note that when adding a new record using either the Execute method of the Connection object or the AddNew method of the Recordset object, you must pass values to all fields that cannot be NULL.

The Unique Key

Most of the time in database programming, each table that stores your data has a field that holds unique values. This field is called the primary key of the table and the type can be text or numeric. An example is the LoginName field in the Users table, in which you store all login information and user profiles.

When a user first registers and selects a login name, you must make sure that the login name selected has not been used by an existing user. Recall when you were told to choose another login name when you tried to get your free e-mail account. This occurred because the system rejects duplicate login names.

The primary key does not have to be visible to the user. Another common practice in maintaining a unique key is to create a new field of type autonumber as the primary key. This field normally starts from 1 and is incremented by one for each new record. Most, if not all, modern database servers support autonumber or identity fields that you can use for this purpose. In the event that you do not have this feature, you have to detect the highest number used by the table and increment it by one for the new record.

Using an autonumber for the primary key eliminates one major problem that you would need to solve when using a text field primary key. This problem and how to solve it is addressed next. Let's look at an example of adding a new record to a table that uses an autonumber as the primary key.

Suppose you have an Orders table that, for simplicity sake, has four fields: OrderID, CustomerID, ProductID, and Quantity. You may have guessed that the OrderID is the primary key of the Orders table. CustomerID, ProductID, and Quantity store the ID of the customer who places the order, the ID of the product being ordered, and the order quantity, respectively. When using an autonumber field, you must not include it in your SQL statement or pass a value to the field when using the Recordset object's AddNew method.

If you are using the Connection object's Execute method, your SQL statement looks like this:

```
INSERT INTO Orders (CustomerID, ProductID, Quantity) VALUES (34, 45, 120)
```

When using the Recordset object's AddNew method, your code looks the one in Listing 4-14:

Listing 4-14

```
Dim rs As ADODB.Recordset
Dim strSQL As String

' Build the recordset structure
strSQL = "SELECT * FROM Orders WHERE OrderID=0"
Set rs = New ADODB.Recordset
rs.Open strSQL, "Atom", adOpenForwardOnly, adLockOptimistic
rs.AddNew
rs.Fields("CustomerID") = 34
rs.Fields("ProductID") = 45
rs.Fields("Quantity") = 120
rs.Update
rs.Close
Set rs = Nothing
```

In circumstances where autonumber fields are not available, however, inserting a new record consists of two steps: Getting the next ID (in this example, the next OrderID) and inserting the new record. Your code should look like the one in Listing 4-15:

Listing 4-15

```
Private Sub Orders_Add()

    Dim cn As ADODB.Connection
    Dim rs As ADODB.Recordset
    Dim strSQL As String
```

```
Dim lngNextOrderID As Long

Set cn = New ADODB.Connection
Set rs = New ADODB.Recordset
cn.Open "Atom"

' Step 1: Get the next ID
strSQL = "SELECT MAX(OrderID) FROM Orders"
rs.Open strSQL, cn, adOpenForwardOnly, adLockReadOnly
lngNextOrderID = CLng("0" & rs(0)) + 1

' Step 2: Insert the new record
strSQL = "INSERT INTO Orders (OrderID, CustomerID, ProductID," & _
    " Quantity)" & _
    " VALUES (" & lngNextOrderID & ",2,3,44)"
cn.Execute strSQL

rs.Close
Set rs = Nothing
cn.Close
Set cn = Nothing

End Sub
```

You first get the maximum OrderID in the Orders table by using the Recordset object's Open method.

```
strSQL = "SELECT MAX(OrderID) FROM Orders"
rs.Open strSQL, cn, adOpenForwardOnly, adLockReadOnly
```

Please note that the number returned by the MAX function is not necessarily the same as the number of records in the table. You may have five orders with OrderID's 1, 2, 3, 4, and 5. If you delete the order with OrderID 3, the maximum OrderID is still 5, but there are now only four records in the Orders table.

The following line of code stores the value of the maximum OrderID plus one in lngNextOrderID.

```
lngNextOrderID = CLng("0" & rs(0)) + 1
```

The CLng function is needed to anticipate when the rs(0) is NULL when adding the first record.

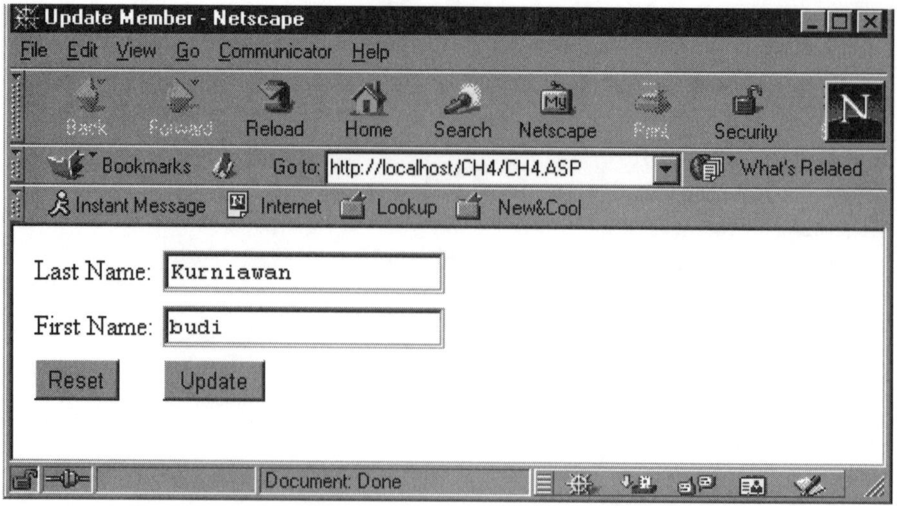

Figure 4-17: The Update page

Updating a Record

To update a record, you need to know for sure which record you want to update and how to pull the record out of the database. You then send the record to the Web browser as an HTML form containing the field values that are updatable. Along with these values, there is normally a primary key that distinguishes one record from another. This primary key is sent as a hidden element in the HTML form. Upon submit, all the values are sent back to the server, triggering a special event designed to handle the update.

In the following example, there is a record from the Members table. It has three fields: ID, LastName, and FirstName. The ID field is the primary key of the table and therefore is not updatable. This ID is sent as a hidden element in the HTML form. The other two fields, LastName and FirstName, are updatable and sent to the Web browser in text boxes. Users can then change these two values and submit the form. The value of the Form's Action attribute is the URL for the Update event in the custom WebItem Members.

The HTML form looks similar to Figure 4-17.

The code is given in Listing 4-16.

Listing 4-16

```
Private Sub WebClass_Start()

    Dim rs As New ADODB.Recordset
    Dim strSQL As String


    ' build SQL statement to pull out the record to edit
```

```
  strSQL = "SELECT ID, LastName, FirstName" & _
    " FROM Members WHERE ID=1"
  rs.Open strSQL, "Atom", adOpenForwardOnly, adLockReadOnly


  If Not (rs.BOF And rs.EOF) Then
  ' Send the HTML page containing a form with two text boxes and
  ' one hidden element. The hidden element's value is the Member ID
    Response.Write "<html>" & vbCr & _
      "<head>" & vbCr & _
      "<title>Update Member</title>" & vbCr & _
      "</head>" & vbCr & _
      "<body>" & vbCr & _
      "<form method=post action=" & URLFor(Members, "Update") & _
      ">" & vbCr & _
      "<input type=hidden name=ID value=" & rs("ID") & ">" & vbCr & _
      "<table>" & vbCr & _
      "  <tr>" & vbCr & _
      "    <td>Last Name:</td>" & vbCr & _
      "    <td><input name=LastName value=""" & rs("LastName") & _
      """></td>" & vbCr & _
      "  </tr>" & vbCr & _
      "  <tr>" & vbCr & _
      "    <td>First Name:</td>" & vbCr & _
      "    <td><input name=FirstName value=""" & rs("FirstName") & _
      """></td>" & vbCr & _
      "  </tr>" & vbCr & _
      "  <tr>" & vbCr & _
      "    <td><input type=reset value=Reset></td>" & vbCr & _
      "    <td><input type=submit value=Update></td>" & vbCr & _
      "  </tr>" & vbCr & _
      "</table>" & vbCr & _
      "</form>" & vbCr & _
      "</body>" & vbCr & _
      "</html>"
  End If


  rs.Close
  Set rs = Nothing
End Sub

Private Sub Members_Update()

  Dim cn As New ADODB.Connection
```

```
Dim strSQL As String

strSQL = "UPDATE Members SET " & _
    " LastName='" & Replace(Request.Form("LastName"), "'", "''") & _
    "'," & _
    " FirstName='" & Replace(Request.Form("FirstName"), "'", "''") & _
    "'" & _
    " WHERE ID=" & Request.Form("ID")

cn.Open "Atom"
cn.Execute strSQL
cn.Close
Set cn = Nothing
Response.Write "Record updated."

End Sub
```

Deleting a Record

Like the record update, when deleting a record you need to know for certain
which record you want to delete. The following example is very similar to the previous example, except that none of the fields is updatable, so the values won't be
in any text boxes. However, the hidden field is still needed, which is the primary
key of the table. In many cases, the ID is not visible to the end user, even though
displaying it probably wouldn't do any harm.

The HTML page is shown in Figure 4-18.

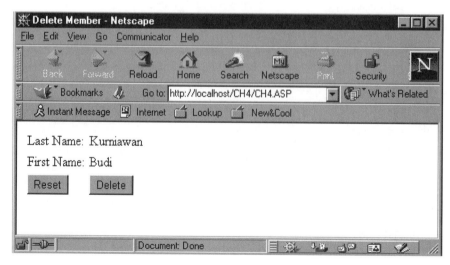

Figure 4-18. The Delete page

The code is outlined in Listing 4-17.

Listing 4-17

```
Private Sub WebClass_Start()

    Dim rs As New ADODB.Recordset
    Dim strSQL As String

    ' build SQL statement to pull out the record to delete
    strSQL = "SELECT ID, LastName, FirstName" & _
        " FROM Members WHERE ID=1"
    rs.Open strSQL, "Atom", adOpenForwardOnly, adLockReadOnly

    ' Send the HTML page containing a form with two text boxes and
    ' one hidden element. The hidden element's value is the Member ID
    If Not (rs.BOF And rs.EOF) Then
        Response.Write "<html>" & vbCr & _
            "<head>" & vbCr & _
            "<title>Delete Member</title>" & vbCr & _
            "</head>" & vbCr & _
            "<body>" & vbCr & _
            "<form method=post action=" & URLFor(Members, "Delete") & _
            ">" & vbCr & _
            "<input type=hidden name=ID value=" & rs("ID") & ">" & vbCr & _
            "<table>" & vbCr & _
            "   <tr>" & vbCr & _
            "       <td>Last Name:</td>" & vbCr & _
            "       <td>" & rs("LastName") & "</td>" & vbCr & _
            "   </tr>" & vbCr & _
            "   <tr>" & vbCr & _
            "       <td>First Name:</td>" & vbCr & _
            "       <td>" & rs("FirstName") & "</td>" & vbCr & _
            "   </tr>" & vbCr & _
            "   <tr>" & vbCr & _
            "       <td><input type=reset value=Reset></td>" & vbCr & _
            "       <td><input type=submit value=Delete></td>" & vbCr & _
            "   </tr>" & vbCr & _
            "</table>" & vbCr & _
            "</form>" & vbCr & _
            "</body>" & vbCr & _
            "</html>"
    End If
```

```
        rs.Close
        Set rs = Nothing

End Sub
Private Sub Members_Delete()

    Dim cn As New ADODB.Connection
    Dim strSQL As String

    strSQL = "DELETE FROM Members " & _
      " WHERE ID=" & Request.Form("ID")

    cn.Open "Atom"
    cn.Execute strSQL
    cn.Close
    Set cn = Nothing
    Response.Write "Record deleted."

End Sub
```

Connection String

So far you have used the ODBC DSN as the connection string to open a connection to a given database. With ADO, you have a variety of ways of building a connection string. The ODBC DSN has been used because it is the simplest way and most of you are familiar with it. To conclude this chapter, I discuss the other forms of building a connection string.

Even though ODBC proves effective, you will sometimes feel a need to use the native OLE DB provider for a certain database. Because using a native provider eliminates one layer (ODBC driver) in the data communication, it should be faster. Another reason to choose an OLE DB provider is that some providers expose features not available in others. Using ODBC DSN has one disadvantage, which is that you need to set up the DSN on the machine that hosts the Web server.

The connection string can be assigned to the ConnectionString property of the Connection object prior to calling the Open method of the Connection object or passed as a parameter of the Open method. If you decide not to create a Connection object explicitly, you can pass the connection string as a parameter of the Recordset object's Open method. All approaches have been described in the examples in this chapter.

The connection string specifies a data source and all of the other information you need to provide by passing a series of arguments to ADO. Each argument is provided in the *argument = value* format separated by semicolons. Although officially there are seven arguments in a connection string, there could be more. Any argument that ADO doesn't recognize will be passed directly to the data provider.

What kind of information does ADO need in the connection string? First, the ADO needs to know what type of database you want to connect to. Is it an Oracle database or a Microsoft SQL Server database? The argument to pass this information to is the Provider argument.

Second, ADO needs to know the location of the database server. If you are using an Access database, for example, you need to tell ADO where the .mdb file resides. If you are using a Microsoft SQL Server database, you need to tell ADO where it is. It may reside on the same machine as your application or it may be in another computer in the LAN.

ADO also needs to know your user name and password. These are not used when you are connecting to a database that is not password protected. This information is necessary because ADO needs to prove that it is an authorized user.

The list of arguments is shown in Table 4-4.

If you are new to ADO, you might find its flexibility confusing. The following list summarizes the available methods to connect to a database. In a nutshell, you can connect to a database in a couple of ways. Note that when you use an ODBC driver, ADO actually uses both the OLE DB provider for ODBC and the ODBC driver itself.

Table 4-4. The List of Arguments in a Connection String

ARGUMENT	DESCRIPTION
Provider	The name of the underlying OLE DB data provider for the connection.
Data Source	The name of a data source for the underlying data provider.
User ID	The username to use when establishing the connection.
Password	The password to use when establishing the connection.
File Name	The name of a data provider specific file. This could, for example, represent a text file containing preset connection information. Using a File Name element in your connection string loads the provider into memory. For this reason, you cannot have both a Provider and a File Name element in your ConnectionString property.
Remote Provider	The name of the data provider to set on the server when opening a client-side connection. This is only for use with Remote Data Services.
Remote Server	The path name of the remote server to use when opening a client-side connection. This is only for use with Remote Data Services.

- Using an ODBC driver, you can set up a DSN and refer to this DSN as the connection string.

- Using an ODBC driver, you can use a DSN-less method. You don't need to set up an ODBC DSN, but you need to pass the same information in a string. For example:

```
DRIVER={Microsoft Access Driver (*.mdb)};DBQ=C:\CompanySecret.mdb
```

- Using an ODBC driver, you can store the connection information in a file and transfer the file to another computer.

- You can use the native OLE DB provider for the database you want to connect to and pass the information in the *argument=value* format in the connection string. For example, for a Microsoft Access database connection:

```
Provider=Microsoft.Jet.OLEDB.4.0;Data Source=C:\CompanySecrets.mdb;
```

or, for an SQL Server:

```
Provider=MSDASQL.1;User ID=sa;Password=;Data Source=BigDaddy;
Initial Catalog=pubs;
```

- You can use the native OLE DB provider for the database you want to connect to, store the information in a file, and refer to this file each time you want to open a connection.

CHAPTER 5

Database Access Optimization

WHILE CHAPTER 4 CONTAINS ENOUGH BEGINNING information on accessing databases for most practical purposes, there is more to learn on the subject, especially when it comes to optimization. Database access plays such an important role in your application that speeding up database access will affect the entire application. Beef up your database access, and you'll get overall better performance.

This chapter deals with other intermediate and advanced topics. Not only will you learn how to write faster code, you'll how to make your life more enjoyable by writing easy-to-maintain logic, even if it does mean sacrificing some speed. In coding, as in life, there are small tradeoffs that always remind us that there is no such a thing as a free lunch.

Speeding Up Your Code with Stored Procedures

Every time you pass a Structured Query Language (SQL) statement to the database server, it needs to be parsed and compiled before it can be executed. This takes time. Using stored procedures will boost performance because a stored procedure, unless otherwise specified, is only compiled once, the first time it is used.

Although stored procedures are more difficult to code, you should always consider using them whenever possible. Using stored procedures not only speeds up your code, but also forces all the database related commands to reside in one place: the database server.

Using the GetString Method to Retrieve Data

In Chapter 4, I describe how to retrieve data from the database by reading the value of each individual field in a record in the recordset and sending those values to the browser as strings. If you need to send more than one record, you have to scroll through the recordset, usually by using the MoveNext method. However, composing strings containing these records can be done faster using the GetString method of the Recordset object. The added bonus to using this method is that your code is simpler.

The GetString method has the following syntax:

```
Set Variant = recordset.GetString(StringFormat, NumRows,
    ColumnDelimiter, RowDelimiter, NullExpr)
```

or

```
String = recordset.GetString(StringFormat, NumRows, ColumnDelimiter,
    RowDelimiter, NullExpr)
```

The latter syntax is the one you use with Visual Basic.
The GetString method has the following parameters:

- *StringFormat:* According to Microsoft's documentation, this parameter must take the adClipString constant as the value. However, my testing revealed that this parameter can be ignored without making a difference.

- *NumRows* (optional): The number of rows in the recordset to convert. If *NumRows* is not specified or if it is greater than the total number of rows in the recordset, then all the rows in the recordset are converted.

- *ColumnDelimiter* (optional): Delimiter used between columns if specified; otherwise the tab character is used.

- *RowDelimiter* (optional): Delimiter used between rows if specified; otherwise the carriage return character is used.

- *NullExpr* (optional): Expression used in place of a NULL value if specified; otherwise the empty string is used.

Some examples using this method are given in this section. The first example, shown in Listing 5-1, is the code for displaying table data in an HTML table. Do pay special attention to the lines in bold. The "</td><td>" is used as the column delimiter and the "</td></tr><tr><td>" is used as the row delimiter. All NULL values will be replaced by , which translates into a blank space in HTML as the result of passing this string as the NullExpr parameter.

Listing 5-1

```
Private Sub Members_DisplayAllMembers()

    Dim rs As New ADODB.Recordset
    Dim strSQL As String
    Dim strData As String
```

```
Dim strConnectionString as String

strConnectionString = "Provider=Microsoft.Jet.OLEDB.4.0;" & _
   "Data Source=C:\ClubMembers.mdb;"


' build SQL statement to pull out the record to delete
strSQL = "SELECT LastName, FirstName" & _
   " FROM Members"
rs.Open strSQL, strConnectionString, adOpenForwardOnly, adLockReadOnly

strData = rs.GetString(, , "</td><td>", "</td></tr><tr><td>", " ")

rs.Close
Set rs = Nothing

' Send the table data to the browser
Response.Write "<table border=2><tr><td>"
Response.Write strData
Response.Write "</td></tr></table>"

End Sub
```

You can, of course, write the last three Response.Write statements in Listing 5-1 in one single call. Note that using the GetString method, as in the previous example, sends an extra table row to the browser because this method also sends the row delimiter after the last row. This is acceptable in many cases where the table border is set to invisible.

What about formatting the HTML table produced this way? You certainly can do that, but you lose some flexibility when using the GetString method. You can still format the HTML table because you can write the table heading. All subsequent elements in the HTML table will have the same format as the heading. In other words, once you set the attributes for individual column headings, the rest of the cells in the column will have the same attributes, for example, colors, width, and so on.

Look at the next example in Listing 5-2. It is similar to the previous example, with some additional formatting for the table heading.

Listing 5-2
```
Private Sub WebClass_Start()

Dim rs As New ADODB.Recordset
Dim strSQL As String
Dim strData As String
```

```
Dim strConnectionString as String

strConnectionString = "Provider=Microsoft.Jet.OLEDB.4.0;" & _
    "Data Source=C:\ClubMembers.mdb;"

' build SQL statement to pull out the record to delete
strSQL = "SELECT LastName, FirstName" & _
    " FROM Members"
rs.Open strSQL, strConnectionString, adOpenForwardOnly, adLockReadOnly

strData = rs.GetString(, , "</td><td>", "</td></tr><tr><td>", " ")

rs.Close
Set rs = Nothing

' Send the table data to the browser
Response.Write "<table border=2>" & vbCr & _
    "   <tr>" & vbCr & _
    "      <td width=120><b>Last Name</b></td>" & vbCr & _
    "      <td width=100><b>First Name</b></td>" & vbCr & _
    "   </tr>" & vbCr & _
    "   <tr>" & vbCr & _
    "      <td>" & vbCr & _
    strData & vbCr & _
    "      </td>" & vbCr & _
    "   </tr>" & vbCr & _
    "</table>"

End Sub
```

Note that you can also add some additional strings to the SQL statement to produce a recordset that suits your needs. The next example embeds the HTML code for a checkbox. The SQL statement uses the ampersand character (&) to concatenate the strings with the field name ID. This SQL statement is for a Microsoft Access database. Different databases may use different characters for concatenating strings.

To try this example, just copy and paste the code in Listing 5-3 into your WebClass. The results of this code are shown in Figure 5-1.

Listing 5-3

```
Private Sub WebClass_Start()

    Dim rs As New ADODB.Recordset
```

```
Dim strSQL As String
Dim strData As String
Dim strConnectionString as String

strConnectionString = "Provider=Microsoft.Jet.OLEDB.4.0;" & _
  "Data Source=C:\ClubMembers.mdb;"

' build SQL statement to pull out the record to delete
strSQL = "SELECT LastName, FirstName, " & _
  " '<input type=checkbox name=MemberID value=' & ID & '>'" & _
  " FROM Members"
rs.Open strSQL, strConnectionString, adOpenForwardOnly, adLockReadOnly

' Send the table data to the browser
strData = rs.GetString(, , "</td>" & vbCr & "<td>", _
  "</td></tr>" & vbCr & "<tr><td>", " ")

rs.Close
Set rs = Nothing

Response.Write "<form method=post action=" & _
  URLFor(Members, "BulkDelete") & ">" & vbCr & _
  "<table border=2>" & vbCr & _
  "  <tr>" & vbCr & _
  "    <td width=100>Last Name</td>" & vbCr & _
  "    <td width=120>First Name</td>" & vbCr & _
  "    <td width=50>Delete</td>" & vbCr & _
  "  </tr>" & vbCr & _
  "  <tr>" & vbCr & _
  "    <td>" & _
  strData & _
  "    </td>" & vbCr & _
  "  </tr>" & vbCr & _
  "  <tr>" & vbCr & _
  "    <td colspan=3 align=center>" & _
  "<input type=submit value=""Delete Member"">" & _
  "    </td>" & vbCr & _
  "  </tr>" & vbCr & _
  "</table>" & _
  "</form>"


End Sub
```

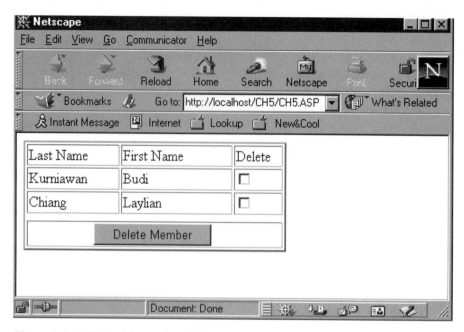

Figure 5-1. HTML table produced by the GetString *method*

The data adds a checkbox for each record. These checkboxes have the same name, which is legal in HTML. When you submit the form, the MemberID has all the values of the checkboxes selected. These values are separated by commas. You can then use this input to delete the selected records.

The GetString method is also a good choice to populate a Select box as in Listing 5-4. However, this method writes a blank item at the end of the list. To get around this problem, embed the tags in the SQL statement as demonstrated by the example in Listing 5-5.

Listing 5-4

```
Private Sub PopulateSelectBox()

  Dim rs As New ADODB.Recordset
  Dim strSQL As String
  Dim strData As String
  Dim strConnectionString as String

  strConnectionString = "Provider=Microsoft.Jet.OLEDB.4.0;" & _
    "Data Source=C:\CommonDB.mdb;"

  ' build SQL statement to pull out records for the Select element
  strSQL = "SELECT State FROM States ORDER BY State"
```

```
rs.Open strSQL, strConnectionString, adOpenForwardOnly, adLockReadOnly

' Send the table data to the browser
strData = rs.GetString(, , "", _
  "</option>" & vbCr & "<option>", " ")

rs.Close
Set rs = Nothing

Response.Write "<select Name=State>" & vbCr & _
  "<option>" & strData & "</option>" & _
  "</select>"

End Sub
```

Listing 5-5

```
Private Sub PopulateSelectBox()

  Dim rs As New ADODB.Recordset
  Dim strSQL As String
  Dim strData As String
  Dim strConnectionString as String

  strConnectionString = "Provider=Microsoft.Jet.OLEDB.4.0;" & _
    "Data Source=C:\CommonDB.mdb;"

  ' build SQL statement to select the name of the states
  strSQL = "SELECT '<option>' & State & '</option>'" & _
    " FROM States ORDER BY State"
  rs.Open strSQL, strConnectionString, adOpenForwardOnly, adLockReadOnly

  rs.Close
  Set rs = Nothing

  ' Send the table data to the browser
  strData = rs.GetString(, , "", "", "")
  Response.Write "<select Name=State>" & vbCr & _
    strData & _
    "</select>"

End Sub
```

Or, if you want to include the value for each item, consider the example in
Listing 5-6.

Listing 5-6

```
Private Sub PopulateSelectBox()

  Dim rs As New ADODB.Recordset
  Dim strSQL As String
  Dim strData As String
  Dim strConnectionString as String

  strConnectionString = "Provider=Microsoft.Jet.OLEDB.4.0;" & _
    "Data Source=C:\CommonDB.mdb;"

  ' build SQL statement to select the name of the states
  strSQL = "SELECT '<option value=' & ID & '>' & State & '</option>'" & _
    " FROM States ORDER BY State"
  rs.Open strSQL, strConnectionString, adOpenForwardOnly, adLockReadOnly

  rs.Close
  Set rs = Nothing

  ' Send the table data to the browser
  strData = rs.GetString(, , "", "", "")
  Response.Write "<select Name=State>" & vbCr & _
    strData & _
    "</select>"

End Sub
```

If you are using SQL Server, you can't use the ampersand character (&) to con-catenate strings. Use the plus (+) sign instead. For example, the SQL statement in Listing 5-6 will look like this:

```
strSQL = "SELECT '<option value=' + ID & '>' + State + '</option>'" & _
    " FROM States ORDER BY State"
```

Generic Function to Insert a Record

More often than not, your table will have more fields than it can comfortably maintain. This book has presented examples in which the tables typically have no more than four or five fields. In reality, you sometimes have to deal with dozens of fields in a table.

This presents a challenge when you need to insert or update a record into a table. First, you need to write the code that caters to all fields in your HTML form.

Second, after painful value checking, you need to build an SQL statement for inserting or updating a record. Looping through and making sure you don't leave out a field and ensuring that all fields are correctly spelled is no easy task. This chore becomes even more annoying when case sensitivity in the field names matter as it does when using Oracle or Sybase databases.

The technique you are about to learn won't speed up your code, in fact, it will make your code a little slower. However, for the price of some small degradation in speed, you are awarded with easier to program and more readable code, not to mention the ease of use that you give to the people who inherit your code.

The technique is very simple: For each element in your HTML form, prefix it with either s_ or n_. Instead of having an element named *FieldName*, you have n_*FieldName* or s_*FieldName*, where *FieldName* is the exact name of your table field. Use n_ if the data is of type numeric or boolean; otherwise use s_. Date fields must also have names like s_DateField. Other form elements that don't have anything to do with the table must not be prefixed with s_ or n_.

Upon receiving the Request object that carries all the values the user has entered, you loop through the Form collection to grab the field names and values to form the SQL statement on the fly. This way, you don't need to worry about how many fields your table has. No spell checking is necessary either, provided the HTML form contains the correct spellings.

The routine in Listing 5-7 checks every single element of the Form collection of the Request object if its name starts with s_ or n_. If the object's name starts with s_ or n_ and the value of the element is not a blank string, the field name/value pair is then added to the SQL statement.

Listing 5-7

```
Private Sub Members_InsertRecordWithManyFields()
  Dim intCounter As Integer
  Dim strFields As String
  Dim strValues As String
  Dim strSQL As String
  Dim strKey As String
  Dim cn As New ADODB.Connection
  Dim strConnectionString As String

  strConnectionString = "Provider=MSDASQL.1;User ID=sa;Password=;" & _
    "Data Source=BigDaddy;Initial Catalog=pubs;"

  For intCounter = 1 To Request.Form.Count
    If Request.Form.Item(intCounter) <> "" Then
      strKey = Request.Form.Key(intCounter)
      If Left$(strKey, 2) = "s_" Then
        strFields = strFields & Mid$(strKey, 3) & ","
```

```
            strValues = strValues & " '" & _
              Replace(Request.Form.Item(intCounter), "'", "''") & "',"
          ElseIf Left$(strKey, 2) = "n_" Then
            strFields = strFields & Mid$(strKey, 3) & ","
            strValues = strValues & Request.Form.Item(i) & ","
          End If
        End If
      Next

      'Remove the last commas from strFields and strValues
      strFields = Left$(strFields, Len(strFields) - 1)
      strValues = Left$(strValues, Len(strValues) - 1)

      strSQL = "INSERT INTO TableName (" & strFields & ")" & _
        " VALUES (" & strValues & ")"

      cn.Open strConnectionString

      cn.Execute strSQL
      cn.Close
      Set cn = Nothing

  End Sub
```

When using this method, check to make sure that all non-nullable fields have values before calling this method. The checking can easily be done on the client-side, as explained in Chapter 6.

Generic Function to Update a Record

When updating a record with many fields, you'll encounter the same problems as described in the previous section of this chapter. You can, however, use a generic function to update a record containing many fields. The code is shown in Listing 5-8.

Listing 5-8

```
Private Sub Members_UpdateRecordWithManyFields()
  Dim intCounter As Integer
  Dim strValues As String
  Dim strSQL As String
  Dim strKey As String
  Dim cn As New ADODB.Connection
```

```
Dim strConnectionString As String

strConnectionString = "Provider=MSDASQL.1;User ID=sa;Password=;" & _
  "Data Source=BigDaddy;Initial Catalog=pubs;"


For intCounter = 1 To Request.Form.Count
  strKey = Request.Form.Key(intCounter)
  If Left$(strKey, 2) = "s_" Then
    strValues = strValues & Mid$(strKey, 3) & "=" & _
      "'" & Replace(Request.Form.Item(intCounter), "'", "''") & "',"
  ElseIf Left$(strKey, 2) = "n_" Then
    strValues = strValues & Mid$(strKey, 3) & "=" & _
      Request.Form.Item(intCounter) & ","
  End If
Next

'Remove the last commas from strFields and strValues
strValues = Left$(strValues, Len(strValues) - 1)

strSQL = "UPDATE TableName SET " & strValues & _
  " WHERE PrimaryKey=" & Request.Form.Item("PrimaryKeyValue")

cn.Open strConnectionString
cn.Execute strSQL

End Sub
```

One major difference between the routine to insert a record and the routine to update a record concerns blank values. In the routine in Listing 5-7, all blank values are not added to the SQL statement; they are given their default values at the server. With the Update routine, all fields, including those whose values are blank, are included in the SQL statement.

Splitting a Large Form into Smaller Ones

A number of reasons exist why you might want to split a form into several smaller ones, but the most significant reason is to increase user-friendliness. This is especially true when you have a form with more than 20 input elements. Even with a smaller number of elements, you sometimes want to separate inputs of different topics. For example, for an online job application, you may want to separate the questions related to education from those related to work experience.

Although form splitting does make your application more user-friendly, it doesn't reduce the processing time or server workload, and it also means extra work for you. You are also faced with the challenge of transferring user input from the previous forms to the next. But if you have to, then you have to.

There are a couple of ways of passing values from one form to another, and this topic is worth a chapter of its own. What is relevant for this discussion is how to pass these values before finally reaching the database.

For this purpose, you can use the Hidden element. A Hidden element is similar to a Text element, but Hidden elements are invisible on the HTML page. However, they can be seen if the user views the source code of the page.

For example, let's decide to split the preliminary part of a job application form into three parts. The first two parts will be regular input forms, and the last part will be the confirmation form, which displays the values the user has entered in the previous forms. Only when the user submits the last form will the values be entered into the database.

For the sake of simplicity, the first form will have only three text boxes: Last Name, First Name, and Date of Birth. The second form will have the Street, City, State/Province, and Country. The third form will have a submit button for the user to confirm the values he has entered. There are three HTML templates, which are simply called Page1, Page2, and Page3.

Page1 is the first form, which you can send to the browser directly from the WebClass_Start() event procedure or after some processing. Page1 contains a form, and the form's onSubmit event is connected to the Page2 WebItem. Because the onSubmit event is not explicitly connected to any event in Page2, the event will trigger the Respond event of Page2, which in turns calls the WriteTemplate method of Page2. As you can see in Chapter 2, every call to this method triggers the ProcessTag event, so this is where you insert code to pass the values from Page1 as hidden elements in Page2.

Page2 also has a form, which is connected to Page3. By the same token, the form is connected to the Page3 WebItem. Similar to Page2, in the Respond event procedure, you call the WriteTemplate method of Page3. It then triggers the ProcessTag event of Page3 and runs the code. Note that there is different code for these two ProcessTag events. On Page2 there are only three hidden values, but when there are more values, a generic function that loops through the Request object's Form collection is helpful.

To get this example running, create three HTML pages named Page1.htm, Page2.htm, and Page3.htm, and add them as HTML templates. The three HTML pages are given in Listings 5-9 to 5-11.

Listing 5-9

```
<html>
<head>
<title>Application Form -- Step 1</title>
```

```
</head>
<body>
<center>
<form method=post>
<table>
  <tr>
    <td>Last Name:</td>
    <td><input type=text name=LastName></td>
  </tr>
  <tr>
    <td>First Name:</td>
    <td><input type=text name=FirstName></td>
  </tr>
  <tr>
    <td>Date Of Birth:</td>
    <td><input type=text name=DateOfBirth></td>
  </tr>
  <tr>
    <td> </td>
    <td><input type=submit value=Continue></td>
  </tr>
</table>
</form>
</center>
</body>
</html>
```

Listing 5-10

```
<html>
<head>
<title>Application Form -- Step 2</title>
</head>
<body>
<center>
<form method=post>
<WC@HIDDENVALUES>Insert values from Page1</WC@HIDDENVALUES>
<table>
  <tr>
    <td>Street:</td>
    <td><input type=text name=Street ></td>
  </tr>
  <tr>
    <td>City:</td>
```

```
        <td><input type=text name=City ></td>
    </tr>
    <tr>
      <td>State:</td>
      <td><input type=text name=State ></td>
    </tr>
    <tr>
      <td>Post Code:</td>
      <td><input type=text name=PostCode ></td>
    </tr>
    <tr>
      <td> </td>
      <td><input type=submit value=Continue></td>
    </tr>
  </table>
</form>
</center>
</body>
</html>
```

Listing 5-11

```
<html>
<head>
<title>Application Form -- Step 3</title>
</head>
<body>
<center>
You have entered your details.
<br>If everything is correct,
<br>please click the Submit button to submit your application.

<form method=post>
<WC@HIDDENVALUES>Insert values from Page2</WC@HIDDENVALUES>
<table>
  <tr>
    <td>Last Name:</td>
    <td><WC@LastName></WC@LastName></td>
  </tr>
  <tr>
    <td>First Name:</td>
    <td><WC@FirstName></WC@FirstName></td>
  </tr>
  <tr>
```

```
    <td>Date Of Birth:</td>
    <td><WC@DateOfBirth></WC@DateOfBirth></td>
  </tr>
  <tr>
    <td colspan=2><hr></td>
  </tr>
  <tr>
    <td>Street:</td>
    <td><WC@Street></WC@Street></td>
  </tr>
  <tr>
    <td>City:</td>
    <td><WC@City></WC@City></td>
  </tr>
  <tr>
    <td>State:</td>
    <td><WC@State></WC@State></td>
  </tr>
  <tr>
    <td>Post Code:</td>
    <td><WC@PostCode></WC@PostCode></td>
  </tr>
  <tr>
    <td colspan=2><hr></td>
  </tr>
  <tr>
    <td> </td>
    <td><input type=submit value=Submit></td>
  </tr>
</table>
</form>
</center>
</body>
</html>
```

The code in Listing 5-12 provides the event procedures that you need to create in conjunction with the HTML templates.

Listing 5-12

```
Private Sub WebClass_Start()

  Page1.WriteTemplate
```

```
        End Sub

        Private Sub Page2_ProcessTag(ByVal TagName As String, _
          TagContents As String, SendTags As Boolean)

          TagContents = "<input type=hidden name=LastName" & _
            " value=""" & Request.Form("LastName") & """>" & vbCr & _
            "<input type=hidden name=FirstName" & _
            " value=""" & Request.Form("FirstName") & """>" & vbCr & _
            "<input type=hidden name=DateOfBirth" & _
            " value=""" & Request.Form("DateOfBirth") & """>"
        End Sub

        Private Sub Page2_Respond()

          Page2.WriteTemplate

        End Sub

        Private Sub Page3_ProcessTag(ByVal TagName As String, _
          TagContents As String, SendTags As Boolean)

          Select Case TagName
            Case "WC@HIDDENVALUES"
              Dim strTemp As String
              Dim intCounter As Integer
              For intCounter = 1 To Request.Form.Count
                strTemp = strTemp & "<input type=hidden name=" & _
                  Request.Form.Key(intCounter) & _
                  " value=""" & Request.Form.item(intCounter) & """>" & vbCr
              Next intCounter
              TagContents = strTemp
            Case "WC@LastName"
              TagContents = Request.Form.item("LastName")
            Case "WC@FirstName"
              TagContents = Request.Form.item("FirstName")
            Case "WC@DateOfBirth"
              TagContents = Request.Form.item("DateOfBirth")
            Case "WC@Street"
              TagContents = Request.Form.item("Street")
            Case "WC@City"
              TagContents = Request.Form.item("City")
            Case "WC@State"
              TagContents = Request.Form.item("State")
```

```
    Case "WC@PostCode"
        TagContents = Request.Form.item("PostCode")
    End Select
End Sub

Private Sub Page3_Respond()
    Page3.WriteTemplate
End Sub
```

Referring to a Recordset Field by Its Index

Referring to a Recordset field by its name is a valid and convenient way of getting and storing a value. For instance, it's easy to get too comfortable using expressions such as the following without realizing that you're using a more expensive way of retrieving and storing data.

```
lngID = rs("ID")
strLastName = rs("LastName")
    and

rs.AddNew
rs("FirstName") = Request.Form("FirstName")
rs("LastName") = Request.Form("LastName")
rs.Update
```

Referring to a Recordset field by its index is surely faster, and you should always use this method whenever possible, that is, when the number of fields is not so large that it's confusing to refer to a field by its index. Even so, there is a work around that you can easily implement.

In my experience, referring to a field by its index, as opposed to calling its name, is 20 to 25 percent faster. You can easily test the speed gain by using the Timer function in VB, as in the following two pieces of code. The first, in Listing 5-13, uses the field names luxuriously; the second, in Listing 5-14, is an attempt to be a bit thrifty.

Listing 5-13

```
Dim rs As New ADODB.Recordset
Dim strSQL As String
Dim t1

strSQL = "SELECT ID, LastName, FirstName" & _
    " FROM Members "
```

```
rs.Open strSQL, "Atom", adOpenForwardOnly, adLockReadOnly

t1 = Timer
While Not rs.EOF
  Response.Write rs("ID") & rs("LastName") & rs("FirstName") & "<br>"
  rs.MoveNext
Wend
Response.Write Timer - t1
rs.Close
Set rs = Nothing
```

And, for the sake of comparison, replace the following line

```
Response.Write rs("ID") & rs("LastName") & rs("FirstName") & "<br>"
```

with this line:

```
Response.Write rs(0) & rs(1) & rs(2) & "<br>"
```

The result is shown in the code in Listing 5-14.

Listing 5-14

```
Dim rs As New ADODB.Recordset
  Dim strSQL As String
  Dim t1

  strSQL = "SELECT ID, LastName, FirstName" & _
    " FROM Members "
  rs.Open strSQL, "Atom", adOpenForwardOnly, adLockReadOnly

  t1 = Timer
  While Not rs.EOF
    Response.Write rs(0) & rs(1) & rs(2) & "<br>"
    rs.MoveNext
  Wend
  Response.Write Timer - t1
  rs.Close
  Set rs = Nothing
```

To notice a difference, your table must have a sufficient number of records (approximately 120 rows on an AMD 330MHz machine). If the displayed time is 0, it means the time taken to display all the records is too little, and you need more data in your table.

Using the index will of course reduce the readability of your code. However, you can use some constants as the replacements of field names. Your code will then look like the code in Listing 5-15.

Listing 5-15

```
Const ID = 0
Const LAST_NAME = 1
Const FIRST_NAME = 2

Dim rs As New ADODB.Recordset
Dim strSQL As String

strSQL = "SELECT ID, LastName, FirstName" & _
    " FROM Members "
rs.Open strSQL, "Atom", adOpenForwardOnly, adLockReadOnly

While Not rs.EOF
    Response.Write rs(ID) & rs(LAST_NAME) & rs(FIRST_NAME) & "<br>"
    rs.MoveNext
Wend

rs.Close
Set rs = Nothing
```

The Command Object

Back in Chapter 4, the ADO object model is discussed. In that discussion, I note that the ADO has three major objects: Connection, Command, and Recordset. I've held off on explaining the Command object until now, for a good reason.

The hierarchy of the ADO object model is very loose. You can, for instance, populate a Recordset object with data from your database table without first creating a Connection object explicitly, as in the examples in Chapter 4. When you do this, however, you still need a Connection object. Every time you use the Open method of the Recordset object and pass a connection string, ADO automatically creates a Connection object in the background. As a result, you can enjoy having database access with fewer objects to worry about.

What was not discussed in Chapter 4 was that ADO also creates a Command object for every operation involving ADO when you don't explicitly create one. For example, this occurs when you populate a Recordset object and when you use the Execute method of the Connection object to run an action query. However, in most cases, it is okay to forget about the Command object because this object is taken care of by ADO.

It is perfectly valid to perform a task without the Command object. The Recordset object and the Connection object can perform most tasks with the same speed; however, there will be times when you need to create a Command object explicitly—for example, when you need to get an output parameter from a stored procedure or when you need to speed up your code when running the same query repeatedly.

The Command object is basically a definition of a specific command that you want to execute against a data source. It has two collections, the Parameters and the Properties collections, and three methods: Cancel, CreateParameter, and Execute. A complete reference is given in Appendix C.

You use the Command object's Execute method to run an action query or populate a recordset. When using the Command object, you need to assign values to a few properties before calling the Execute method. You can, as in the Connection and the Recordset objects, pass these properties as arguments to the Execute method.

When using the Command object, you need to specify the SQL statement in the CommandText property and tell ADO what type of SQL statement is used and whether it is an SQL query that needs to be parsed, a name of a stored procedure, or another type. Equally important, you need to pass an active Connection object or a valid connection string to its ActiveConnection property. The example in Listing 5-16 demonstrates how to return a recordset using the Command object.

Listing 5-16

```
Const ID = 0
Const LAST_NAME = 1
Const FIRST_NAME = 2

Dim cmd As New ADODB.Command
Dim rs As New ADODB.Recordset
Dim strSQL As String
Dim strConnectionString As String

strConnectionString = "DRIVER={Microsoft Access Driver (*.mdb)}; " & _
  " DBQ=" & Server.MapPath("dbs\db01.mdb")

strSQL = "SELECT ID, LastName, FirstName" & _
  " FROM Members "
cmd.CommandType = adCmdText
cmd.CommandText = strSQL
cmd.ActiveConnection = strConnectionString
Set rs = cmd.Execute

While Not rs.EOF
  Response.Write rs(ID) & rs(LAST_NAME) & rs(FIRST_NAME) & "<br>"
```

```
    rs.MoveNext
Wend

rs.Close
Set rs = Nothing
Set cmd = Nothing
```

However, the previous code can be rewritten without using the Command object. So, when do you need a Command object? In some cases, for instance, when you need to execute the same action query repeatedly. Consider the code in Listing 5-17.

Listing 5-17

```
Dim strSQL As String
Dim intCounter As Integer
Dim cn As New ADODB.Connection
Dim strConnectionString As String

strConnectionString = "DRIVER={Microsoft Access Driver (*.mdb)}; " & _
   " DBQ=" & Server.MapPath("dbs\db01.mdb")

strSQL = "INSERT INTO Members (ID, LastName, FirstName)" & _
   " VALUES (1, 'Pasternak', 'Boris')"
cn.Open strConnectionString

For intCounter = 1 To 100
  cn.Execute strSQL
Next intCounter
Set cn = Nothing
```

Using the Connection object's Execute method, the same query of each of the 100 record inserts will need to be parsed and compiled by the database server each time the Execute method is called. Parsing and compiling do take time. With the Command object, your SQL statement will only be parsed and compiled once, and the query can persist for the entire life of the Command object. In the case in which you need to run the same action query 100 times, as in the previous example, using the Command object will result in much faster code.

Using the Command object, the previous code can be rewritten as in Listing 5-18.

Listing 5-18

```
Dim cmd As New ADODB.Command
Dim strSQL As String
```

```
Dim intCounter As Integer
Dim strConnectionString As String

strConnectionString = "DRIVER={Microsoft Access Driver (*.mdb)}; " & _
   " DBQ=" & Server.MapPath("dbs\db01.mdb")


strSQL = "INSERT INTO Members (ID, LastName, FirstName)" & _
   " VALUES (1, 'Pasternak', 'Boris')"
cmd.CommandType = adCmdText
cmd.CommandText = strSQL
cmd.ActiveConnection = strConnectionString

cmd.Prepared = True
For intCounter = 1 To 100
   cmd.Execute
Next intCounter

Set cmd = Nothing
```

Notice that the Prepared property of the Command object is used (in bold in Listing 5-18). Without this property, using the Command object will be slower than simply using the Connection object, but setting the Prepared property to True will outrun the Connection object approach, and can result in improved performance only if you execute the command more than once.

If the Prepared property is set to True, ADO tells the database server to create a temporary stored procedure to execute the query. It's the reason the Command object is faster for executing the same SQL statement repeatedly. A stored procedure is created when the Command object's Execute method is first called and is then retained for the next calls. If you are actually calling a stored procedure in a database server, there is no point in using a Command object. Use the Connection object instead.

The Command object is also useful when you need to run a stored procedure that takes parameters. For this purpose, one approach is to create each parameter needed by the stored procedure and add it to the Parameters collection. The following code illustrates the use of the Command object to run the sp_GetCountryDescription stored procedure that takes one parameter: ID. This stored procedure returns the country name whose ID is passed in the ID parameter.

The stored procedure used in the next example was created in a Microsoft SQL Server 7 database.

```
CREATE PROCEDURE dbo.sp_GetCountryDescription;1
  (@ID numeric)

AS
  SELECT CountryName FROM dbo.COUNTRIES
  WHERE CountryID = @ID
```

The code is provided in Listing 5-19.

Listing 5-19

```
Dim cn As New ADODB.Connection
Dim rs As New ADODB.Recordset
Dim strSQL As String
Dim cmd As New ADODB.Command
Dim prm As New ADODB.Parameter

strSQL = "sp_GetCountryDescription"
cn.Open "myString", "sa", " myPassword"
cmd.CommandText = strSQL
cmd.CommandType = adCmdStoredProc

Set prm = cmd.CreateParameter("ID", adInteger, adParamInput, , 2)
cmd.Parameters.Append prm
Set cmd.ActiveConnection = cn
Set rs = cmd.Execute


Debug.Print rs(0)
```

The previous example, of course, is more easily implemented with a Connection object as given in Listing 5-20.

Listing 5-20

```
Dim cn As New ADODB.Connection
Dim rs As New ADODB.Recordset
Dim strSQL As String
Dim cmd As New ADODB.Command
Dim prm As New ADODB.Parameter

strSQL = "sp_GetCountryDescription 2"
cn.Open "myString", "sa", "myPassword"

Set rs = cn.Execute(strSQL)

Debug.Print rs(0)
```

When you use the Connection object, as in Listing 5-20, a Command object is created implicitly in the background.

You can see from the previous examples that in most cases you don't need to create the Command object explicitly. It is actually recommended that you don't. Use an explicit Command object only when you really need it. For instance, the Command object is irreplaceable when you need to grab the return value from a stored procedure. Consider the following stored procedure called sp_CheckProduct. It has one input parameter (@ProductID) and one output parameter (@InStock).

```
CREATE PROCEDURE sp_CheckProduct
  @ProductID numeric, @InStock numeric OUTPUT
AS
  SELECT @InStock = SUM(QuantityInStock) FROM ProductsInStock
  WHERE ProductID = @ProductID
  RETURN @InStock
GO
```

The code that uses the stored procedure is provided in Listing 5-21.

Listing 5-21

```
Dim cn As New ADODB.Connection
Dim cmd As New ADODB.Command
Dim prm As New ADODB.Parameter

cn.Open "pubs"
cmd.CommandText = "sp_CheckProduct"
cmd.CommandType = adCmdStoredProc

Set prm = cmd.CreateParameter("ProductID", adInteger, adParamInput, , 1)
cmd.Parameters.Append prm
Set prm = cmd.CreateParameter("InStock", adInteger, adParamOutput)
cmd.Parameters.Append prm
Set cmd.ActiveConnection = cn

cmd.Execute (strSQL)
Debug.Print cmd.Parameters("InStock")
```

But, hang on. Why do you want to use a stored procedure with output parameters? Can't you just pass the return value in a single-row recordset? You could, but when using a recordset, the query results returned by the data source object include data and metadata. Often the metadata is much larger than the data or is a significant part of the query results. Consequently, creating a recordset when you can use an output parameter will result in slower code.

Using the Options Parameter in the Recordset Object's Open Method

The syntax of the Recordset object's Open method is

```
recordset.Open Source, ActiveConnection, CursorType, LockType, Options
```

In previous examples, both in Chapter 4 and this chapter, I did not use the optional *Options* parameter. You should look at this parameter if you want to further speed up your code, specifying the Options parameter can increase the speed of your database access. How?

The Options parameter is a Long value that indicates how the provider should evaluate the *Source* argument if it represents something other than a Command object or if the Recordset object should be restored from a file where it was previously saved. The possible values for the Options parameter are given in Table 5-1.

> **NOTE:** *The optional* Source *parameter specifies a Variant that evaluates to a valid* Command *object variable name, an SQL statement, a table name, a stored procedure call, or the filename of a persisted Recordset.*

Table 5-1: Possible Values for the Options Parameter

CONSTANT	DESCRIPTION
adCmdText	Indicates that the provider should evaluate *Source* as a textual definition of a command.
adCmdTable	Indicates that ADO should generate an SQL query to return all rows from the table named in *Source*.
adCmdTableDirect	Indicates that the provider should return all rows from the table named in *Source*.
adCmdStoredProc	Indicates that the provider should evaluate *Source* as a stored procedure.
adCmdUnknown	Indicates that the type of command in the *Source* argument is not known.
adCommandFile	Indicates that the persisted (saved) recordset should be restored from the file named in *Source*.
adExecuteAsync	Indicates that the *Source* should be executed asynchronously.
adFetchAsync	Indicates that after the initial quantity specified in the CacheSize property is fetched, any remaining rows should be fetched asynchronously.

If you don't pass a `Command` object in the *Source* argument, you can use the *Options* argument to optimize the evaluation of the *Source* argument. If the *Options* argument is not defined, you may experience diminished performance because ADO must make calls to the provider to determine if the argument is an SQL statement, a stored procedure, or a table name. Setting the *Options* argument instructs ADO to jump directly to the relevant code. If the *Options* argument does not match the *Source* type, an error occurs.

If no connection is associated with the recordset, the default for the *Options* argument is `adCommandFile`. This will typically be the case for persisted `Recordset` objects.

Asynchronous Operations

Normally your code is synchronous, meaning that each line of code is completed before the processing goes to the next line. However, when dealing with databases, a large portion of CPU time is probably spent on waiting for the database server to finish the operation.

You can switch to the asynchronous operation, as long as you do so with care. When opening a connection, for example, you can let the database driver handle it while assigning some other operations to your CPU. You must be careful when using this type of operation. Before you try to open a recordset that uses the Connection object that you tried to open, you must make sure that the Connection object has been completely opened.

To indicate that you want to do asynchronous operations, you must use the constants `adAsyncConnect`, `adAsyncFetch`, or `adAsyncExecute`. When you pass one of these constants as an Options parameter, you tell ADO to return control to your application immediately after launching the operation.

To open a connection in asynchronous mode, pass the `adAsyncConnect` constant after the Password parameter, as follows:

```
cn.Open strConnectionString, , , adAsyncConnect
```

Before you use the connection, for example, to open a `Recordset` object, make sure that the `Connection` object has been opened. Consider the code in Listing 5-22.

Listing 5-22
```
Dim cn As New ADODB.Connection
Dim rs As New ADODB.Recordset
Dim strSQL As String

cn.Open "Pubs", Options:=adAsyncConnect
```

```
strSQL = "SELECT * FROM Authors"
rs.Open strSQL, cn, adOpenForwardOnly, adLockReadOnly
```

When you run Listing 5-22 on your server, unless your computer is extremely slow, VB will raise the error "Run-time error '3713': Invalid operation on object while still connecting." This means that you just attempted to use a Connection object that is not yet open.

Before you perform a function that needs the completion of the previous asynchronous operation, in this case opening a Connection object, you need to make sure that the Connection object is already open. You can check if a Connection object is open using the State property of the Connection object. The code for that is given in Listing 5-23.

Listing 5-23

```
Dim cn As New ADODB.Connection
Dim rs As New ADODB.Recordset
Dim strSQL As String

cn.Open "pubs", , , adAsyncConnect

'Do something here while waiting for connection

strSQL = "SELECT * FROM dbo.discounts"

While cn.State <> adStateOpen
   DoEvents
Wend
rs.Open strSQL, cn, adOpenForwardOnly, adLockReadOnly
```

The code in bold waits until the connection is open before trying to open the recordset.

Another application of asynchronous operations uses the Execute method as shown in Listing 5-24. For example, for an online store, you can stash products that the user has placed in the shopping bag in a table. This is an ideal situation for using an asynchronous operation because you can get back to the user without having to wait for the database server to finish inserting a record in the table.

Listing 5-24

```
Dim cn As New ADODB.Connection
Dim strSQL As String
cn.Open "pubs"

strSQL = "INSERT INTO Products VALUES ('abc', 3, 3, 4)"
cn.Execute strSQL, , adAsyncExecute
```

Table 5-2. Possible Values for the State *Property*

CONSTANT	VALUE	DESCRIPTION
adStateClosed	0	The object is closed.
adStateOpen	1	The object is open.
adStateConnecting	2	The Connection object is in the process of opening.
adStateExecuting	4	The object is still executing a query.
adStateFetching	8	The object is executing or opening.

The possible values for the State property are provided in Table 5-2.

Note that when a Connection object is executing a query, the State returns both adStateOpen and adStateExecuting. To check whether it has finished executing, use the following code:

```
While cn.State = adStateOpen + adStateExecuting
   DoEvents
Wend
```

instead of this:

```
While cn.State = adStateExecuting
   DoEvents
Wend
```

Although asynchronous operations are more difficult to code, using them properly will give your application superior performance. The key is to handle them with care.

Data Shaping

When using a join to retrieve data from more than one table, there is almost always some redundancy in the recordset produced. Consider the following query, which tries to retrieve a list of customers and their orders:

```
SELECT C.Company, O.Quantity, P.ProductName FROM Customers C,
Orders O, Products P
WHERE C.CustomerID = O.CustomerID AND O.ProductID = P.ProductID
```

This query results in a single recordset as shown in Figure 5-2.

C. Company	O. Quantity	P. ProductName
MicroLite	44	Microfuge Lite
MicroLite	2	Beckman Balancer
Labsale Pty.	43	PH Electron
Labsale Pty.	4	Rais Centrifuge
Biomatic	5	Rais Centrifuge
Biomatic	55	Beckman Balancer
Biomatic	3	Rais Centrifuge
Biomatic	2	PH Electron
Biomatic	7	Microfuge Lite

*Figure 5-2. The single recordset resulting
from the query*

Although the Customers table has only three records, the resulting recordset has nine records. This means that there is redundancy because the Company field values are repeated for each order.

ADO 2.0 introduced a more efficient way of retrieving data from more than one table: hierarchical recordset, which is more widely known as *data shaping*. The principal idea behind data shaping is that a main recordset can have columns that contain instances of child recordsets. In the previous example, the main recordset is the one that gets data from the Customers table. This main recordset, which has a number of child recordsets, is depicted in Figure 5-3.

Each child recordset in Figures 5.4a through 5.4c holds order details on each customer.

Each child recordset can be a NULL recordset and can also have a column containing other child recordsets. The level of nesting is limited only by your computer's capacity.

To implement data shaping, an OLE DB data source provider must supply data that will be passed to another provider, which will perform the data shaping. The data source provider is specified in the Connection object connect string as "Shape Provider=*YourDataSource*". The provider supplying data shaping support

Company	CustomerOrd
MicroLite Industries	Child recordset
Labsale Pty. Ltd.	Child recordset
Biomatic Vision	Child recordset

Figure 5-3. The main recordset

O. Quantity	P. ProductName
44	Microfuge Lite
2	Beckman Balancer

O. Quantity	P. ProductName
43	PH Electron
4	Rais Centrifuge

O. Quantity	P. ProductName
5	Rais Centrifuge
55	Beckman Balancer
3	Rais Centrifuge
2	PH Electron
7	Microfuge Lite

Figure 5-4. Child recordsets

is specified in the Connection object's `Provider` property as "MSDataShape"; for example:

```
Dim cnn As New ADODB.Connection
cnn.Provider = "MSDataShape"
cnn.Open "Shape Provider=MSDASQL;DSN=FoxBusiness;uid=sa;pwd=;database=pubs"
```

ADO 2.0 also introduced a new Shape data manipulation language syntax, which allows you to make queries that result in a hierarchical recordset. A Shape language command is issued in the same way as any other ADO command string. The Shape language is built into the ADO Client Cursor Engine.

The Shape language enables you to make hierarchical Recordset objects in two ways. The first appends a child recordset to the parent recordset, whereas the second computes an aggregate operation on a child recordset and generates a parent recordset.

The Shape `APPEND` command assigns a child recordset to the `Value` property of `Field` objects in a parent recordset. It has the following syntax:

```
SHAPE {parent-command} [[AS] table-alias]
APPEND {child-command}
RELATE(parent-column TO child-column)
```

The parts of this command consist of:

- `parent-command`, `child-command`: query command that returns a Recordset object. The command is issued to the underlying data provider, and its syntax depends on the requirements of that provider. This will typically be SQL, although ADO doesn't require any particular query language.

- `parent-column`: column in the recordset returned by the `parent-command`.

- `child-column`: column in the recordset returned by *the child-command.*

- `table-alias`: alias used to refer to the recordset returned by the *parent-command.*

The Client Cursor Engine will issue the parent-command to the provider, which will return a parent recordset. Then the child-command will be issued, which will return a child recordset.

For example, the parent-command could return a recordset of customers for a company from a Customers database, and the child-command could return a recordset of orders for all customers from an Orders database.

The parent and child Recordset objects must have a column in common. The columns are named in the RELATE clause, parent-column first, then child-column. The columns may have different names in their respective Recordset objects, but must refer to the same information in order to specify a meaningful relation.

For example, the Customers and Orders recordsets could have a CustomerID field in common.

The Client Cursor Engine internally creates a new column and literally appends it to the parent recordset. The values of the fields in the new column are references to rows in the child recordset that satisfy the RELATE clause.

The appended column will be automatically named "chapter" and be of data type adChapter. If you wish to navigate through the child recordset, specify the appended column in the Recordset object Fields collection and retrieve the recordset from the Field object's Value property. Assign the retrieved recordset to an empty Recordset object, and then navigate through that recordset as you would any other.

Shape commands may be parameterized. For example, you can specify the following:

```
SHAPE {SELECT * FROM customer}
APPEND {SELECT * FROM orders WHERE cust_id = ?}
RELATE (cust_id TO PARAMETER 0)
```

In this case, parent and child tables happen to have a column name in common, cust_id. The child-command has a placeholder (that is, ?) to which the RELATE clause refers (that is, ...PARAMETER 0). In effect, the relation is between the explicitly identified parent-column and the child-column implicitly identified by the placeholder.

When the Shape command is executed, the following happens:

1. An empty column is appended to the parent recordset.

2. The parent-command is executed and returns a row from the customer table.

3. The value of the customer.cust_ID column replaces the placeholder and the child-command is executed.

4. All the rows from the Orders table where the orders.cust_ID column matches the customer.cust column are retrieved.

5. A reference to the retrieved child rows is placed in the current row of the column appended to the parent recordset.

6. The next parent row is retrieved from the customer table and the cycle repeats until all rows are retrieved.

The code in Listing 5-25 demonstrates the use of data shaping to retrieve data from the Customers, Orders, and Products tables, which are the same tables used to describe data shaping.

Listing 5-25

```
Private Sub WebClass_Start()

  Dim cn As New ADODB.Connection
  Dim rsCustomer As New ADODB.Recordset
  Dim rsOrder As New ADODB.Recordset
  Dim strSQL As String

  strSQL = "SHAPE { SELECT * FROM Customers } AS Customers" & _
    " APPEND (" & _
    " { SELECT O.CustomerID, O.Quantity, P.ProductName " & _
    "   FROM Orders O, Products P" & _
    "   WHERE O.ProductID = P.ProductID" & _
    " } AS Orders" & _
    " RELATE CustomerID TO CustomerID) AS CustomerOrder"
```

```
cn.Provider = "MSDataShape"
cn.Open "atom"   ' atom is a DSN
rsCustomer.Open strSQL, cn


' the same as saying
' rsCustomer.Open strSQL, "Provider=MSDataShape;DSN=atom"

Do Until rsCustomer.EOF
  Response.Write "<b>" & rsCustomer("Company") & "</b><br>"
  Set rsOrder = rsCustomer("CustomerOrder").Value
    Do Until rsOrder.EOF
      Response.Write "   " & rsOrder("ProductName") & _
        "   " & rsOrder("Quantity") & "<br>"
      rsOrder.MoveNext
    Loop
    Response.Write "<br>"
  rsCustomer.MoveNext
Loop

End Sub
```

The result of this code is shown in Figure 5-5.

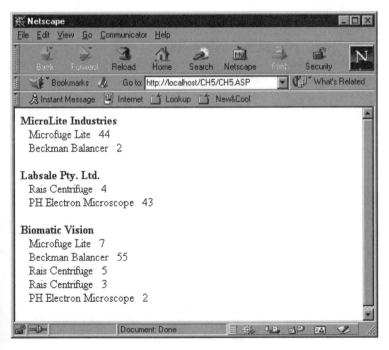

Figure 5-5. The result of data shaping

Use Text Files to Populate Select Elements

When developing Web applications, Select elements are sometimes inevitable. There are many cases where you will want to use them. For example, you may want to use them for displaying a list of products sold in an online store, displaying the list of job categories job seekers can search for, and so on. These situations require you to populate the Select elements with lookup data, which is normally stored in lookup tables.

No matter how fast your database server and network are, and no matter how clever you code your way to grab the lookup data, it's still faster to produce text without going to the database. Using the GetString method is a good choice, but in some situations you can increase the speed of your application by not accessing the database at all.

You can do this by storing lookup data in a text file. Then, when you need to populate a Select element with some lookup data, the data can simply be taken from the text file. This technique is at least 20 times faster than accessing the database, creating the recordset, and populating the Select box.

You can create a text file in .txt format and read the content. However, VB provides you with HTML templates, which are easier to use. For example, you can have an HTML template called States that contains the following string.

```
<select Name=State>
<option value=1>ACT</option>
<option value=2>NSW</option>
<option value=3>NT</option>
<option value=4>QLD</option>
<option value=5>SA</option>
<option value=6>TAS</option>
<option value=7>VIC</option>
<option value=9>WA</option>
</select>
```

All you need to do is call the WriteTemplate method, as follows:

```
Private Sub PopulateSelectBox ()

  States.WriteTemplate

End Sub
```

Of course, this is not suitable in all cases. It is appropriate for lookup tables whose values don't change a lot. With State names, for example, any change to a state (name change) would probably not happen for many years, if at all.

Using an HTML template for this purpose is not as fast as opening the text file yourself. When using an HTML template, VB will search the HTML template for tags that need replacement. VB does this, despite the fact there is no code in the ProcessTag event procedure. Unfortunately, no way exists to turn this feature off. Writing your own function to read the text file and output its contents using the Response object's Write method will eliminate this unnecessary processing. However, an HTML template is much easier to use.

For lookup tables that change occasionally, you are faced with a maintenance problem. You have to make sure that you don't forget to update the text file whenever you delete or insert a new record into the lookup table or whenever you update a record. It is true that when the data changes, you just need to edit the text file and don't need to recompile your application. However, you can use the technique that I have implemented in one of my consultation projects to automate this updating process.

So, let's make this process clear. To move the lookup data to a table, you need to edit it whenever the data changes. If the data changes quite often, there is a compelling reason to automate this process. There are a couple of ways to do this. One of the ways to automate this process includes scheduling the task so that the file gets updated regularly, regardless of whether or not there is a change to the data. Although this seems to be a good solution, there are at least two problems with using a scheduler. First, when a change happens in the lookup table, the change is not reflected immediately. Second, maintaining a scheduled program means your code is more scattered than it should be

Another solution that I personally propose seems to work well: Use a trigger to update a text file whenever there is an insert, update, or delete operation performed on the lookup table. A trigger is a special type of stored procedure that is automatically invoked whenever the data in the table is modified. Triggers are invoked in response to INSERT, UPDATE, or DELETE statements. The good news is that most modern relational database servers support triggers, even though you won't find triggers in desktop databases, such as Microsoft Access.

But how do you update the text file? If you are using Microsoft SQL Server, then you are in luck because you can use the xp_cmdshell extended stored procedure. If your database is not Microsoft SQL Server, there is normally an equivalent of this extended stored procedure. For example, Sybase Adaptive Server also has the xp_cmdshell extended stored procedure that does the same job. Again, if you are using Microsoft SQL Server you can also use the isql tool to update your text file. This tool allows you to enter Transact-SQL statements, system procedures, and script files. It uses DB-Library to communicate with Microsoft SQL Server.

The following example uses the ever popular *pubs* database that comes with the standard installation of Microsoft SQL Server. Maintenance is also easy because you need to run the script given in Listing 5-26 only once.

Listing 5-26

```
USE pubs
GO
IF EXISTS (SELECT name FROM sysobjects
  WHERE name = 'myTrigger' AND type = 'TR')
  DROP TRIGGER myTrigger
GO
CREATE TRIGGER myTrigger
ON authors
FOR INSERT, UPDATE, DELETE
AS
EXEC master..xp_cmdshell 'isql -Usa -P -SmyServer -dpubs -h-1
  -o "C:\test.txt" -c; -Q "SET NOCOUNT ON; SELECT ''<OPTION VALUE=''
  + au_id + ''>'' + au_lname + ''</OPTION>'' FROM authors" '
GO
```

The script basically creates a trigger called myTrigger on the authors table, which is invoked on INSERT, UPDATE, or DELETE statements to run the xp_cmdshell extended stored procedure that in turn updates the text file using the isql utility.

The first two lines in Listing 5-26 force the script to use the pubs database:

```
USE pubs
GO
```

Then, it checks to see if a trigger with the same name already exists. If it does, the trigger is deleted. The code for performing this function is given in the next three lines in Listing 5-26.

```
IF EXISTS (SELECT name FROM sysobjects
  WHERE name = 'myTrigger' AND type = 'TR')
    DROP TRIGGER myTrigger
GO
```

The remaining lines in Listing 5-26 create the triggers that when invoked will call the xp_cmdshell extended stored procedure in the master database. The syntax of the CREATE TRIGGER statement can be found in the *SQL Server Books Online* that comes with the installation of Microsoft SQL Server.

The xp_cmdshell extended procedure executes a given command string as an operating system command shell and returns any output as rows of text.

The isql tool has the following syntax. Remember that you must write the whole statement in one line.

```
isql -U login_id [-e] [-E] [-p] [-n] [-d db_name] [-Q "query"]
  [-q "query"] [-c cmd_end] [-h headers] [-w column_width]
  [-s col_separator] [-t time_out] [-m error_level] [-L] [-?]
  [-r {0 | 1}] [-H wksta_name] [-P password] [-S server_name]
  [-i input_file] [-o output_file] [-a packet_size] [-b] [-O]
  [-l time_out] [-x max_text_size]
```

The arguments are as follows.

- **-U** *login_id*: The user login ID. Login IDs are case sensitive.

- **-e**: Echoes input.

- **-E:** Uses a trusted connection instead of requesting a password.

- **-p**: Prints performance statistics.

- **-n** Removes numbering and the prompt symbol (>) from input lines.

- **-d** *db_name*: Issues a USE *db_name* statement when isql is started.

- **-Q** "*query*": Executes a query and immediately exits isql when the query completes. Use double quotation marks around the query and single quotation marks around any characters embedded in the query.

- **-q** "*query*": Executes a query when isql starts, but does not exit isql when the query completes. (Note that the query statement should *not* include GO.) If you issue a query from a batch file, you can use %variables. Environment %variables% also work.

- **-c** *cmd_end*: Specifies the command terminator. By default, commands are terminated and sent to SQL Server by entering GO on a line by itself. When you reset the command terminator, do not use SQL reserved words or characters that have special meaning to the operating system, whether preceded by a backslash or not.

- **-h** *headers*: Specifies the number of rows to print between column headings. The default is to print headings one time for each set of query results. Use -1 to specify that no headers will be printed. If using -1, there must be no space between the parameter and the setting (-h-1, not -h -1).

- **-w** *column_width*: Allows the user to set the screen width for output. The default is 80 characters. When an output line has reached its maximum screen width, it is broken into multiple lines.

- **-s** *col_separator*: Specifies the column-separator character, which is a blank space by default. To use characters that have a special meaning to the operating system (for example, | ; & < >), enclose the character in double quotation marks (").

- **-t** *time_out*: Specifies the number of seconds before a command times out. If no *time_out* value is specified, a command runs indefinitely; the default time-out for logging in to isql is eight seconds.

- **-m** *error_level*: Customizes the display of error messages. The message number, state, and error level are displayed for errors of the specified severity level or higher. Nothing is displayed for errors of severity levels lower than the specified level. Use -1 to specify that all headers are returned with messages, even informational messages. If using -1, there must be no space between the parameter and the setting (-m-1, not -m -1).

- **-L**: Lists the locally configured servers and the names of the servers broadcasting on the network.

- **-?**: Displays the syntax summary of isql switches.

- **-r** {**0** | **1**}: Redirects message output to the screen (stderr). If you don't specify a parameter or if you specify 0, only error messages with severity 17 or higher are redirected. If you specify 1, all message output (including "print") is redirected.

- **-H** *wksta_name*: A workstation name. The workstation name is stored in sysprocesses.hostname and is displayed by sp_who. If not specified, the current computer name is assumed.

- **-P** *password*: Is a user-specified password. If the -P option is not used, isql prompts for a password. If the -P option is used at the end of the command prompt without any password, isql uses the default password (NULL). Passwords are case-sensitive.

- **-S** *server_name*: Specifies which SQL Server installation to connect to. The *server_name* is the name of the server computer on the network. This option is required if you are executing isql from a remote computer.

- **-i** *input_file*: Identifies the file that contains a batch of SQL statements or stored procedures. The less than (<) comparison operator can be used in place of -i.

- **-o** *output_file*: Identifies the file that receives output from isql. The greater than (>) comparison operator can be used in place of -o.

- **-a** *packet_size*: Allows you to request a different size packet. The valid values for *packet_size* are 512 through 65535. The default value for the Microsoft Windows NT version of isql is 8192; otherwise, the default value is 512 for MS-DOS, although larger sizes can be requested with that version as well. Increased packet size can enhance performance on larger script execution where the amount of SQL statements between GO commands is substantial. Microsoft testing indicates that 8192 is typically the fastest setting for bulk copy operations. A larger packet size can be requested, but isql defaults to 512 if the request cannot be granted.

- **-b**: Specifies that isql exits and returns a DOS ERRORLEVEL value when an error occurs. The value returned to the DOS ERRORLEVEL variable is 1 when the SQL Server error message has a severity of 10 or greater; otherwise the value returned is 0. MS-DOS batch files can test the value of DOS ERRORLEVEL and handle the error appropriately.

- **-O:** Specifies that isql reverts to the behavior of earlier versions. It also sets the default DOS ERRORLEVEL value to -1. The following features are deactivated:

  - EOF batch processing

  - Automatic console width scaling

  - Wide messages

- **-l** *time_out*: Specifies the number of seconds before an isql login times out. If no *time_out* value is specified, a command runs indefinitely. The default time-out for login to isql is eight seconds.

- **-x** *max_text_size*: Specifies, in bytes, the maximum length of text data to return. Text values longer than *max_text_size* are truncated. If *max_text_size* is not specified, text data is truncated at 4096 bytes.

The isql tool in Listing 5-26 must be written in one line. For ease of reading it is rewritten here.

```
EXEC master..xp_cmdshell 'isql -Usa -P -SmyServer -dpubs -h-1
  -o "C:\test.txt" -c; -Q "SET NOCOUNT ON; SELECT ''<OPTION VALUE=''
  + au_id + ''>'' + au_lname + ''</OPTION>'' FROM authors" '
```

From the argument, it is known that the isql is used to access the pubs database in myServer server using the sa user account with a blank password. The –h–1 argument is used to suppress the heading and the output will be written to the test.txt file in C drive. The –c; argument indicates that the sql statements in the query are separated by semicolons. The query consists of two SQL statements. The first statement is

```
SET NOCOUNT ON
```

The previous statement is used to prevent the row count from appearing in the output. The second SQL statement is

```
SELECT '<OPTION VALUE=' + au_id + '>' + au_lname + '</OPTION>'
  FROM authors
```

Note that every single quote in the previous SQL statement is escaped using another single quote in the complete EXEC command.

The previous SQL statement is used to retrieve the au_id and the au_lname field values from the authors table. The strings "<OPTION VALUE=" and ">" and "</OPTION>" are added to compose the options for the Select element. The text file will look something like this:

```
<OPTION VALUE=409-56-7008>Bennet</OPTION>
<OPTION VALUE=648-92-1872>Blotchet-Halls</OPTION>
<OPTION VALUE=238-95-7766>Carson</OPTION>
<OPTION VALUE=722-51-5454>DeFrance</OPTION>
<OPTION VALUE=712-45-1867>del Castillo</OPTION>
<OPTION VALUE=427-17-2319>Dull</OPTION>
```

More information on the isql tool can be found in *SQL Server Books Online.*

If you are not using Microsoft SQL Server and you can't find a similar utility to build your text file, you can write your own program that is called by the xp_cmdshell extended stored procedure. Alternatively you can use a .vbs script. When you install IIS, Windows Scripting Host (WSH) will also be installed. WSH allows you to run any .vbs file as if it is a compiled program. Information on WSH can be found at Microsoft's Web site.

CHAPTER 6

Client-side Processing

So far you have seen examples of IIS applications where the processing is done on the server-side. The server handles the workload and the client receives processed plain text in the form of HTML tags. Even though this works well the way it is, moving some of the work to the client-side could mean significant improvement in overall performance and less network traffic.

Consider the case in which you have an HTML registration form that contains fields that must be filled in by users. With purely server-side processing, you have to check whether or not the user has entered all mandatory values. Even if one mandatory field is not filled in, your code sends an error message. The error message can be sent within a different HTML page or in the same registration page. If you choose the first option, the user can then click the Back button of his Web browser to return to the previous page. If you decide to embed the error message in the same registration form, you have to resend the form and make sure that the previously entered values are also sent back to the user to save the user from having to re-enter the same values.

With whichever method you choose, the extra round trip to the server can be avoided. Not only can this extra trip frustrate the user if the connection is very slow, it also creates an unnecessary workload for the Web server. What's more, input validation doesn't end here. You still need to check whether the user has entered correct values for all inputs, that is, numeric values for numeric type of data and so forth. If one of the input fields is incorrect, you have to send a message to the user to request that a correction be made.

Wouldn't it be nice if all input values are sent to the server only when they are all valid and their leading and trailing spaces, if any, have been truncated? You can do this with JavaScript client-side processing. Why JavaScript? you may be wondering. Why not use VBScript that looks and feels like Visual Basic? The reason is simple: JavaScript is understood by the two reigning browsers: Microsoft Internet Explorer and Netscape Navigator. VBScript, unfortunately, can only be used for Internet Explorer and is not, and probably never will be, supported by Netscape.

Many VB developers must be thinking, but JavaScript looks weird and difficult. I have met lots and lots of VB and ASP programmers who simply do not like JavaScript because it means they have to learn a new language. I would say that three out of four, or should I say nine out of ten, ASP heroes don't use JavaScript and always depend on the server-side processing for input validation. Or they ask someone, usually the only one, in the team to write the JavaScript code for them.

They also use robots, well, I mean some commercial software to write the undesirable parts of their program. What a shame.

For an Internet developer, an understanding of JavaScript is just as important as an understanding of HTML. Although the latter is generally accepted without complaint because of its simplicity, JavaScript is still considered an annoyance.

Asking an ASP/VB programmer to learn JavaScript is like asking a programmer to learn to touch-type. Oh, well. All programmers know that being able to touch-type will make them much more productive. However, how many programmers out of a hundred are willing to learn to touch-type? One, or maybe five?

This chapter is intended for those who have zero or very little understanding of JavaScript and "still haven't got time" to learn it thoroughly. Those who are already experts in JavaScript might still find some useful tricks here. This chapter is a cookbook for JavaScript. It contains recipes for the simplest and most useful JavaScript scripts, but is not intended as a complete textbook for those who want to seriously learn JavaScript.

JavaScript is still growing, so refer to some good books on the market for a complete discussion and reference. After reading this chapter, I hope you will come to realize that mastering JavaScript will make you more marketable and help you cope with your JavaScript-phobia so that you can start learning it and increase your productivity. Learn to touch-type, too, if you have the time.

In addition to client-side input validation as previously mentioned, JavaScript can help you do a lot of useful and exciting tasks including but not limited to:

- Simple and complex mathematical calculations

- Animation

- Writing to the Web browser status bar

- Populating HTML form elements

- Checking the browser type and version

- Reading and writing cookies

- Controlling a Java applet

This chapter starts with an introduction of JavaScript and proceeds with some useful functions for client-side input validation. Examples on how to use these functions are then given, followed by examples on how to populate HTML form element values using JavaScript. Animation follows, and at the end of the chapter, a reference for the most commonly used JavaScript objects is given.

What Is JavaScript?

JavaScript is an interpreted language. Originally called LiveScript, JavaScript has nothing to do with Java, even though at first glance they look similar. The similarity of names is purely a marketing ploy. JavaScript was created by Netscape, whereas Java is a product of Sun Microsystems.

Although JavaScript is a complete and mature language of its own, JavaScript as discussed in this book means the JavaScript as implemented in Web browsers, that is, client-side JavaScript. Another important fact to remember is that JavaScript is implemented somewhat differently in Internet Explorer than it is in Netscape Navigator. Microsoft has even developed its own version of JavaScript called JScript. This book uses the portion of JavaScript that is implemented by both browsers, especially by version 3.0 and later.

Comparing JavaScript with Visual Basic

A good place to start is by noting some characteristics of JavaScript as compared to some characteristics of VB.

- JavaScript is case sensitive; therefore, a variable called `myString` is different from one called `MyString` or `MYSTRING`. The event handler that responds to a mouse click must be written as `onclick` in JavaScript. However, it can be written as `onClick` or `OnClick` in HTML because HTML is not case sensitive.

    Unfortunately, all objects and their methods and properties added to the core language are case insensitive in Internet Explorer. Date and Math, for example, are built-in objects in JavaScript, therefore they are case sensitive in IE as are all user-defined variables, functions, and objects. Therefore, you should apply strict case sensitivity in your code to maintain compatibility between Internet Explorer and Netscape Navigator.

    The reason for some case insensitivity in IE is that IE allows the same client-side objects to be used by VBScript, which, like VB, is not case sensitive. So, Microsoft assumes that client-side objects must not be either. Because of Microsoft's requirement for VBScript, it's not likely that the client-side objects will become case sensitive in future versions of IE. Consequently, you can't take advantage of Navigator's case sensitivity to create different variables with the same spelling but different capitalization.

- All lines in JavaScript end with an *optional* semicolon. For example, it is legal to write these two lines without semicolons:

```
str = "Cockroaches can live up to one year. "
a = 3
```

But, if you put *more than one statement* in a single line, the semicolons are required.

```
str = "Cockroaches can live up to one year. "; a = 3;
```

Therefore, it is good programming practice with JavaScript to always use a semicolon.

- JavaScript has two styles of comments: the // for commenting one single line, and the /* .. */ pair for comments that are one line long or longer. For example:

```
// the calculation starts here.
a = 89 / 2;
/* First multiply it with 52
        and then take the larger between A and B.*/
```

- Strings in JavaScript can be enclosed within single or double quotes. For example, both of the following lines are legal in JavaScript.

```
str = "Silk was discovered in about 3000 BC.";
s = 'Silk was first discovered in China.';
```

Further, double-quote characters may be contained within strings delimited by single-quote characters, and single-quote characters may be contained within strings delimited by double quotes. For example, these are valid statements:

```
str = "His name is O'Connor.";
s = 'You can call him John "The Great".';
```

If you insist on adhering to one programming style with strings, you can use a preceding backslash character (\ ) before the single quote or the double quote. The previous two strings can be rewritten as:

```
str = 'His name is O\'Connor.';
s = "You can call him John \"The Great\".";
```

- To concatenate strings, use a plus sign. For example:

```
str = 'His name is O\'Connor.';
s = "You can call him John \"The Great\".";
str2 = str + ' ' + s;
```

> **NOTE:** *Concatenating strings with a plus sign in VB is a bad VB programming habit. Use an ampersand instead.*

- JavaScript is untyped, which means variables can hold values of any data type. This is similar to being forced to use variant data types for all variables in VB. Expectedly, there are functions to convert one data type to another.

- You can use a variable without first declaring it. This is similar to not including the `Option Explicit` statement at the beginning of your VB code. However, you should always declare your variables for the same reason you should always use the Option Explicit statement in your VB code. You declare a variable using the `var` keyword followed by the variable name as in:

```
var a;
```

- You can initialize a variable at the same time you declare it. For example:

```
var a = 10;
```

or even when the first occurrence of the variable is in a statement:

```
for (var i = 0; i < 100; i++)
```

- The `if` statement has the following syntax:

```
if (expression) {
    statement-1
    statement-2
    .
    .
    .
    statement-m
}
[else {
statement-n
statement-o
.
.
.
statement-z
}]
```

Unlike VB, the brackets enclosing the *expression* are required. Also note that it's only correct to use if, and not If or IF or iF.

Where you place the curly brackets ({}) is a matter of preference. You can also omit the curly brackets if there is only one statement; for example:

```
if (a==b)
        str = 'The two numbers are equal.';
else {
        a = b + 12;
        str = 'The two numbers are not equal.';
}
```

You should always use the curly brackets, however, if omitting them could lead to ambiguity and misinterpretation; for example:

```
if (a==b) {
        if (x!y)
            str = 'The two numbers are equal.';
}
else {
        a = b + 12;
        str = 'The two numbers are not equal.';
}
```

- The while loop has the following syntax:

```
while (expression) {
  statement-1
  statement-2

      .

      .

      .

  statement-m
}
```

There is no Wend for enclosing the statements that are to be executed if the expression is true. Again, you can omit the curly brackets if there is only one statement.

- The for loop has the following syntax:

```
for (initialize ; test ; increment) {
   statement-1
   statement-2
   .
   .
   .
   statement-m
}
```

which is the same as the following while loop:

```
initialize;
while (test) {
   statement-1
   statement-2
   .
   .
   .
   statement-m
   increment;
}
```

The curly brackets can be omitted if there is only one statement; for example:

```
for (i = 0; i < 10; i++)
   document.write(i);
```

Note that in JavaScript the syntax i++ is an efficient way to increment the variable *i* by one.

If there is no statement in the for loop, you can use a semicolon; for example:

```
for (i = 0; i < 100000; i++)
   ;
```

is the same as the following in VB:

```
For i = 0 To 100000
Next i
```

- JavaScript also has a with keyword, which is similar to the one used in VB. The syntax is this:

```
with (object) {
   statement-1
   statement-2

      .

      .

      .

   statement-m
}
```

So, instead of writing

```
x = Math.sin(a);
y = Math.cos(a);
```

Table 6-1 Reserved Words in JavaScript

break	if	true
continue	in	typeof
delete	new	var
else	null	void
false	return	while
for	this	with
function		

Table 6-2 Java Keywords Reserved by JavaScript

abstract	final	private
boolean	finally	protected
byte	float	public
case	goto	short
catch	implements	static
char	import	super
class	instanceof	switch
const	int	synchronized
default	interface	throw
do	long	throws
double	native	transient
extends	package	try

it is safe to write

```
with(Math) {
    x = sin(a);
    y = cos(a);
}
```

- To evaluate an expression, use == and != in JavaScript, which are equivalent to = and <> in VB. Use ! as a Not. For example:

Table 6-3 Identifiers to Avoid

alert	history	Packages
Anchor	Image	parent
Area	isNaN	parseFloat
Array	java	parseInt
assign	JavaArray	password
blur	JavaClass	Plugin
Boolean	JavaObject	prompt
Button	JavaPackage	prototype
Checkbox	length	Radio
clearTimeout	Link	ref
close	Location	Reset
closed	location	scroll
confirm	Math	Select
Date	MimeType	self
defaultStatus	name	setTimeout
Document	navigate	status
document	Navigator	String
Element	navigator	Submit
escape	netscape	sun
eval	Number	taint
FileUpload	Object	Text
focus	onblur	Textarea
Form	onerror	top
Frame	onfocus	toString
frames	onload	unescape
Function	onunload	untaint
getClass	open	valueOf
hidden	opener	Window
History	Option	window

```
if (a==b)
  str = 'The two numbers are equal.';
else {
  a = b + 12;
  str = 'The two numbers are not equal.';
}
```

- Use the double ampersand (&&) as the logical AND and the double pipe characters (||) as the logical OR. However, use a single ampersand (&) as the bitwise AND and a single pipe character (|) as the bitwise OR.

To conclude this introduction to JavaScript, Tables 6-1, 6-2, and 6-3 contain reserved words that you must *not* use as identifiers in your code.

Although the identifiers in Table 6-3 are not strictly reserved, they may be in the future.

Writing JavaScript in HTML Pages

JavaScript scripts are embedded in the HTML page and are seen by your server-side application and Web server as text. To a JavaScript-enabled Web browser, this piece of text has special meaning.

Using <script> and <head> Tags

To tell the Web browser that the text is actually client-side JavaScript code, you enclose it between the <script> and </script> tags, as in the following example.

```
<script language="JavaScript" type="text/javascript">

  // your scripts go here

</script>
```

Actually, unless you want your HTML page to pass the validation by a W3 HTML validating machine, you don't need the type attribute in the script tag. The language attribute is necessary because more than one scripting language can be embedded between the <script> and </script> tags. By specifying in the <script> tag what language a script is written in, the browser can decide whether or not it should try to interpret it. If it is written in a language the Web browser doesn't understand, the script is skipped.

You can write your JavaScript code anywhere in the HTML page. For example, take a look at the following listings.

You can write your JavaScript scripts between the <head> and </head> tags, like the code in Listing 6-1.

Listing 6-1

```
<html>
<head>
<script language="JavaScript" type="text/javascript">

  // your scripts go here

</script>
</head>
<body>

Here is your HTML body

</body>
</html>
```

Or as an alternative, put it in the body section, like the code in Listings 6-2 and 6-3.

Listing 6-2

```
<html>
<head>
</head>
<body>
<script language="JavaScript" type="text/javascript">

  // your scripts go here

</script>

Here is your HTML body

</body>
</html>
```

Listing 6-3

```
<html>
<head>
</head>
<body>
```

```
Here is your HTML body

<script language="JavaScript" type="text/javascript">

  // your scripts go here

</script>
</body>
</html>
```

The `<script>` and `</script>` tags can even appear more than once in different sections if necessary.

Like other HTML tags, the JavaScript code is executed whenever the Web browser sees it. If you put your JavaScript code in the Head section, it will be executed before the HTML tags in the Body section are parsed. If the processing time takes too long, however, the user might see a delay and find it annoying.

The example in Listing 6-4 uses JavaScript to send a string to the HTML page.

Listing 6-4

```
<html>
<head>
  <title>JavaScript testing</title>
</head>
<body>
<script Language="JavaScript">
  document.write("Hello.");
</script>
</body>
</html>
```

This code simply writes "Hello" to the HTML page and is the same as writing the code you see in Listing 6-5.

Listing 6-5

```
<html>
<head>
  <title>JavaScript testing</title>
</head>
<body>
Hello.
</body>
</html>
```

Of course, JavaScript is of little use if it is only used for writing strings as in the previous example. As you proceed through this chapter, you will see more practical uses of JavaScript.

Enclosing the Body of a Script in HTML Comments

When programming with JavaScript, you should always remember that even though Web browsers are in their fourth or fifth generation, you can expect that some people still use very old browsers that don't recognize the <script> tag, let alone JavaScript. These very old browsers ignore the <script> tags and treat the JavaScript code between them as text to be displayed.

In order to prevent any embarrassment, you should enclose the body of your scripts within HTML comments using the format shown in the example in Listing 6-6.

Listing 6-6

```
<script Language="JavaScript">
<!-- hide JavaScript code

  // Your JavaScript scripts go here

  // end of HTML comment -->
</script>
```

Calling Functions

As in any other programming language, functions are an important part of JavaScript. The concept of functions in JavaScript is the same as in VB. In JavaScript, functions can appear anywhere throughout the HTML page. When you call a function, however, you must make sure that the function exists when it is called. The function "exists" when the Web browser passes the point where the function is defined in the HTML page. A function can be defined as in the following code:

```
function functionName(arg-1, arg-2, ... arg-n)
{
  statement-1;
  statement-2;
  .
  .
  .
  statement-m;
}
```

Listing 6-7 defines the factorial function that computes factorials.

Listing 6-7

```
function factorial(n)
{
  if (n <=1)
    return 1;
  else
    return n * factorial(n-1);
}
```

When functions are discussed in any programming language, one question always arises: How do arguments get passed, by value or by reference? Although an argument is passed by reference in VB by default, you can specify otherwise if you wish to do so. In JavaScript, you have no control over passing arguments.

Whether an argument is passed by value or by reference depends on the type of the argument. The basic rule states that primitive types are manipulated by value and reference types by reference. Examples of primitive types include numbers and booleans. They are primitive because they consist of nothing more than a small fixed number of bytes, which are easily manipulated at the low (primitive) levels of the JavaScript interpreter.

On the other hand, objects and arrays are reference types. These data types can contain arbitrary numbers of properties or elements. Because objects and arrays can become very large, it doesn't make sense to manipulate these types by value because doing so could involve an inefficient copying and comparing of large amounts of memory. However, there is an anomaly in the string data type. Strings are passed by reference, but when you compare a string in your function, it is the value that is being compared, not the reference.

Working with the String Object and String Data Type

In JavaScript, you can declare a variable that contains a string, as in the following lines of code:

```
var str;
str = 'The magic of JavaScript.';
```

You may find it surprising that the string variable can act like an object, as demonstrated in the following code lines.

```
var str, a;
str = 'The magic of JavaScript.';
a = str.length;
```

The variable str is treated as if it is an object that has the length property.

The String object exists to provide methods for operating on string values. The String object, for example, has the length property that specifies the number of characters in the string. It also has useful methods, such as charAt, which extracts the character at a given position from the string, and toUpperCase, which returns a copy of the string with all characters converted to uppercase. More about the String object can be found in "A Brief Window Object and String Object Reference" at the end of this chapter.

When you need to use a property or any method of the String object for your string value, you don't need to create a String object explicitly. You can just pretend that your string value is a String object! This explains why the following line is valid and legal in JavaScript:

```
a = str.length;
```

When you call any method or use the length property of the String object with your string value, the JavaScript interpreter creates a String object in the background for you.

Another method worth noting is the substring method. It has the following syntax:

```
string.substring(from, to)
```

It returns a new string of length to-from, which contains a substring of string. The new string contains characters copied from position from to to-1 of string.

If you find the use of the String object's methods in the coming examples confusing, refer to the section "A Brief Window Object and String Object Reference" at the end of this chapter for more information.

Examining the JavaScript Object Model

Before proceeding to more advanced topics, let's take a look at the big picture: the JavaScript object model. Figure 6-1 shows a portion of the JavaScript object model.

In this object model, the Window object is the central object. It represents the Web browser window. It has a number of child objects: the Location object, the Document object, the History object, and others that are not shown in the Figure 6-1.

Each Window object contains a document property that refers to the Document object associated with the window. The convention in JavaScript is that the Window object is referenced by default. This means that to use one of its

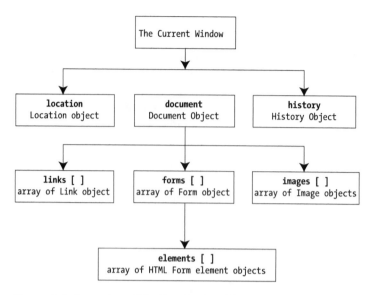

Figure 6-1. A portion of the JavaScript object model

child objects or properties, you just mention the child object, the property, or the method in your code.

To refer to an object in the lower hierarchy, you use a period to separate it from its parent object. For example, to refer to the first HTML element in the second form in the HTML page use the following line:

```
Document.forms[1].elements[0]
```

The Window object itself also has a number of methods, such as alert(), confirm(), and prompt(). As mentioned earlier, you can use the Window object's methods without mentioning the Window object in your code, as in

```
alert('Please enter a value in the "First Name" box.');
```

which is the same as writing

```
window.alert('Please enter a value in the "First Name" box.');
```

A summary of the Window object is given in the "A Brief Window Object and String Object Reference" at the end of this chapter.

Event Handling

HTML was extended by the addition of new attributes to various tags that define objects. JavaScript added a new dimension to the previously boring and static HTML by making it event-driven. For example, to define an event procedure that is invoked when the user clicks a button, you can add the onClick attribute to the button tag in the form:

```
<Input type=button Name=Send onClick="displayPassword">
```

There are fewer events in JavaScript than in VB. For example, there is no double-click event. However, JavaScript does have enough events to make your HTML page lively. For example, most of the form elements recognize the Blur event, which is equivalent to the LostFocus event in VB. These elements also recognize the Focus event, which is the same as GotFocus in VB.

Table 6-4 lists event handlers that each object supports.

Unfortunately, some incompatibilities exist between browsers running on a Unix platform and those running in Windows. Netscape Navigator for Windows, for instance, doesn't recognize the Click event for an Area element. In Netscape Navigator for Unix, some form elements, such as area, button, checkbox, radio, reset, select, and submit only recognize the Click event, but not the Blur and Focus events.

Table 6-4 HTML elements and their events

ELEMENT	EVENT HANDLERS
Area	OnClick, onMouseOut, onMouseOver
Button	OnBlur, onClick, onFocus
Checkbox	OnBlur, onClick, onFocus
FileUpload	OnBlur, onChange, onFocus
Form	OnReset, onSubmit
Frame	OnLoad, onUnload
Image	OnAbort, onError, onLoad
Link	OnClick, onMouseOut, onMouseOver
Radio	OnBlur, onClick, onFocus
Reset	OnBlur, onClick, onFocus
Select	OnBlur, onChange, onFocus
Submit	OnBlur, onClick, onFocus
Text	OnBlur, onChange, onFocus
Textarea	OnBlur, onChange, onFocus
Window	OnBlur, onError, onFocus, onLoad, onUnload

Another type of event is not triggered by user interaction: the Timer event. This event gets triggered when specified periods of time have elapsed and can be useful for animation.

Input Validation

One of the uses of JavaScript that is emphasized in this chapter is client-side input validation, i.e. checking the input values before an HTML form is submitted.

The strategy is to write some code for the onsubmit event handler that will respond to the user clicking the Submit button. This function returns true if all input values are valid, and returns false otherwise. If the validation function returns false, the Web browser cancels the form submission and tells the user what is wrong with his or her input values.

With the HTML form, you need to include the onsubmit attribute in the form tag; for example:

```
<form method=post onsubmit="return validateForm()">
```

The form won't be submitted if the validateForm function returns false.

Consider an HTML page with a form that has three text boxes, as in Listing 6-8. Before the form is submitted, you want to make sure that the user has typed something in each of the text boxes. In other words, you don't want a blank value.

Listing 6-8

```
<html>
<head>
<title>Registration Page</title>
<script language="JavaScript">
  function validateForm()
  {
    if (document.forms[0].LastName.value=='')
    {
      alert('Please enter a value in the "Last Name" box.');
      document.forms[0].LastName.focus();
      return false;
    }
    if (document.forms[0].FirstName.value=='')
    {
      alert('Please enter a value in the "First Name" box.');
      document.forms[0].FirstName.focus();
      return false;
```

```
    }
    if (document.forms[0].Email.value=='')
    {
      alert('Please enter a value in the "Email" box.');
      document.forms[0].Email.focus();
      return false;
    }
    return true;
  }
</script>
</head>

<body>
<form method=post onSubmit="return validateForm()">
<table>
  <tr>
    <td>Last Name:</td>
    <td><input type=text name=LastName ></td>
  </tr>
  <tr>
    <td>First Name:</td>
    <td><input type=text name=FirstName ></td>
  </tr>
  <tr>
    <td>Email:</td>
    <td><input type=text name=Email ></td>
  </tr>
  <tr>
    <td><input type=reset value="Reset"></td>
    <td><input type=submit value="Register"></td>
  </tr>
</table>
</form>
</body>
</html>
```

In the HTML page in Listing 6-8, the validateForm function is declared and defined in the Head section. The function itself consists of three main if statements, each of which checks an input box for a value. Notice how you can refer to the HTML input box as shown in the following line of code:

```
if (document.forms[0].LastName.value=='')
```

In this line, document refers to the HTML page itself, forms[0] refers to the first form in the document, and LastName refers to the LastName text box. The text box has a property called value, which is the value entered into the text box. This simply means that a document object has a forms collection and forms[0] simply refers to the first member of the collection. Each form in turn has a collection called *elements*. In the previous example, the first form in the document has five elements: three input boxes, one Submit button, and one Reset button.

To refer to the first member of the form's elements collection, you can refer to its index instead of its name. Therefore, the line

```
if (document.forms[0].LastName.value=='')
```

can be replaced by

```
if (document.forms[0].elements[0].value=='')
```

The same also applies to the forms collection. Instead of bearing the pain of having to know the order of forms (if you have more than one form in the HTML page), you can refer to a form by its name, once you give the form a name. The following code line

```
<form method=post onSubmit="return validateForm()">
```

should be rewritten as shown in the following line, so that the form can be referred to by its name:

```
<form Name=mainForm method=post onSubmit="return validateForm()">
```

Using the form name instead of its position in the forms collection and using the keyword with to avoid typing document repeatedly, you get a slightly different validateForm function, as shown in Listing 6-9.

Listing 6-9

```
function validateForm()
{
  with (document)
  {
    if (mainForm.LastName.value=='')
    {
      alert('Please enter a value in the "Last Name" box.');
      mainForm.LastName.focus();
      return false;
    }
```

```
    if (mainForm.FirstName.value=='')
    {
      alert('Please enter a value in the "First Name" box.');
      mainForm.FirstName.focus();
      return false;
    }
    if (mainForm.Email.value=='')
    {
      alert('Please enter a value in the "Email" box.');
      mainForm.Email.focus();
      return false;
    }
  }
  return true;
}
```

When the user clicks the Submit button to submit the form, the browser invokes the validateForm() function. If one of the input boxes is empty, JavaScript does the following:

- Executes the alert method, which displays a dialog box, like the one shown in Figure 6-2, passing a string to the dialog box.

- Executes the focus() method of the input box, which moves the focus to the input box.

- Returns false as the return value of the function. Wherever JavaScript encounters a return statement in a function, it also stops executing the function and returns to the calling function or statement.

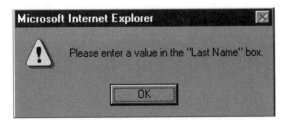

Figure 6-2. A dialog box warning the user that something is still wrong with the input

The trim *Function*

Checking a text box for a blank value as demonstrated in the preceding example is not flawless. If the user enters a space, he or she will escape the validation algorithm in the JavaScript code. To catch this, you can do what is normally done in VB: Use the Trim$ function.

There is no equivalent Trim function in JavaScript, but you can easily write one. Listing 6-10 provides an example.

Listing 6-10

```
function trim(str)
  {
    //this function is like the Trim function in VB
    while (str.charAt(str.length - 1)==" ")
      str = str.substring(0, str.length - 1);
    while (str.charAt(0)==" ")
      str = str.substring(1, str.length);
    return str;
  }
```

The function is very simple and requires one parameter. The brains of this function are the two while loops. The first while loop continually checks the last character of the string and truncates the last character if it is a space.

```
while (str.charAt(str.length - 1)==" ")
  str = str.substring(0, str.length - 1);
```

The second while loop checks the first character in the string and removes the first character if it is a space.

```
while (str.charAt(0)==" ")
  str = str.substring(1, str.length);
```

It then returns the truncated string:

```
return str;
```

The JavaScript modified script in the HTML page now includes two functions: the validateForm and the trim function. The complete script is given in Listing 6-11.

Listing 6-11

```
<script language="JavaScript">

  function trim(str) {
    //this function is like the Trim function in VB
    while (str.charAt(str.length - 1)==" ")
      str = str.substring(0, str.length - 1);
    while (str.charAt(0)==" ")
      str = str.substring(1, str.length);
    return str;
  }

  function validateForm()
  {
    with (document)
    {
      if (trim(mainForm.LastName.value)=='')
      {
        alert('Please enter a value in the "Last Name" box.');
        mainForm.LastName.focus();
        return false;
      }
      if (trim(mainForm.FirstName.value)=='')
      {
        alert('Please enter a value in the "First Name" box.');
        mainForm.FirstName.focus();
        return false;
      }
      if (trim(mainForm.Email.value)=='')
      {
        alert('Please enter a value in the "Email" box.');
        mainForm.Email.focus();
        return false;
      }
    }
    return true;
  }

</script>
```

Note that the called function (trim) can come after or before the calling function (formValidate) provided the called function exists when it is called. If you put the trim function at the end of the Body section on a slow connection, for exam-ple, the user could click the Submit button even before the text that comprises the trim function arrives. It is a good programming practice to put the called function ahead of the calling function.

Some Other Validation Functions

Validation can be accomplished by checking whether the user has entered the correct value. For example, the isNumeric function, as given in Listing 6-12, re-turns true only if all the characters that compose the string argument str are characters 0 through 9, inclusively.

Note the use of a do loop that resembles the Do loop in VB. The function loops through the string argument from character 0 to character str.length, from the first character to the last. It compares each character with a pattern and stops and returns false once it finds a character that does not match the characters that compose the pattern.

Listing 6-12

```
function isNumeric(str) {
  var pattern = "0123456789"
  var i = 0;
  do {
    var pos = 0;
    for (var j=0; j<pattern.length; j++)
      if (str.charAt(i)==pattern.charAt(j))
        pos = 1;
    i++;
  } while (pos==1 && i<str.length)
  if (pos==0)
    return false;
  return true;
}
```

Besides using it to validate a positive numeric value, you can also use isNumeric to check a postcode.

Similar functions can be derived from the isNumeric function simply by changing the pattern string. Examples include the isValidPhoneNumber and the isMoney functions in Listing 6-13.

Listing 6-13

```
function isValidPhoneNumber(str) {
  var pattern = "0123456789( )-"
  var i = 0;
```

```
do {
  var pos = 0;
  for (var j=0; j<pattern.length; j++)
    if (str.charAt(i)==pattern.charAt(j))
      pos = 1;
  i++;
} while (pos==1 && i<str.length)
if (pos==0)
  return false;
return true;
}


function isMoney(str) {
  var pattern = "0123456789,.";
  var i = 0;
  do {
    var pos = 0;
    for (var j=0; j<pattern.length; j++)
      if (str.charAt(i)==pattern.charAt(j))
        pos = 1;
    i++;
  } while (pos==1 && i<str.length)
  if (pos==0)
    return false;
  return true;
}
```

Remember: When validating a string that represents a monetary value, even though the comma can be in the string (such as in 4,500), when passing the value, you must first remove the comma if you don't want to remove it on the server. The function removeComma in Listing 6-14 does the job.

Listing 6-14
```
function removeComma(str) {
  var result = "";
  for (var i=0; i<str.length; i++)
    if (str.charAt(i)!=",")
      result += str.charAt(i);
  return result;
}
```

It checks the whole string for a comma character and recomposes the result from str. The result variable now contains no comma.

The other data type that also needs attention is date. The various formats of dates always adds complexity to your code. A good idea is to make three select boxes with valid options, one for the day, one for the month, and one for the year. However, if your design does not permit you to do so, and you can only have one text box, the two functions in Listing 6-15 can help.

Both functions, isUSDate and isOZDate, assume that a valid date must be ten characters and have two backslash characters as separators. Therefore, if the day or the month in the date is only one character long, it must be padded with a zero character. For example, May 5, 2001 must be 05/05/2001.

The difference between the two functions lies in the order of the day and the month. The isUSDate function takes a date as valid if the format is mm/dd/yyyy. The isOZDate, on the other hand, thinks that a valid date must have a dd/mm/yyyy format.

Listing 6-15

```
function isUSDate(str) {
  if (str.length!=10 || str.charAt(2)!="/" || str.charAt(5)!="/" ||
    !isNumeric(str.substring(0,2)+str.substring(3,5)+str.substring(6,10)))
    return false;
  var d = str.substring(3,5) - 0;
  var m = str.substring(0,2) - 0;
  var y = str.substring(6,10) - 0;
  if (m>12) return false;
  if (m==1 || m==3 || m==5 || m==7 || m==8 || m==10 || m==12)
    var dmax = 31;
  else
    if (m==4 || m==6 || m==9 || m==11) dmax = 30;
    else
      if ((y%400==0) || (y%4==0 && y%100!=0)) dmax = 29;
      else dmax = 28;
  if (d>dmax) return false;
  return true;
}

function isOZDate(str) {
  if (str.length!=10 || str.charAt(2)!="/" || str.charAt(5)!="/" ||
    !isNumeric(str.substring(0,2)+str.substring(3,5)+str.substring(6,10)))
    return false;
  var d = str.substring(0,2) - 0;
  var m = str.substring(3,5) - 0;
  var y = str.substring(6,10) - 0;
  if (m>12) return false;
  if (m==1 || m==3 || m==5 || m==7 || m==8 || m==10 || m==12)
```

```
  var dmax = 31;
 else
   if (m==4 || m==6 || m==9 || m==11) dmax = 30;
   else
    if ((y%400==0) || (y%4==0 && y%100!=0)) dmax = 29;
    else dmax = 28;
 if (d>dmax) return false;
 return true;
}
```

If you happen to use different date formats in the client- and server-side, you need to convert your dates upon submitting the form to avoid the same processing on the server. For example, if you want to publish your Web site in the UK, but the data goes directly to a server in the U.S., you need to validate the dates using the isOZDate function and convert it to a U.S. format.

The solution is provided in Listing 6-16. The convertToUSDate function converts an already valid date in dd/mm/yyyy format to a mm/dd/yyyy format. The opposite of the convertToUSDate is the convertToOZDate that does the reverse.

Listing 6-16

```
function convertToUSDate(str) {
   return (str.substring(3,5) + "/" + str.substring(0,2) + "/" +
str.substring(6,10));
}

function convertToOZDate(str) {
   return (str.substring(3,5) + "/" + str.substring(0,2) + "/" +
str.substring(6,10));
}
```

Were you surprised to find out that the two functions differ only in their names?

Populating HTML Form Elements

In reading Chapter 4, you learned how to populate HTML form elements for editing by the user. Recall how painful it was to select the index of a select box. You had to go through all the options and compare the value from the database with each of the Select element's options. If a match was found, you then wrote the sacred "selected" string for that option. As promised, there is a better way to populate HTML form elements, namely with JavaScript.

Populating a Text element is easy. To set the index of a Select element presents a bit of a challenge. You still need to go through all the options, but this time it is done by the JavaScript interpreter in the user's Web browser. It is no longer a burden to your server.

Consider the setSelectIndex function in Listing 6-17. It does the job as expected provided you supply it with the select box name and the index. Where do you get the index? It comes from the table in your database where you previously stored the index value. If you didn't store the index, but instead stored the text of the select box, you have a problem. Either your application needs special treatment or you didn't stick to the rule of good database design.

Listing 6-17

```
function setSelectIndex(ctrl, index) {
  for (var i=0; i<ctrl.length; i++)
    if (index==ctrl.options[i].value) {
      ctrl.selectedIndex = i;
      return;
    }
  ctrl.selectedIndex = -1;
}
```

Before you get too excited, hold on a second. The previous function assumes that the value is the same as the index. It's like saying that your HTML code for that select box looks like the following code when viewed from the Source page.

```
<Select Name=Product>
  <option value=0>--Please select a product--</option>
  <option value=1>Happy 550g Chocolate</option>
  <option value=2>Herman Candy</option>
  <option value=3>Robusta Coffee</option>
  <option value=4>Sulista Beer</option>
  <option value=5>WaggaWagga Wine</option>
</select>
```

The function won't work if the values are not the same as the indexes, as in the following code.

```
<Select Name=Product>
  <option value=0>--Please select a product--</option>
  <option value=41>Happy 550g Chocolate</option>
  <option value=52>Herman Candy</option>
  <option value=43>Robusta Coffee</option>
  <option value=44>Sulista Beer</option>
  <option value=5>WaggaWagga Wine</option>
</select>
```

In this case, you must first get the index of the value using the getIndex function, and use the return value as an argument to the setSelectIndex function, as shown in Listing 6-18.

Listing 6-18

```
function getIndex(ctrl, value) {
  for (var i=0; i<ctrl.length; i++)
    if (value==ctrl.options[i].value)
      return i;
  return -1;
}
```

The following example uses JavaScript to "push" the values of the HTML form elements. The page is for users to edit their order. The form contains one Select element and one Text element. Populating the Select element is accomplished by using the getIndex function. The function returns the correct option index of the Product Select element given the ProductID of the product. Knowing the option index allows you to select the correct option.

The example is implemented using an HTML template WebItem called EditOrder, as shown in Listing 6-19.

Listing 6-19

```
<html>
<head>
<title>Edit your order</title>
<script language="JavaScript">
function setSelectIndex(ctrl, index) {
  for (var i=0; i<ctrl.length; i++)
    if (index==ctrl.options[i].value) {
      ctrl.selectedIndex = i;
      return;
    }
  ctrl.selectedIndex = -1;
}

function getIndex(ctrl, value) {
  for (var i=0; i<ctrl.length; i++)
    if (value==ctrl.options[i].value)
      return i;
  return -1;
}

</script>
```

```
</head>
<body>
<center>
<h3>Edit Order</h3>
<br>
<form action=buy.ASP?WCI=Order&amp;WCE=Edit&amp;WCU method=post>
<table>
  <tr>
    <td>Product</td>
    <td><WC@ProductList></WC@ProductList></td>
  </tr>
  <tr>
    <td>Quantity:</td>
    <td><input name=Quantity></td>
  </tr>
  <tr>
    <td> </td>
    <td><input type=submit value="EDIT"></td>
  </tr>
</table>
</form>
</center>
<WC@PopulateElements></WC@PopulateElements>
</body>
</html>
```

You then need the code in Listing 6-20 to process the Process_Tags event.

Listing 6-20

```
Private Sub EditOrder_ProcessTag(ByVal TagName As String, _
TagContents As String, SendTags As Boolean)

  If TagName = "WC@ProductList" Then
    ' The list of products has been hardcoded here,
    ' but it could also have come from a lookup table or
    ' from a text file
    TagContents = "<Select Name=Product>" & vbCr & _
      "<option value=0>--Please select a product--</option>" & vbCr & _
      "<option value=41>Happy 550g Chocolate</option>" & vbCr & _
      "<option value=52>Herman Candy</option>" & vbCr & _
      "<option value=43>Robusta Coffee</option>" & vbCr & _
      "<option value=44>Sulista Beer</option>" & vbCr & _
      "<option value=5>WaggaWagga Wine</option>" & vbCr & _
```

```
      "</select>"
  Else
    Dim rs As adodb.Recordset
    Dim strSQL As String
    Dim strConnectionString As String
    Dim intProductID As Integer
    Dim lngQuantity As Long

    strConnectionString = "DRIVER={Microsoft Access Driver (*.mdb)}; " &_
      "DBQ=" & Server.MapPath("dbs\db01.mdb")
    strSQL = "SELECT ProductID, Quantity FROM Orders" & _
      " WHERE ProductID=" & Request.Form("ProductID")
    Set rs = New adodb.Recordset
    rs.Open strSQL, strConnectionString
    If Not (rs.BOF And rs.EOF) Then
      intProductID = rs(0)
      lngQuantity = rs(1)
    End If
    rs.Close
    Set rs = Nothing
    TagContents = "<script language=""JavaScript"">" & vbCr & _
      "document.forms[0].Quantity.value=" & lngQuantity & ";" & vbCr & _
      "var i = getIndex(document.forms[0].Product, " & _
          intProductID & ");" & vbCr & _
      "document.forms[0].Product.options[i].selected=true;" & vbCr & _
      "</script>"

  End If

End Sub
```

It is assumed that the HTML template has been called by a previous page, which passed the ProductID in the Request object's Form collection.

The output in the Web browser is shown in Figure 6-3.

Viewed from the Source page of the browser, the listing of the HTML page is similar to Listing 6-21.

Listing 6-21

```
<html>
<head>
<title>Edit your order</title>
<script language="JavaScript">
```

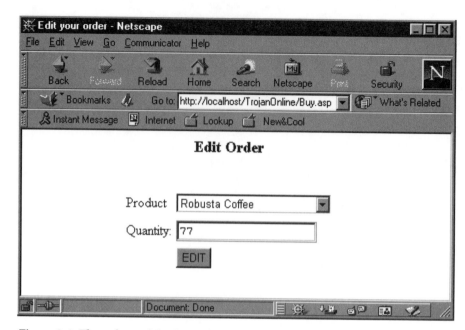

Figure 6-3. The values of the form elements set by JavaScript code

```
function setSelectIndex(ctrl, index) {
  for (var i=0; i<ctrl.length; i++)
    if (index==ctrl.options[i].value) {
      ctrl.selectedIndex = i;
      return;
    }
  ctrl.selectedIndex = -1;
}


function getIndex(ctrl, value) {
  for (var i=0; i<ctrl.length; i++)
    if (value==ctrl.options[i].value)
      return i;
  return -1;
}



</script>
</head>
<body>
<center>
<h3>Edit Order</h3>
<br>
```

```
<form action=buy.ASP?WCI=Order&amp;WCE=Edit&amp;WCU method=post>
<table>
  <tr>
    <td>Product</td>
    <td><Select Name=Product>
<option value=0>--Please select a product--</option>
<option value=41>Happy 550g Chocolate</option>
<option value=52>Herman Candy</option>
<option value=43>Robusta Coffee</option>
<option value=44>Sulista Beer</option>
<option value=5>WaggaWagga Wine</option>
</select></td>
  </tr>
  <tr>
    <td>Quantity:</td>
    <td><input name=Quantity></td>
  </tr>
  <tr>
    <td> </td>
    <td><input type=submit value="EDIT"></td>
  </tr>
</table>
</form>
</center>
<script language="JavaScript">

document.forms[0].Quantity.value=77;
var i = getIndex(document.forms[0].Product, 43);
document.forms[0].Product.options[i].selected=true;

</script>
</body>
</html>
```

Animation

Some amount of animation will make your site more lively. The first choice for
Web animation is probably animated .gif files. However, JavaScript can go beyond
the .gif files limitation. For example, .gif files are limited to performing just one
kind of function, whereas JavaScript can animate the text, continuously change
the text in the browser status bar, or even scroll the window.

The key to doing animation using JavaScript is the Window object's setTimeout method. This method acts like the Timer object in VB by executing some given function or code after a certain period of time elapses. The syntax of this method is

```
setTimeout(code, delay)
```

The code component is a string that contains the JavaScript code to be executed and the delay component is the amount of time in milliseconds before the JavaScript statements in the string are executed.

The following script scrolls the window up and down. Working together with the setTimeout method is the scroll method, which is another useful method of the Window object. The scroll method moves the window's document within the window, so that a pair of new (x, y) coordinates of the document appear in the upper-left corner of the window. The x coordinate increases as the window moves to the right, and the y coordinate increases as the window moves down the page. The method has the following syntax:

```
scroll(x, y)
```

The example in Listing 6-22 creates a simple animation by repeatedly calling the scrollMyself function every 20 milliseconds.

Listing 6-22

```
<script language="JavaScript">

  var pos=0;
  var up=true;

  function scrollMyself() {
    if (up)
      pos += 0.2;
    else
      pos -=0.2;

    scroll(0,pos);
    if (pos>=360) up=false;
    if (pos<=0) up=true;
    setTimeout("scrollMyself()", 20);
  }

  setTimeout("scrollMyself()", 0);

</script>
```

The animation starts when the JavaScript interpreter sees the following line of code, which immediately calls the scrollMyself function.

```
setTimeout("scrollMyself()", 0);
```

It is immediate because 0 is used as the delay. The function scrollMyself makes the document move downward and upward. First it moves the document downward by incrementing the position variable *pos* by a certain amount (0.2). After reaching a certain point (360 in this case), it changes the up flag so that the position variable is decremented by 0.2. The flag is then changed back when the position variable reaches 0. To create the animation effect, you call another setTimeout method at the end of the function, which triggers the same function in 20 milliseconds' time, as shown:

```
setTimeout("scrollMyself()", 20);
```

A Brief Window Object and String Object Reference

To conclude this chapter, this section offers a brief reference for two of the most valuable objects: Window and String.

Window Object

The Window object represents a browser window or frame. It is the root of the JavaScript object hierarchy.

Window object properties include the following:

- *closed*: A read-only boolean that specifies whether a window has been closed.

- *defaultStatus*: A read/write string that specifies the default message to appear in the status line.

- *document*: A reference to the Document object contained in the window.

- *frames[]*: An array of frames contained by this window.

- *history*: A reference to the History object for this window.

- *java*: A reference to the JavaPackage object that is the top of the package name hierarchy for the core Java packages that comprise the Java language.

- *length*: A read-only value that evaluates to the number of elements in the frames[] array.

- *location*: A reference to the Location object for this window.

- *Math*: A reference to an object holding various mathematical functions and constants.

- *name*: A string that contains the name of the window. The name is optionally specified when the window is created with the open() method.

- *navigator*: A reference to the Navigator object that applies to this and all other windows.

- *netscape*: A reference to the JavaPackage object which is the top of the Java package name hierarchy for the netscape Java packages from Netscape.

- *opener*: A read/write property that refers to the Window object that called open() to create this window.

- *packages*: A reference to a JavaPackage object that represents the top of the Java package name hierarchy.

- *parent*: A reference to the parent window or frame of the current window. Only useful when the current window is a frame rather than a top-level window.

- *self*: A reference to the window itself. A synonym of window.

- *status*: read/write string that specifies the current contents of the status line.

- *sun*: A reference to the JavaPackage object, which is the top of the Java package name hierarchy for the sun Java packages from Sun Microsystems.

- *top*: A reference to the top-level window that contains the current window. Only useful when the current window is a frame rather than a top-level window.

- *window*: A reference to the window itself. A synonym of self.

Window object methods include the following:

- *alert()*: Displays a simple message in a dialog box.

- *blur()*: Takes keyboard focus from the top-level browser window; this sends the window to the background on most platforms.

- *clearTimeout()*: Cancels a pending timeout operation.

- *close()*: Closes a window.

- *confirm()*: Asks a yes or no question with a dialog box.

- *focus()*: Gives the top-level browser window keyboard focus; this brings the window to the front on most platforms.

- *open()*: Creates and opens a new window.

- *prompt()*: Asks for simple string input with a dialog box.

- *scroll()*: Scrolls the document displayed in the window.

- *setTimeout()*: Executes code after a specified amount of time elapses.

The String Object

The String object provides methods for operating on string values. A property of the String object is length, which is the number of characters in the string.
String object methods include the following:

- *anchor()*: Returns a copy of the string in an <A Name=> environment.

- *big()*: Returns a copy of the string in a <BIG> environment.

- *blink()*: Returns a copy of the string in a <BLINK> environment.

- *bold()*: Returns a copy of the string, in a <B> environment.

- *charAt()*: Extracts the character at a given position from a string.

- *fixed()*: Returns a copy of the string in a <TT> environment.

- *fontcolor()*: Returns a copy of the string in a <FONT COLOR=> environment.

- *fontsize()*: Returns a copy of the string in a <FONT SIZE=> environment.

- *indexOf()*: Searches the string for a character or substring.

- *italics()*: Returns a copy of the string in an <I> environment.

- *lastIndexOf()*: Searches the string backward for a character or substring.

- *link()*: Returns a copy of the string in an <A HREF=> environment.

- *small()*: Returns a copy of the string in a <SMALL> environment.

- *split()*: Converts a string to an array of strings using a specified delimiter character.

- *strike()*: Returns a copy of the string in a <STRIKE> environment.

- *sub()*: Returns a copy of the string in a <SUB> environment.

- *substring()*: Extracts a substring of a string.

- *sup()*: Returns a copy of the string in a <SUP> environment.

- *toLowerCase()*: Returns a copy of the string with all characters converted to lowercase.

- *toUpperCase()*: Returns a copy of the string with all characters converted to uppercase.

CHAPTER 7

State Management

Unlike elephants, Web servers and Internet applications do forget things. This is to say more precisely, Internet applications are *stateless*—they don't remember the states of previous requests. The HTTP protocol that passes requests and responses between the Web server and the browser is not capable of maintaining information between each request. As a result, your Web application doesn't remember whether a request is coming from a user for the tenth time in the last two minutes or from a user who is visiting your Web site for the first time.

In the context of WebClasses, this also means that you don't know whether a request to a page comes because the user clicked a link in the previous page or because the user typed in the URL in the Address or Location box of his or her Web browser. This presents a serious security issue if your site contains sensitive data.

For example, if you require a user to log in before being able to see a CompanySecret page, you pass this page to the user only upon the user logging in successfully. In this case, you probably use the WriteTemplate method of the CompanySecret HTML Template WebItem in a Member_LoggedIn event. However, if someone knows the URL to the CompanySecret HTML Template WebItem, that person can bypass your Login page and avoid entering a password to see the supposedly confidential information.

Another important issue to consider is that you don't know who is doing what with your application. Consider an online wine store. Normally, the user is allowed to choose from a variety of products before proceeding to the checkout. The process of selecting products requires the user to go back and forth between pages in the application. The user selects a product, puts it in the shopping basket, goes to the page where a variety of different brands are on sale, chooses two or three other products, and puts those in the same shopping basket. At the end of the shopping process, the user goes to the checkout counter to pay.

The server has to know for certain exactly what a user has selected. Because HTTP cannot remember state information between requests, it is important to use other strategies to work around this problem (otherwise the Internet would end up a commerce-free zone).

A number of ways are available to maintain state information in an IIS application:

- Use the URLData property.

- Use the Session object.

- Store the state information in a database.

- Use cookies.

- Use hidden fields to move state information back and forth between the server and the browser on each request.

Each of these approaches has its own advantages and drawbacks. The Session object is most convenient to work with, but it consumes a lot of memory resources. Storing the state information in a database is less resource consumptive, but it requires that you manage connections and recordsets, and access to a database is always slower. Cookies and hidden fields are the hardest to code, but they give you the most scalability.

It's up to you as a developer to choose one or more ways to manage state. Before you make a decision, you should understand how each method works as well as the consequences of each method.

Using the URLData Property to Store State

The WebClass object has a property called URLData that you can use to store state information across the browser's requests. As the name implies, the URLData property stores pieces of information in the URL.

The disadvantage of using the URLData property is that the value can easily be seen, and the URLData is restricted in the amount of data it can send. The size limitation varies from browser to browser, but most browsers can handle about 2000 bytes in the URL.

The URLData property can add information to URLs in the WebClass's responses in two ways: when the WebClass calls the WriteTemplate method of an HTML Template WebItem, and when the WebClass calls the WebClass's URLFor method.

When used with the WriteTemplate method, the WebClass generates a response that involves formatting a template file to send to the browser. The URLData property tells the WebClass to perform additional processing on the template. The WebClass must append the URLData property value to each URL in the template file. This value is then augmented to the WCU parameter in the URL.

If you are not using a template file, the URLData property value is still appended to any URL when you use the URLFor method.

Consider the HTML Template WebItem called `LoginPage` in Listing 7-1.

Listing 7-1

```
<html>
<head>
<title>Login Page</title>
</head>

<body>
<center>
Please type in your login name and password.
<form action=CH7.ASP?WCI=Members&amp;WCE=VerifyLogin&amp;WCU
  method=post>
<table>
  <tr>
    <td>Login:</td>
    <td><input name=Login></td>
  </tr>
  <tr>
    <td>Password:</td>
    <td><input type=password name=UserPassword></td>
  </tr>
  <tr>
    <td> </td>
    <td><input type=submit value=Login></td>
  </tr>
</table>
</form>
</center>
</body>
</html>
```

When you connect the form to a WebItem, Visual Basic modifies the ACTION attribute of the form in the template (printed in bold in the code in Listing 7-1). So far, the role of the WCU parameter has been a mystery, and as you can see, the mystery is now solved.

If you are not using the URLData property, you can safely take out the WCU parameter, so that the bold line in Listing 7-1 looks like this:

```
<form action=CH7.ASP?WCI=Members&amp;WCE=VerifyLogin&amp; method=post>
```

However, if you are using the URLData property, you must leave the WCU parameter intact, either in a form's ACTION attribute or in other URLs. Otherwise, the URLData property value will be lost.

The code in Listing 7-2, using the LoginPage HTML Template WebItem in Listing 7-1, shows the use of the URLData property to pass a value to the next page.

Listing 7-2

```
Private Sub WebClass_Start()

  'Assign a value to the URLData property
  URLData = 123


  LoginPage.WriteTemplate

End Sub
```

Once the template is sent to the browser, you can open the browser's source page to see the HTML tags. The code on the source page should look similar to that in Listing 7-3.

Listing 7-3

```
<html>
<head>
</head>

<body>
<center>
Please type in your login name and password.
<form action=CH7.ASP?WCI=Members&amp;WCE=VerifyLogin&amp;WCU=123
  method=post>
<table>
  <tr>
    <td>Login:</td>
    <td><input name=Login></td>
  </tr>
  <tr>
    <td>Password:</td>
    <td><input type=password name=UserPassword></td>
  </tr>
  <tr>
    <td> </td>
    <td><input type=submit value=Login></td>
  </tr>
</table>
</form>
</center>
</body>
</html>
```

Notice in Listing 7-3 how the URLData property value has been appended to the URL, which is the ACTION attribute of the form. When the user clicks the Submit button, the value is passed back to your application.

You can retrieve the value of the URLData property as easily as you can assign a value to it. For example, the event procedure in Listing 7-4 sends a greeting to the user if he or she has successfully logged in.

Listing 7-4

```
Private Sub Members_VerifyLogin()

  Dim cn As ADODB.Connection
  Dim rs As ADODB.Recordset
  Dim strSQL As String

  ' Compose the SQL statement that retrieves the record
  ' with specific Login name and password.
  strSQL = "SELECT COUNT(*) FROM Users" & _
    " WHERE Login='" & Request.Form("Login") & "'" & _
    " AND Password='" & Request.Form("UserPassword") & "'"

  Set rs = New ADODB.Recordset
  rs.Open strSQL, "Atom", adOpenForwardOnly, adLockReadOnly

  If rs(0) = 0 Then
    ' recordset is empty, login failed
    Response.Redirect URLFor(LoginPage)
  Else
    ' login was successful, send greeting.
    Response.Write "Welcome Agent " & URLData
  End If

  rs.Close
  Set rs = Nothing

End Sub
```

On a successful login, the user's browser displays the string "Welcome Agent 123," as shown in Figure 7-1. Pay special attention to the URL.

If the user has supplied the wrong user ID or password, the user is redirected to the same Login Page using the Redirect method of the Response object shown here:

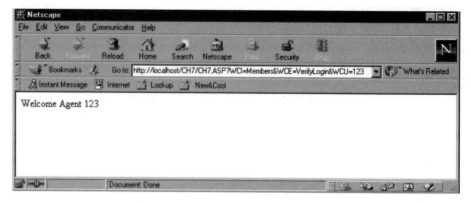

Figure 7-1. Passing values using the URLData property

```
If rs(0) = 0 Then
   ' recordset is empty, login failed
   Response.Redirect URLFor(LoginPage)
Else
   ' login was successful, send greeting.
   Response.Write "Welcome Agent " & URLData
End If
```

The `Response.Redirect URLFor(LoginPage)` triggers the Respond event of the LoginPage template.

```
Private Sub LoginPage_Respond()

    LoginPage.WriteTemplate

End Sub
```

The use of the `Redirect` method to redirect the user to an HTML template is not efficient in this case because you still need to use the `WriteTemplate` method in the Respond event procedure. So, you might as well just replace it with the `WriteTemplate` method. The `Redirect` method, however, is irreplaceable if you need to redirect the user to another Web site.

When the user sees the Login page again as a result of a redirection, the URL of the page will have the `URLData` property value attached to it (see Figure 7-2).

Note that the following line of code:

```
Response.Write "Welcome Agent " & URLData
```

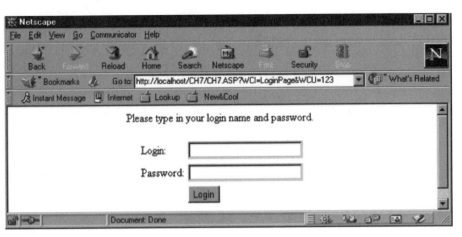

Figure 7-2. The URLData property value is also passed on redirection.

is basically the same as this:

```
Response.Write "Welcome Agent " & Request.QueryString("WCU")
```

Note also that the WCU parameter does not appear on the first Login page, even though it came from the same source, the LoginPage HTML Template WebItem. The first Login page is sent to the browser by the following line in the WebClass's Start event procedure:

```
LoginPage.WriteTemplate
```

Even though the URLData property has been assigned a value prior to calling the WriteTemplate method in the WebClass's Start event procedure, this method doesn't append the WCU parameter or the URLData property value. It is not necessary anyway. However, upon calling the LoginPage HTML Template WebItem's WriteTemplate method a second time when the user fails to log in, VB appends the WCU parameter and the URLData property value to all URLs in the template itself.

The second Login page has the WCU parameter as a result of calling the URLFor method in the following line:

```
Response.Redirect URLFor(LoginPage)
```

Note that when the WebClass assigns the URL data to the WCU parameters, it scans the file for all occurrences of &WCU and ?WCU and assigns the value of the URLData property to them in the format &WCU=*URL data*. If, for some reason, you want the letters ?WCU or &WCU to appear as part of your template's text and you want the WebClass to ignore this text when it parses the file, enter the text as **?WCUWCU** or

&WCUWCU. When the WebClass runtime finds such a string, it strips out the extra WCU and leaves the text as you intended. This extra level of encoding is only necessary if you assign a value to the URLData property.

The previous example demonstrates how to pass one value. If a few values need to be passed to the next page, you can do this by building a string of values delimited by certain characters. On the receiving end, that is, when you need to retrieve each individual value, you just need to parse the string.

In the simple example in Listing 7-5, three values are passed, strField1, strField2, and strField3, separated by vbTab characters.

Listing 7-5

```
Dim strField1 As String
Dim strField2 As String
Dim strfield3 As String

strField1 = "1"
strField2 = "2"
strfield3 = "3"

URLData = strField1 & vbTab & strField2 & vbTab & strfield3
```

To retrieve the values, use the Split function as demonstrated by the code in Listing 7-6.

Listing 7-6

```
' retrieve the values
Dim strArray() As String
Dim strValue1 As String
Dim strValue2 As String
Dim strValue3 As String

strArray = Split(URLData, vbTab)
strValue1 = strArray(0)
strValue2 = strArray(1)
strValue3 = strArray(2)
```

Make sure that you use the same order in assigning and retrieving values.

Storing State in the Session Object

Although the URLData property is a good way of storing state, it has some disadvantages, which sometimes makes it unsuitable for an application. One of its disadvantages is the fact that everybody can see the information stored by just glancing at the user's screen.

When you need to retain sensitive information, such as a password, storing it in the Session object is probably the best method to use. However, before you jump into coding using this object, it's better to have good understanding of what a session and a Session object are.

How Session Objects Work with Session IDs

Every time a new user requests a page in your application, the Web server sends back a response plus a special number to the browser. This special number is invisible to the user and is called a Session ID. This number is guaranteed unique during the life of IIS and becomes an identifier for that user. Note that when you restart IIS, the Session IDs generated previously may be duplicated, so you should not use Session IDs as identifiers that must remain unique for the entire life of your IIS application.

In addition to creating the Session ID, the Web server also creates a Session object for each user. This Session object is associated with the Session ID. On the client side, the browser keeps the Session ID and sends it back to the Web server on the next request. This Session ID tells the Web browser that this request is not a first visit by the user and that a Session object has been created for this user. Instead of creating another Session object, the Web server then looks for a Session object with the same Session ID and associates the request with the Session object.

Consider a scenario in which three users, Tom, Sally, and Bonnie, access a Web application at http://www.labsale.com. Tom is first, so his request is given a Session ID 1001. In addition to the response, the Web browser sends the Session ID to Tom's browser. The browser then keeps it in Tom's computer at least until he closes his browser. This Session ID is associated with http://www.labsale.com, so if Tom goes to other Web sites after his first request to http://www.labsale.com and comes back to request a second page, the Session ID from http://www.labsale.com will still be sent with his request. Remember that on the server there is a Session object with Session ID 1001, which belongs to Tom.

Sally is next. She is given a Session ID 1002. The Web server also creates a Session object with Session ID 1002 for Sally. Sally's Session object is accessible only to Sally because only Sally's browser carries the Session ID 1002. When Bonnie comes in as the third person, the Web server just repeats the procedure, giving Bonnie a Session ID 1003 and creating a new Session object. All Session objects are created in the Web server memory, so it consumes RAM. The more users, the more RAM is used for storing Session objects.

Nevertheless, the three users get what they want and are happy with the service. However, what if Tom decides to go to bed after he requests the fourth page? What happens to the Session object with Session ID 1001? The Web server is patient. It will wait for twenty minutes (or any other period of time you set in the Web server settings) starting from the *last time* Tom sends a request for a page. When time runs out, the Session object is destroyed and the part of memory used for Tom's Session object is reclaimed.

Session ID 1001 also becomes history. It won't be reused. The next user will get a new Session ID 1004. The Web server does not run out of unique numbers because Session IDs are sequential numbers that are 32 bits long.

You can store state information in the Session object. For example, you can have a variable called LoginName that you store in the Session object. It will become a session-level variable. You can store a session-level variable anywhere in your code with the syntax in the following line:

```
Session("LoginName") = "Tom"
```

In theory, you can have as many variables as you want in the Session object. To retrieve the value of a session-level variable, write this line of code:

```
strPassword = Session("Password")
```

In the preceding example, the Web server allocates memory space for three Session objects, as illustrated in Figure 7-3.

Each Session object contains variables, the first being Session ID and the second being LoginName. The first session object was created for Tom. In this Session object, the value of the SessionID variable is 1001 and the value of the LoginName variable is Tom. It is assumed that there are more than two session-level variables in Tom's Session object because Tom requested other pages that Sally and Bonnie

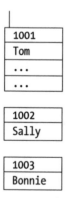

Figure 7-3. Memory space allocation for Session objects

didn't. The other pages happen to assign more variables to the Session object. The Session object can grow indefinitely, and each Session object can have a different size.

Now comes the not so good news. The Web server always creates a Session ID for a newcomer and creates a Session object associated with the Session ID. The Session ID is then sent to the browser with the hope that the browser is willing to keep it for a while so that the Session ID can be sent back on the next request.

The Session ID is sent to the browser as a cookie. If the browser, for security or other reasons, is not willing to accept cookies, the Session ID won't be stored in the client computer and the next request will *not* carry with it the Session ID previously given to the browser. As a result, the Web server will think that the request is from a new user and will give it a new Session ID and create a new Session object as well.

You can see that using the Session object requires users' willingness to accept cookies. Also note that the Session ID stored as a cookie is erased when the user closes his or her browser, either deliberately or by accident. For example, if the user's computer crashes during a session with a Web site, all session variables set previously cannot be retrieved because the browser is given a new Session ID.

Testing Whether a Browser Accepts Cookies

If you use Session objects to store state information, make sure that you test the user's browser for acceptance of cookies (for more information on cookies, see the section "Using Cookies" later in this chapter). An easy way to test this is to use the SessionID property of the Session object and the WebClass's URLData property. The idea is to make use of the fact that the Web server always assigns a new Session ID to a request that doesn't carry with it a Session ID. If a browser doesn't accept cookies, it won't return to the server the Session ID assigned to it from the previous response.

The code in Listing 7-7 assigns a session ID in the response to the browser and stores the same session ID on the page itself using the URLData property. It then instantly forces the browser to make another request. The value in the URLData property doesn't depend on cookies to work. Therefore, on the second request, it can check whether or not the browser accepts cookies by comparing the session ID stored in the URLData property to the current Session ID. If they are the same, it means the server didn't assign a new Session ID for the second request because it found a Session ID in the second request.

A check needs to be run only once, the first time the user requests the .asp file. In the next example, the code is written in the Browser custom WebItem's Respond event procedure, so you need to create this WebItem if you want to test the code. If the browser accepts cookies, the application returns the LoginPage HTML Template WebItem. If not, it displays an error message. The code is provided in Listing 7-7.

Listing 7-7

```
Private Sub WebClass_Start()

  Set NextItem = Browser

End Sub

Private Sub Browser_Respond()

  If URLData = "" Then
    'The first request
    URLData = Session.SessionID
    'Redirect browser to the Browser's Respond event procedure
    Response.Redirect URLFor(Browser)
  Else
    'The second request
    If URLData = Session.SessionID Then
      'browser accepts cookies.
      LoginPage.WriteTemplate
    Else
      'Oops, browser does not accept cookies.
      Response.Write "This application requires that" & _
        " your browser accept cookies."
    End If
  End If

End Sub
```

The code starts when the user requests the .asp file, which passes the control to the WebClass's Start event procedure. Control is then passed to the Browser's Respond event procedure using the WebClass's NextItem property, as shown next:

```
Set NextItem = Browser
```

In the Respond event procedure of the Browser custom WebItem, you need to store the Session object's SessionID property value in the URLData property only on the first request. You'll know that it is the first request if nothing is in the URLData property.

```
If URLData = "" Then
    URLData = Session.SessionID
```

After storing the session ID, it then uses the `Redirect` method of the `Response` object to force the browser to make another request to the Web server, as follows:

```
Response.Redirect URLFor(Browser)
```

The `URLFor(Browser)` makes the browser request the same URL, that is, the `Respond` event procedure of the `Browser` custom WebItem.

On the second request, it compares the current Session ID with the one stored in the `URLData` property, as follows:

```
If URLData = Session.SessionID Then
    'User browser accepts cookies.
    LoginPage.WriteTemplate
Else
    'Oops, user browser does not accept cookies.
    Response.Write "This application requires that" & _
        " your browser accept cookies."
End If
```

Note that the use of the `URLData` property makes the URL carry the `SessionID` property value in its `WCU` argument, as shown in Figure 7-4.

The `WCU` value remains in the URL until you assign a new value to it. Some developers might find this annoying and will want to take it off. Even though you can't make the `WCU` argument disappear, you can remove its value immediately after you do the cookies' test. You just need to assign a blank string as its value, as in the code in Listing 7-8.

Figure 7-4. Testing the user's willingness to accept cookies

Listing 7-8

```
If URLData = Session.SessionID Then
  'User browser accepts cookies.
  URLData = ""
  LoginPage.WriteTemplate
Else
  'Oops, user browser does not accept cookies.
  Response.Write "This application requires that" & _
    " your browser accept cookies."
End If
```

Storing and Retrieving State in the Session Object

Once you are confident that your users are using a cookies-enabled browser, storing and retrieving state in the Session object is easy.

To store a value, just create a session-level variable and assign a value to it; for example:

```
Session("ApplicationID") = rs("ApplicationID")
```

You don't need to declare a Session object's variable before use. It is created automatically. To retrieve the value, use code similar to the following:

```
LngApplicationID = Session("ApplicationID")
```

Unfortunately, using the Session object means allocating some part of the server memory for it. The common policy is to use as few session-level variables as possible. The use of this kind of variable is often limited to the holding of a very important piece of information. For instance, the following example uses the Session object's variable to store one piece of information only: whether or not the user has successfully logged in. In your code, you set the LoggedIn session variable to True when the user supplies the correct user name and password. On all other routines, you check this variable before granting access to the user or performing other functions.

The next example assumes that your users employ cookies-enabled browsers. The testing is therefore not performed again in this code.

The example uses the standard Members_VerifyLogin event procedure, which is given in Listing 7-9. Upon successful login, the user is redirected to the Admin page in Listing 7-10.

Listing 7-9

```
Private Sub Members_VerifyLogin()

  Dim cn As ADODB.Connection
  Dim rs As ADODB.Recordset
  Dim strSQL As String

  ' Compose the SQL statement that retrieves the record that
  ' with specific Login name and password.
  strSQL = "SELECT COUNT(*) FROM Users" & _
    " WHERE Login='" & Request.Form("Login") & "'" & _
    " AND Password='" & Request.Form("UserPassword") & "'"

  Set rs = New ADODB.Recordset
  ' Uses DSN called Atom.
  rs.Open strSQL, "Atom", adOpenForwardOnly, adLockReadOnly

  If rs(0) = 0 Then
    ' recordset is empty, login failed
    Response.Redirect URLFor(LoginPage)
  Else
    ' login was successful, set the Session("LoggedIn") to True
    ' and then proceed to another page.
    Session("LoggedIn") = True
    Set NextItem = Admin
  End If

  rs.Close
  Set rs = Nothing

End Sub
```

In the Admin WebItem's Respond event, you write the code in Listing 7-10.

Listing 7-10

```
Private Sub Admin_Respond()

  If Not Session("LoggedIn") Then
    Response.Redirect URLFor(LoginPage)
  End If

  ' perform the function here...


End Sub
```

This code redirects the user to the Login page if the user has not successfully logged in. For example, if a smart user types **http://localhost/CH7/CH7.ASP? WCI=Admin** in order to bypass the Login page in the browser's Location box without first logging in, the user will be redirected to the Login page.

You need to check the Session object's LoggedIn variable in every event procedure.

However, if an authorized user leaves the browser for longer than a certain period of time set in IIS, the Session object will be destroyed. The user will then have to log in again.

> **NOTE:** *With ASP 3.0, you can use the* Remove *and* RemoveAll *methods to delete session variables stored in a* Session *object.*

Storing State in the Application Object

Although session-level variables have session scope, you can use the Application object to store global variables. You can have many Session objects throughout the life of your application, but only one Application object for each application. Any variable that you store in the Application object has application scope and therefore is accessible by all users. Once set, an application-level variable lives until the server is shut down. Candidates for application-level variables include the connection string and the application counter.

Typically, to access a database, all users employ the same connection string. For example, the following line:

```
rs.Open strSQL, Application("ConnectionString")
```

uses the Application object's ConnectionString variable as the connection string in a Recordset object's Open method.

Also, the example in Listing 7-11 uses the Application object to store a counter.

Listing 7-11

```
Private Sub WebClass_Start()

  Application.Lock
  Application("Counter") = Application("Counter") + 1
  Application.UnLock

  Set NextItem = Browser
End Sub
```

The previous code increments the Counter every time someone accesses the ASP page. The Lock method is called to prevent other users from changing any of the Application object's variables.

> **NOTE:** *With ASP 2.0, you can't destroy an application-level variable. With ASP 3.0, however, you can use the* Remove *and* RemoveAll *methods to delete application-level variables that are no longer needed.*

A question arises: How do you initialize an application-level variable? There are at least two answers: Use the WebClass's Start event, or use the global.asa file. The example in Listing 7-12 demonstrates the use of the first approach.

Listing 7-12

```
Private Sub WebClass_Start()

  If Not Application("Initialized") Then
    Application.Lock
    Application("Counter") = 0
    Application("ConnectionString") = "atom"
    Application("Initialized") = True
    Application.UnLock
  End If

  LoginPage.WriteTemplate

End Sub
```

You can also use the global.asa file to perform initialization. The next section explains the global.asa file.

Examining the Global.asa File

When you first start your WebClass project, one of the files Visuals Basic creates is the global.asa file. By default, this is a blank file and deleted when you end your IIS application.

The global.asa file is an optional file in which you can specify event scripts and declare objects that have session or application scope. It is not a content file displayed to the users; instead it stores event information and objects used globally by the application. This file must reside in the root directory of the application. An application can only have one global.asa file.

With IIS applications, you must create your own global.asa file using a text editor. If you just add code to the global.asa file that VB creates when you run the application, your global.asa file will be deleted when you end the application.

Global.asa files can contain only the following:

- Application object's events: `Application_OnStart` and `Application_OnEnd`

- Session object's events: `Session_OnStart` and `Session_OnEnd`

- Object declarations

- Type Library declarations

The first two items in the previous list are of interest in regard to this chapter, and the snippet in Listing 7-13 is a typical global.asa file.

Listing 7-13

```
<Script Language="VBScript" RUNAT=SERVER>

Sub Application_OnStart
' your code goes here

End Sub

Sub Application_OnEnd
' your code goes here

End Sub

Sub Session_OnStart
' your code goes here

End Sub

Sub Session_OnEnd
' your code goes here

End Sub
</Script>
```

If you include script that is not enclosed by the `<script>` .. `</script>` tags, or that defines an object that does not have session or application scope, the server returns an error. The server ignores both tagged scripts that the application or session events do not use as well as any HTML in the file.

The scripts contained in the global.asa file may be written in any supported scripting language. If multiple event or object scripts use the same scripting language, they can be combined inside a single set of <script> tags.

The four events in the global.asa file—Application_OnStart, Application_OnEnd, Session_OnStart, and Session_OnEnd—are optional, and each event is independent from one other. This means that the Application_OnEnd event procedure does not have to be present when there is an Application_OnStart subroutine in the global.asa file and so forth.

When present, the Application_OnStart event is triggered when the first client requests a page within your application. The Application_OnStart is triggered only once during the life of your application and is normally used for initialization. An example of the use of the Application_OnStart event is given in Listing 7-14.

Listing 7-14

```
Sub Application_OnStart

  ' Initialize variables
  Application("Counter") = 0
  Application("ConnectionString") = "atom"

End Sub
```

The Application_OnEnd event, on the other hand, is executed when the Web server is shut down. It can be used, for example, for storing application-level variables in a database or a file.

The two Session object's events, Session_OnStart and Session_OnEnd, are triggered when a client requests a page for the first time and when the user's session times out (the user does not come back to request a page for a certain period of time). To be exact, the Session_OnStart is triggered when a request from a Web browser doesn't carry with it a Session ID, even though the same user requested a page not long before. This is normally the case when the browser doesn't support cookies. The Session_OnEnd procedure also executes when a script explicitly calls the Session object's Abandon method.

You can write code to count the number of users in the Session_OnStart. The example in Listing 7-15 uses this event to increment an application-level variable that counts the number of visitors to your Web site.

Listing 7-15

```
Sub Session_OnStart

  ' Increment counter for each new user
  Application("NumberOfUsers") = Application("NumberOfUsers") + 1

End Sub
```

The use of the Session_OnEnd event is often found in an online store, where it is used to delete temporary orders that are based on the Session ID. When a user selects a product, the product code is stored in a temporary table in a database and is identified by the user's Session ID. When the user doesn't return to the site after a certain period of time, it is assumed that the user has decided not to proceed with the purchase, hence, the products the user has selected must be deleted from the temporary table.

According to Microsoft, when you save changes to the global.asa file, the server finishes processing all the current application requests before it *recompiles* the global.asa file. During that time, the server refuses additional requests and returns an error message stating that a request cannot be processed while the application is being restarted.

After all the current user requests have been processed, the server deletes all active sessions, calls the Session_OnEnd event for each session it deletes, closes the application, and calls the Application_OnEnd event. The global.asa file is then recompiled. Subsequent user requests will start the application, create new sessions, and trigger the Application_OnStart and Session_OnStart events.

In reality, unfortunately, things don't always go this smoothly. After you change the contents of the global.asa file, you are forced to reboot the machine in order for the changes to the global.asa file to take effect. Restarting the Web server alone doesn't help.

A final note on the global.asa file: Even though the global.asa file looks pretty handy, whether or not you use it really depends on the application you're developing. Some applications require the presence of this file, and others are easier to code if global.asa is used. However, the absence of a global.asa file increases the access speed for the first requested page in your application because running the global.asa file and then running the requested page will always be slower than running just the requested page. If possible, avoid using global.asa, and if you have to use it, use with care.

Storing State in the WebClass Object

As mentioned earlier, the Web server creates and destroys the WebClass object for each request, preventing the Web server from remembering the previous request.

Using the Session object, you can also set up your WebClass to remain instantiated between requests. This way, you can store state information in member variables of the WebClass object. You can make the objects stay instantiated in two ways: by storing them in the Session or Application objects, or by referencing them in member variables of the WebClass itself if the WebClass's StateManagement property is set to wcRetainInstance. By default, this property is set to wcNoState and this value makes the WebClass stateless.

If you choose to keep the WebClass alive between requests, the runtime DLL instantiates the WebClass when the first request occurs and does not destroy it until the application terminates. This enables you to use variables within the WebClass to store information between browser requests. However, this solution is not recommended, so if you must use this approach, use it with care.

Keeping the WebClass alive between requests affects the scalability of your application because WebClasses that stay alive are stored in the Session object. Consequently, some memory is allocated for the Session object, and the Web server must take action to ensure that the correct thread is used to process the request. If you choose to keep the WebClass alive between requests, you can use the ReleaseInstance method to terminate an instance of a WebClass you have kept alive across requests. When you use this method in a procedure, the runtime DLL terminates the instance of the WebClass at the end of the procedure. If you don't use this method to explicitly terminate the instance, the Session object that is used to store your WebClass is destroyed 20 minutes (or any designated period of time) after the last request from the same user.

To keep the WebClass alive between requests, click the name of the WebClass in the Properties window, and then set the StateManagement property to 2- wcRetainInstance].

Using Cookies to Retain State

Unlike Session objects that consume resources in the Web server, using cookies is generally considered safe for the Web server. This approach, however, still requires the Web browser to allow the Web server to write to the client's machine.

Both Request and Response objects have the Cookies collection. You use the Cookies collection of the Response object to send cookies to the browser, and the Cookies collection of the Request object to retrieve cookies from the Web browser. Before you start using cookies, here's a brief overview.

A *cookie* is a small piece of information from a Web server that is stored by the Web browser in the client's machine. This information is sent to the server each time the client requests a page from the same area in which the information was received. By default, the cookie will only be sent back during the same session with the Web server.

The cookie expires when users close their Web browsers. You can change this behavior by setting the expiry date to a date later than the system's date. Cookies received by a browser are not recognized by other types of browsers. If you go to a Web site using Internet Explorer and get a cookie that is valid for a year, the cookie won't be sent back when you browse the same site using the Netscape Navigator browser.

Examining Attributes of Cookies

Cookies are sent to the client using a Set-Cookie HTTP response header in the following format:

```
Set-Cookie: Name=Value; expires=Date; domain=DOMAIN_NAME; path=PATH; secure
```

The syntax breaks down as follows. All attributes are optional except the NAME=VALUE pair.

- NAME=VALUE: The name/value pair of the specific cookie the Web server wants saved on the client machine. The value can contain any character except a word space, comma, or semicolon.

- EXPIRES: A date after which the browser can dispose of the cookie. If no EXPIRES attribute is given, the cookie will expire at the end of the current HTTP session. The format for the expire date is

```
Wdy, DD-Mon-YYYY HH:MM:SS GMT
```

Only Greenwich mean times are allowed.

- DOMAIN: Each time the user navigates to a specific URL, the DOMAIN attributes of all the cookies on the client's machine are compared against the domain of the URL. If the DOMAIN attribute of any cookie on the client's machine matches the last two segments of the full domain name, the cookie is sent in the header of the HTTP request to that URL.

  A domain must have at least two periods in its name to set the DOMAIN attribute of a cookie sent to the client. For example, www.labsale.com can send cookies to a client's machine, but labsale.com can't. The actual value of the Labsale-related cookie DOMAIN attribute would be Labsale.com. This cookie would therefore be sent to any URL ending with Labsale.com including www.Labsale.com and products.Labsale.com.

In a similar manner, only pages within this domain can set cookies with this DOMAIN attribute. If no DOMAIN attribute is present in the cookie sent to the browser, the default is the domain name of the sender of the cookie.

You may have problems when trying to set a domain for a cookie from your intranet Web server because local Web servers normally don't have domain names that contain at least two periods.

- PATH: The Path is a subset of URLs within the domain defined by the cookie's DOMAIN attribute. Its value determines whether or not the cookie is sent back to the server. If no PATH attribute is sent, the default is the path of the document the browser is viewing. Because the client of a WebClass always goes through the same .asp file regardless of which page is being displayed, this attribute can be ignored in most cases.

- SECURE: When present for a cookie, this attribute tells the browser to send this cookie only to pages within the path specified in the Path property if the server and browser are communicating over a secure channel.

The Cookies collection of the Request object as well as the Cookies collection of the Response object have the following properties:

- Item: Represents the value of a specific cookie in the collection. To specify a cookie, you can use an index number or a key.

- Key: Represents the name of a specific element in the Cookies collection. Each element's name is represented by its Key property.

- Count: Represents the number of elements in the collection.

You can set or retrieve the value of any field in the Cookies collection by using the Item property. For example, to send a cookie to the browser, use the following code:

```
Response.Cookies.Item("Login") = Request.Form("Login")
```

which can be abbreviated to

```
Response.Cookies("Login") = Request.Form("Login")
```

And, to retrieve a cookie, use the following code:

```
strLoginName = Request.Cookies.Item("Login")
```

or use

```
strLoginName = Request.Cookies("Login")
```

When sending a cookie to the browser, you can also set attributes other than the name. An example of sending a cookie is given in Listing 7-16.

Listing 7-16

```
Response.Cookies("LastName") = strLastName
Response.Cookies("LastName").Expires = #12/12/2000#
Response.Cookies("LastName").Domain = "Labsale.com"
Response.Cookies("LastName").Path = "/Products/Search"
Response.Cookies("LastName").Secure = True
```

The following example uses a cookie to maintain the user's Login name. The cookie is sent after the user has successfully logged in. With the expiry date set a day later, the cookie will last for 24 hours even after the user closes his browser. The next time the user logs in, his or her login name is automatically presented in the Login box.

This example uses a LoginPage HTML Template WebItem provided in Listing 7-17, which is similar to the templates you have seen so far, but with a little modification (printed in bold).

Listing 7-17

```
<html>
<head>
<title>Login Page</title>
</head>

<body>
<center>
Please type in your login details.
<form action=CH7.ASP?WCI=Members&amp;WCE=VerifyLogin&amp;
  WCU method=post>
<table>
  <tr>
    <td>Login:</td>
    <td><input name=Login Value="<WC@Login></WC@Login>">
</td>
  </tr>
  <tr>
    <td>Password:</td>
    <td><input type=password name=UserPassword></td>
  </tr>
```

```
<tr>
  <td> </td>
  <td><input type=submit value=Login></td>
</tr>
</table>
</form>
</center>
</body>
</html>
```

To use this example, you must also paste the code in Listing 7-18 into your WebClass. Note that the form in the LoginPage is connected to the VerifyLogin event of the Members WebItem.

Listing 7-18

```
Private Sub WebClass_Start()

  LoginPage.WriteTemplate

End Sub

Private Sub LoginPage_ProcessTag(ByVal TagName As String, _
  TagContents As String, SendTags As Boolean)

  If Request.Cookies("Login") <> "" Then
    TagContents = Request.Cookies("Login")
  End If

End Sub

Private Sub Members_VerifyLogin()

Dim rs As ADODB.Recordset
  Dim strSQL As String

  ' Compose the SQL statement that retrieves the record that
  ' with specific Login name and password.
  strSQL = "SELECT Login FROM Users" & _
    " WHERE Login='" & Request.Form("Login") & "'" & _
    " AND Password='" & Request.Form("UserPassword") & "'"

  Set rs = New ADODB.Recordset
  rs.Open strSQL, "Atom", adOpenForwardOnly, adLockReadOnly
```

```
If rs.BOF And rs.EOF Then
  ' recordset is empty, login failed
  LoginPage.WriteTemplate
Else
  ' login was successful, set the cookies
  Response.Cookies("Login") = Request.Form("Login")
  ' Make the cookie last for 1 day
  Response.Cookies("Login").Expires = Now() + 1
  Response.Write "Welcome " & Request.Form("Login")
End If


rs.Close
Set rs = Nothing


End Sub
```

When you run the project, the WebClass sends the content of LoginPage. The call to the WriteTemplate method triggers the ProcessTag event of the same template, which contains the following procedure:

```
If Request.Cookies("Login") <> "" Then
  TagContents = Request.Cookies("Login")
End If
```

This checks the presence of the cookie called Login. If it is present (as a result of previous successful login), VB replaces the WC@Login tag with the cookie's value.

After the user logs in, the Request is redirected to the VerifyLogin event of the Members custom WebItem. If login fails, the user is prompted to log in again. A successful login will send a cookie to the browser and greet the user with a brief message, as in the following lines:

```
If rs.BOF And rs.EOF Then
  ' recordset is empty, login failed
  LoginPage.WriteTemplate
Else
  ' login was successful, set the cookies
  Response.Cookies("Login") = Request.Form("Login")
  ' Make the cookie last for 1 day
  Response.Cookies("Login").Expires = Now() + 1
  Response.Write "Welcome " & Request.Form("Login")
End If
```

Cookies have their limitations, which differ from browser to browser. For example, Netscape browsers can have only

- 300 total cookies in the cookie file.

- 4 kilobytes per cookie, for the sum of both the cookie's name and value.

- 20 cookies per server or domain (completely specified hosts and domains are treated as separate entities and have a 20-cookie limitation for each, not combined).

Accessing Cookies on the Browser with JavaScript

Cookies can also be manipulated on the client side. For example, the browser can create a cookie and send it to the server. Or, the browser can delete a cookie that it has received from the Web server. Although you can't use simple HTML to perform these manipulations, JavaScript can help.

Manipulating cookies with JavaScript is one of the most difficult parts of JavaScript and therefore, requires advanced mastery of the language. It is often-times tricky, debugging the JavaScript code involves cookies, and it is time con-suming and psychologically stressing. Also, before you release an application that has browser-side cookies, make sure you have thoroughly tested the code in every browser your users will be launching. From personal experience, I find that Internet Explorer is more forgiving than Netscape. Even though it sounds taxing, the rewards from using cookies on the browser are well worth it.

Some JavaScript functions for manipulating cookies are given in the following code listings. They include the getCookie function to read a cookie value, the setCookie function to create a cookie, and deleteCookie to delete a cookie.

The function getCookie, provided in Listing 7-19, has one argument: name. This argument is the name of the cookie whose value you want to retrieve.

Listing 7-19

```
function getCookie(name) {
  var cName = name + "=";
  var dc = document.cookie;
  if (dc.length>0) {
    begin = dc.indexOf(cName);
    if (begin != -1) {
      begin += cName.length;
      end = dc.indexOf(";", begin);
      if (end == -1) end = dc.length;
        return unescape(dc.substring(begin,end));
    }
  }
  return null;
}
```

The function setCookie, in Listing 7-20, creates a cookie. It has six arguments, but only the name and value arguments need to be present. For any argument that's not present, an optional argument is given its default value.

Listing 7-20

```
function setCookie(name, value, expires, path, domain, secure) {
  document.cookie = name + "=" + escape(value) +
    ((expires) ? "; expires=" + expires.toGMTString() : "") +
    ((path) ? "; path=" + path : "") +
    ((domain) ? "; domain=" + domain : "") +
    ((secure) ? "; secure" : "");
}
```

For example, to create a cookie called UserID with the value P4, use the following JavaScript command:

```
setCookie('UserID', ' P4');
```

This cookie exists until the user closes the browser. If you want to set the expire date so that the cookie can last longer than the current browser session, you need to pass a date as the expires argument. However, due to a bug in some browsers, you need to use the fixDate to "repair" your date before being passed to the setCookie function, as in Listing 7-21.

Listing 7-21

```
// date - any instance of the Date object
// hand all instances of the Date object to this function for "repairs"
function fixDate(date) {
  var base = new Date(0);
  var skew = base.getTime();
  if (skew > 0) date.setTime(date.getTime() - skew);
}
```

The example in Listing 7-22 sets a cookie called authorizationLevel with the value of 2 and an expiry date one year after it is set. Notice how the date is repaired before being passed to the function.

Listing 7-22

```
var expiryDate = new Date();
fixDate(expiryDate);
expiryDate.setTime(expiryDate.getTime() + 365 * 24 * 60 * 60 * 1000);
setCookie("authorizationLevel", 2, expiryDate);
```

The deleteCookie function, given in Listing 7-23, deletes a cookie in the client's machine. It works by setting the cookie expiry date to a date much earlier than the current date. Before it tries to change the expiry date to make the cookie expire, it makes sure that the cookie exists.

Listing 7-23

```
function deleteCookie (name, path, domain) {
  if (getCookie(name)) {
    document.cookie = name + "=" +
    ((path==null) ? "" : "; path=" + path) +
    ((domain==null) ? "" : "; domain=" + domain) +
    "; expires=Thu, 01-Jan-70 )):00:01 GMT";
  }
}
```

The example in Listings 7-24, 7-25, and 7-26 are modifications of the preceding example. The code still sets a cookie following a successful user verification, however, it also gives the user the option to completely log out if she wishes. In addition to greeting the user, the WebClass also sends a button for the user to delete the cookie. The entire code is the same, but you modify the Members_ VerifyLogin event procedure, so that it sends a Welcome HTML template on successful login by the user.

The Login page template is given in Listing 7-24, the Welcome HTML template is given in Listing 7-25, and Listing 7-26 provides the code that you need to paste into your WebClass in order to test this example.

Listing 7-24

```
<html>
<head>
<title>Login Page</title>
</head>

<body>
<center>
Please type in your login details.
<form action=CH7.ASP?WCI=Members&amp;WCE=VerifyLogin&amp;WCU
  method=post>
<table>
  <tr>
    <td>Login:</td>
    <td><input name=Login Value="<WC@Login></WC@Login>">
</td>
  </tr>
```

```
   <tr>
     <td>Password:</td>
     <td><input type=password name=UserPassword></td>
   </tr>
   <tr>
     <td> </td>
     <td><input type=submit value=Login></td>
   </tr>
</table>
</form>
</center>
</body>
</html>
```

Listing 7-25

```
<html>
<head>
<title>Welcome</title>
<script language="JavaScript">
function fixDate(date) {
  var base = new Date(0);
  var skew = base.getTime();
  if (skew > 0) date.setTime(date.getTime() - skew);
}

function setCookie(name, value, expires, path, domain, secure) {
  document.cookie = name + "=" + escape(value) +
    ((expires) ? "; expires=" + expires.toGMTString() : "") +
    ((path) ? "; path=" + path : "") +
    ((domain) ? "; domain=" + domain : "") +
    ((secure) ? "; secure" : "");
}

function eraseCookie(name, path) {
  var expiryDate = new Date();
  fixDate(expiryDate);
  expiryDate.setTime(expiryDate.getTime() + 24 * 60 * 60 * 1000);
  setCookie(name, '', expiryDate, path);
}

</script>
</head>

<body>
```

```
  Welcome.
<br><br>
<form action="" method=post>
  <input type=button value="Log Out Completely"
    onClick="eraseCookie('Login', '/CH7')">
</form>

</body>
</html>
```

Listing 7-26

```
Private Sub WebClass_Start()

  LoginPage.WriteTemplate

End Sub

Private Sub LoginPage_ProcessTag(ByVal TagName As String,
  TagContents As String, SendTags As Boolean)

  If Request.Cookies("Login") <> "" Then
      TagContents = Request.Cookies("Login")
  End If

End Sub

Private Sub Members_VerifyLogin()

  Dim rs As ADODB.Recordset
  Dim strSQL As String

  ' Compose the SQL statement that retrieves the record that
  ' with specific Login name and password.
  strSQL = "SELECT Login FROM Users" & _
    " WHERE Login='" & Request.Form("Login") & "'" & _
    " AND Password='" & Request.Form("UserPassword") & "'"

  Set rs = New ADODB.Recordset
  rs.Open strSQL, "Atom", adOpenForwardOnly, adLockReadOnly

  If rs.BOF And rs.EOF Then
    ' recordset is empty, login failed
    LoginPage.WriteTemplate
  Else
```

```
' login was successful, set the cookies
Dim cookiename As String
Response.Cookies("Login") = Request.Form("Login")
' Make the cookie last for 1 day
Response.Cookies("Login").Expires = Now() + 1
Response.Cookies("Login").Path = "/CH7"
Welcome.WriteTemplate
End If


rs.Close
Set rs = Nothing

End Sub
```

The Welcome HTML Template WebItem contains JavaScript code for manipulating cookies. When the user has successfully logged in, the user's login name is remembered by the browser. The next time the user logs in, the login name is already typed in for the user, so he or she just needs to type in a password.

You can also use a facility to log out completely when the user doesn't want the browser to remember his or her login name. This is done by deleting the cookie when the user clicks the Log Out Completely button. Note that this is client-side cookie processing. Nothing is sent to the Web server; the JavaScript functions work quietly to destroy the cookie on the client's machine.

Hidden Fields

When you cannot guarantee that your users' browsers support cookies or have cookies enabled, you can still transfer state information across the network. In this case, you don't use cookies. Instead, you embed the state in hidden fields.

There are two disadvantages to using hidden fields:

1. The state information is visible to other people who have access to the user's computer. Anybody who can find the page in the cache can easily see the state information by viewing the source page. This situation can become critical if the information you store in the hidden fields is sensitive, such as user passwords or credit card details.

2. You must have a form to use hidden fields. The advantage of using hidden fields is that they don't use cookies, and there is no practical restriction to the length of information you can send.

The following example is an Admin page that adds a product to a table called Products. The example involves three pages: The first is the Login page, where the user must type in the correct user ID and password, the second is the Add Product page, and the third is the confirmation page. The second and third pages are displayed only if the user types in the correct user ID and password.

Upon verification, the user ID and password are passed to the second page, which in turn forwards the information back to the server when the user submits the Add Product form. Before the product is actually added, another user verification process takes place. Apart from the couple of disadvantages of using hidden fields that I mentioned, this process prevents an unauthorized person from adding a product.

This example also uses a custom WebItem called `Products`, which has a custom event called `Add`.

The form in the `LoginPage` HTML Template WebItem is connected to the `AddProduct` HTML Template WebItem. You may recall that in the absence of a `WCE` argument, the form is actually connected to the default event `Respond`. After being connected, the template looks similar to the following listing.

The `LoginPage` HTML template is given in Listing 7-27, and the `AddProduct` HTML template is given in Listing 7-28. The code that you need to paste into your WebClass is presented in Listing 7-29.

Listing 7-27

```
<html>
<head>
<title>Login Page</title>
</head>

<body>
<center>
Please type in your login name and password.
<form action=CH7.ASP?WCI=AddProduct&amp;WCU method=post>
<table>
  <tr>
    <td>Login:</td>
    <td><input name=Login></td>
  </tr>
  <tr>
    <td>Password:</td>
    <td><input type=password name=UserPassword></td>
  </tr>
  <tr>
    <td> </td>
    <td><input type=submit value=Login></td>
  </tr>
```

```
</table>
</form>
</center>
</body>
</html>
```

The form in the AddProduct HTML Template WebItem is connected to the Add event of the Products custom WebItem. You need to manually edit the template to connect it to a custom event. After the connection occurs, the template looks like the following listing. Notice the two hidden values for login and password. Both are printed in bold in Listing 7-28.

Listing 7-28

```
<html>
<head>
<title>Add Product</title>
</head>
<body>
<center>
Add Product
<br>
<form action=CH7.ASP?WCI=Products&amp;WCE=Add&amp;WCU method=post>
<table>
  <tr>
    <td>Product Code:</td>
    <td><input name=ProductCode></td>
  </tr>
  <tr>
    <td>Product Description:</td>
    <td><input name=ProductDescription></td>
  </tr>
  <tr>
    <td>Quantity:</td>
    <td><input name=Quantity></td>
  </tr>
  <tr>
    <td> </td>
    <td><input type=submit value="ADD"></td>
  </tr>
</table>
<input type=hidden Name=Login Value="<WC@Login>Login</WC@Login>">
<input type=hidden Name=UserPassword
  Value="<WC@UserPassword>User Password</WC@UserPassword>">
</form>
```

```
</center>
</body>
</html>
```

Listing 7-29

```
Function VerifyLogin(ByVal strUserID As String, _
  ByVal strPassword As String) As Boolean

  Dim rs As New ADODB.Recordset
  Dim strSQL As String

  ' Compose the SQL statement that retrieves the record that
  ' with specific Login name and password.
  strSQL = "SELECT Login FROM Users" & _
    " WHERE Login='" & Replace(strUserID, "'", "''") & "'" & _
    " AND Password='" & Replace(strPassword, "'", "''") & "'"

  rs.Open strSQL, "Atom", adOpenForwardOnly, adLockReadOnly

  If Not (rs.BOF And rs.EOF) Then
    ' recordset is not empty, user successfully logged in
    VerifyLogin = True
  End If
  rs.Close
  Set rs = Nothing

End Function

Private Sub WebClass_Start()

  LoginPage.WriteTemplate

End Sub

Private Sub AddProduct_Respond()

  If VerifyLogin(Request.Form("Login"), _
    Request.Form("UserPassword")) Then
    AddProduct.WriteTemplate
  Else
    LoginPage.WriteTemplate
  End If

End Sub
```

```
Private Sub AddProduct_ProcessTag(ByVal TagName As String, _
  TagContents As String, SendTags As Boolean)
  Select Case TagName
    Case "WC@Login"
      TagContents = Request.Form("Login")
    Case "WC@UserPassword"
      TagContents = Request.Form("UserPassword")
  End Select

End Sub


Private Sub Products_Add()

  If VerifyLogin(Request.Form("Login"), Request.Form("UserPassword")) Then

    'go to the function that adds the product
    ' . . .
    Response.Write "The product has been added."

  Else
    'oops, user is trying to bypass the login page.
    LoginPage.WriteTemplate
  End If

End Sub
```

A session starts with the Start event procedure of the WebClass object, where you use the WriteTemplate method to display the Login Page.

```
LoginPage.WriteTemplate
```

This displays the standard Login page.

When the user clicks the Submit button, the Web server passes the request to the WebClass, which in turn triggers the AddProduct HTML Template WebItem's Respond event.

```
If VerifyLogin(Request.Form("Login"), Request.Form("UserPassword")) Then
    AddProduct.WriteTemplate
  Else
    LoginPage.WriteTemplate
  End If
```

You use the VerifyLogin function to verify the user login name and password. If the function returns false, VB sends the Login page back to the browser in order for the user to try to log in again. The function returning True, by contrast, means that the user has successfully logged in. As a reward VB runs this line of code:

```
AddProduct.WriteTemplate
```

You may remember that calling the WriteTemplate method triggers the ProcessTag event, which scans the template for any replacement prior to sending the template to the browser.

```
Private Sub AddProduct_ProcessTag(ByVal TagName As String, _
  TagContents As String, SendTags As Boolean)
  Select Case TagName
    Case "WC@Login"
      TagContents = Request.Form("Login")
    Case "WC@UserPassword"
      TagContents = Request.Form("UserPassword")
  End Select

End Sub
```

The subroutine replaces the WC@Login tag with the login name entered by the user and the WC@UserPassword with the user password.

The Add Product HTML page looks like Figure 7-5 in the Netscape browser.

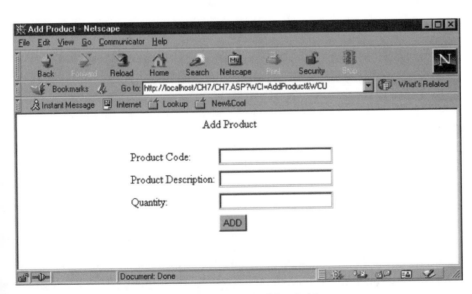

Figure 7-5. The Add Product page that uses hidden fields

You should spend some time viewing the HTML source code. Open the source of the HTML page to find the hidden values transferred back to the browser: the login name sa and the password QUR370. The HTML page as seen from the source page of the Web browser is given in Listing 7-30.

Listing 7-30

```
<html>
<head>
<title>Add Product</title>
</head>
<body>
<center>
Add Product
<br>
<form action=CH7.ASP?WCI=Products&amp;WCE=Add&amp;WCU method=post>
<table>
  <tr>
    <td>Product Code:</td>
    <td><input name=ProductCode></td>
  </tr>
  <tr>
    <td>Product Description:</td>
    <td><input name=ProductDescription></td>
  </tr>
  <tr>
    <td>Quantity:</td>
    <td><input name=Quantity></td>
  </tr>
  <tr>
    <td> </td>
    <td><input type=submit value="ADD"></td>
  </tr>
</table>
<input type=hidden Name=Login Value="sa">
<input type=hidden Name=UserPassword Value="QUR370">
</form>
</center>
</body>
</html>
```

If you don't want other people to be able to see the hidden values, you can create your own encoding scheme. For example, you can encrypt the strings so that the ASCII value of each character is less than a certain value; consequently, it will be seen as boxes such as this:

```
<input type=hidden Name=Login Value="□□">
<input type=hidden Name=UserPassword Value="□□□□□□">
```

Even though this is not perfectly secure, it will take some effort for curious people to discover just what the sensitive information is.

CHAPTER 8
File Uploading

Have you ever used a Web-based e-mail service, such as Hotmail or Yahoo Mail, and wondered how you can send a file from your hard drive as an attachment? Although submitting input can be easily done by using a form in an HTML page, as you saw in previous chapters of this book, submitting a file to the Web server is a different matter. It requires you to manipulate the raw data sent in the HTTP request.

So far in this book, the HTTP protocol has been taken for granted, and there hasn't been any real need to delve deeper into the lower levels of HTTP when a browser requests a page and your application sends a response. In this chapter, you'll be dealing with uploading files from the browser to the Web server, but unfortunately, the usual code to retrieve the HTTP request will not work here. A totally different approach is needed, and it's critical that you have a clear understanding of the HTTP request. That's why I've prefaced this chapter with the HTTP request structure.

The remainder of the chapter examines the code for uploading files from the Web browser to the server. This includes a discussion on how to store an uploaded file in a database.

The HTTP Request Structure

If you dissect an HTTP request, it has the following components:

- Method, Uniform Resource Identifier (URI), and protocol version

- Headers

- Carriage-return line-feed sequence

- Entity-body

The first part of the first component, the method, indicates the method used in the HTTP request. Various methods will work, and each method has a different functionality. The three most common HTTP methods are Get, Head, and Post. The Get method is the default, which explains why a form is always submitted using this method when the Method attribute is not present.

The URI fully specifies an Internet resource. A URL is actually a type of URI. (See `http://info.internet.isi.edu/in-notes/rfe/fles/rfc2396.txt/` for more details.) A URI is usually interpreted as being relative to the server's root WWW directory. Thus, it should always begin with a forward slash (/). In an IIS application, you can expect a URI that looks like this:

```
/localhost/FindMember.asp
```

The protocol version represents the version of the HTTP protocol being used. Combining the three sub-components, the first component of an HTTP request may look similar to this:

```
POST /localhost/FindMember.asp HTTP/1.1
```

The second component of an HTTP request consists of a number of HTTP headers. Three of the four types of HTTP headers are present in an HTTP request. They are general, entity, and request headers. The fourth type of the HTTP header is the response header, which, as the name implies, is found in HTTP responses. The first two types, the general and entity headers, are present in both HTTP requests and responses. The request headers are present only in HTTP requests.

Tables 8-1, 8-2, and 8-3 summarize the general, entity, and request headers. The response headers are very similar to the request headers, but won't be discussed in this chapter because, as stated earlier, they are only present in HTTP responses and are not of concern when uploading files.

In IIS applications, you can see these headers using the elements of the Request object's ServerVariables collection: ALL_HTTP and ALL_RAW. The following line of code, for example, retrieves all the headers:

```
Request.ServerVariables("ALL_RAW"))
```

Table 8-1. General Headers

HEADER	DESCRIPTION
Pragma	The Pragma general header is used to include implementation-specific directives that may apply to any recipient along the request/response chain. That is, pragmas notify the servers that are used to send this request to behave in a certain way. The Pragma header may contain multiple values. For example, the line of code `Pragma: no-cache` informs all proxy servers that relay this request to *not* use a cached version of the object, but to download the object from the specified location instead.
Date	The Date general header represents the date and time at which the message was originated.

Table 8-2. Entity Headers

HEADER	DESCRIPTION
Allow	This header lists the set of methods supported by the resource identified by the requested URL. The purpose of this field is strictly to inform the recipient of valid methods associated with the resource. The Allow header is not permitted in a request using the `Post` method, and therefore should be ignored if it is received as part of a Post entity. For instance, `Allow: GET, HEAD`
Content-Encoding	This header is used to describe the type of encoding used on the entity. When present, its value indicates the decoding mechanism that must be applied to obtain the media type referenced by the Content-Type header. For example, `Content-Encoding: x-gzip`
Content-Length	This header indicates the size of the entity-body, in a decimal number of octets, sent to the recipient or, in the case of the `Head` method, the size of the entity-body that would have been sent had the request been a `Get`. Applications should use this field to indicate the size of the entity-body to be transferred, regardless of the media type of the entity. A valid `Content-Length` field value is required on all HTTP/1.0 request messages containing an entity-body. Any Content-Length header greater than or equal to zero is a valid value. For example, `Content-Length: 123452`
Content-Type	The Content-Type header indicates the media type of the entity-body sent to the recipient or, in the case of the `Head` method, the media type that would have been sent had the request been a `Get`. For example, `Content-Type: text/html`
Expires	The Expires header gives the date and time after which the entity should be considered invalid. This allows information providers to suggest the volatility of the resource or a date after which the information may no longer be accurate. Applications must not cache this entity beyond the date given. The presence of an Expires header does not imply that the original resource will change or cease to exist at, before, or after that time. However, information providers should include an `Expires` header with that date. For example, `Expires: Thu, 10 Aug 2000 13:00:00 GMT`
Last-Modified	The Last-Modified header indicates the date and time at which the sender believes the resource was last modified. The exact semantics of this field are defined in terms of how the recipient should interpret it: If the recipient has a copy of this resource that is older than the date given by the `Last-Modified` field, then the copy should be considered stale. For example, `Last-Modified: Thu, 10 Aug 2000 12:12:12 GMT`

Table 8-3. Request Headers

HEADER	DESCRIPTION
From	The From header specifies who is taking responsibility for the request. This field contains the e-mail address of the user submitting the request. For example, `From: rembrant@labsale.com`
Accept	This header contains a semicolon-separated list of Multipurpose Internet Mail Extensions (MIME) representation schemes that are accepted by the client. The server uses this information to determine which data types are safe to send to the client in the HTTP response. Although the `Accept` field can contain multiple values, the `Accept` line itself can also be used more than once to specify additional accept types (this has the same effect as specifying multiple accept types on a single line). If the `Accept` field is not used in the request header, the default accept types of `text/plain` and `text/html` are assumed. For example, `Accept: text/plain; text/html` and `Accept; image/gif; image/jpeg`
Accept-Encoding	This header is very similar to the Accept header in syntax. However, it specifies the content-encoding schemes that are acceptable in the response. For instance, `Accept-Encoding: x-compress; x-zip`
Accept-Language	This header is also similar to the Accept header. It specifies the preferred response language. The following example specifies English as the accepted language: `Accept-Language: en`
User-Agent	The User-Agent, if present, specifies the name of the client browser. The first word should be the name of the software followed by a slash and an optional version number. Any other product names that are part of the complete software package may also be included. Each name/version pair should be separated by white space. This field is used mostly for statistical purposes. It allows servers to track software usage and protocol violation. For example, `User-Agent: Mozilla/4.0 (compatible; MSIE 4.01; Windows 98)`
Referer	This header specifies the URI that contained the URI in the request header. In HTML, it would be the address of the page that contained the link to the requested object. Like the User-Agent header, this header is not required, but is mostly for the server's statistical and tracking purpose. For example, `Referer: http://localhost/Atoms/Details.htm`
Authorization	The Authorization header contains authorization information. The first word contained in this header specifies the type of authorization system to use. Then, separated by a white space, it should be followed by the authorization information, such as a user name, password, and so forth. For example, `Authorization: user ken:dragonlancer`
If-Modified-Since	This header is used with the `GET` method to make it conditional. Basically, if the object hasn't changed since the date and time specified by this header, the object is not sent. A local cached copy of the object is used instead. For example, `If-Modified-Since: Thu, 10 Aug 2000 12:12:29 GMT`

The ServerVariables collection's element ALL_RAW is a long string containing all the HTTP headers in their original state as sent by the client browser. This element is very similar to the ALL_HTTP element. The main difference is that the ALL_HTTP values are all prefixed with HTTP_ and the header name is always capitalized. The following is an example of an HTTP header:

```
Accept: application/vnd.ms-excel, application/msword, */*
Accept-Language: en-gb
Connection: Keep-Alive
Host: localhost
Referer: http://localhost/ch8/SendDetails.htm
User-Agent: Mozilla/4.0 (compatible; MSIE 4.01; Windows 98)
Cookie: ASPSESSIONIDFFFENQAB=HCALPOADCPAHJDPAMNHBPPKE
Content-Length: 32
Content-Type: application/x-www-form-urlencoded
Accept-Encoding: gzip, deflate
```

```
LastName=sawaki&FirstName=tomoko
```

Numerous values are revealed in the previous HTTP header. The first line tells you that the browser that sent this request can accept a number of file formats including Microsoft Excel and Microsoft Word. It is followed by the language used (in this case, British English), the type of connection (*keep-alive*, which means a persistent connection is being used), and the name of the host (localhost). By using persistents, a client can use a single or reduced number of connections for multiple requests. It also tells the server that the request is sent from the SendDetails.htm file, which is located in the ch8 virtual root.

In the User-Agent entry, the Request tells that the user is using Microsoft Internet Explorer version 4.01, which is compatible with Netscape 4.0. The user's operating system is also recorded as Windows 98. The Cookie header contains the cookie(s) sent from the browser; the Content-Length header specifies the number of bytes in the content (in this example, 32); the Content-Type header indicates the media type of the entity-body sent to the recipient (application/x-www-form-urlencoded); and the Accept-Encoding header reveals that gzip and deflate are accepted by the browser.

Two pairs of carriage-return line-feed characters follow the header. The length of this separator is 4 bytes because each carriage-return line-feed character pair consists of the ASCII characters numbers 13 and 10. From the previous HTTP header you can also see that the entity-body of the HTTP request consists of the following code, which is obviously from a form with two input boxes, one called LastName with the value sawaki and the other named FirstName with the value tomoko:

```
LastName=sawaki&FirstName=tomoko
```

Note that the length of `LastName=sawaki&FirstName=tomoko` is 32. Note also that the entity-body is separated from the headers by a carriage return line-feed sequence (blank line). Only requests that need to send data need to use an entity-body.

Now that the HTTP Request anatomy has been clarified, you are ready to write code for a file upload. Take a look at what needs to be on the browser's side first, and then you can write code to grab the file details.

Uploading Files on the Client Side

Prior to the Request For Comments (RFC) 1867 that was issued in November 1995, which defined specifications for form-based file upload in HTML, there were eight possible values for the TYPE attribute of an INPUT element: CHECKBOX, HIDDEN, IMAGE, PASSWORD, RADIO, RESET, SUBMIT, and TEXT. Although these form elements were proven useful in a wide variety of applications in which input from the user needed to be transferred to the server, none were useful for sending a file, either text or binary.

To enable file upload from an HTML form, it was then proposed in RFC 1867 that the TYPE attribute of an HTML INPUT element have another possible value: FILE. In addition, RFC 1867 defined a new MIME media type, multipart/form-data, and specified the behavior of HTML user agents when interpreting a form with ENCTYPE="multipart/form-data" and/or <INPUT type="file"> tags. This specification was adopted by major browser makers and as a result, you can upload files from an HTML form using current browsers.

To perform file upload, you need to have a form tag with attributes as in the following line and an Input tag of type File:

```
<FORM ENCTYPE="multipart/form-data" ACTION="_URL_" METHOD=POST>
File to process: <INPUT NAME="userfile1" TYPE="file">
<INPUT TYPE="submit" VALUE="Send File">
</FORM>
```

When an INPUT tag of type File is encountered, the browser shows a box similar to the TEXT element as well as a Browse button. Selecting the Browse button causes the browser to enter into a file selection mode appropriate for the platform. Windows-based browsers might display a file selection window, for example.

Retrieving Uploaded Files on the Server Side

To retrieve the content of a file sent by the browser, the key method is the Request object's BinaryRead method, which, as the name indicates, reads binary data. It has the following syntax:

```
variant = Request.BinaryRead(count)
```

where `variant` contains an array of unsigned bytes returned by this method, and the `count` parameter specifies how many bytes to read from the client.

After the `BinaryRead` method returns, `count` contains the number of bytes successfully read from the client. The total number of bytes that is actually read is less than or equal to `Request.TotalBytes`.

The `BinaryRead` method retrieves data sent to the server from the client as part of a `Post` request. This method retrieves the data from the client and stores it in a SafeArray. A SafeArray is an array that contains information about the number of its dimensions and the bounds of those dimensions.

The `BinaryRead` method is used for low-level access to this data as opposed to, for example, using the `Request.Form` collection to view form data sent in a `Post` request. Once you call `BinaryRead`, referring to any variable in the `Request.Form` collection will cause an error. Conversely, once you refer to a variable in the `Request.Form` collection, calling `BinaryWrite` is also taboo. If you do so, you will get the following error message: ' 006~ASP 0206' error message: Cannot call BinaryRead after using Request.Form collection. If you access a variable in the `Request` object without specifying which collection it belongs to, the `Request.Form` collection may be searched, bringing this rule into force.

Despite having a powerful method at your disposal, such as `BinaryRead`, the process of retrieving the file content is not as straightforward as retrieving the values in the `Request` object's `Form` collection. Like me, you may wish that you could write the following line of code to retrieve the content of a file uploaded to the server:

```
Request.Form("MyFile")
```

Or, after reading the next few paragraphs, you might wish that you could obtain the file name by writing this line of code:

```
strFilename = Request.Form("Filename")
```

Unfortunately, to retrieve the file name and the file content, you have to read and parse the raw data of the entity-body part of the HTTP header.

Although the idea of reading the raw data sounds threatening, the following examples will hopefully provide you with valuable information to make this process easier. And, although it takes a bit of programming, the structure of the HTTP Request is definite, making it possible to be processed.

For example, if you try to upload the test.bat file from the C drive of your computer whose content is a single line of text such as this:

```
PATH=C:\WINDOWS;C:\WINDOWS\COMMAND;D:\BINN;
```

the entity-body part of the HTTP request would look like the following if you could capture it using a text editor:

```
---------------------------7d03841b594
Content-Disposition: form-data; name="Filename"; filename="C:\test.bat"
Content-Type: text/plain

PATH=C:\WINDOWS;C:\WINDOWS\COMMAND;D:\BINN;
---------------------------7d03841b594--
```

And, the following is the entity-body part when uploading a .gif file called b1.gif from the client computer's F:\ps directory:

```
---------------------------7d02c6384d4
Content-Disposition: form-data; name="Filename"; filename="F:\ps\b1.gif"
Content-Type: image/gif

GIF89a ÕÿÀÀÀ__ìªª_§§___
_ŸŸ____œœ__›Î˜•Ü—ò—•Ü""_'"ò''_''_˜_^^_‡‡_……_„„_|
|_{{_zz_yy_ww_pp_oo_ooõmm_ll_kkõcc_bb_aa_[ZöXX_XXöVV_UU_TT_JJ_!ù__,
_7@_pH,___Aa'__†FgÒ___%EÃ_" "Ë_D_:(˜NÈ4_*2-Ñ)¥ *>¨_āh 1;;
--------------------------- 7d02c6384d4--
```

The previous two examples make the structure of the entity-body of the HTTP request clear. It starts and ends with a delimiter of a set of hyphens followed by an unknown number on the first line. The first line and the second line are indeed separated by a vbCrLf (ASCII characters numbers 13 and 10). On the second line is a string of text with information, such as the complete file path and content type. And after that, two pairs of carriage-return line-feed characters signal the beginning of the file. The file content ends with a vbCrLf and the closing delimiter. The closing delimiter is followed by two hyphens and another vbCrLf.

Knowing the structure of the entity-body, retrieving the content of an uploaded file involves the following steps:

1. Read the TotalBytes property of the Request object. This value contains the number of bytes in the entity-body part of the HTTP header.

2. Obtain the file name by parsing the string after the starting delimiter.

3. Mark the beginning and the end of the file content. The beginning of the file starts right after the first occurrence of the two pairs of carriage-return line-feed characters.

4. Retrieve the file content by writing it to a file on the server or inserting it into a database table.

The following example demonstrates how to retrieve the uploaded file on the server. The example uses an HTML Template WebItem called UploadFile as given in Listing 8-1.

Listing 8-1

```html
<html>
<head>
<title>File Upload</title>
</head>

<body>
<form enctype="multipart/form-data" action=CH8.ASP?WCI=UploadFile&amp;WCU
method=post>
<br>
Select file to upload
<br>
<input type=file Name=Filename>
<br>
<input type=submit value="Upload File">
</form>
</body>
</html>
```

The HTML template is sent to the browser, so that the user can select a file to upload in the browser. In a Windows-based browser, the page will have an appearance similar to Figure 8-1.

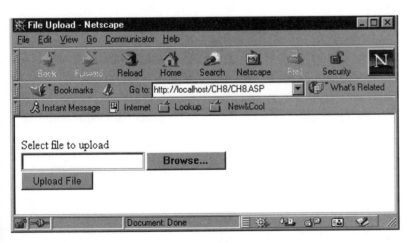

Figure 8-1. File upload selection in HTML

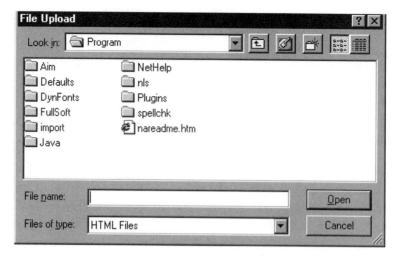

Figure 8-2. The dialog box for selecting the file to upload

When the user clicks the Browse button, another dialog box will appear, allowing the user to browse the file system and select a file. The dialog box is shown in Figure 8-2.

Once the file is selected by highlighting the file name and clicking Open, the user can submit the file by clicking the Upload File button.

Returning to Listing 8-1, note that the form is connected to the UploadFile WebItem.

In your WebClass, you need to write code in the WebClass's Start event procedure to send the UploadFile HTML template to the browser and in the UploadFile's Respond event procedure to process the uploaded file. In the following example, the file is simply written to another file with the same name in the application's path. The complete code is given in Listing 8-2.

Listing 8-2

```
Private Sub WebClass_Start()

  UploadFile.WriteTemplate

End Sub

Private Sub UploadFile_Respond()
  Dim lngTotalBytes As Long
  Dim bytArray() As Byte
  Dim lngFileDataStart As Long
  Dim lngFileDataEnd As Long
  Dim strHeader As String
```

```
Dim strDelimiter As String
Dim intPathNameStart As String
Dim strPathName As String
Dim strFilepath As String
Dim strFilename As String
Dim intFileNameStart As Integer
Dim intFileNameEnd As Integer
Dim lngCount As Long
Dim lngFileSize As Long
Dim intFileHandle As Integer

On Error GoTo ErrHandler
lngTotalBytes = Request.TotalBytes
ReDim bytArray(lngTotalBytes)
bytArray = Request.BinaryRead(CVar(lngTotalBytes))

' Parse header data of first element from byte array
Do Until Right$(strHeader, 4) = vbCrLf & vbCrLf
  strHeader = strHeader & Chr$(bytArray(lngCount))
  lngCount = lngCount + 1
  If lngCount > lngTotalBytes Then
    Response.Write "HTTP header error. Please try again."
    Exit Sub
  End If
Loop

intPathNameStart = InStr(strHeader, "filename=") + 10
intFileNameEnd = InStr(intPathNameStart, strHeader, vbCrLf) - 1

If intPathNameStart = intFileNameEnd Then
  Response.Write "No file uploaded."
  Exit Sub
End If

strPathName = Mid$(strHeader, intPathNameStart, _
  intFileNameEnd - intPathNameStart)
strFilename = Right$(strPathName, Len(strPathName) - _
  InStrRev(strPathName, "\"))
strDelimiter = Left$(strHeader, InStr(strHeader, vbCrLf) - 1)

lngFileDataStart = Len(strHeader) + 1
lngFileDataEnd = lngTotalBytes - Len(strDelimiter) - 6
lngFileSize = lngFileDataEnd - lngFileDataStart + 1
```

```
      intFileHandle = FreeFile

      strFilepath = App.Path & "\" & strFilename

      If Len(Dir$(strFilepath)) Then
        Response.Write "Error. File with the same name already " & _
          "exists in this directory."
        Exit Sub
      End If

      Open strFilepath For Binary Access Write As #intFileHandle
      For lngCount = lngFileDataStart - 1 To lngFileDataEnd - 1
        Put #1, , (bytArray(lngCount))
      Next
      Close #intFileHandle
      Response.Write "Successfully uploaded file: " & strFilename & _
        "<br>File size=" & lngFileSize

      Exit Sub

ErrHandler:
      Response.Write Err.Description
      On Error Resume Next
      Response.Write "Error uploading file"
      If Len(Dir$(strFilepath)) Then Kill strFilepath
    End Sub
```

Now, I'll step through the code while discussing each section in Listing 8-2. After the variable declaration and error handling statement, the code continues with these three lines:

```
    lngTotalBytes = Request.TotalBytes
    ReDim bytArray(lngTotalBytes)
    bytArray = Request.BinaryRead(CVar(lngTotalBytes))
```

The first line reads the TotalBytes property of the Request object into the lngTotalBytes variables, the second line redimensions the bytArray array variable to make it as long as lngTotalBytes, and the third line reads the raw data of the Request object using the BinaryRead method. Conversion of the value of lngTotalBytes to the VARIANT type is needed because the BinaryRead method requires an argument of type VARIANT.

The next code segment includes the do loop to parse the header data prior to the file content. This is easily achieved because you know that the file content starts right after the first occurrence of the double vbCrLf. You just need to read the raw data starting from the first byte and add the bytes read to the strHeader string variable until the last four characters are a double vbCrLf.

```
' Parse header data of first element from byte array
  Do Until Right$(strHeader, 4) = vbCrLf & vbCrLf
    strHeader = strHeader & Chr$(bytArray(lngCount))
    lngCount = lngCount + 1
    If lngCount > lngTotalBytes Then
      Response.Write "HTTP header error. Please try again."
      Exit Sub
    End If
  Loop
```

The Chr$ function in the previous code segment returns a string containing the character associated with the specified character code. Note that because the string prior to the file content consists of ASCII characters, you can safely use string functions Chr$ and Right$ rather than their companions Chr and Right functions, which return variants.

You then need to retrieve the complete path from the strHeader variable. Remember that the complete file path is embedded in the string after the starting delimiter. At this point, the strHeader variable has a value similar to the following, where the last four characters are two vbCrLf.

```
---------------------------7d03841b594
Content-Disposition: form-data; name="Filename"; filename="C:\test.bat"
Content-Type: text/plain
```

The starting position of the file name can easily be retrieved with the following line:

```
intPathNameStart = InStr(strHeader, "filename=") + 10
```

And the ending can be retrieved just as easily knowing that the file name ends with a double quote character and a vbCrLf:

```
intFileNameEnd = InStr(intPathNameStart, strHeader, vbCrLf) - 1
```

You then try to trap the error caused by the user sending the form before the user selects a file at all, as shown next:

```
If intPathNameStart = intFileNameEnd Then
  Response.Write "No file uploaded."
  Exit Sub
End If
```

The path name is then the substring starting from the beginning of the path name (intPathNameStart) with the length of intFileNameEnd - intPathNameStart:

```
strPathName = Mid$(strHeader, intPathNameStart, intFileNameEnd -
intPathNameStart)
```

The file name, in turn, can easily be retrieved using the InStrRev function, which is the long awaited added function in Visual Basic 6:

```
strFilename = Right$(strPathName, Len(strPathName) - _
  InStrRev(strPathName, "\"))
```

The InStrRev function is similar to the InStr function in that both return the position of the first occurrence of one string within another. The difference is that the InStrRev function starts the search from the rightmost character.

Because the file content is terminated with a closing delimiter, which is the same as the starting delimiter, obtaining the value of the starting delimiter helps you determine where the file content ends.

```
strDelimiter = Left$(strHeader, InStr(strHeader, vbCrLf) - 1)
```

To get the file content, you need to know the position of the first byte and the last byte of the file content in the raw data. The starting position is obvious, it is right after the first double vbCrLf, which means it is right after the strHeader. Therefore, the starting position of the file content is retrievable using this line:

```
lngFileDataStart = Len(strHeader) + 1
```

The end position is not as straightforward. This is where the delimiter string helps out. Knowing the length of the delimiter helps you to find out where the file content ends.

```
lngFileDataEnd = lngTotalBytes - Len(strDelimiter) - 6
```

The 6 is used to offset the fact that there is a vbCrLf between the last byte of the file content and the closing delimiter and that two hyphens and a vbCrLf are after the closing delimiter.

Knowing the starting and ending position of the file content leads you straight to the file size:

```
lngFileSize = lngFileDataEnd - lngFileDataStart + 1
```

The next lines of code attempt to write the file to a file. In this case, the location of the file is in the application path.

```
intFileHandle = FreeFile

strFilepath = App.Path & "\" & strFilename
```

The code in this example doesn't overwrite the file with the same name. Instead, it raises an error if a file with the same name is already present in the directory.

```
If Len(Dir$(strFilepath)) Then
  Response.Write "Error. File with the same name already " & _
    "exists in this directory."
  Exit Sub
End If
```

Writing to the file is accomplished by the following code. Because the array element starts with a zero, position x in the array has an index of x – 1.

```
Open strFilepath For Binary Access Write As #intFileHandle
For lngCount = lngFileDataStart - 1 To lngFileDataEnd - 1
  Put #1, , (bytArray(lngCount))
Next
Close #intFileHandle
Response.Write "Successfully uploaded file: " & strFilename & _
  "<br>File size=" & lngFileSize

Exit Sub

ErrHandler:
  Response.Write Err.Description
  On Error Resume Next
  Response.Write "Error uploading file"
  If Len(Dir$(strFilepath)) Then Kill strFilepath
```

When writing the code for file upload, you need to pay attention to two details. First, you may want to restrict the size of the file uploaded. In the previous example, this is accomplished by checking the file size after this line:

```
lngFileSize = lngFileDataEnd - lngFileDataStart + 1
```

If lngFileSize exceeds a predetermined value, you can stop processing the file and throw an error message to the user.

Unless you use an ActiveX control that only Internet Explorer can understand, there is no way of obtaining the file size on the browser side. Forget using JavaScript because the security scheme in JavaScript prevents it from reading a file in the client's computer.

Second, when uploading a big file, the server may be forced to time out before the whole file is uploaded. As a result, the user will receive an error message, too. To overcome this problem, you need to set the ScriptTimeout property to a reasonable value. The ScriptTimeout property specifies the maximum length of time a script can run before it is terminated.

For example, you can add the following line to the top of your code in the UploadFile_Respond event procedure, where NumSeconds is the maximum number of seconds the script can run before it times out:

```
Server.ScriptTimeout = NumSeconds
```

Adding Additional Form Elements

If you want to have other elements in the same form as the one used to select the file to be uploaded, nothing prevents you from doing so. But, remember that you have to process the raw data at the server side to retrieve the element value. As noted in the previous section, you are limited by not being able to use Request.Form after or before calling the BinaryRead method.

The following HTML template adds a text element called Author to the form in the preceding example. Considering the amount of extra work to retrieve this value, you might want to put the additional element in another form on another HTML page, and then use one of the methods described in Chapter 7 to pass the value to the next page. Listing 8-3 shows the HTML template file for file upload with an extra HTML element.

Listing 8-3

```
<html>
<head>
<title>File Upload with Author Name</title>
</head>

<body>
<form enctype="multipart/form-data" action=CH8.ASP?WCI=UploadFile&amp;
  WCU method=post>
<br>
Select file to upload
```

```
<br>
<input type=text Name=Author>
<br>
<input type=file Name=Filename>
<br>
<input type=submit value="Upload File">
</form>
</body>
</html>
```

On the server side, the entity-body of the HTTP request is as follows:

```
-----------------------------7d033423b64
Content-Disposition: form-data; name="Author"

budi
-----------------------------7d033423b64
Content-Disposition: form-data; name="Filename"; filename="C:\test.bat"
Content-Type: text/plain

PATH=C:\WINDOWS;C:\WINDOWS\COMMAND;D:\BINN;

-----------------------------7d033423b64--
```

Two vbCrLf's are between name="Author" and budi, the element value, and vbCrLf's are also between the text/plain and the start of the file content. You have to modify your code to take into consideration the first form element that appears before the file name and file content.

Multiple File Uploading

Uploading more than one file at a time is also possible. All you need to do on the client side is add another FILE element to the form, as in the HTML template in Listing 8-4.

Listing 8-4
```
<html>
<head>
<title>Multiple File Upload</title>
</head>

<body>
```

```
<form enctype="multipart/form-data" action=CH8.ASP?
WCI=UploadMultipleFile&amp;WCU method=post>
<br>
Select file to upload
<br>
<input type=file Name=Filename1>
<br>
<input type=file Name=Filename2>
<br>
<input type=submit value="Upload File">
</form>
</body>
</html>
```

To get an idea of what the Request raw data looks like, try uploading two text files, 1.txt and 2.txt. 1.txt is a single line of text that contains the following string:

```
This is the first file.
```

2.txt is also as simple, containing the following single string of text:

```
This is the second file.
```

The following code is the header plus the contents of the two files, as you may have expected:

```
---------------------------7d012c15b64
Content-Disposition: form-data; name="Filename1"; filename="C:\1.txt"
Content-Type: text/plain

This is the first file.
---------------------------7d012c15b64
Content-Disposition: form-data; name="Filename2"; filename="C:\2.txt"
Content-Type: text/plain

This is the second file.
---------------------------7d012c15b64--
```

Knowing the structure of the entity-body will give you enough information to write the code for uploading multiple files.

Storing Uploaded Files in a Database

Is it possible to store a text or binary file in a database table? It certainly is. All modern relational databases from Microsoft Access to Sybase Adaptive Server to Oracle have at least one data type for binary data. Is it recommended? No, it isn't. If possible, avoid reading and writing files to a database. It's better to store your file in the file server and store only the file name and the ID of that file in a database. Storing a file in a database is a slower process. What's more, it is more difficult to program and debug.

However, if you really have to read and write files to a database, you may find the following information useful.

You can store a file in a database table as Binary Large Object (BLOB) data. In Microsoft SQL Server, the Text and Image data types are provided. Both types can have a length of $2^{31}-1$ (2,147,483,647) characters/bytes. Even though the Text data type gives you the impression that it is only for ASCII characters, the reality that isn't so. You can use the Text data type to store binary data as well. In fact, in my experiments, I find Text data types are easier to manage. In the following examples, I use the Text data type to store my binary data. But before you try these functions, read on.

When you are working with binary data, you sometimes deal with a very large data file. This raises an issue that doesn't exist with small-sized data: When you try to read from or write to a database, your server may not have enough memory. This forces you to work with chunks of data.

You can only use the Value property of the ADO's Field object if the whole BLOB data can be retrieved in a single operation, which oftentimes is not the case. This means that if you have a 200MB file that you want to store in the database, instead of writing it in one large chunk, you feed the database server, say, 200 1MB chunks. However, without your realizing it, this creates another problem: You need to choose how large a chunk it's going to be.

Choosing too large a chunk size increases the risk that your server may not have enough memory, and choosing a chunk size that is too small means that the operation will take longer because each chunk requires another trip to the database server.

You also need to be selective in using the driver for database connection. The OLE DB provider for ODBC is not a good choice to open your connection when working with chunks of data. My experiments did not show good results. Sometimes it read fewer bytes than it was supposed to. Also, if you don't use a server-side cursor, all the BLOB columns must be to the right of all the non-BLOB columns. Using the SQLOLEDB data provider for Microsoft SQL Server seems to work just fine.

The two functions in Listing 8-5, InsertFileToDatabase and GetFileFrom Database, write a file to and read a file from a database.

Listing 8-5

```
Option Base 1

Private Function InsertFileToDatabase(ByVal strFilepath As String) _
  As Boolean
  Dim t() As Byte
  Dim rs As New ADODB.Recordset
  Dim strConnectionString As String
  Dim intFileHandle As Integer
  Dim lngFilesize As Long
  Dim lngChunkCount As Long
  Dim ChunkSize As Long
  Dim lngRemainder As Long
  Dim strSQL As String
  Dim i As Integer

  On Error GoTo ErrHandler

  strConnectionString = "Provider=SQLOLEDB;Data Source=SERVERNT0023;" & _
    "Initial Catalog=pubs;User ID=sa;Password=;"

  intFileHandle = FreeFile
  Open strFilepath For Binary Access Read As #intFileHandle
  lngFilesize = FileLen(strFilepath)
  lngChunkCount = lngFilesize \ CHUNK_SIZE
  lngRemainder = lngFilesize Mod CHUNK_SIZE

  strSQL = "SELECT * FROM Blobs WHERE ID=0"
  rs.Open strSQL, strConnectionString, adOpenKeyset, adLockOptimistic
  rs.AddNew
  ReDim t(CHUNK_SIZE)
  For i = 1 To lngChunkCount
    Get #intFileHandle, , t()
    rs("File").AppendChunk t()
  Next i

  If lngRemainder > 0 Then
    ReDim t(lngRemainder)
    Get #intFileHandle, , t()
    rs("File").AppendChunk t()
```

```vbnet
   End If

   rs.Update
   rs.Close
   Set rs = Nothing
   Close #intFileHandle
   InsertFileToDatabase = True
   Exit Function

ErrHandler:
   Response.Write Err.Description
End Function


Private Function GetFileFromDatabase(ByVal lngID As Long, _
   ByVal strFilename As String) As Boolean

   On Error GoTo ErrHandler

   Dim t() As Byte
   Dim rs As New ADODB.Recordset
   Dim strSQL As String
   Dim strConnectionString As String
   Dim intFileHandle As Integer
   Dim strPath As String
   Dim lngFilesize As Long
   Dim lngRemainder As Long
   Dim strChunk As String
   Dim lngChunkCount As Long
   Dim i As Integer

   strConnectionString = "Provider=SQLOLEDB;Data Source=SERVERNT0023;" & _
      "Initial Catalog=pubs;User ID=sa;Password=;"
   intFileHandle = FreeFile

   strPath = Request.ServerVariables("PATH_TRANSLATED")
   strPath = Left$(strPath, InStrRev(strPath, "\"))

   Open strPath & strFilename For Binary Access Write As #intFileHandle

   strSQL = "SELECT * FROM Blobs WHERE ID=" & lngID
   rs.CursorType = adOpenStatic
   rs.Open strSQL, strConnectionString
```

```
If Not (rs.BOF And rs.EOF) Then
  lngFilesize = rs("File").ActualSize
  lngChunkCount = lngFilesize \ CHUNK_SIZE
  lngRemainder = lngFilesize Mod CHUNK_SIZE

  For i = 1 To lngChunkCount
    strChunk = rs("File").GetChunk(CHUNK_SIZE)
    Put #intFileHandle, , strChunk
  Next i

  If lngRemainder > 0 Then
    strChunk = rs("File").GetChunk(lngRemainder)
    Put #intFileHandle, , strChunk
  End If
End If

rs.Close
Set rs = Nothing
Close #intFileHandle
GetFileFromDatabase = True
Exit Function

ErrHandler:
  Response.Write Err.Description
End Function
```

Both functions assume that you have a table called Blobs in your pubs database. This table has two columns, ID and File. ID has an integer data type and is also an identity column, which is used for storing the file ID. File is a Text data type.

When using these functions, you must make sure to include the Option Base 1 statement at the beginning of your module. This statement makes your array start with an index number of 1. By default, the Option Base 0 is implied. If you want to use Option Base 0, you need to subtract the number of array elements by 1.

If the array number starts from 0, such as when using the default, the t array variable will have 11 elements, element 0 through element 10:

```
Redim t(10)
```

When you state Option Base 1 at the beginning of your module, the t array variable will have 10 elements, element 1 through element 10.

The InsertFileToDatabase function stores a file in the database. It takes one argument, strFilepath, which must consist of the complete physical path in the server where the file to be stored is located. The t variable is an array of bytes that is used to store your chunks of data temporarily.

The InsertFileToDatabase function starts by declaring the connection string that uses the SQLOLEDB provider to access the pubs database in the SERVERNT0023 server. The user ID is sa and there is currently no password set for user sa:

```
strConnectionString = "Provider=SQLOLEDB;Data Source=SERVERNT0023;" & _
    "Initial Catalog=pubs;User ID=sa;Password=;"
```

The code then tries to open a file to read. The filepath is specified in strFilepath. The filesize can be obtained using the FileLen function, as follows:

```
intFileHandle = FreeFile
Open strFilepath For Binary Access Read As #intFileHandle
lngFilesize = FileLen(strFilepath)
```

From the filesize, you can then calculate the number of chunks by dividing the filesize by the CHUNK_SIZE constant:

```
lngChunkCount = lngFilesize \ CHUNK_SIZE
```

The remainder is stored in the lngRemainder variable, as shown:

```
lngRemainder = lngFilesize Mod CHUNK_SIZE
```

Knowing the number of chunks and the remainder allows you to continue with the database access. The SQL statement is meant to acquire the structure of the recordset only, giving back no record:

```
strSQL = "SELECT * FROM Blobs WHERE ID=0"
rs.Open strSQL, strConnectionString, adOpenKeyset, adLockOptimistic
rs.AddNew
```

You then redimension the t array variable, as follows:

```
ReDim t(CHUNK_SIZE)
```

After getting the number of chunks and the chunk size, you perform a loop to write all the chunks to the table. The Get function retrieves byte data from the file and stores this data in t. To store the chunk to the table, use the AppendChunk method, as follows:

```
For i = 1 To lngChunkCount
  Get #intFileHandle, , t()
  rs("File").AppendChunk t()
Next i
```

The loop guarantees that all the chunks are written to the table. The next loop makes sure the remainder, if any, is also written to the database:

```
If lngRemainder > 0 Then
  ReDim t(lngRemainder)
  Get #intFileHandle, , t()
  rs("File").AppendChunk t()
End If
```

The rest of the code performs the standard tasks, such as updating the recordset, closing it, and setting it to nothing to release the memory. After these tasks are complete, you close the file and exit the function:

```
rs.Update
rs.Close
Set rs = Nothing
Close #intFileHandle
InsertFileToDatabase = True
Exit Function

ErrHandler:
  Response.Write Err.Description
End Function
```

The GetFileFromDatabase does the reverse. It reads a BLOB from a table and writes it to a file. The GetFileFromDatabase function takes two arguments: the file ID and the name of the file the BLOB should be written to. Like the InsertFileToDatabase function, it starts with the connection string:

```
strConnectionString = "Provider=SQLOLEDB;Data Source=SERVERNT0023;" & _
  "Initial Catalog=pubs;User ID=sa;Password=;"
```

It then opens a file for write:

```
intFileHandle = FreeFile
```

The PATH_TRANSLATED element of the ServerVariables collection of the Request object returns the ASP filepath. You can remove the file name by using these two lines of code:

```
strPath = Request.ServerVariables("PATH_TRANSLATED")
strPath = Left$(strPath, InStrRev(strPath, "\"))
```

Concatenating strPath with strFilename gives you the full path to the same directory as your WebClass:

```
Open strPath & strFilename For Binary Access Write As #intFileHandle
```

You can then open the recordset and select the record that has the given ID, as shown here:

```
strSQL = "SELECT * FROM Blobs WHERE ID=" & lngID
rs.CursorType = adOpenStatic
rs.Open strSQL, strConnectionString
```

The next few lines then check to make sure that the recordset has at least one record before trying to process the File column value. You can get the length of the BLOB by calling the ActualSize property:

```
If Not (rs.BOF And rs.EOF) Then
  lngFilesize = rs("File").ActualSize
  lngChunkCount = lngFilesize \ CHUNK_SIZE
  lngRemainder = lngFilesize Mod CHUNK_SIZE
```

The GetChunk method is used to read the chunks of the column value:

```
  For i = 1 To lngChunkCount
    strChunk = rs("File").GetChunk(CHUNK_SIZE)
    Put #intFileHandle, , strChunk
  Next i

  If lngRemainder > 0 Then
    strChunk = rs("File").GetChunk(lngRemainder)
    Put #intFileHandle, , strChunk
  End If
End If
```

The rest of the code closes the recordset, sets it to nothing to release the memory it used, and then closes the file:

```
rs.Close
Set rs = Nothing
Close #intFileHandle
GetFileFromDatabase = True
Exit Function


ErrHandler:
  Response.Write Err.Description
End Function
```

File Uploading for ASP Developers

This book encourages you to use Visual Basic's compiled objects. However, file upload with ASP pages is a task that many ASP developers consider impossible. I believe some, if not many, developers who read this book are also ASP developers who are looking for a better alternative.

So far, all ASP books that mention file uploading always suggest using available components. These components range from the free Posting Acceptor that ships with Microsoft Site Server Express 3.0 and can be downloaded from Microsoft's Web site to some commercial components, such as ASPUpload from Persits Software and SA-FileUp from Software Artisans

Even though these components are great products, serious consequences arise out of not being able to do file uploading without a component. Many not so lucky individuals and companies out there don't own a Web server. They rely on service providers to provide hard disk space for their ASP application, and they use pure ASP without components. They do this not because their programmers aren't aware of the benefits of using compiled objects, but because it is very difficult to persuade service providers to allow them to install their custom components. Unless you have a considerable amount of shares in an ISP company, the ISP will not compromise the security of its server.

Because I don't think I am hardy enough to write an ASP book in order to share the following code after finishing this book, I would like to at least present what I have found while doing extensive research for this chapter: how to file upload without a component. With this code in hand, I hope ASP developers can add a file upload feature to their application.

You have to overcome two obstacles when trying to upload a file using an ASP page. First, you need to read the `SafeArray` from the page. Second, after you read and parse the raw HTTP request data, you need to write the content of the file uploaded to the server. This second obstacle normally pressures an ASP programmer into giving up.

Because it is not possible to write directly from an ASP page, I use the FileSystemObject object. But wait, didn't I say that service providers won't allow you to use objects? Yes, but they usually don't mind your using standard objects that come with IIS. They know that these objects from Microsoft are safe. The FileSystemObject object is one of these, and I haven't found a service provider yet that provides ASP and doesn't have this object.

The FileSystemObject object is instantiated directly from the Microsoft Scripting runtime DLL. The name of this file is scrrun.dll. This DLL contains functionality that is not in the native ASP objects nor in the VBScript runtime (vbscript.dll) itself. From the scripting DLL, you can instantiate objects that provide your application with extensive file manipulation capabilities.

Isn't this object only for manipulating text files? Yes, according to the official documentation. However, with the code in Listing 8-6, you can upload not only text files, but also binary files. So, enjoy.

Listing 8-6

```
<%
  server.scripttimeout = 1200        'seconds
  Const ForWriting = 2

  varTotalBytes = Request.TotalBytes
  binArray = Request.BinaryRead(varTotalBytes)

  intCount = 1
  Do Until Right(strHeader, 4) = vbCrLf & vbCrLf
    strHeader = strHeader & Chr(AscB(MidB(binArray, intCount, 1)))
    intCount = intCount + 1
    If intCount > varTotalBytes Then
      Response.Write "HTTP header error. Please try again."
      Response.End
    End If
  Loop

  intPathNameStart = InStr(strHeader, "filename=") + 10
  intFileNameEnd = InStr(intPathNameStart, strHeader, vbCrLf) - 1

  PathName = Mid(strHeader, intPathNameStart, intFileNameEnd - _
    intPathNameStart)
  Filename = Right(PathName, Len(PathName) - InStrRev(PathName, "\"))
  StrDelimiter = Left(strHeader, InStr(strHeader, vbCrLf) - 1)
```

```
Response.Write "<br>Filename:" & Filename

If intPathNameStart = intFileNameEnd Then
  Response.Write "No file uploaded."
  Response.End
End If


lngFileDataStart = Len(strHeader) + 1
lngFileDataEnd = CLng(varTotalBytes) - Len(StrDelimiter) - 6
lngFileSize = lngFileDataEnd - lngFileDataStart + 1

Set fso = Server.CreateObject("Scripting.FileSystemObject")

FilePath = Request.ServerVariables("PATH_TRANSLATED")
FilePath = Left(FilePath, InstrRev(FilePath, "\")) & Filename

Set ts = fso.CreateTextFile(FilePath, True, False)    'overwrite, ASCII

  For lngCount = lngFileDataStart To lngFileDataEnd
    ts.Write(Chr(AscB(MidB(binArray, lngCount, 1))))
  Next

  Set ts = Nothing
  Set fso = Nothing
%>
```

The uploaded file will be written to the same directory as the ASP file and will have the same file name as the uploaded file.

CHAPTER 9

Working with E-mail

THIS CHAPTER IS ABOUT SENDING AND RECEIVING E-MAIL. In it you will find sample
code that you can use to send and receive e-mails. In addition, I explain how the
e-mail system works, what an e-mail server is, what the protocols are, and which
format is used in each e-mail to guarantee that your e-mail arrives at its destination intact. This chapter begins with the relevant protocols that will help you understand the big picture of how the whole system works.

E-mail Protocols

The process of sending and receiving of e-mail is accomplished by mail servers.
The communication between two mail servers, the sending and receiving servers,
is achieved through a protocol. Currently, there are two protocols: Simple Mail
Transfer Protocol (SMTP) and X.400.

SMTP is the Internet standard for e-mail and was developed through the early
research and development efforts of the Internet. It was made a standard by the
Internet Engineering Task Force (IETF). X.400 was developed by the International
Telecommunications Union-Telecommunications Standards Sector (ITU-TSS)
and the International Organization for Standardization (ISO).

X.400, which was first specified by the ITU in 1984 and later updated in 1988,
is a very complex and robust protocol. SMTP, on the other hand, which was
defined in 1982, is a relatively simple but not so robust protocol. Even though it
lacks some of the rich features of X.400, SMTP has gained much wider acceptance
due to its simplicity and can be considered today's de facto standard. Consequently, this chapter focuses solely on SMTP. Nevertheless, it is worth mentioning
the differences between SMTP and X.400.

Briefly, SMTP has

- Simplicity

- Wide acceptance

- Public domain implementations

- Public domain user interfaces

- Lots of new, but optional, features such as MIME and delivery reports

By comparison, X.400 has

- Acceptance in the standards communities

- Commercial vendors of service

- Defined ways to transfer information other than ASCII text (but only a few applications have included it)

- Standard notifications of delivery to a user's mailbox and notification of a message being read by the user (these features are very often in software implementations)

Because X.400 stipulates a number of possible address characteristics that SMTP does not, an X.400 address can be long and cumbersome. X.400 also offers more capabilities than SMTP does. However, many of these capabilities are seldom used.

The E-mail Server

Communication is performed by mail servers, but does this mean that everyone needs a mail server to send e-mail? The answer is yes, even though the mail server does not have to reside on your own computer. There needs to be a way to transport the e-mail to the mail server. When you connect to the Internet through an Internet Service Provider (ISP), you can send and receive e-mail from your computer, even though you don't have a mail server.

The role of an e-mail server can be likened to that of a post office. With a non-electronic mail system, when you want to send a letter, you go to the nearest post office and drop your letter in a mailbox. That's all you need to do. The rest is taken care of by the postal service. When someone sends a letter to you, the letter is first delivered to your local post office before its delivered to your mailbox. Of course, the post office does not service only one person. People who live in the same area can also send letters through the same post office.

With an e-mail server, you drop your e-mail into one particular directory dedicated for delivery, and the e-mail server will do the rest to guarantee that the e-mail arrives at its destination. The e-mail server normally serves users on the same network. For example, all employees in a company usually share the same e-mail server, just as residents of the same suburb share the same post office. When someone sends you an e-mail, the e-mail arrives in the same e-mail server that you use for sending e-mails, more specifically in a directory called Drop, and so will the e-mail sent to other people who use that e-mail server.

The transportation of your e-mail from your computer to the mail server involves two other protocols, Post Office Protocol 3 (POP3) or Internet Message Access Protocol (IMAP). These protocols let the user save messages in a server mailbox and download them periodically from the server. These protocols are used because SMTP does not provide any mailbox facility or any special features beyond mail transport. For these reasons, SMTP is not a good choice for hosts situated behind highly unpredictable lines (such as modems). SMTP works best if your machine has a reliable connection to the Internet.

Users typically employ a program that uses SMTP for sending e-mail. That program must also understand either POP3 or IMAP, so that e-mail that has been received for users at their local server can be transferred to their own computers.

Most e-mail programs let you specify both an SMTP server and a POP server. On Unix-based systems, Sendmail is the most widely used SMTP server for e-mail. A commercial package, Sendmail includes a POP3 server and also comes in a version for Windows NT.

An e-mail server that understands the SMTP protocol can be called an SMTP server. SMTP, documented in RFC 821, is the Internet's standard host-to-host mail transport protocol and traditionally operates over TCP port 25. SMTP provides mechanisms for the direct transmission of electronic mails from the sending e-mail server to the receiving e-mail server when the two e-mail servers are connected to the same transport service. If the source e-mail server and the destination e-mail server are not connected to the same transport service, communication is done via one or more relay SMTP servers.

The SMTP design is based on the following model of communication: As the result of a user mail request, the sender-SMTP establishes a two-way transmission channel to a receiver-SMTP. The receiver-SMTP may be either the ultimate destination or an intermediate destination. SMTP commands are generated by the sender SMTP and sent to the receiver SMTP. In turn, SMTP replies are sent from the receiver SMTP to the sender SMTP in response to the commands.

After the transmission channel is established, the SMTP sender sends a `MAIL` command indicating the sender of the mail. If the SMTP receiver can accept mail, it responds with an OK reply. The SMTP sender then sends a `RCPT` command identifying a recipient of the mail. If the SMTP receiver can accept mail for that recipient, it responds with an OK reply; if not, it responds with a reply rejecting that recipient (but not the whole mail transaction).

The SMTP sender and SMTP receiver may negotiate several recipients. When the recipients have been negotiated, the SMTP sender sends the mail data, terminating the data with a special sequence. If the SMTP receiver successfully processes the mail data, it responds with an OK reply. These alternating dialogs are purposely lockstep, one-at-a-time.

SMTP servers come in many flavors. Some work on Windows operating systems, some reside on Unix machines, and some work with Macintosh computers. They speak the same language; therefore, they can communicate with each other.

Setting Up the Microsoft SMTP Server

To use the e-mail facility as discussed in this chapter, you need a Microsoft SMTP server. If you are using Windows NT 4.0 Server, you can install the Microsoft SMTP server from the Windows NT Option Pack 4 CD or download it from Microsoft's Web site. Note that you can't install the SMTP server on a Windows NT workstation.

If you are using Windows 2000 Server, chances are the SMTP server has already been installed because SMTP Service is part of Internet Information Server (IIS), and IIS is fully integrated into the Windows 2000 Server operating system. If you don't have the SMTP Server on your Windows 2000 Server, you'll need to run the Setup from the Add/Remove Programs application in the Control Panel to add the Windows 2000 SMTP Service components. You can find the SMTP Server as a subcomponent of IIS.

Administration of the SMTP Service is accomplished using the same tools as those used for IIS. These tools are briefly described in Chapter 1. In Windows NT 4.0 Server, the Microsoft Management Console (MMC) looks similar to Figure 9-1.

In Windows 2000 Server, the IIS snap-in looks similar to Figure 9-1 except the Internet Information Server is now called Internet Information Service, and Default SMTP Site has become Default SMTP Virtual Server.

The Setup program for the SMTP Service creates the MailRoot directory under the InetPub directory. In the MailRoot directory, Setup installs five default subdirectories, so that Microsoft SMTP Service can process messages. The directories are described in Table 9-1.

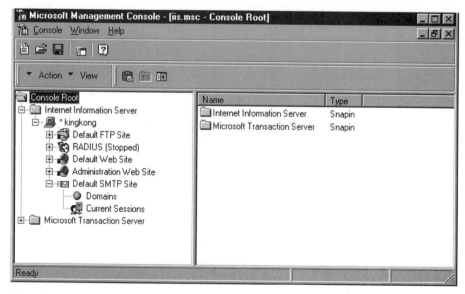

Figure 9-1. Microsoft Management Console in Windows NT 4.0

Table 9-1. The Five Default Subdirectories under MailRoot

DIRECTORY	DESCRIPTION
Badmail	Stores undeliverable messages that cannot be returned to the sender.
Drop	Receives all incoming messages for all of the domains hosted on the computer. You can assign any directory to be the Drop directory except one that has already been designated as the Pickup directory.
Pickup	Processes outgoing messages that are created as text files and are copied to the directory. As soon as a text message is copied to the Pickup directory, Microsoft SMTP Service collects it and initiates delivery.
Queue	Holds messages for delivery. If a message cannot be delivered because the connection is busy or down, the message is stored in the queue and sent again at designated intervals.
SortTemp	Stores temporary files.

Finally, to make the SMTP Server ready, set it up using its property sheets. The following steps describe the minimum settings you must configure.

First, you need to launch the Internet Service Manager MMC in Windows NT 4.0 Server or the IIS snap-in MMC in Windows 2000 Server. Second, you need to perform the following steps:

1. Right-click the Default SMTP Site node (Windows NT 4.0 Server) or the Default SMTP Virtual Server node (Windows 2000 Server), and select Properties. The Properties dialog opens.

2. Select the Delivery tab of the dialog.

3. Enter the URL of your server in the `Fully Qualified Domain Name` box, if it hasn't already been set by the IIS Setup program. This is the identity of the source of the mail, and by default, the IP address or the name of the SMTP server machine that will be used.

4. In the same dialog, you can change the settings for the `Remote Queue`, which controls how many times and at what intervals the SMTP service will attempt to send messages.

Understanding E-mail Formatting

Earlier I described how similar an e-mail server is to a post office, To send a letter, you go to the post office and drop the letter in the mailbox. To send an e-mail, all you need to do is copy a text file to the Pickup directory.

Of course, you must comply with a certain format in order for your e-mail to be delivered. This format is defined in RFC 822. According to RFC 822, messages are viewed as having an envelope and contents. The envelope contains whatever information is needed to accomplish transmission and delivery. The contents constitute the object to be delivered to the recipient. A message consists of header fields and, optionally, a body. The body is simply a sequence of lines containing ASCII characters. It is separated from the headers by a blank line (carriage return line feed characters).

A typical e-mail message might look like the following:

```
From: <Ken@labsale.com>
To: <budi@labsale.com>
Subject: First project meeting
Date: Tue, 29 Feb 2000 16:32:12 +0100

Budi, fyi: where: C-107, when: Wednesday next week
```

The first four lines are the header, analogous to an envelope in traditional mail. The last line is the body of the message. The e-mails received by your mail server are saved as files in the Drop directory. Each file has an .eml extension, which is basically a text file that you can read with a text editor.

Field Names

An e-mail message must have three mandatory fields: Date, From, and To, and the three fields must not be empty. The RFC 822 also specifies another valid message, which can consist of the Date, From, and Bcc fields, where the Bcc field cannot be empty.

The field name must consist of printable ASCII characters (that is, characters that have values between 33 and 126 except the colon). The field-body may be composed of any ASCII characters. The field names that can be present in an e-mail message are described next.

Return Path

This field is added by the final transport system that delivers the message to its recipient. The field is intended to contain definitive information about the address and route back to the message's originator. Note that the Reply-To field is added by the originator and serves to direct replies, whereas the Return-Path field is used to identify a path back to the originator. Although the syntax indicates that a route specification is optional, every attempt should be made to provide that information in this field.

Received

A copy of this field is added by each transport service that relays the message. The information in this field can be quite useful for tracing transport problems. The names of the sending and receiving hosts and time of receipt may be specified.

- The via parameter may be used to indicate what physical mechanism the message was sent over, such as Arpanet or Phonenet.

- The with parameter may be used to indicate the mail- or connection-level protocol that was used, such as the SMTP mail protocol or the X.25 transport protocol. **Note:** Several with parameters may be included to fully specify the set of protocols that was used.

- Some transport services queue mail; the internal message identifier that is assigned to the message may be noted using the id parameter.

- When the sending host uses a destination address specification that the receiving host reinterprets by expansion or transformation, the receiving host may wish to record the original specification using the for parameter. For example, when a copy of mail is sent to the member of a distribution list, this parameter may be used to record the original address that was used to specify the list.

From/Resent-From

This field contains the identity of the person(s) who sent this message. The message creation process should default this field to be a single, authenticated machine address indicating the *Agent* (person, system, or process) entering the message. If this is not done, the *Sender* field *must* be present. If the From field *is* defaulted this way, the Sender field is optional and is redundant with the From field. In all cases, addresses in the From field must be machine usable (addr-specs) and may not contain named lists (groups).

Sender/Resent-Sender

This field contains the authenticated identity of the *Agent* (person, system, or process) that sends the message. It is intended for use when the sender is not the author of the message or to indicate who among a group of authors actually sent the message. If the contents of the Sender field is completely redundant with the From field, then the Sender field need not be present, and its use is discouraged (though still legal). In particular, the Sender field *must* be present if it is *not* the same as the From Field.

The Sender mailbox specification includes a word sequence, which must correspond to a specific agent (that is, a human user or a computer program), rather than a standard address. This indicates the expectation that the field will identify the single *Agent* (person, system, or process) responsible for sending the mail and not simply include the name of a mailbox from which the mail was sent. For example, in the case of a shared login name, the name by itself would not be adequate. The local-part address unit, which refers to this agent, is expected to be a computer system term, and *not* (for example) a generalized person reference that can be used outside the network text message context. Because the critical function served by the Sender field is identification of the agent responsible for sending mail and because computer programs cannot be held accountable for their behavior, it is strongly recommended that when a computer program generates a message, the *human* who is responsible for that program be referenced as part of the Sender field mailbox specification.

Reply-To/Resent-Reply-To

This field provides a general mechanism for indicating any mailbox(es) to which responses are to be sent. Three typical uses for this feature can be distinguished. In the first case, the author(s) may not have regular machine-based mailboxes, and therefore wish(es) to indicate an alternate machine address. In the second case, an author may wish additional persons to be made aware of or be responsible for replies. A somewhat different third use may be of some help to "text message teleconferencing" groups equipped with automatic distribution services: Include the address of that service in the Reply-To field of all messages submitted to the teleconference; participants can then "reply" to conference submissions to guarantee the correct distribution of any submission of their own.

> **NOTE:** *The Return-Path field is added by the mail transport service at the time of final delivery. It is intended to identify a path back to the originator of the message. The Reply-To field is added by the message originator and is intended to direct replies.*

To/Resent-To

This field contains the identity of the primary recipients of the message.

Cc/Resent-Cc

This field contains the identity of the secondary (informational) recipients of the message.

Note that technically To and Cc are identical. Cc (carbon copy) refers to the time when documents were created on typewriters and carbon paper was used to produce duplicates.

Bcc/Resent-Bcc

This field contains the identity of additional recipients of the message. The contents of this field are not included in copies of the message sent to the primary and secondary recipients. Bcc (blind carbon copy) recipients receive the message in the same manner as To and Cc recipients, but they are not listed in the addressee list. Some implementations may show the Bcc list to all Bcc recipients, but the Bcc list should never be shown to the To or Cc recipients.

Message-ID/Resent-Message-ID

This field contains a unique identifier (the local-part address unit), which refers to *this* version of *this* message. The uniqueness of the message identifier is guaranteed by the host that generates it. This identifier is intended to be machine readable and not necessarily meaningful to humans. A message identifier pertains to exactly one instantiation of a particular message; subsequent revisions to the message should each receive a new message identifier.

In-Reply-To

The contents of this field identify previous correspondence that this message answers. Note that if message identifiers are used in this field, they must use the msg-id specification format.

References

The contents of this field identify other correspondence that this message references. Note that if message identifiers are used, they must use the msg-id specification format.

Keywords

This field contains keywords or phrases separated by commas.

Subject

This field is intended to provide a summary or indicate the nature of the message.

Comments

This field permits adding text comments onto the message without disturbing the contents of the message's body.

Encrypted

Sometimes, data encryption is used to increase the privacy of message contents. If the body of a message has been encrypted to keep its contents private, the Encrypted field can be used to note this fact and to indicate the nature of the encryption. The first <word> parameter indicates the software used to encrypt the body, and the second, optional <word> is intended to aid the recipient in selecting the proper decryption key. This code word may be viewed as an index to a table of keys held by the recipient.

> **NOTE:** *Unfortunately, headers must contain envelope as well as contents information. Consequently, it is necessary that they remain unencrypted, so that mail transport services may access them. Because names, addresses, and Subject field contents may contain sensitive information, this requirement limits total message privacy.*

Names of encryption software are registered with the Network Information Center, SRI International, Menlo Park, California.

<Extension-Field>

A limited number of common fields have been defined in RFC 822. As network mail requirements dictate, additional fields may be standardized. To provide user-defined fields with a measure of safety in name selection, such as Extension-Fields, they will never have names that begin with the string "X-".

Names of Extension-Fields are registered with the Network Information Center, SRI International, Menlo Park, California.

<User-Defined-Field>

Individual users of network mail are free to define and use additional header fields. Such fields must have names that are not already used in the current specification or in any definitions of Extension-Fields, and the overall syntax of these User-Defined-Fields must conform to this specification's rules for delimiting and folding fields. Due to the Extension-Field publishing process, the name of a User-Defined-Field may be preempted.

> **NOTE:** *The prefatory string "X-" will never be used in the names of Extension-Fields. This provides User-Defined Fields with a protected set of names.*

Date

This field specifies the day of the week, date, month, year, hour, and time zone. If included, day-of-week must be the day implied by the date specification.

The time zone may be indicated in any one of several ways. UT is Universal Time (formerly called Greenwich Mean Time [GMT]); GMT is permitted as a reference to Universal Time. The military standard uses a single character for each zone. "Z" is Universal Time. "A" indicates one hour earlier, and "M" indicates 12 hours earlier; "N" is one hour later, and "Y" is 12 hours later. The letter "J" is not used. The other remaining two forms are taken from ANSI standard X3.51-1975. One allows explicit indication of the amount of offset from UT; the other uses common 3-character strings for indicating time zones in North America.

Encoding Methods

Although the format specified in RFC 822 is sufficient for text-based messages, you sometimes need to attach binary files, such as images and sound files in e-mail messages. This cannot be handled by the e-mail format in RFC 822 because it handles only 7-bit ASCII text. To compensate this shortcoming, some encoding methods were introduced, one of which was Multipurpose Internet Mail Extensions (MIME). MIME supplements RFC 822 and allows the encapsulation of multimedia (nontext) messages inside a standard e-mail message. MIME uses Base64 encoding to convert complex files into ASCII.

MIME is a relatively new standard, and there may be a chance that some e-mail applications do not support MIME. If that is the case, you will have to use one of the other encoding methods: BinHex or uuencode. BinHex or Binary Hexadecimal is considered by some to be a Macintosh version of MIME.

Uuencode stands for Unix-to-Unix Encoding because of its Unix origin, even though now it is supported by many non-UNIX platforms as well. MIME, BinHex, and uuencode do the same job; they convert nontext files to a format that can be sent in text messages.

The following is an example of an e-mail message that includes an attachment.

```
x-sender: ken@labsale.com
x-receiver: budi@pc302923.labsale.com
Received: from mail pickup service by Labsale with Microsoft SMTPSVC;
        Mon, 6 Mar 2000 17:35:13 +1000
From: <ken@labsale.au>
To: <budi@labsale.com>
Subject: The two files
Date: Mon, 6 Mar 2000 17:27:30 +1000
X-MimeOLE: Produced By Microsoft MimeOLE V4.72.3110.3
Message-ID: <000b43117020199PC302923@labsale.com>


Budi, Please find attached two files: Test.txt and Test2.txt


begin 666 Test.djf
M6V))O;WO@;&]A9&55R70T*=&EM96]U=#TS, T*9&5F8755L=#UM=6QT:2@P*61I
M<VLH,"ER9&ES:R@R4R!A<G1I=&EO;B!B@Q*5Q0724Y.5 T*6V]P97)A=&EN9R!S
M>7-T96US70T*;75L=#&DH,"ED:7-K=R8# I<F1I<VLH," EP87))T:71I;;VXH,2E<
M5TE.3E0](E=I;;F1<=,@3E0@4V5R=F5R+"!%<;G9)E<;GIR:7-(;($$<5D
M5F5R<VEO;B!T+C P($#0IM=6QT:2@P*61I<VLH,"ER9&ES:R@R4R!A<G1I
M=&EO;;;B!B@Q*5Q0724Y.5#TB5E25B9]=W<R!.5S)W<R!;'<R5397!397=;
M161I=&EO;;;B!;697)S)S:6]N(#$@&5R<;'=)I<V4@<TH:@;W(\')I<V4@<T
M<V]D=F5R<V5R+"!F5S)2<V5R+B!&;W(\VLH-ON,R @6U%<;9U9'02I;M-3;5E<V@V
M<V]D=F5R<V5R+"!F6$=R;@-"0TVLH-ON,R @6U%<;9U9'02I; M5$<V@V
M:F5R<V5R+"!F.5D;W<R.5D;W-"0TVLH-ON,R @6U%<;9U9'02I; N:B]5
M6&5R<VEO;B!5;696W-;'297957979I9&5O("]S;W-;;, -
!"@`
`
`
end


begin 666 Test2.rtf
52&5L;RP-"1'R'G1H:7,@:T:,@;;:9@,@T*
`
end
```

Because sending an e-mail is basically composing a text file with the correct format and placing it in the Pickup directory, you need to be familiar with the format and know how to embed any attachment in your e-mail file. Also, because all incoming e-mail is saved as files in the Drop directory, you will inevitably need to access each individual file to extract all the components of an e-mail, such as the sender, subject, message, time received, and so on. This is clearly not something that you will voluntarily do. Your task will be more tedious when you need to extract the attachment, too, if any.

Writing Code for Sending and Receiving E-mail

Fortunately, components are already available that can help you with the task of sending and receiving e-mail. Some components only support the sending parts because sending e-mail is relatively easier than receiving it. Some of these components are commercially available and some good ones are free. Within the Microsoft framework, Collaboration Data Objects (CDO), Collaboration Data Objects for Windows NT Server (CDONTS), and Collaboration Data Objects for Windows 2000 are the components to use for e-mailing.

CDO was originally known as OLE Messaging, and its version 1.1 was called Active Messaging. This object library, now in version 1.2, ships with Microsoft Exchange Server 5.5 and is also available from Microsoft's Web site. CDO is backwards compatible, so that code written using Active Messaging 1.1 requires no modifications to be able to run in a CDO setup. With CDO, you can utilize Microsoft Exchange Server capabilities to provide calendaring, collaborating, and workflow functionality as well as sending and receiving e-mail.

CDONTS provides a subset of the functionality of CDO and is suitable for applications that need e-mailing capabilities but don't require calendaring and workflow facilities in the Exchange Server. CDONTS is installed as part of the SMTP Service in Windows NT 4.0 and is included as an optional component for Windows 2000 Server. CDONTS can be used to access the SMTP Service in Windows NT as well as the SMTP Service in Windows 2000 Server.

CDO for Windows 2000 ships with all versions of Windows 2000. Like CDONTS, CDO for Windows 2000 is designed to enable SMTP Messaging. However, the two are not code compatible. CDO for Windows 2000 is therefore not a direct replacement for CDONTS and both can be used on the same system concurrently, if required.

Because CDONTS is still the most widely used component, this book will base all its examples on CDONTS. The CDONTS object model is shown in Figure 9-2.

At the root of the hierarchy are two objects: NewMail and Session. The NewMail object is only used for sending e-mail. The Session object and all its child objects can be used for both sending and receiving e-mail. The complete reference on CDONTS is given in Appendix E.

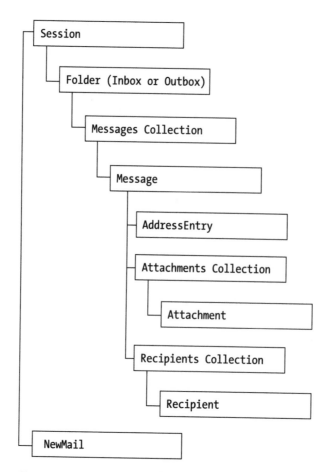

Figure 9-2. The CDONTS Object Model

CDONTS is installed automatically when you install the Microsoft SMTP Server. With CDONTS, you can only log on to the SMTP Server on the same server where CDONTS is installed because remote login is not available. This means that you have to work with a Windows NT Server when developing a program that uses CDONTS because you can only install the SMTP Server on a Windows NT Server.

Before you start a project, reference select Project → References. Then select Microsoft CDO for NTS 1.2 Library from the list of available references.

Sending E-mail

Sending e-mails with or without attachments is very easy with the NewMail object. It can be done with a few lines of code. The example in Listing 9-1 shows how to send an e-mail from budi@labsale.com to ceo@ITDirectContract.com with two attachments. The e-mail has a subject, which is "VB Programmer," and the message is "Please find attached my cover letter and resume."

Listing 9-1

```
Dim objNewMail As New CDONTS.NewMail
objNewMail.From = "budi@labsale.com"
objNewMail.To = "ceo@ITDirectContract.com"
objNewMail.Subject = "VB Programmer "
objNewMail.Body = "Please find attached my cover letter and resume."
objNewMail.AttachFile "C:\Data\MyCoverLetter.doc"
objNewMail.AttachFile "C:\Data\ MyCV.doc"
objNewMail.Send
Set objNewMail = Nothing
```

You will also learn how to send e-mail using the Message object, in the example near the end of this chapter that demonstrates how to forward an e-mail message.

Receiving E-mail

Receiving e-mail is far trickier than sending it. First, you need to know your domain and host name. That part is easy. If your domain is labsale.com, for example, and the e-mail server name is postman, then people can send e-mail to you by addressing it to *whatever*@postman.labsale.com.

If you are not sure about the naming convention, don't hesitate to ask your network administrator. The word before the @ sign can be any valid name. You can have an unlimited number of e-mail addresses, such as ceo@postman.labsale.com, director@postman.labsale.com, and so on.

All e-mail addressed with the host and domain name of postman.labsale.com will arrive in the Drop folder. In other words, with one SMTP server, you can give e-mail accounts to all the employees in the company. Once you are sure that all e-mail you receive is being placed in this folder, it's then up to you to distribute these e-mails. Each incoming e-mail message is saved as a text file. However, this file won't have a .txt extension. Instead, it will have an .eml extension. If the e-mail has attachments, the attachments will be embedded in the same file, as explained earlier in the "E-mail Formatting" section.

The file name of each e-mail message may seem arbitrary, so don't be surprised you if find files named, for example, 002264950041d20MYDEAR SERVER.eml in your Drop directory.

When you try to read messages for a given user, the messages will be sorted based on the file name. For example, let's say that User A has three messages, which are stored in the following file names:

FILE NAME	SUBJECT
002264950041d20MYDEARSERVER.eml	What about lunch
00b264950041d20MYDEARSERVER.eml	Hello
003264950041d20MYDEARSERVER.eml	New boss

The incoming e-mail will be sorted on the file name, not the date or time of arrival.

Message 1 has the subject line "What about lunch," message 2 has the subject line "New boss," and message 3 has "Hello" as its subject line. As you will see shortly, the fact that the messages are sorted on the file name can be an issue.

To read an e-mail message, you need to log in to the SMTP server and retrieve the Inbox object. The Inbox object is a type of Folder object. As its name implies, the Inbox object holds the Messages collection. Consider Listing 9-2, which illustrates the initial part of the code for retrieving all of a user's e-mail.

Listing 9-2

```
Dim objSession As New CDONTS.Session
Dim objInbox As CDONTS.Folder
Dim colMessages As CDONTS.Messages
Dim objMessage As CDONTS.Message

objSession.LogonSMTP "myMail", "budi@postman.labsale.com"
Set objInbox = objSession.Inbox
Set colMessages = objInbox.Messages
```

To log in to the SMTP server, you use the Session object's LogonSMTP method. This method requires two arguments: the display name and the e-mail address of the user who is logging in to the system. But where is the password? There is no password. Nevertheless, you should check a user's identity before allowing him or her to get to this point. As the developer, you should guarantee that no one can read other people's e-mail. Did you notice that the code in Listing 9-1 did not even require the user to log in to send an e-mail?

After logging in, you can easily obtain the Messages collection for the user whose e-mail address was passed as the second argument to the LogonSMTP method. With the Messages collection in hand, you can scroll through each element in the collection to read each individual message. As usual, a collection member can be retrieved using the index. The index in the Messages collection starts with 1. For example, the first message in the collection can be referred to as colMessages.Item(1). The second message is colMessages.Item(2), and so on. The number of elements in the Messages collection can be retrieved by reading its Count property.

Now, this is a consequence of the messages being sorted on the file name. I am using the example from the Field Names section to describe the problem.

When you try to use the message index as a unique identifier for each message, you would think that after displaying the first page of a list of e-mails (subject, time received, and so forth) the user could click an e-mail (say the first e-mail with the subject "What about lunch?") to see the details. However, if between the moment the list is displayed and the microsecond it takes for the user to click an e-mail to see the details, another e-mail arrives with the file name 000264950041d20MYDEARSERVER.eml, this new e-mail will have the index 1 on the list. The details displayed will then belong to this new e-mail. The user will be confused because the e-mail details will be different than what was expected.

That's why another way is needed to make a unique identifier. Fortunately, each message has a few properties, such as `TimeSent` and `TimeReceived`.

The code in Listing 9-3 and 9-4 is a simple mail system with which you can send e-mail with attachments and read e-mail. In addition, you can also download the attachment of the e-mail you are reading and reply and forward that e-mail to other people.

The example project has one HTML template called Login and one WebItem called Mail. The latter has 11 custom events that together support the system (see Figure 9-3). To make this work, you need to add these objects and copy Listing 9-4 to your IIS Application.

The system also uses a directory called Members under the virtual directory. Under the Members directory, you must create a directory for each user, which

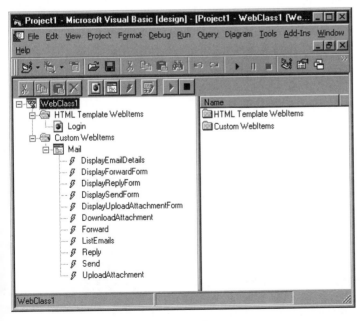

Figure 9-3. The list of WebItems and events

should be created automatically when a user registers. The Registration page is not included. These directories are intended to store temporary files when the user attaches a file in an e-mail. Each directory must also be cleared on a regular basis. This code clears each directory when the user receives a list of e-mail.

The Login HTML file is given in Listing 9-3.

Listing 9-3

```html
<html>
<head>
  <title>Login Page</title>
</head>
<body>
<form action=WebClass1.ASP?WCI=Mail&amp;WCE=ListEmails method=post>
<table>
  <tr>
    <td>Login Name:</td>
    <td><input name=LoginName></td>
  </tr>
  <tr>
    <td>Password:</td>
    <td><input name=Password type=password></td>
  </tr>
  <tr>
    <td><input type=reset value=Reset></td>
    <td><input type=submit value=Login></td>
  </tr>
</table>
</form>
</body>
</html>
```

And the code for your WebClass is given in Listing 9-4.

Listing 9-4

```vb
Option Explicit
Option Compare Text
Private m_strLoginName As String
Const DOMAIN_NAME = "Kingkong"

Private Function ValidateUser() As Boolean

  'The absence of the collection in the Request object will make
  'IIS search the object. So, if the LoginName and Password are
```

```
'present in the Form collection, these will be used
'or else, the Cookies collection's values will be used.
'If these values are not present anywhere,
'ValidateUser will return false.

Dim strLoginName As String
Dim strPassword As String

strLoginName = Request.Cookies("LoginName")
strPassword = Request.Cookies("Password")

If strLoginName = "" Then
  strLoginName = Request.Form("LoginName")
  strPassword = Request.Form("Password")
End If

If strLoginName = "budi" And strPassword = "password" Then
  Response.Cookies("LoginName") = strLoginName
  Response.Cookies("Password") = strPassword
  m_strLoginName = strLoginName
  ValidateUser = True
End If

End Function

Private Sub Mail_DisplayEmailDetails()
  If Not ValidateUser Then
    Login.WriteTemplate
    Exit Sub
  End If

  Dim objSession As New CDONTS.Session
  Dim objInbox As CDONTS.Folder
  Dim colMessages As CDONTS.Messages
  Dim objMessage As CDONTS.Message

  objSession.LogonSMTP "myMail", m_strLoginName & "@" & DOMAIN_NAME
  Set objInbox = objSession.Inbox
  Set colMessages = objInbox.Messages

  Dim lngMsgCount As Long
  lngMsgCount = colMessages.Count

  Dim strMessageID As String
  strMessageID = URLData
```

```
Dim lngCounter As Long
For lngCounter = 1 To lngMsgCount
  Set objMessage = colMessages.Item(lngCounter)
  If strMessageID = Replace(objMessage.TimeSent & _
    objMessage.TimeReceived, " ", "") Then
    Response.Write "<br><b>Date:</b> " & _
      objMessage.TimeReceived & vbCr & _
      "<br><b>From:</b> " & objMessage.Sender & vbCr & _
      "<br><b>Subject:</b> " & objMessage.Subject & vbCr & _
      "<br><TextArea rows=10 cols=70>" & _
        objMessage.Text & "</TextArea>" & vbCr

      Dim lngAttachmentCount As Long
      lngAttachmentCount = objMessage.Attachments.Count
      Dim lngAttachmentCounter As Long

      Response.Write "<br><b>Attachments</b>"
      For lngAttachmentCounter = 1 To lngAttachmentCount
        Dim objAttachment As CDONTS.Attachment
        Set objAttachment = _
          objMessage.Attachments.Item(lngAttachmentCounter)
        If Len(objAttachment.Name) > 0 Then
          URLData = strMessageID & "_" & lngAttachmentCounter
          Response.Write "<br><a href=" & _
            URLFor(Mail, "DownloadAttachment") & _
            ">" & objAttachment.Name & "</a>"
        End If
        'you must not remove the following line,
        'or your IIS will crash
        Set objAttachment = Nothing
      Next

    Exit For
  End If
Next

Set objMessage = Nothing
Set colMessages = Nothing
Set objInbox = Nothing
Set objSession = Nothing

'Button for Reply and Forward
URLData = strMessageID
```

```
  Response.Write "<br><form method=""post"" action=""" & _
    URLFor(Mail, "DisplayReplyForm") & """>" & vbCr & _
    "<input type=submit value=""REPLY"">" & vbCr & _
    "</form>"
  Response.Write " <form method=""post"" action=""" & _
    URLFor(Mail, "DisplayForwardForm") & """>" & vbCr & _
    "<input type=submit value=""FORWARD"">" & vbCr & _
    "</form>"


End Sub

Private Sub Mail_DisplayForwardForm()

  If Not ValidateUser Then
    Login.WriteTemplate
    Exit Sub
  End If

  Dim objSession As New CDONTS.Session
  Dim objInbox As CDONTS.Folder
  Dim colMessages As CDONTS.Messages
  Dim objMessage As CDONTS.Message

  objSession.LogonSMTP "myMail", m_strLoginName & "@" & DOMAIN_NAME
  Set objInbox = objSession.Inbox
  Set colMessages = objInbox.Messages

  Dim lngMsgCount As Long
  lngMsgCount = colMessages.Count

  Dim strMessageID As String
  strMessageID = URLData

  Dim lngCounter As Long
  For lngCounter = 1 To lngMsgCount
    Set objMessage = colMessages.Item(lngCounter)
    If strMessageID = Replace(objMessage.TimeSent & _
      objMessage.TimeReceived, " ", "") Then
      Response.Write "<form method=""post"" action=""" & _
        URLFor(Mail, "Forward") & _
        """>" & _
        "Forward To: <input type=""text"" Name=""Recipient"">" & _
        "<br><b>Date:</b> " & objMessage.TimeReceived & vbCr & _
```

```
                    "<br><b>From:</b> " & objMessage.Sender & vbCr & _
                    "<br><b>Subject:</b> " & objMessage.Subject & vbCr & _
                    "<br><TextArea rows=10 cols=70>" & objMessage.Text & _
                      "</TextArea>" & vbCr

                Dim lngAttachmentCount As Long
                lngAttachmentCount = objMessage.Attachments.Count
                Dim lngAttachmentCounter As Long

                Response.Write "<br><b>Attachments</b>"
                For lngAttachmentCounter = 1 To lngAttachmentCount
                  Dim objAttachment As CDONTS.Attachment
                  Set objAttachment = _
                    objMessage.Attachments.Item(lngAttachmentCounter)
                  If Len(objAttachment.Name) > 0 Then
                    URLData = strMessageID & "_" & lngAttachmentCounter
                    Response.Write "<br><a href=" & _
                      URLFor(Mail, "DownloadAttachment") & _
                      ">" & objAttachment.Name & "</a>"
                  End If
                  'you must not remove the following line, or your IIS will crash
                  Set objAttachment = Nothing
                Next

            Exit For
          End If
      Next

      Set objMessage = Nothing
      Set colMessages = Nothing
      Set objInbox = Nothing
      Set objSession = Nothing

      'Button for Send
      URLData = strMessageID
      Response.Write "<br><input type=submit value=""SEND"">" & vbCr & _
        "</form>"

End Sub


Private Sub Mail_DisplayReplyForm()

  If Not ValidateUser Then
    Login.WriteTemplate
```

```
  Exit Sub
End If

Dim objSession As New CDONTS.Session
Dim objInbox As CDONTS.Folder
Dim colMessages As CDONTS.Messages
Dim objMessage As CDONTS.Message

objSession.LogonSMTP "myMail", m_strLoginName & "@" & DOMAIN_NAME
Set objInbox = objSession.Inbox
Set colMessages = objInbox.Messages

Dim lngMsgCount As Long
lngMsgCount = colMessages.Count

Dim strMessageID As String
strMessageID = URLData

Dim lngCounter As Long
For lngCounter = 1 To lngMsgCount
  Set objMessage = colMessages.Item(lngCounter)
  If strMessageID = Replace(objMessage.TimeSent & _
    objMessage.TimeReceived, " ", "") Then
    Response.Write "<form method=""post"" action=""" & _
      URLFor(Mail, "Reply") & """>" & _
      "Reply To: <input type=""text"" Name=""Recipient"" value=""" & _
      objMessage.Sender & """>" & vbCr & _
      "<br><b>Date:</b> " & objMessage.TimeReceived & vbCr & _
      "<br><b>From:</b> " & objMessage.Sender & vbCr & _
      "<br><b>Subject:</b> " & objMessage.Subject & vbCr & _
      "<input type=""hidden"" name=""Subject"" value=""" & _
      objMessage.Subject & """>" & vbCr & _
      "<br><TextArea Name=""Body"" rows=10 cols=70>" & vbCr & _
      objMessage.Text & "</TextArea>" & vbCr

    Dim lngAttachmentCount As Long
    lngAttachmentCount = objMessage.Attachments.Count
    Dim lngAttachmentCounter As Long

    Response.Write "<br><b>Attachments</b>"
    For lngAttachmentCounter = 1 To lngAttachmentCount
      Dim objAttachment As CDONTS.Attachment
      Set objAttachment = _
        objMessage.Attachments.Item(lngAttachmentCounter)
```

```
                    If Len(objAttachment.Name) > 0 Then
                      URLData = strMessageID & "_" & lngAttachmentCounter
                      Response.Write "<br><a href=" & _
                        URLFor(Mail, "DownloadAttachment") & _
                        ">" & objAttachment.Name & "</a>"
                    End If
                    'you must not remove the following line,
                    'or your IIS will crash
                    Set objAttachment = Nothing
                  Next

              Exit For
            End If
        Next

        Set objMessage = Nothing
        Set colMessages = Nothing
        Set objInbox = Nothing
        Set objSession = Nothing

        'Button for Send
        URLData = strMessageID
        Response.Write "<br><input type=submit value=""SEND"">" & vbCr & _
          "</form>"

End Sub

Private Sub Mail_DisplaySendForm()

    If Not ValidateUser Then
      Login.WriteTemplate
      Exit Sub
    End If

    Response.Write "<html>" & vbCr & _
      "<head>" & vbCr & _
      "<script language=""JavaScript"">" & vbCr & _
      "function openWindow() {" & vbCr & _
        "window.open('" & URLFor(Mail, "DisplayUploadAttachmentForm") & _
          "','AttachFile');" & vbCr & _
      "}" & vbCr & _
      "</script>" & vbCr & _
      "</head>" & vbCr
```

```vb
  Response.Write "<body>" & vbCr & _
    "<form method=post Action=""" & _
    URLFor(Mail, "Send") & """>" & vbCr & _
    "<table>" & vbCr & _
      "<tr>" & vbCr & _
        "<td>To:</td>" & vbCr & _
        "<td><input type=text Name=""Recipient""></td>" & vbCr & _
      "</tr>" & vbCr & _
      "<tr>" & vbCr & _
        "<td>Subject:</td>" & vbCr & _
        "<td><input type=text Name=""Subject""></td>" & vbCr & _
      "</tr>" & vbCr & _
      "<tr>" & vbCr & _
        "<td>Message:</td>" & vbCr & _
        "<td><textarea Name=""Body"" rows=10 cols=40>" & _
          "</textarea></td>" & vbCr & _
      "</tr>" & vbCr & _
      "<tr>" & vbCr & _
        "<td><a href=javascript:openWindow()>" & "Attach File" & _
          "</a></td>" & vbCr & _
        "<td><input type=""submit"" value=""Send""></td>" & vbCr & _
      "</tr>" & vbCr & _
    "</table>" & vbCr & _
    "</form>" & vbCr & _
    "</body>" & vbCr & _
    "</html>"
End Sub

Private Sub Mail_DisplayUploadAttachmentForm()

  If Not ValidateUser Then
    Login.WriteTemplate
    Exit Sub
  End If

  Response.Write "<html>" & vbCr & _
    "<head>" & vbCr & _
    "<title>Attach File</title>" & vbCr & _
    "</head>" & vbCr & _
    "<body>" & vbCr & _
    "<b>Attachment(s):</b>" & vbCr

  'List all attachments in the member directory
  Dim strAttachment As String
```

```
      strAttachment = Dir$(App.Path & "\Members\" & m_strLoginName & "\*.*")
      Do Until strAttachment = ""
        Response.Write "<br>" & strAttachment
        strAttachment = Dir$
      Loop

      'Display the form
      Response.Write "<br><form enctype=""multipart/form-data""" & _
        " action=""" & _
        URLFor(Mail, "UploadAttachment") & """ method=post>" & vbCr & _
        "<br>Select file to attach" & vbCr & _
        "<br><input type=file Name=Filename>" & vbCr & _
        "<br><input type=submit value=""Attach"">" & vbCr & _
        "</form>" & vbCr & _
        "</body>" & vbCr & _
        "</html>"

End Sub

Private Sub Mail_DownloadAttachment()

  If Not ValidateUser Then
    Login.WriteTemplate
    Exit Sub
  End If

  Dim objSession As New CDONTS.Session
  Dim objInbox As CDONTS.Folder
  Dim colMessages As CDONTS.Messages
  Dim objMessage As CDONTS.Message

  objSession.LogonSMTP "myMail", _
    m_strLoginName & "@" & DOMAIN_NAME
  Set objInbox = objSession.Inbox
  Set colMessages = objInbox.Messages

  Dim lngMsgCount As Long
  lngMsgCount = colMessages.Count
  Dim strMessageID As String
  Dim intAttachmentIndex As Integer

  strMessageID = Left$(URLData, InStr(URLData, "_") - 1)
  intAttachmentIndex = Mid$(URLData, InStr(URLData, "_") + 1)
```

```vb
Dim lngCounter As Long
For lngCounter = 1 To lngMsgCount
  Set objMessage = colMessages.Item(lngCounter)
  If strMessageID = Replace(objMessage.TimeSent & _
    objMessage.TimeReceived, " ", "") Then
    Dim objAttachment As CDONTS.Attachment
    Set objAttachment = objMessage.Attachments.Item(intAttachmentIndex)
    Dim strFilename As String
    strFilename = objAttachment.Name
    objAttachment.WriteToFile App.Path & "\Members\" & _
      m_strLoginName & "\" & strFilename
    Set objAttachment = Nothing
    Response.Redirect "Members/" & m_strLoginName & "/" & strFilename
  End If
Next

Set objMessage = Nothing
Set colMessages = Nothing
Set objInbox = Nothing
Set objSession = Nothing

End Sub

Private Sub Mail_Forward()

  If Not ValidateUser Then
    Login.WriteTemplate
    Exit Sub
  End If

  Dim objSession As New CDONTS.Session
  Dim objInbox As CDONTS.Folder
  Dim colMessages As CDONTS.Messages
  Dim objMessage As CDONTS.Message

  'The session name will appear as the sender of any message sent
  objSession.LogonSMTP m_strLoginName & "@" & DOMAIN_NAME, _
    m_strLoginName & "@" & DOMAIN_NAME
  Set objInbox = objSession.Inbox
  Set colMessages = objInbox.Messages

  Dim lngMsgCount As Long
  lngMsgCount = colMessages.Count
```

```
Dim strMessageID As String
strMessageID = URLData

Dim lngCounter As Long
For lngCounter = 1 To lngMsgCount
  Set objMessage = colMessages.Item(lngCounter)
  If strMessageID = Replace(objMessage.TimeSent & _
    objMessage.TimeReceived, " ", "") Then
    Dim objOutbox As CDONTS.Folder
    Dim objNewMessage As CDONTS.Message
    Dim objRecipient As CDONTS.Recipient
    Dim objNewAttachment As CDONTS.Attachment

    Set objOutbox = objSession.Outbox
    'Create a new message in the Outbox
    Set objNewMessage = objOutbox.Messages.Add
    Set objRecipient = objNewMessage.Recipients.Add("", _
      Request.Form("Recipient"))
    objNewMessage.Subject = "Fwd: " & objMessage.Subject

    objNewMessage.MessageFormat = CdoMime
    Set objNewAttachment = objNewMessage.Attachments.Add("", _
      CdoEmbeddedMessage, objMessage)
    objNewMessage.Send

    Set objRecipient = Nothing
    Set objNewAttachment = Nothing
    Set objNewMessage = Nothing

    Exit For
  End If
Next

Response.Write "Mail Forwarded."
Set objMessage = Nothing
Set colMessages = Nothing
Set objInbox = Nothing
Set objSession = Nothing

End Sub


Private Sub Mail_ListEmails()
```

```
If Not ValidateUser Then
  Login.WriteTemplate
  Exit Sub
End If

'Clear the personal folder here
Dim strFilename As String
strFilename = Dir$(App.Path & "\Members\" & m_strLoginName & "\*.*")
Do Until strFilename = ""
  Kill (App.Path & "\Members\" & m_strLoginName & "\" & strFilename)
  strFilename = Dir$
Loop

Dim objSession As New CDONTS.Session
Dim objInbox As CDONTS.Folder
Dim colMessages As CDONTS.Messages
Dim objMessage As CDONTS.Message

objSession.LogonSMTP "myMail", m_strLoginName & "@" & DOMAIN_NAME
Set objInbox = objSession.Inbox
Set colMessages = objInbox.Messages

Dim lngMsgCount As Long
Dim lngCounter As Long
lngMsgCount = colMessages.Count

Response.Write "<table border=1><tr>" & vbCr & _
  "<td width=100><b>From</b></td>" & vbCr & _
  "<td><b>Date</b></td>" & vbCr & _
  "<td><b>Subject</b></td>" & vbCr & _
  "<td><b>Size</b></td></tr>" & vbCr
For lngCounter = 1 To lngMsgCount
  Set objMessage = colMessages.Item(lngCounter)
  Dim strMessageID As String
  strMessageID = Replace(objMessage.TimeSent & _
    objMessage.TimeReceived, " ", "")
  URLData = strMessageID
  Response.Write "<tr><td>" & objMessage.Sender & "</td>" & vbCr & _
    "<td>" & objMessage.TimeReceived & "</td>" & vbCr & _
    "<td><a href=" & URLFor(Mail, "DisplayEmailDetails") & ">" & _
    objMessage.Subject & "</a></td>" & vbCr & _
    "<td>" & objMessage.Size & vbCr
  If objMessage.Attachments.Count > 0 Then
    Response.Write "<img src=""images/Attachment.gif"">"
```

```
      End If
      Response.Write "</td></tr>"


   Next
   Response.Write "</table>"
   Set objMessage = Nothing


   'whatever happens, the next lines must be completed
   On Error Resume Next
   Set colMessages = Nothing
   Set objInbox = Nothing
   Set objSession = Nothing


   Response.Write "<br><a href=""" & _
      URLFor(Mail, "DisplaySendForm") & """>Send Email</a>"
End Sub


Private Sub Mail_Reply()

   If Not ValidateUser Then
      Login.WriteTemplate
      Exit Sub
   End If


   Dim objNewMail As New CDONTS.NewMail
   objNewMail.From = m_strLoginName & "@" & DOMAIN_NAME
   objNewMail.To = Request.Form("Recipient")
   objNewMail.Subject = Request.Form("Subject")
   objNewMail.Body = Request.Form("Body")
   objNewMail.Send
   Set objNewMail = Nothing


   Response.Write "Mail Sent."

End Sub


Private Sub Mail_Send()

   If Not ValidateUser Then
      Login.WriteTemplate
      Exit Sub
   End If


   Dim objNewMail As New CDONTS.NewMail
   objNewMail.From = m_strLoginName & "@" & DOMAIN_NAME
```

```
objNewMail.To = Request.Form("Recipient")
objNewMail.Subject = Request.Form("Subject")
objNewMail.Body = Request.Form("Body")

'Attach all files in the Member's directory
Dim strAttachment As String
strAttachment = Dir$(App.Path & "\Members\" & m_strLoginName & "\*.*")
Do Until strAttachment = ""
  objNewMail.AttachFile App.Path & "\Members\" & _
    m_strLoginName & "\" & strAttachment
  strAttachment = Dir$
Loop

objNewMail.Send
Set objNewMail = Nothing

Response.Write "Mail Sent."

End Sub

Private Sub Mail_UploadAttachment()

  If Not ValidateUser Then
    Login.WriteTemplate
    Exit Sub
  End If

  Dim lngTotalBytes As Long
  Dim bytArray() As Byte
  Dim lngFileDataStart As Long
  Dim lngFileDataEnd As Long
  Dim strHeader As String
  Dim intPathNameStart As String
  Dim strPathName As String
  Dim strFilepath As String
  Dim strFilename As String
  Dim strDelimiter As String
  Dim intFileNameStart As Integer
  Dim intFileNameEnd As Integer
  Dim lngCount As Long
  Dim lngFileSize As Long
  Dim intFileHandle As Integer

  On Error GoTo ErrHandler
  lngTotalBytes = Request.TotalBytes
```

```
ReDim bytArray(lngTotalBytes)
bytArray = Request.BinaryRead(CVar(lngTotalBytes))

' Parse header data of first element from byte array
Do Until Right$(strHeader, 4) = vbCrLf & vbCrLf
  strHeader = strHeader & Chr$(bytArray(lngCount))
  lngCount = lngCount + 1
  If lngCount > lngTotalBytes Then
    Response.Write "HTTP header error. Please try again."
    Exit Sub
  End If
Loop

intPathNameStart = InStr(strHeader, "filename=") + 10
intFileNameEnd = InStr(intPathNameStart, strHeader, vbCrLf) - 1

If intPathNameStart = intFileNameEnd Then
  Response.Write "No file uploaded."
  Exit Sub
End If

strPathName = Mid$(strHeader, intPathNameStart, _
  intFileNameEnd - intPathNameStart)
strFilename = Right$(strPathName, _
  Len(strPathName) - InStrRev(strPathName, "\"))
strDelimiter = Left$(strHeader, InStr(strHeader, vbCrLf) - 1)

lngFileDataStart = Len(strHeader) + 1
lngFileDataEnd = lngTotalBytes - Len(strDelimiter) - 6
lngFileSize = lngFileDataEnd - lngFileDataStart + 1

intFileHandle = FreeFile

'Cookies collection must be mentioned here or else IIS will try to
'access the Form collection,
'which is not permitted after the BinaryRead
'method is called
strFilepath = App.Path & "\Members\" & _
  Request.Cookies("LoginName") & "\" & strFilename

Open strFilepath For Binary Access Write As #intFileHandle
For lngCount = lngFileDataStart - 1 To lngFileDataEnd - 1
  Put #1, , (bytArray(lngCount))
```

```
Next
Close #intFileHandle

Mail_DisplayUploadAttachmentForm
Exit Sub

ErrHandler:
   Response.Write Err.Description
   On Error Resume Next
   Response.Write "Error uploading file"
   If Len(Dir$(strFilepath)) Then Kill strFilepath
End Sub

Private Sub WebClass_Start()

   'Display Login page
   Login.WriteTemplate

End Sub
```

Each of the functions in Listing 9-4 is explained in the following sections.

Validating Users

The system starts by displaying the Login page. All users must be validated before they can send or read their e-mail. The validation is done through the ValidateUser function. This function returns True if the user trying to enter the system is an authorized user, and returns False otherwise. The function uses cookies to pass values between pages. The cookies don't have an expiry date, therefore, they lose the values when the user closes the browser.

When the function fails to validate the user, the user is redirected to the Login page. The function can receive the login name and password from either the Cookies collection of the Request object or the Form collection of the Request object. It receives the values from the Form collection only when the function is called when the user first logs in. When the function is called from other event procedures, the function gets the login name and password from the Cookies collection.

How does the function know where it is called from? By examining the cookie called LoginName. If it is blank or if it does not exist, it means the user has just tried to log in or someone is trying to bypass the Login page. Either way, the function will try to use the Login Name and Password from the Form collection. The function is represented again in Listing 9-5 for your reading convenience.

Listing 9-5

```
Private Function ValidateUser() As Boolean

  'The absence of the collection in the Request object will make
  'IIS search the object. So, if the LoginName and Password are
  'present in the Form collection, these will be used
  'or else, the Cookies collection's values will be used.
  'If these values are not present anywhere,
  'ValidateUser will return false.

  Dim strLoginName As String
  Dim strPassword As String

  strLoginName = Request.Cookies("LoginName")
  strPassword = Request.Cookies("Password")

  If strLoginName = "" Then
    strLoginName = Request.Form("LoginName")
    strPassword = Request.Form("Password")
  End If

  If strLoginName = "budi" And strPassword = "password" Then
    Response.Cookies("LoginName") = strLoginName
    Response.Cookies("Password") = strPassword
    m_strLoginName = strLoginName
    ValidateUser = True
  End If

End Function
```

The function has hardcoded the login name and password for the sake of simplicity, as in

```
If strLoginName = "budi" And strPassword = "password" Then
```

It means that a user can only pass the validation if he types in "budi" as the login name and "password" as the password. In the actual system, however, you should use a proper lookup to the table that contains all the authorized users.

The HTML page looks like Figure 9-4 in the Web browser.

After the validation, the user is brought to the main page, the page that displays the ListEmail page.

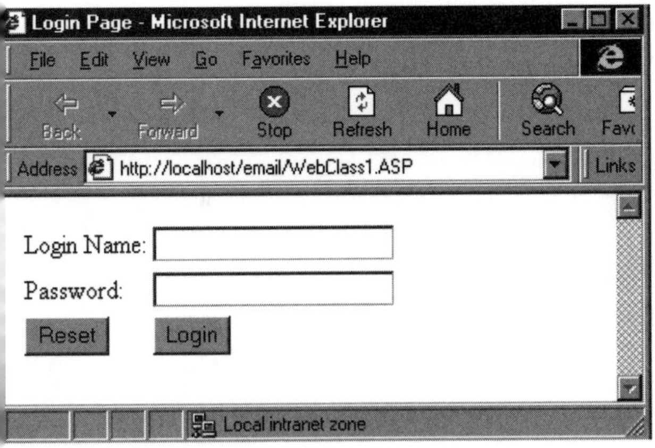

Figure 9-4. The validation page

Displaying the List of Received E-mails

This function is accomplished by the ListEmails event in the Mail custom WebItem. As with all other events, the same four lines of code shown next always appear at the top to prevent users from bypassing the Login page:

```
If Not ValidateUser Then
    Login.WriteTemplate
    Exit Sub
End If
```

The complete function is given in Listing 9-6.

Listing 9-6

```
Private Sub Mail_ListEmails()

If Not ValidateUser Then
    Login.WriteTemplate
    Exit Sub
End If

'Clear the personal folder here
Dim strFilename As String
strFilename = Dir$(App.Path & "\Members\" & m_strLoginName & "\*.*")
Do Until strFilename = ""
    Kill (App.Path & "\Members\" & m_strLoginName & "\" & strFilename)
    strFilename = Dir$
Loop
```

```
Dim objSession As New CDONTS.Session
Dim objInbox As CDONTS.Folder
Dim colMessages As CDONTS.Messages
Dim objMessage As CDONTS.Message

objSession.LogonSMTP "myMail", m_strLoginName & "@" & DOMAIN_NAME
Set objInbox = objSession.Inbox
Set colMessages = objInbox.Messages

Dim lngMsgCount As Long
Dim lngCounter As Long
lngMsgCount = colMessages.Count

Response.Write "<table border=1><tr>" & vbCr & _
  "<td width=100><b>From</b></td>" & vbCr & _
  "<td><b>Date</b></td>" & vbCr & _
  "<td><b>Subject</b></td>" & vbCr & _
  "<td><b>Size</b></td></tr>" & vbCr
For lngCounter = 1 To lngMsgCount
  Set objMessage = colMessages.Item(lngCounter)
  Dim strMessageID As String
  strMessageID = Replace(objMessage.TimeSent & _
    objMessage.TimeReceived, " ", "")
  URLData = strMessageID
  Response.Write "<tr><td>" & objMessage.Sender & "</td>" & vbCr & _
    "<td>" & objMessage.TimeReceived & "</td>" & vbCr & _
    "<td><a href=" & URLFor(Mail, "DisplayEmailDetails") & ">" & _
    objMessage.Subject & "</a></td>" & vbCr & _
    "<td>" & objMessage.Size & vbCr
  If objMessage.Attachments.Count > 0 Then
    Response.Write "<img src=""images/Attachment.gif"">"
  End If
  Response.Write "</td></tr>"

Next
Response.Write "</table>"
Set objMessage = Nothing

'whatever happens, the next lines must be completed
On Error Resume Next
Set colMessages = Nothing
Set objInbox = Nothing
Set objSession = Nothing
```

```
Response.Write "<br><a href="""" & _
    URLFor(Mail, "DisplaySendForm") & """">Send Email</a>"
End Sub
```

After user validation, the function cleans the user's personal folder by browsing through the personal folder and deleting every file there. It gets the file name in the personal folder using the `Dir$` function. The `Dir$` returns the name of the first file in the directory when a directory name is present as its argument. When there is no argument present, the `Dir$` function returns the next file name after the one returned by the previous `Dir$` function.

```
strFilename = Dir$(App.Path & "\Members\" & m_strLoginName & "\*.*")
Do Until strFilename = ""
    Kill (App.Path & "\Members\" & m_strLoginName & "\" & strFilename)
    strFilename = Dir$
Loop
```

The `Kill` method is used to delete a file.

You can find all e-mails for a given user in the `Messages` collection in the user's Inbox. Note that all messages in the Inbox are read-only. Before you can access the `Messages` collection, however, you must first login to the SMTP server:

```
Dim objSession As New CDONTS.Session
Dim objInbox As CDONTS.Folder
Dim colMessages As CDONTS.Messages
Dim objMessage As CDONTS.Message

objSession.LogonSMTP "myMail", m_strLoginName & "@" & DOMAIN_NAME
Set objInbox = objSession.Inbox
Set colMessages = objInbox.Messages
```

Note that you only need a user name to log in. No password is required. This is why you need to perform user validation before the user enters the page.

After getting the `Messages` collection in the `colMessages` variable, you can read each individual e-mail. As mentioned before, the incoming e-mails are ordered by their file names, which are not accessible from CDONTS. If you want to display e-mail in a certain order, you must do your own sorting here.

The number of messages in the collection can be obtained from the `Count` property of the `Messages` collection, as in the following line:

```
lngMsgCount = colMessages.Count
```

Knowing the number of the messages, you can loop through the Messages collection to display each individual e-mail message, as follows:

```
For lngCounter = 1 To lngMsgCount
  Set objMessage = colMessages.Item(lngCounter)
  Dim strMessageID As String
  strMessageID = Replace(objMessage.TimeSent & _
    objMessage.TimeReceived, " ", "")
  URLData = strMessageID
  Response.Write "<tr><td>" & objMessage.Sender & "</td>" & vbCr & _
    "<td>" & objMessage.TimeReceived & "</td>" & vbCr & _
    "<td><a href=" & URLFor(Mail, "DisplayEmailDetails") & ">" & _
    objMessage.Subject & "</a></td>" & vbCr & _
    "<td>" & objMessage.Size & vbCr

  If objMessage.Attachments.Count > 0 Then
    Response.Write "<img src=""images/Attachment.gif"">"
  End If
  Response.Write "</td></tr>"

Next
```

You can access an individual message by assigning the Messages collection member to the objMessage object variable. Note that you can use the combination of the TimeSent and the TimeReceived properties of the Message object as a unique identifier for each message. You store this in the strMessageID variable and copy the value to URLData so it will get passed to the next page. For each message, you display the Sender, TimeReceived, Subject, and Size properties. You return the subject in the form of a hyperlink for the user to click when he or she wants to see the details.

You can also obtain the number of attachments in each message from the Count property of the Attachments collection of the Message object. You display the image Attachment.gif in the Images directory when a message has attachments, that is, when the Count property contains a positive value.

Before leaving the function, you release the memory used by all object variables. Actually this is done automatically when the control leaves the function. However, it is good practice to do it explicitly, as shown here:

```
Set colMessages = Nothing
Set objInbox = Nothing
Set objSession = Nothing
```

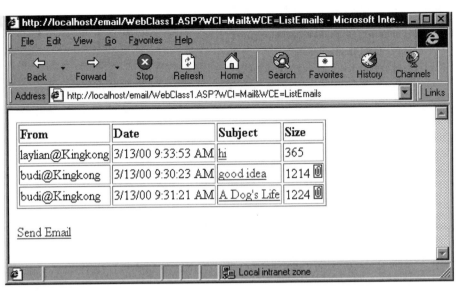

Figure 9-5. Displaying the summary of a user's incoming e-mail

Just before the function reaches the end, you return the code for displaying the link for sending e-mails:

```
Response.Write "<br><a href=""" & _
    URLFor(Mail, "DisplaySendForm") & """>Send E-mail</a>"
```

Figure 9-5 shows the page that displays the list of e-mail messages for a specific user.

Displaying the E-mail Details

The `DisplayEmailDetails` event procedure of the `Mail` custom WebItem displays the details of each e-mail selected from the previous page. Remember that when the user clicks the subject of an e-mail, this action also passes the message ID. This message ID is important to determine which message the user intends to view. The function is given in Listing 9-7.

Listing 9-7

```
Private Sub Mail_DisplayEmailDetails()
  If Not ValidateUser Then
    Login.WriteTemplate
    Exit Sub
  End If

  Dim objSession As New CDONTS.Session
  Dim objInbox As CDONTS.Folder
  Dim colMessages As CDONTS.Messages
  Dim objMessage As CDONTS.Message

  objSession.LogonSMTP "myMail", m_strLoginName & "@" & DOMAIN_NAME
  Set objInbox = objSession.Inbox
  Set colMessages = objInbox.Messages

  Dim lngMsgCount As Long
  lngMsgCount = colMessages.Count

  Dim strMessageID As String
  strMessageID = URLData

  Dim lngCounter As Long
  For lngCounter = 1 To lngMsgCount
    Set objMessage = colMessages.Item(lngCounter)
    If strMessageID = Replace(objMessage.TimeSent & _
      objMessage.TimeReceived, " ", "") Then
      Response.Write "<br><b>Date:</b> " & _
        objMessage.TimeReceived & vbCr & _
        "<br><b>From:</b> " & objMessage.Sender & vbCr & _
        "<br><b>Subject:</b> " & objMessage.Subject & vbCr & _
        "<br><TextArea rows=10 cols=70>" & objMessage.Text & _
          "</TextArea>" & vbCr

      Dim lngAttachmentCount As Long
      lngAttachmentCount = objMessage.Attachments.Count
      Dim lngAttachmentCounter As Long

      Response.Write "<br><b>Attachments</b>"
      For lngAttachmentCounter = 1 To lngAttachmentCount
        Dim objAttachment As CDONTS.Attachment
        Set objAttachment = _
          objMessage.Attachments.Item(lngAttachmentCounter)
```

```
        If Len(objAttachment.Name) > 0 Then
          URLData = strMessageID & "_" & lngAttachmentCounter
          Response.Write "<br><a href=" & _
            URLFor(Mail, "DownloadAttachment") & _
            ">" & objAttachment.Name & "</a>"
        End If
        'you must not remove the following line, or your IIS will crash
        Set objAttachment = Nothing
      Next

    Exit For
  End If
Next

Set objMessage = Nothing
Set colMessages = Nothing
Set objInbox = Nothing
Set objSession = Nothing

'Button for Reply and Forward
URLData = strMessageID
Response.Write "<br><form method=""post"" action=""" & _
  URLFor(Mail, "DisplayReplyForm") & """>" & vbCr & _
  "<input type=submit value=""REPLY"">" & vbCr & _
  "</form>"
Response.Write " <form method=""post"" action=""" & _
  URLFor(Mail, "DisplayForwardForm") & """>" & vbCr & _
  "<input type=submit value=""FORWARD"">" & vbCr & _
  "</form>"

End Sub
```

The beginning of the event procedure is very similar to ListEmails. It starts with user validation and logs in to the SMTP server using the user login name. It then gets the Messages collection in the Inbox. The code is meant for obtaining one particular message, the one that has a specific message ID. The message ID is obtained from URLData, as follows:

```
strMessageID = URLData
```

It then browses through the Messages collection to obtain the one whose message ID is the same as the one from the previous page.

```
        For lngCounter = 1 To lngMsgCount
          Set objMessage = colMessages.Item(lngCounter)
```

To find the intended message, it just compares the message ID. When the right message is found, it displays the details and lists the attachments, if any:

```
        If strMessageID = Replace(objMessage.TimeSent & _
          objMessage.TimeReceived, " ", "") Then
          Response.Write "<br><b>Date:</b> " & _
            objMessage.TimeReceived & vbCr & _
            "<br><b>From:</b> " & objMessage.Sender & vbCr & _
            "<br><b>Subject:</b> " & objMessage.Subject & vbCr & _
            "<br><TextArea rows=10 cols=70>" & objMessage.Text & _
              "</TextArea>" & vbCr

          Dim lngAttachmentCount As Long
          lngAttachmentCount = objMessage.Attachments.Count
          Dim lngAttachmentCounter As Long

          Response.Write "<br><b>Attachments</b>"
          For lngAttachmentCounter = 1 To lngAttachmentCount
            Dim objAttachment As CDONTS.Attachment
            Set objAttachment = _
              objMessage.Attachments.Item(lngAttachmentCounter)
            If Len(objAttachment.Name) > 0 Then
              URLData = strMessageID & "_" & lngAttachmentCounter
              Response.Write "<br><a href=" & _
                URLFor(Mail, "DownloadAttachment") & _
                ">" & objAttachment.Name & "</a>"
            End If
            'you must not remove the following line, or your IIS will crash
            Set objAttachment = Nothing
          Next

        Exit For
      End If
    Next
```

For each attachment, two items are important: the message ID and the attachment index. Both are forwarded to the next page in the following format:

```
MessageID_AttachmentIndex
```

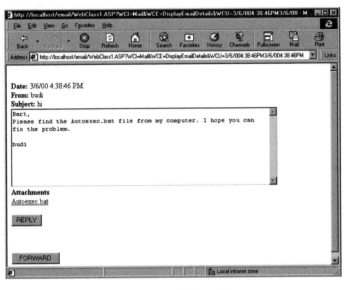

Figure 9-6. Displaying an e-mail's details

They appear as shown in the following line:

```
URLData = strMessageID & "_" & lngAttachmentCounter
```

The user can download the attachment by clicking the attachment name. This action calls the DownloadAttachment event procedure. The page that displays the e-mail details and all the attachments is shown in Figure 9-6.

Downloading Attachments

When the user clicks the name of an attachment, it passes the message ID and attachment index to the DownloadAttachment event procedure. The DownloadAttachment event procedure then does the following: searches the message, finds the attachment index, and saves the attachment to a file in the user's personal folder. Once saved as a file, downloading the attachment is a matter of redirecting the user to the file.

The event procedure is given in Listing 9-8.

Listing 9-8
```
Private Sub Mail_DownloadAttachment()

  If Not ValidateUser Then
    Login.WriteTemplate
    Exit Sub
```

```
        End If

        Dim objSession As New CDONTS.Session
        Dim objInbox As CDONTS.Folder
        Dim colMessages As CDONTS.Messages
        Dim objMessage As CDONTS.Message

        objSession.LogonSMTP "myMail", m_strLoginName & "@" & DOMAIN_NAME
        Set objInbox = objSession.Inbox
        Set colMessages = objInbox.Messages

        Dim lngMsgCount As Long
        lngMsgCount = colMessages.Count
        Dim strMessageID As String
        Dim intAttachmentIndex As Integer

        strMessageID = Left$(URLData, InStr(URLData, "_") - 1)
        intAttachmentIndex = Mid$(URLData, InStr(URLData, "_") + 1)

        Dim lngCounter As Long
        For lngCounter = 1 To lngMsgCount
          Set objMessage = colMessages.Item(lngCounter)
          If strMessageID = Replace(objMessage.TimeSent & _
            objMessage.TimeReceived, " ", "") Then
            Dim objAttachment As CDONTS.Attachment
            Set objAttachment = objMessage.Attachments.Item(intAttachmentIndex)
            Dim strFilename As String
            strFilename = objAttachment.Name
            objAttachment.WriteToFile App.Path & "\Members\" & _
              m_strLoginName & "\" & strFilename
            Set objAttachment = Nothing
            Response.Redirect "Members/" & m_strLoginName & "/" & strFilename
          End If
        Next

        Set objMessage = Nothing
        Set colMessages = Nothing
        Set objInbox = Nothing
        Set objSession = Nothing

    End Sub
```

Sending E-mail

In the page that lists the e-mail received, the user can click the Send Email hyperlink to get to the Send Email form. It is an ordinary HTML form defined in Listing 9-9.

Listing 9-9

```
Private Sub Mail_DisplaySendForm()

  If Not ValidateUser Then
    Login.WriteTemplate
    Exit Sub
  End If

  Response.Write "<html>" & vbCr & _
    "<head>" & vbCr & _
    "<script language=""JavaScript"">" & vbCr & _
    "function openWindow() {" & vbCr & _
      "window.open('" & URLFor(Mail, "DisplayUploadAttachmentForm") & _
        "','AttachFile');" & vbCr & _
    "}" & vbCr & _
    "</script>" & vbCr & _
    "</head>" & vbCr

  Response.Write "<body>" & vbCr & _
    "<form method=post Action=""" & _
    URLFor(Mail, "Send") & """>" & vbCr & _
    "<table>" & vbCr & _
      "<tr>" & vbCr & _
        "<td>To:</td>" & vbCr & _
        "<td><input type=text Name=""Recipient""></td>" & vbCr & _
      "</tr>" & vbCr & _
      "<tr>" & vbCr & _
        "<td>Subject:</td>" & vbCr & _
        "<td><input type=text Name=""Subject""></td>" & vbCr & _
      "</tr>" & vbCr & _
      "<tr>" & vbCr & _
        "<td>Message:</td>" & vbCr & _
        "<td><textarea Name=""Body"" rows=10 cols=40>" & _
        "</textarea></td>" & vbCr & _
      "</tr>" & vbCr & _
      "<tr>" & vbCr & _
        "<td><a href=javascript:openWindow()>" & "Attach File" & _
```

```
        "</a></td>" & vbCr & _
      "<td><input type=""submit"" value=""Send""></td>" & vbCr & _
    "</tr>" & vbCr & _
  "</table>" & vbCr & _
  "</form>" & vbCr & _
  "</body>" & vbCr & _
  "</html>"
End Sub
```

The form gives the user boxes for the recipient, the subject, and the body. The sender name is embedded in the page as a hidden field. Note the line that displays the hyperlink where the user can attach files:

```
<td><a href=javascript:openWindow()>Attach File</a></td>
```

When clicked, the code that is run in the Web browser calls the JavaScript openWindow function, which in the browser is parsed like this:

```
<script language="JavaScript">
function openWindow() {
  window.open('WebClass1.asp?' +
    'WCI=Mail&WCE=DisplayUploadAttachmentForm&WCU=','AttachFile');
}
</script>
```

This function opens a new browser window. The description of the code to upload an attachment is given in the next section.

After the user types in the information for the e-mail, he or she can send the e-mail by clicking the Send button, which triggers the Mail_Send event procedure. The event procedure is given in Listing 9-10.

Listing 9-10

```
Private Sub Mail_Send()

  If Not ValidateUser Then
    Login.WriteTemplate
    Exit Sub
  End If

  Dim objNewMail As New CDONTS.NewMail
  objNewMail.From = m_strLoginName & "@" & DOMAIN_NAME
  objNewMail.To = Request.Form("Recipient")
  objNewMail.Subject = Request.Form("Subject")
  objNewMail.Body = Request.Form("Body")
```

```
'Attach all files in the Member's directory
Dim strAttachment As String
strAttachment = Dir$(App.Path & "\Members\" & _
  strLoginName & "\*.*")
Do Until strAttachment = ""
  objNewMail.AttachFile App.Path & "\Members\" & _
    m_strLoginName & "\" & strAttachment
  strAttachment = Dir$
Loop

objNewMail.Send
Set objNewMail = Nothing

Response.Write "Mail Sent."
```

End Sub

The code is very simple and straightforward. Before it concludes by calling the Send method of the NewMail object, it attaches all files in the personal folder, again using the Dir$ function. Figure 9-7 shows the page for sending an e-mail.

Uploading Attachments

You can use the same code to enable users to select files from their hard disks and upload them as attachments. (File uploading is also discussed in Chapter 8.) Users can attach as many files as they like, but can upload only one file at a time.

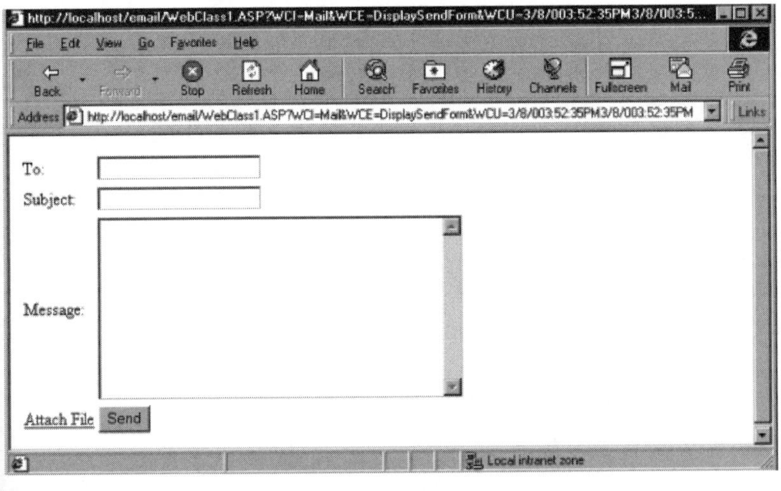

Figure 9-7. The page for sending an e-mail

The uploaded files are stored on the personal folder of each user. That way, no file gets overwritten if two users upload files with the same name at the same time. It is assumed, of course, that no two users log in to the system using the same login name.

For file upload, two event procedures can be used: Mail_DisplayUpload AttachmentForm and Mail_UploadAttachment. In addition to displaying the form for file upload, the Mail_DisplayUploadAttachmentForm event procedure also displays all files that have been uploaded. It does so by using the Dir$ function as in event procedures noted previously in this chapter. The Mail_DisplayUploadAttachment Form event procedure is given in Listing 9-11 and the Mail_UploadAttachment event procedure is given in Listing 9-12.

Listing 9-11

```
Private Sub Mail_DisplayUploadAttachmentForm()

  If Not ValidateUser Then
    Login.WriteTemplate
    Exit Sub
  End If

  Response.Write "<html>" & vbCr & _
    "<head>" & vbCr & _
    "<title>Attach File</title>" & vbCr & _
    "</head>" & vbCr & _
    "<body>" & vbCr & _
    "<b>Attachment(s):</b>" & vbCr

  'List all attachments in the member directory
  Dim strAttachment As String
  strAttachment = Dir$(App.Path & "\Members\" & m_strLoginName & "\*.*")
  Do Until strAttachment = ""
    Response.Write "<br>" & strAttachment
    strAttachment = Dir$
  Loop

  'Display the form
  Response.Write "<br><form enctype=""multipart/form-data""" & _
    " action=""" & _
    URLFor(Mail, "UploadAttachment") & """ method=post>" & vbCr & _
    "<br>Select file to attach" & vbCr & _
    "<br><input type=file Name=Filename>" & vbCr & _
    "<br><input type=submit value=""Attach"">" & vbCr & _
    "</form>" & vbCr & _
```

```
"</body>" & vbCr & _
"</html>"
```

End Sub

The `Mail_UploadAttachment` receives the attachment and writes the file to the user's personal folder. (A description of this function is given in Chapter 8.) After it does its job, the function returns control to the `Mail_DisplayUploadAttachment` Form event procedure. Figure 9-8 shows the page for uploading an attachment.

Listing 9-12

```
Private Sub Mail_UploadAttachment()

  If Not ValidateUser Then
    Login.WriteTemplate
    Exit Sub
  End If

  Dim lngTotalBytes As Long
  Dim bytArray() As Byte
  Dim lngFileDataStart As Long
  Dim lngFileDataEnd As Long
  Dim strHeader As String
  Dim intPathNameStart As String
  Dim strPathName As String
  Dim strFilepath As String
  Dim strFilename As String
  Dim strDelimiter As String
  Dim intFileNameStart As Integer
  Dim intFileNameEnd As Integer
  Dim lngCount As Long
  Dim lngFileSize As Long
  Dim intFileHandle As Integer

  On Error GoTo ErrHandler
  lngTotalBytes = Request.TotalBytes
  ReDim bytArray(lngTotalBytes)
  bytArray = Request.BinaryRead(CVar(lngTotalBytes))

  ' Parse header data of first element from byte array
  Do Until Right$(strHeader, 4) = vbCrLf & vbCrLf
    strHeader = strHeader & Chr$(bytArray(lngCount))
    lngCount = lngCount + 1
```

```
      If lngCount > lngTotalBytes Then
        Response.Write "HTTP header error. Please try again."
        Exit Sub
      End If
  Loop

  intPathNameStart = InStr(strHeader, "filename=") + 10
  intFileNameEnd = InStr(intPathNameStart, strHeader, vbCrLf) - 1

  If intPathNameStart = intFileNameEnd Then
    Response.Write "No file uploaded."
    Exit Sub
  End If

  strPathName = Mid$(strHeader, intPathNameStart, _
    intFileNameEnd - intPathNameStart)
  strFilename = Right$(strPathName, _
    Len(strPathName) - InStrRev(strPathName, "\"))
  strDelimiter = Left$(strHeader, InStr(strHeader, vbCrLf) - 1)

  lngFileDataStart = Len(strHeader) + 1
  lngFileDataEnd = lngTotalBytes - Len(strDelimiter) - 6
  lngFileSize = lngFileDataEnd - lngFileDataStart + 1

  intFileHandle = FreeFile

  'Cookies collection must be mentioned here or else IIS will try to
  'access the Form collection,
  'which is not permitted after the BinaryRead
  'method is called
  strFilepath = App.Path & "\Members\" & _
    Request.Cookies("LoginName") & "\" & strFilename

  Open strFilepath For Binary Access Write As #intFileHandle
  For lngCount = lngFileDataStart - 1 To lngFileDataEnd - 1
    Put #1, , (bytArray(lngCount))
  Next
  Close #intFileHandle

  Mail_DisplayUploadAttachmentForm
  Exit Sub
```

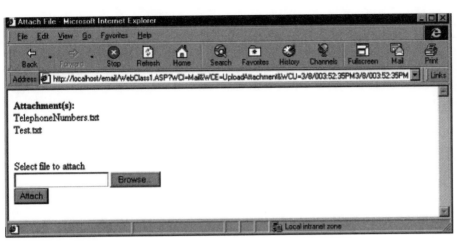

Figure 9-8. The form for uploading an attachment

```
ErrHandler:
  Response.Write Err.Description
  On Error Resume Next
  Response.Write "Error uploading file"
  If Len(Dir$(strFilepath)) Then Kill strFilepath
End Sub
```

Replying to E-mail

Replying to an e-mail message is very similar to sending an e-mail. In Reply, however, the recipient is the e-mail's sender. The subject is also the same as the incoming e-mail. In this example, the subject is prefixed by "Re:". Also, you don't
send back the attachments, if any, to the sender. The code is given in Listing 9-13.
You need two event procedures: one for displaying the form where users can type
a reply and one for sending the reply itself.

The page for replying to an e-mail is shown in Figure 9-9.

Listing 9-13

```
Private Sub Mail_DisplayReplyForm()

  If Not ValidateUser Then
    Login.WriteTemplate
    Exit Sub
  End If
```

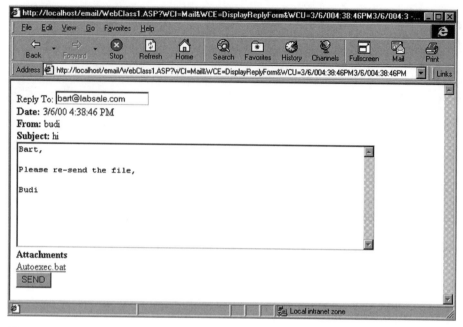

Figure 9-9. The form for replying to an e-mail

```
Dim objSession As New CDONTS.Session
Dim objInbox As CDONTS.Folder
Dim colMessages As CDONTS.Messages
Dim objMessage As CDONTS.Message

objSession.LogonSMTP "myMail", m_strLoginName & "@" & DOMAIN_NAME
Set objInbox = objSession.Inbox
Set colMessages = objInbox.Messages

Dim lngMsgCount As Long
lngMsgCount = colMessages.Count

Dim strMessageID As String
strMessageID = URLData

Dim lngCounter As Long
For lngCounter = 1 To lngMsgCount
  Set objMessage = colMessages.Item(lngCounter)
  If strMessageID = Replace(objMessage.TimeSent & _
    objMessage.TimeReceived, " ", "") Then
    Response.Write "<form method=""post"" action=""" & _
```

```vba
        URLFor(Mail, "Reply") & """>" & _
        "Reply To: <input type=""text"" Name=""Recipient"" value=""" & _
        objMessage.Sender & """>" & vbCr & _
        "<br><b>Date:</b> " & objMessage.TimeReceived & vbCr & _
        "<br><b>From:</b> " & objMessage.Sender & vbCr & _
        "<br><b>Subject:</b> " & objMessage.Subject & vbCr & _
        "<input type=""hidden"" name=""Subject"" value=""" & _
        objMessage.Subject & """>" & vbCr & _
        "<br><TextArea Name=""Body"" rows=10 cols=70>" & vbCr & _
        objMessage.Text & "</TextArea>" & vbCr

        Dim lngAttachmentCount As Long
        lngAttachmentCount = objMessage.Attachments.Count
        Dim lngAttachmentCounter As Long

        Response.Write "<br><b>Attachments</b>"
        For lngAttachmentCounter = 1 To lngAttachmentCount
          Dim objAttachment As CDONTS.Attachment
          Set objAttachment = _
            objMessage.Attachments.Item(lngAttachmentCounter)
          If Len(objAttachment.Name) > 0 Then
            URLData = strMessageID & "_" & lngAttachmentCounter
            Response.Write "<br><a href=" & _
              URLFor(Mail, "DownloadAttachment") & _
              ">" & objAttachment.Name & "</a>"
          End If
          'you must not remove the following line, or your IIS will crash
          Set objAttachment = Nothing
        Next

    Exit For
  End If
Next

Set objMessage = Nothing
Set colMessages = Nothing
Set objInbox = Nothing
Set objSession = Nothing

'Button for Send
URLData = strMessageID
Response.Write "<br><input type=submit value=""SEND"">" & vbCr & _
```

```
              "</form>"

End Sub


Private Sub Mail_Reply()

  If Not ValidateUser Then
    Login.WriteTemplate
    Exit Sub
  End If


  Dim objNewMail As New CDONTS.NewMail
  objNewMail.From = m_strLoginName & "@" & DOMAIN_NAME
  objNewMail.To = Request.Form("Recipient")
  objNewMail.Subject = Request.Form("Subject")
  objNewMail.Body = Request.Form("Body")
  objNewMail.Send
  Set objNewMail = Nothing


  Response.Write "Mail Sent."

End Sub
```

Forwarding E-mail

Forwarding e-mail is basically the same process as Reply. However, when there is
an attachment, the attachment must also be sent to the recipient. There are two
approaches to forwarding an e-mail. The first is to use the NewMail object to
write all attachments to files in the user's personal folder. When sending the
e-mail, you need to attach all e-mails in the personal folder. With the second
approach, you use the Message object and let it take care of any existing
attachments. The second method is the one used in this example.

Again, this involves two event procedures: `Mail_DisplayForwardForm` displays
the form for the user to type in the recipient and `Mail_Forward` is the event procedure that does the forwarding. Both event procedures are given in Listing 9-14.

Listing 9-14

```
Private Sub Mail_DisplayForwardForm()

  If Not ValidateUser Then
    Login.WriteTemplate
    Exit Sub
  End If
```

```
Dim objSession As New CDONTS.Session
Dim objInbox As CDONTS.Folder
Dim colMessages As CDONTS.Messages
Dim objMessage As CDONTS.Message

objSession.LogonSMTP "myMail", m_strLoginName & "@" & DOMAIN_NAME
Set objInbox = objSession.Inbox
Set colMessages = objInbox.Messages

Dim lngMsgCount As Long
lngMsgCount = colMessages.Count

Dim strMessageID As String
strMessageID = URLData

Dim lngCounter As Long
For lngCounter = 1 To lngMsgCount
  Set objMessage = colMessages.Item(lngCounter)
  If strMessageID = Replace(objMessage.TimeSent & _
    objMessage.TimeReceived, " ", "") Then
    Response.Write "<form method=""post"" action=""" & _
      URLFor(Mail, "Forward") & """>" & _
      "Forward To: <input type=""text"" Name=""Recipient"">" & _
      "<br><b>Date:</b> " & objMessage.TimeReceived & vbCr & _
      "<br><b>From:</b> " & objMessage.Sender & vbCr & _
      "<br><b>Subject:</b> " & objMessage.Subject & vbCr & _
      "<br><TextArea rows=10 cols=70>" & _
      objMessage.Text & "</TextArea>" & vbCr

    Dim lngAttachmentCount As Long
    lngAttachmentCount = objMessage.Attachments.Count
    Dim lngAttachmentCounter As Long

    Response.Write "<br><b>Attachments</b>"
    For lngAttachmentCounter = 1 To lngAttachmentCount
      Dim objAttachment As CDONTS.Attachment
      Set objAttachment = _
        objMessage.Attachments.Item(lngAttachmentCounter)
      If Len(objAttachment.Name) > 0 Then
        URLData = strMessageID & "_" & lngAttachmentCounter
        Response.Write "<br><a href=" & _
          URLFor(Mail, "DownloadAttachment") & _
          ">" & objAttachment.Name & "</a>"
```

341

```
                End If
                'you must not remove the following line, or your IIS will crash
                Set objAttachment = Nothing
            Next

        Exit For
      End If
    Next

    Set objMessage = Nothing
    Set colMessages = Nothing
    Set objInbox = Nothing
    Set objSession = Nothing

    'Button for Send
    URLData = strMessageID
    Response.Write "<br><input type=submit value=""""SEND"""">" & vbCr & _
      "</form>"

End Sub

Private Sub Mail_Forward()

  If Not ValidateUser Then
    Login.WriteTemplate
    Exit Sub
  End If

  Dim objSession As New CDONTS.Session
  Dim objInbox As CDONTS.Folder
  Dim colMessages As CDONTS.Messages
  Dim objMessage As CDONTS.Message

  'The session name will appear as the sender of any message sent
  objSession.LogonSMTP m_strLoginName & "@" & DOMAIN_NAME, _
    m_strLoginName & "@" & DOMAIN_NAME
  Set objInbox = objSession.Inbox
  Set colMessages = objInbox.Messages

  Dim lngMsgCount As Long
  lngMsgCount = colMessages.Count

  Dim strMessageID As String
```

```
strMessageID = URLData

Dim lngCounter As Long
For lngCounter = 1 To lngMsgCount
  Set objMessage = colMessages.Item(lngCounter)
  If strMessageID = Replace(objMessage.TimeSent & _
    objMessage.TimeReceived, " ", "") Then
    Dim objOutbox As CDONTS.Folder
    Dim objNewMessage As CDONTS.Message
    Dim objRecipient As CDONTS.Recipient
    Dim objNewAttachment As CDONTS.Attachment

    Set objOutbox = objSession.Outbox
    'Create a new message in the Outbox
    Set objNewMessage = objOutbox.Messages.Add
    Set objRecipient = _
      objNewMessage.Recipients.Add("", Request.Form("Recipient"))
    objNewMessage.Subject = "Fwd: " & objMessage.Subject

    objNewMessage.MessageFormat = CdoMime
    Set objNewAttachment = objNewMessage.Attachments.Add("", _
      CdoEmbeddedMessage, objMessage)
    objNewMessage.Send

    Set objRecipient = Nothing
    Set objNewAttachment = Nothing
    Set objNewMessage = Nothing

    Exit For
  End If
Next

Response.Write "Mail Forwarded."
Set objMessage = Nothing
Set colMessages = Nothing
Set objInbox = Nothing
Set objSession = Nothing

End Sub
```

Unlike the other event procedures, the SMTPLogon method uses different arguments here:

```
objSession.LogonSMTP m_strLoginName & "@" & DOMAIN_NAME, _
    m_strLoginName & "@" & DOMAIN_NAME
```

The first argument, Session, is significant when you send e-mail using the Message object. Also, note that you are using the Outbox folder and not the Inbox to compose your new message:

```
Set objOutbox = objSession.Outbox
'Create a new message in the Outbox
Set objNewMessage = objOutbox.Messages.Add
Set objRecipient = _
  objNewMessage.Recipients.Add("", Request.Form("Recipient"))
objNewMessage.Subject = "Fwd: " & objMessage.Subject

objNewMessage.MessageFormat = CdoMime
Set objNewAttachment = objNewMessage.Attachments.Add("", _
  CdoEmbeddedMessage, objMessage)
objNewMessage.Send
```

You also need to set the MessageFormat property of the Message object to CdoMime, so that when you use the Add method of the Attachments collection, to your surprise, you pass a Message object! You pass the previous Message object to the Add method. The recipient receives the whole message as an attachment. If you don't like this idea, you can always try the more difficult way of attaching the attachments after writing them to files.

CHAPTER 10

Securing Your Server

COMPUTER SECURITY IS A COMPLEX ISSUE. Examples of security breaks include unauthorized users accessing a system, base-level packet data interception, domain name hijacking, denial of service attacks, and so forth. This list grows longer as the technology evolves, and discussing every aspect of computer security could fill a book of its own.

This chapter covers only the most important issues in securing your IIS application. It first covers the security features in IIS that are fully integrated with the Windows NT and Windows 2000 Server operating systems, the types of security that are available, and how to utilize them. The discussion then proceeds to the Secure Sockets Layer (SSL) protocol, including how to obtain and install certificates to support secure transactions for your Web site.

Securing IIS on Windows NT 4.0 and Windows 2000 Servers

In Chapter 7, you can see how to password protect your Web application. This is done by creating a database table, which contains all the login names and passwords of authorized users. You will now find out how to utilize IIS security features.

Windows NT 4.0 supports New Technology File System (NTFS) 4 and FAT file system formats. Windows 2000 supports NTFS 4, NTFS 5, FAT, and FAT32. For you to fully utilize the security features in IIS, you should use NTFS 4 in Windows NT 4.0 and NTFS 5 in Windows 2000. NTFS, among other things, supports what FAT and FAT32 don't: Access Control Lists (ACLs) for directories and files. ACLs contain zero or more access control entries, each of which details a user's access rights to a specific file or directory. You will see how ACLs relate to IIS security features in the section "Anonymous Access," which is coming up.

If the operating system is currently installed on a server using the FAT or FAT32 file system, you can convert it to NTFS by running the CONVERT command. However, after you convert it to NTFS, you cannot convert it back to FAT or FAT32. For more information on the CONVERT command, look up "Convert" under Help.

With IIS 4.0 on Windows NT or IIS 5.0 on Windows 2000 Server installed on an NTFS volume, you can restrict access to any file or directory in your Web application to only those users who have been given permission. That's because NTFS always verifies that only authorized users can access a file or a directory. Different

authentication methods are available on the two operating systems. Windows NT
4.0 is examined here first, and the authentication methods in Windows 2000
Server are discussed later.

Authentication Methods in IIS 4.0 on Windows NT

IIS 4.0 has three authentication methods: Anonymous, Basic, and Windows NT
Challenge/Response. When you first create a virtual directory for your Web application, Anonymous and Windows NT Challenge/Response are selected by default.
However, you can change this default selection and apply one or more authentication methods to each virtual directory. To view the authentication method(s) in
a virtual directory, perform the following steps:

1. Right-click your virtual directory icon in Internet Service Manager, and
   then click Properties.

2. Click the Directory Security tab (see Figure 10-1).

3. In the Anonymous Access and Authentication Control frame, click the
   Edit button.

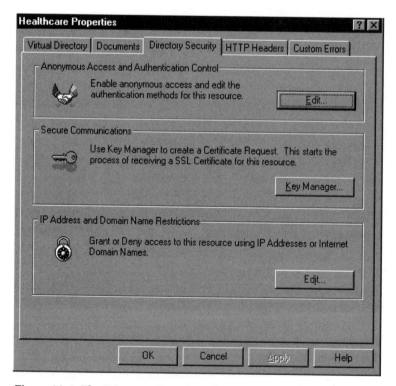

Figure 10-1. The Directory Security tab

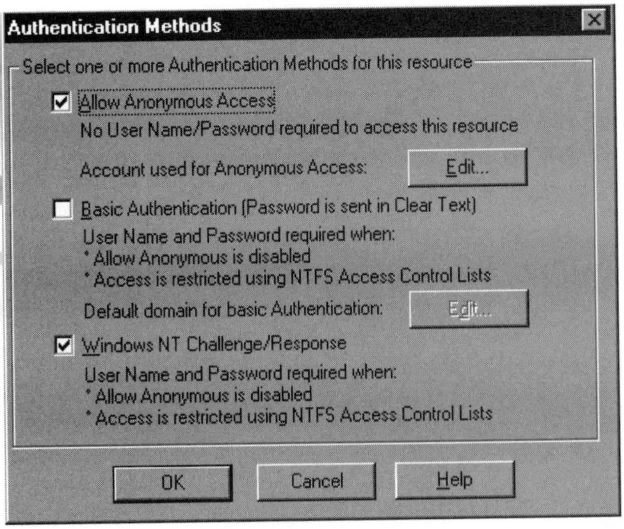

Figure 10-2. The three authentication methods

The Authentication Method dialog box appears (see Figure 10-2), showing all the authentication methods that are available. The three authentication methods are described in the following sections.

Anonymous Access

As mentioned previously, under NTFS every file and directory has a set of permissions that determines which users or groups have been granted access to specific files or directories, and which rights a user may exercise, such as read, write, or execute. You can view the ACL for a file or directory by right-clicking the file or directory in the Windows Explorer, choosing Properties, and then selecting the Permissions button on the Securities tab. The Directory or File Permissions dialog box appears.

Figure 10-3 shows the Directory Permission dialog box for viewing and editing the ACLs for a specific directory. For a file, the dialog box will read File Permissions as its title. The dialog box in Figure 10-3 displays all users and groups who have permissions to the Healthcare directory under the C:\Budi directory. It also shows the types of access each user or group has in the Type of Access list box. The access types are No Access, List, Read, Add, Add & Read, Change, Full Control, Special Directory Access, and Special File Access.

So then, how do your Internet users, whose identities are unknown to the server, have access? Internet users don't have user accounts, do they? When you install IIS, a special account is created for IIS to use. By default, all your Web applications in that server will include this special account in the users' ACLs. When

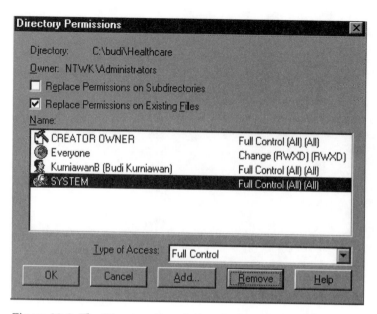

Figure 10-3. The Directory Permission dialog box for viewing and editing the ACLs for a specific directory. For a file, the dialog box will read File Permissions as its title.

an anonymous user needs access to a certain page, IIS employs this special user account to access that page on a user's behalf. You could say that IIS is impersonating the user.

The special user account for IIS is IUSR_*ComputerName*, where *ComputerName* is the name of the server. If your server name is Kingkong, then the name created for IIS is IUSR_Kingkong. Whenever someone unknown to the server requests a page through IIS, IIS will use this name.

By default, this user account has Read permission on the virtual directory. Unless the Allow Anonymous Access checkbox in the Authentication Method dialog box is cleared, IIS will first try to use this method when a user requests a page in the virtual directory.

IIS will try to use the password entered in the Internet Service Manager. If you change this special account's password without changing the one in the Internet Service Manager, the two passwords for the same user will be out of sync. As a result, user authentication using this method will fail. How do you prevent these passwords from being out of sync? By default, IIS keep these passwords in sync. However, you can check them from the Internet Information Manager by using the following steps:

1. From the Internet Information Manager, right-click your virtual directory, and then click Properties.

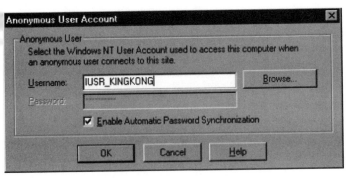

Figure 10-4. Keeping the passwords in sync

2. Click the Directory Security tab.

3. Click the Edit button. The Authentication Method dialog box appears.

4. Click the Edit button at the top. The Anonymous User Account dialog box appears.

5. Make sure that the Enable Automatic Password Synchronization checkbox is selected, as in Figure 10-4.

If you remove the Read permission of the IUSR_*ComputerName* account for a file, an anonymous user will no longer be able to access that file. Removing the Read permission is normally done when you only want specific users to have access to your Web site. If an anonymous user attempts to view a page without the required permission, IIS will try to use other methods of authentication. If neither the Basic nor Challenge/Response method is selected, IIS will send a message to the Web browser telling the user that he or she doesn't have permission to view the requested page.

Basic Authentication

Enabling the Basic and/or Windows NT Response/Challenge authentication methods is only appropriate for a corporate or members-only Web site, where it is important to validate all users accessing the site. If your Web site falls into one of these categories, you must ensure that IIS can't use the IUSR_*ComputerName* account to access the restricted files anonymously. You should remove the Everyone group and the IUSR_*ComputerName* from the access list.

The Basic Authentication method is a widely used, industry-standard method. When you use Basic Authentication, the user name and password that the user types in are sent to the Web server in Base64 encoded form. It is somewhat like sending the user name and password in plain text.

The Basic Authentication method transmits passwords over the network without data encryption. Someone attempting to attack your system security could use a protocol analyzer to examine user passwords during the authentication process. Therefore, Basic Authentication is *not* a very secure method for transmitting user names and passwords. The user name and password are Base64 encoded, which can be decoded easily even by novice hackers, although they still need to access your network and use a TCP/IP packet sniffer to intercept network packets.

The user name and password that the user types into the browser, which get sent to IIS, are used by IIS to execute a "Log on locally" command to the IIS machine. Because IIS then has the login name and password of that user, it can use them to access the requested resource.

Despite its lack of encryption, Basic Authentication should be used in one particular instance: when you need to authenticate users using a browser other than Internet Explorer. For example, Netscape Navigator understands only the Basic Authentication method because this method is the industry standard. If you have Challenge/Response and Basic Authentication selected, Internet Explorer always uses Windows NT Challenge/Response, and Navigator always chooses Basic Authentication. If you have sensitive data, this is a serious security concern.

Windows NT Challenge/Response

Windows NT Challenge/Response is a very secure way to determine who is making a request. The process flow of Challenge/Response is mandatory knowledge for anyone working on IIS.

Windows NT Challenge/Response does not send a password across the network because passwords can be intercepted and deciphered. Windows NT uses a nonreversible algorithm analogous to a meat grinder. You put something in, and out comes a hash. Windows NT uses the Internet standard MD4 hashing algorithm to produce a 16-byte (128-bit) hash. It is theoretically impossible to take both the hash and the algorithm and mathematically reverse the process to determine the password. In other words, the password serves as a "private key." Only someone who has the key can generate a particular hash.

A Windows NT domain controller has a database of user hashes generated from user passwords, but doesn't store the passwords themselves. (Note that this separation of hash and passwords does *not* necessarily make the domain controller less of a target for hackers because sometimes a hash can be used as a password equivalent.)

IIS 4.0 on a Windows NT 4.0 Server will try to use Challenge/Response authentication if all the following are true:

- Allow Anonymous in the Internet Service Manager under WWW Properties is not selected. The IUSR account does not then have sufficient permissions to access the requested resource.

- Windows NT Challenge/Response is selected in the Internet Service Manager.

- The browser making the request understands Challenge/Response (currently, Internet Explorer is the only browser that supports Challenge/Response).

If both Basic and Challenge/Response authentication methods are selected, how does IIS know which authentication method to use? It is fairly simple. IIS sends an "HTTP 401 Access Denied" message back to the browser with a list of authentication methods it accepts, saying in effect: "Hey, this is an exclusive club. Before you can get in, you must first identify yourself. These are the identification methods I accept."

Internet Explorer will always attempt to use Challenge/Response, and other browsers will use Basic.

Authentication Methods in IIS 5.0 on Windows 2000 Server

If you have installed IIS 5.0 on Windows 2000 Server, you have four authentication methods to use: Anonymous, Basic, Digest, and Integrated Windows. The Anonymous and Basic methods are the same as those in IIS 4.0, which were discussed previously in this chapter.

Digest Authentication

The Digest Authentication method is a new feature in IIS 5.0 and is available only on domains with a Windows 2000 domain controller. This method operates much like Basic Authentication except that passwords are sent as hash values. A hash value is a number derived from a text message, from which it is not feasible to decipher the original text.

Digest Authentication proceeds as follows:

1. IIS sends certain information that will be used in the authentication process to the browser.

2. The browser adds this information to its user name and password plus some other information and performs hashing on it.

3. The resulting hash is sent over the network to the server along with the additional information in clear text.

4. The server adds the additional information to a plain text copy it has of the client's password and hashes all of the information.

5. The server then compares the hash value it received with the one it just produced.

6. Access is granted only if the two numbers are identical.

Because the Digest Authentication method is a new feature in HTTP 1.1, not all browsers support it. If a noncompliant browser makes a request on a server that requires this method, the server will reject the request and send an error message to the client.

Integrated Windows Authentication

The Integrated Windows Authentication method is the enhanced version of the previous Windows NT Challenge/Response Authentication method. The Integrated Windows Authentication method can use both the Kerberos v5 authentication protocol and its own challenge/response protocol. If Directory Services is installed on the server and the requesting browser is compatible with the Kerberos v5 authentication protocol, both the Kerberos v5 and the challenge/response protocol are used; otherwise only the challenge/response protocol is used.

The Kerberos v5 authentication protocol is a feature of the Windows 2000 Distributed Services architecture. In order for Kerberos v5 authentication to be successful, both the client and the server must have a trusted connection to a Key Distribution Center (KDC) and the Directory Services must be compatible. More information on this protocol can be found in Windows 2000 Help.

The Integrated Windows Authentication method works like this:

1. Unlike Basic Authentication, it does not initially prompt users for a user name and password. The current Windows user information on the client computer is used instead. You can configure Internet Explorer version 4.0 or later to initially prompt for user information if you wish.

2. If the authentication exchange initially fails to identify the user, the browser will prompt the user for a Windows user account user name and password.

3. Internet Explorer will continue to prompt the user until the user enters a valid user name and password, or it will close the prompt dialog box.

Even though this method is secure, it is only supported by Internet Explorer version 2.0 or later. Integrated Windows Authentication does not work over an HTTP Proxy connection.

Restricting Access from a Specific IP Address

With IIS 4.0 and 5.0, you can prevent certain computers, groups of computers, or entire networks from accessing your Web site. For example, if your intranet server is connected to the Internet and you don't want a particular site to be accessed by Internet users, you can configure IIS so it only grants access to users from your network. Or, if you know that a malicious person is trying to attack your Web site, you can configure IIS to deny that person access.

When this feature is enabled in IIS, IIS checks the IP address of the user's computer against the server's IP address restriction settings.

To deny access to computers, groups of computers, or domains, perform the following steps:

1. In the Internet Service Manager in IIS 4.0 or IIS snap-in in IIS 5.0, right-click a Web site, directory, or file, and select Properties to open its property sheets.

2. Select the appropriate Directory Security or File Security property sheet. Under IP Address and Domain Name Restrictions, click Edit.

3. In the IP Address and Domain Name Restrictions dialog box, select the Granted Access option. When this option is selected, you grant access to all computers and domains except those that you specifically deny access to.

4. Click Add.

5. In the Deny Access On dialog box, select Single Computer, Group of Computers, or Domain Name options.

6. You can click the DNS Lookup button to search for computers or domains by name, rather than by IP address. IIS will search on the current domain for the computer, and if found, will enter its IP address in the IP address text box.

7. Click OK to close both dialog boxes.

Note that a user accessing your Web server through a Proxy server will appear to have the IP address of the Proxy server.

To grant access to computers, groups of computers, or domains, perform the following steps:

1. In the Internet Service Manager in IIS 4.0 or IIS snap-in in IIS 5.0, right-click a Web site, directory, or file, and select Properties to open its property sheets.

2. Select the appropriate Directory Security or File Security property sheet. Under IP Address and Domain Name Restrictions, click Edit.

3. In the IP Address and Domain Name Restrictions dialog box, select the Denied Access option. When this option is selected, you deny access to all computers and domains except those that you specifically grant access to.

4. Click Add.

5. In the Grant Access On dialog box, select Single Computer, Group of Computers, or Domain Name options.

6. You can click the DNS Lookup button to search for computers or domains by name, rather than by IP address. Type in a name.

7. Click OK to close both dialog boxes.

In addition to configuring IIS, you can also prevent certain computers from accessing your Web site through your code. The REMOTE_ADDR server environment variable of the Request object's ServerVariables collection returns the IP address of the client host making the request. Using this server environment variable, you can restrict access by any computer you don't intend to allow into your system.

```
If Request.ServerVariables("REMOTE_ADDR") = "1.2.3.4" Then
   ( Reject access here
   .
   .
   .

End If
```

Using SSL for Encryption, Authentication, and Data Integrity

Now that you know how to ensure that your Web site is accessed only by authorized users, you need to be aware of another type of attack. Like telephone lines that can be tapped, information transferred from a Web browser to a server, and vice versa, can be stolen. When the information is sensitive, you will want to take measures to protect your data.

For encrypting purposes, you don't have much choice other than the Secure Sockets Layer (SSL) protocol. Originally developed by Netscape, SSL is a protocol for transmitting information securely. SSL is the only method that works with the majority of current browsers. SSL uses encryption to guarantee confidentiality and also solves authentication and data integrity issues.

Encryption

SSL encrypts information as it passes back and forth between the Web server and the browser. SSL comes with 40-bit key and 128-bit key encryptions. Of course, the more bits you use, the stronger the encryption is. However, more bits also means more work for the server and browser to encrypt and decrypt the message being passed back and forth.

To prevent the server performance from deteriorating significantly when using SSL, you should apply encryption only to files that will contain and receive sensitive data. Also, keep the files free of elements, such as images, that can be resource hungry. To ease maintenance, you should also create a special directory for these files.

Authentication

SSL also provides something very important to Internet users: authentication. Authentication protects users against any impostor who claims to be someone he or she isn't.

For example, if you go to a Web site to buy books, you might feel confident that it is safe to type in your credit card details. However, it is possible for a clever thief to create a Web site that is indistinguishable from the online bookstore's in order to steal a user's credit card information. To prevent this, you can use SSL for authentication.

Data integrity

When using SSL, whenever a message is sent, the sending and receiving computers each generate code based on the message content. If even a single character in the message content is altered en route, the receiving computer will generate different code, and then alert the recipient that the message is not legitimate. With data integrity, both parties involved in the transaction know that what they're seeing is exactly what the other party sent.

Using Asymmetric Technology for Encryption and Decryption

When encoding and decoding messages, you need an encryption algorithm and a key. The key is used in conjunction with the algorithm to convert the message into scrambled cipher text. Some techniques, such as DES, RC2, and RC5, are known as symmetric key technology because the algorithms use the same key for encrypting and decrypting the message.

Other methods, such as the one implemented in SSL, use two keys—the public key and the private key. The two keys are mathematically related, but it is not feasible to deduce one without knowing the other. The public key is made available to anyone who requires it, but the private key is kept private, known only to the party generating the key pair. If the public key is used for encryption, the private key is used for decryption, and vice versa. Encryption algorithms that use different keys for encryption and decryption are known as *asymmetric* or *public key* technology.

When an Internet user wants to purchase a product from a Web site, the communication between the Web browser and the Web server should happen over a secure channel. This process should happen automatically behind the scenes, making it transparent to the user.

The following example should give you a good idea of the process with a secure site utilizing SSL. Consider the scenario in which Ken, an Internet user, is ready to type in his credit card details to purchase a book from Amazon.com (or another bookseller on the Web). Note that this is not *exactly* what happens when using SSL, however, this should give you a general idea of how the public and private key pair works.

1. The browser Ken is using asks the Web server at Amazon for the server's public key.

2. The server sends its public key to the user. Public keys are freely available to anyone who requests them.

3. The browser uses the server's public key to encrypt the data it is about to send.

4. The data is sent across the network. Even though someone can tap the network and copy the data, that person can't read it because he does not have the server's private key.

5. The server uses its own private key to decrypt the data. The server also knows if the data received is valid because if the data is corrupt, the private key will fail to decrypt it.

Using Digital Certificates for Authentication

Note that the process I described in the previous section resolves only the confidentiality and data integrity issues. What if a malicious person hijacks Amazon's domain name, so that every browser request for http://www.amazon.com does not go to the real site, but instead goes somewhere else? Ken's sensitive data can then be obtained without Ken's knowledge or permission. This is a problem involving authentication. Ken's browser should also authenticate that the server is the one it claims to be.

The authentication issue is resolved by using *digital certificates*. Digital certificates, or just *certificates*, are documents that provide authentication of persons and entities on a network or on the Internet. Proper use of certificates makes it impossible for malicious users to intercept a message or falsify their identities. A certificate contains the following information:

- The certificate issuer's name

- The entity for whom the certificate is being issued

- The public key of the entity for whom the certificate is being issued

- Some time stamps specifying the validation date of the certificate

Certificates can only be issued by a trusted party. This trusted party, whose job is to verify the identity of any person or organization who applies for a certificate, is called a certificate authority (CA). Examples of CAs are VeriSign, Inc. (http://www.verisign.com), Thawte Consulting (http://www.thawte.com, which has now has been acquired by VeriSign), and GTE CyberTrust Solutions (http://www.cybertrust.gte.com).

An Example of Enabling Your Web Site to Use SSL

The entire process of enabling your Web site to use SSL, from generating the public key and the private key pair to using certificates in an e-commerce Web site, is explained in the following step-by-step process in systems utilizing SSL. Consider the scenario of a fictitious company called SoapOnline, which sells soaps on the Internet.

1. SoapOnline generates its own public/private key pair.

2. The public key is sent to a trusted CA.

3. The CA verifies that it is indeed SoapOnline who made the request.

4. Once satisfied that the requester is legitimate, the certificate authority uses its own private key to encrypt SoapOnline's public key, along with some other data such as an expiration date, serial number, name, and so on. This is used as a certificate. The current industry standard is a X.509 v3 certificate.

5. The CA sends the certificate back to SoapOnline.

6. SoapOnline installs the certificate on their Web server. This makes SoapOnline's encrypted public key available to all Internet users who want to purchase soaps from SoapOnline. SoapOnline is now ready for secure e-commerce.

7. When a user is ready to send the sensitive data, such as credit card details, the user's browser will request SoapOnline's public key. This process happens behind the scene, without the user noticing it.

8. SoapOnline's Web server sends its public key to the user's browser. Remember that the public key has been encrypted by the CA using the CA's private key (in Step 4). The browser can use SoapOnline's public key to encrypt the data it's about to send *only if* the browser has the CA's public key.

   Indeed, most browsers include the public keys of a number of common trusted CA's. This situation is similar to someone having a key (in this case the CA's public key) and given a keyhole (an encrypted public key claimed to be SoapOnline's). If the key and the keyhole match (if the public key can be used to decrypt SoapOnline's encrypted public key), then the keyhole is a genuine one (it is really SoapOnline). This step is important to prove the identity of SoapOnline. If the browser manages to obtain a public key after using the CA's public key, then it is indeed SoapOnline's Web site it's been communicating with, and not that of an impostor who has hijacked SoapOnline's domain name.

9. Once satisfied with the authenticity of SoapOnline, the browser uses SoapOnline's public key to encrypt the data it is about to send.

10. The data is sent across the Internet.

11. SoapOnline uses its own private key to decrypt the data.

Configuring Your Server to Use SSL

Configuring your server to use SSL involves three steps. First, you must generate a Certificate Signing Request (CSR) file and an encryption key pair file using Microsoft Key Manager. Second, apply for a server certificate at a third-party certificate authority by sending the CA the certificate request file you generate. Third, after you receive your server certificate, you must install it, again using Microsoft Key Manager.

Generating a Certificate Signing Request (CSR) File

To generate a CSR file, follow these steps:

1. Open the Internet Service Manager or IIS snap-in.

2. Right-click the Web site for which you want to request the certificate, and select Properties. The Properties dialog box appears.

3. Click the Directory Security tab.

4. Click the Key Manager icon. The Key Manager dialog box appears.

5. Click Create New Key from the Key menu. A series of dialog boxes appears. Fill in the text boxes in this series of dialog boxes. The first in the series is shown in Figure 10-5.

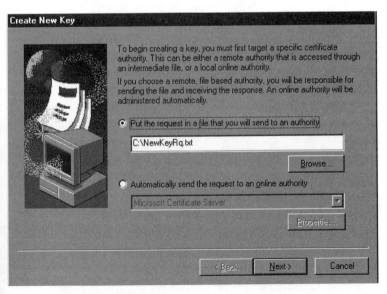

Figure 10-5. Starting the process of generating a key pair

6. Select Put The Request In A File That You Will Send To An Authority.

Subsequent dialog boxes prompt you for the following information:

- Key Name
- Country

- Password
- State/Province

- Bit Length: By default, it is 512.
- City/Locality

- Organization
- Your Name

- Organizational Unit
- Email Address

- Common Name
- Phone Number

Fill in the Key Name field with the name for the key and the Password field with the password that you will use later when installing the certificate. The remainder of the fields should be self-explanatory.

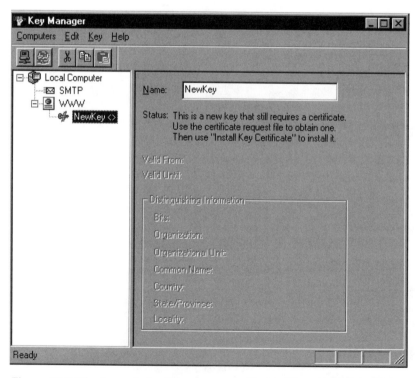

Figure 10-6. The key pair has been generated but still requires a certificate

After you supply this information, a certificate request file will be saved to your hard drive. A broken key will appear in the Key Manager dialog box, stating that a certificate request file has been generated but has not been installed, as shown in the Figure 10-6.

If you open the text file, you will find the following lines:

```
Webmaster: ceo@labsale.com
Phone: 02 90000000
Server: Microsoft Key Manager for IIS Version 4.0

Common-name: www.labsale.com
Organization Unit: Sales
Organization: Labsale
Locality: Sydney
State: NSW
Country: AU

-----BEGIN NEW CERTIFICATE REQUEST-----
MIIBCjCBtQIBADBQMQswCQYDVQQGEwJBVTEMMAoGA1UECBMDT1NXMQ8wDQYDVQQH
EwZTeWRuZXkxCjAIBgNVBAoTAWExCjAIBgNVBAsTAWExCjAIBgNVBAMTAWEwXDAN
BgkqhkiG9w0BAQEFAANLADBIAkEAhIcX93TeyS2wcioV4+WCrmD7CZ+7N9kws52t
ujXgnw+f8X9CKgp4J1SEC17t+gruMMnepNDy45I29n3UuRIH3QIDAQABoAAwDQYJ
KoZIhvcNAQEEBQADQQAZX17ciVoa8CKHpH39XqMdGtMix/DP1FG9IkUBJdVcdPv4
7Hu1WspwCfOkhDYi93YnS3K2pPbl61FsIEdDmhQu
-----END NEW CERTIFICATE REQUEST-----
```

Applying for a Certificate

The easiest way to obtain a digital certificate is go to a Web site for one of the certificate authorities and apply online (see "Using Digital Certificates for Authentication" earlier in this chapter). After your information is verified and the application is approved, you will receive an e-mail that tells you how to obtain your new server certificate.

For more secure systems, you may want to use the 128-bit SSL, rather than the 40-bit version. However, not everyone can obtain the 128-bit SSL. The United States government used to classify the 128-bit SSL as munitions, therefore products such as software utilizing the 128-bit SSL were not permitted to be exported outside the U.S., even though the restriction has been relaxed as of January 2000.

Organizations obtaining a special license from the U.S. government can now export products that use 128-bit SSL to any nongovernment entity and to any commercial government owned entity (except those that produce munitions) in any country except Afghanistan (Taliban-controlled areas), Cuba, Iran, Iraq, Libya, North Korea, Serbia (except Kosovo), Sudan, and Syria. Organizations in those countries can only use the 40-bit SSL.

If you want to get some experience with certificates before making a purchase, CAs will normally give you a free trial for a limited time. Head for one of their Web sites, fill in your identity details, and copy and paste your Certificate Signing Request (CSR) into the page provided. Usually, once you submit your CSR, the CA's Web site will generate your trial certificate straight away. The certificate appears as a string of text. Copy and paste the certificate generated by the CA as a text file. Keep in mind that this is only for testing purposes. You can install the certificate but it will expire within a given short period of time.

You are then ready to install your server certificate.

Installing Your Server Certificate

After you obtain your server certificate from the certification authority, you can install it in your server. To do so, perform the following steps:

1. Open Microsoft Key Manager.

2. Right-click the broken key icon, and choose Install Key Certificate.

3. Browse to the certificate file you received from the Certificate Authority, and double-click the file.

4. Type in the password. This is the same password you used to generate the key.

5. Then, specify the IP address and port to use with SSL. The default port for SSL is 443. It is advisable that you use the default port. When you are finished, an icon of a completed key will appear in the Key Manager.

The server certificate is valid for only a certain period of time. To continue using SSL, you must request a new server certificate before the expiration date.

Enabling SSL in Your Server

After the server certificate is installed in the server, users can request any page from your Web site using the secure protocol.

Users should then be able to access your page using the HTTPS protocol if your application is accessible through the following link:

http://www.yourdomain.com/MetaDetect.asp

then in order to use the secure channel, the link changes to

https://www.yourdomain.com/MetaDetect.asp

If you are using a port other than 443 (the default for SSL), the port number must be present in the link, such as

https://www.yourdomain.com:445/MetaDetect.asp

The application can be accessed by using the HTTP and the HTTPS protocol. To detect whether a user request is handled on the secure port, use the SERVER_PORT_SECURE server environment variable of the Request object's ServerVariables collection. The value of this variable will be the string "1" if the secure channel is used; otherwise, it will be the string "0". An example is given in Listing 10-1.

Listing 10-1

```
If Request.ServerVariables("SERVER_PORT_SECURE") = "1" Then
  ' Secure port
  .
  .

Else
  ' Insecure port
  .
  .

End If
```

In addition, if the page is requested using SSL, some server environment variables whose names are prefixed with CERT_ will contain values related to the server and client certificates.

You may force users to use SSL. However, because requesting a page through SSL takes longer to process, it is not advisable to apply SSL to all files. Secure communication should only be used when transferring sensitive data, such as credit card details.

To enable SSL in a file or a directory, you can do the following:

1. Open the Property page for a directory or a page within the Internet Service Manager, and choose the Directory Security or the File Security tab.

2. Click the Edit button under Secure Communications, and choose Require Secure Channel When Accessing This Resource. See Figure 10-7.

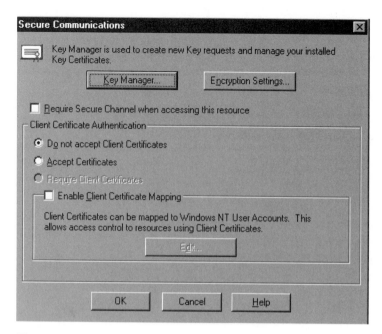

Figure 10-7. Forcing users to use SSL when requesting a page

3.   If you want to require 128-bit SSL, click the button labeled Encryption Settings, and choose Require 128-Bit Encryption.

Please note that the Secure Communications dialog box will not appear unless you have a server certificate installed.

When a page is requested using SSL, in Netscape browsers the padlock in the lower left corner of the window will be closed instead of open. Netscape users can also follow these steps to see what level of encryption is protecting their transactions with your site:

1.   Go to the Web site you want to check.

2.   Click the Security button in the Navigator's toolbar. The Security Info dialog box indicates whether the Web site uses encryption.

3.   If it does, click the Open Page Info button to display more information about the site's security features including the type of encryption used.

In Internet Explorer, a padlock icon appears in the bar at the bottom of Internet Explorer's window. Internet Explorer users can find out a Web site's encryption level by following these steps:

1. Go to the Web site you want to check.

2. Right-click on the Web site's page, and select Properties.

3. Click the Certificates button.

4. In the Fields box, select Encryption Type. The Details box shows you the level of encryption (40-bit or 128-bit).

Redirecting to a Secure Channel in the WebClass

Unlike with ASP applications, in which you normally have one page for every Web page in your site, with IIS applications you have only one ASP page. Therefore, switching to a secure channel requires a different strategy.

Where insecure communication is used, passing another hyperlink is done by using the URLFor function or, in an HTML Template WebItem, by connecting an element to another WebItem. When you are using the HTTPS protocol, however, you need to modify your code as in the following examples.

If you are using the URLFor function, pass the URL by using the following code, where the SERVER_NAME server environment variable is the server's host name, DNS alias, or IP address as it would appear in self-referencing URLs, and the URL server environment variable contains the base portion of the URL.

```
"https://" & Request.ServerVariables("SERVER_NAME") & _
   Left$(Request.ServerVariables("URL"), _
     InStrRev(Request.ServerVariables("URL"), "/")) & _
     URLFor(MyWebItem)
```

Because the URL server variable in the previous code also returns the ASP page name, which is also returned by the URLFor function, you must truncate the URL server environment variable value using the Left$ and InStrRev functions to avoid double ASP page name.

Likewise, in an HTML Template WebItem, you can use the same server environment variables. The following example demonstrates how you can pass the hyperlink in the form's ACTION attribute:

```
<form method=post action=<WC@FormAction></WC@FormAction>
```

In order for the form's ACTION attribute to receive the hyperlink, you must add the code in Listing 10-2 in the ProcessTag event procedure of the same HTML Template WebItem, as shown next:

Listing 10-2

```
Private Sub PayForm_ProcessTag(ByVal TagName As String, TagContents As String, _
SendTags As Boolean)
  If TagName = "WC@FormAction" Then
    TagContents = "https://" & Request.ServerVariables("SERVER_NAME") & _
      Left$(Request.ServerVariables("URL"), _
      InStrRev(Request.ServerVariables("URL"), "/")) & _
      URLFor(MyWebItem)
  End If
End Sub
```

CHAPTER 11

Installable Components

IN ASP APPLICATIONS, MOST SYSTEM RESOURCES are only accessible with the help of COM components that are called from ASP pages. Microsoft has provided quite a few components called installable components for use in ASP applications, so that ASP developers don't have to write their own custom components.

With IIS 5.0, these components are installed by default. If you are using IIS 4.0, however, some of these installable components come with the standard installation of IIS 4.0, and some can be found in the CD included with the IIS Resource Kit.

One of the installable components is the Database Access component, which provides access to databases using ActiveX Data Objects (ADO). This component is described in detail in Chapters 4 and 5. Another installable component is the Browser Capabilities component, which creates a BrowserType object. The BrowserType object is useful in determining the capabilities, type, and version of each browser that accesses your Web site. BrowserType is one of the WebClass's properties, and the BrowserType object is covered in Chapter 3.

The complete list of installable components is given in Table 11-1.

Although the installable components prove very useful in ASP applications, in IIS applications you have Visual Basic built-in functions at your disposal. With these built-in functions, you can write your own code to replace some of the functionality provided by the installable components in ASP applications. Therefore, depending on what you need, you may or may not want to use the installable components in your WebClass.

For instance, to write to a file in an ASP application, you use the File Access component. In IIS applications, however, you can use VB built-in functions to achieve the same goal more efficiently and faster. When accessing databases, however, the Database Access component is irreplaceable.

Another difference between using installable components in ASP applications and using them in IIS applications involves object binding. *Binding* refers to the point at which a system recognizes references to external objects in the compile-run cycle.

For instance, assume you've misspelled a declared object's property name in your code. If you've declared the object with early binding, the VB compiler can check the component's class library and catch any syntax errors before the application fully compiles and runs. If, however, you use the As Object declaration to provide late binding, the VB compiler won't be able to check the component's class library, and the compiler won't detect any syntax errors in the use of the

Table 11-1. Installable Components

COMPONENT	DESCRIPTION
Ad Rotator	Creates an AdRotator object that automatically rotates advertisements displayed on a page according to a specified schedule.
Browser Capabilities	Creates a BrowserType object that determines the capabilities, type, and version of each browser that accesses your Web site.
Content Linking	Creates a NextLink object that creates tables of contents for Web pages and links them together sequentially like pages in a book.
Content Rotator	Automates the rotation of HTML content strings on a Web page.
Counters	Creates a Counters object that can create, store, increment, and retrieve any number of individual counters.
Database Access	Provides access to databases using ADO.
File Access Component	Provides access to file input and output.
Logging Utility	Allows you to read the HTTP activity log files generated by IIS. This component is new in IIS 5.0.
MyInfo	Creates a MyInfo object that keeps track of personal information, such as the site administrator's name, address, and display choices.
Page Counter	Counts and displays the number of times a Web page has been opened.
Permission Checker	Uses the password authentication protocols provided in IIS to determine whether a Web user has been granted permissions to read a file.
Status	Creates a Status object that has properties that contain server status information. Currently, this server status is only available on Personal Web Server for Macintosh and will not be discussed in this chapter.
Tools	Creates a Tools object that provides utilities that enable you to easily add sophisticated functionality to your Web pages.

object. Instead, syntax errors with objects from the COM component will cause runtime errors in your application.

Using early binding also results in faster code because early binding speeds object references. With late binding, VB must include code in the compiled executable that will determine at runtime whether or not an object has a specific method.

When using the COM components in ASP, you have no choice but to use the CreateObject method to late-bind the object. In VB, you have the option of using the New keyword to early bind a COM object as well as the CreateObject function. Although you should always use early binding wherever possible, many COM components don't support the New keyword.

For some installable components, late binding is the only option because the application provides no Object Library to set a reference. The examples in this chapter use early binding wherever possible. With some components, however, early binding is not possible, so the examples for those components use late binding instead. This could change in the future if Microsoft rewrites these components.

The Ad Rotator Component

The Ad Rotator component creates an AdRotator object that automates the rotation of advertisement images on a Web page. Each time a user opens or reloads the Web page, the Ad Rotator component displays a new advertisement based on the information specified in a schedule file.

To use the Ad Rotator component, you must have the AdRot.dll file installed on your computer.

In an ASP application, in addition to the ASP file from which you instantiate the component and the schedule file, there is also a redirection file. Therefore, three files are involved here.

The *schedule file* is basically a text file with two sections. The first section is optional and sets parameters that apply to all advertisement images in the rotation schedule; the second section contains records for all advertisers. Each record in the second section contains the following elements, all are optional.

- The image file to be displayed as a banner.

- The advertiser's Web site address.

- The alternate text that is displayed if the browser does not support graphics, or has its graphics capabilities turned off.

- The percentage of display time that each advertisement should receive.

The first section and the second section are separated by an asterisk.

The syntax of the schedule file is

```
[REDIRECT URL]
[WIDTH numWidth]
[HEIGHT numHeight]
[BORDER numBorder]
*
adURL
adHomePageURL
Text
impressions
```

Parameters

The parameters used in the schedule file are as follows:

- URL: Specifies the path to the dynamic link library (.dll) or application (.asp) file that implements redirection. This path can be specified either fully (http://MyServer/MyDir/redirect.asp) or relative to the virtual directory (/MyDir/redirect.asp).

- numWidth: Specifies the width of the advertisement on the page in pixels. The default is 440 pixels.

- numHeight: Specifies the height of the advertisement on the page in pixels. The default is 60 pixels.

- numBorder: Specifies the thickness of the hyperlink border around the advertisement in pixels. The default is a 1 pixel border. Set this parameter to 0 for no border.

- adURL: The location of the advertisement image file.

- adHomePageURL: The location of the advertiser's home page. If the advertiser does not have a home page, put a hyphen (-) on this line to indicate that there is no link for this ad.

- Text: Alternate text that is displayed if the browser does not support graphics, or has its graphics capabilities turned off.

- impressions: A number between 0 and 4,294,967,295 that indicates the relative weight of the advertisement.

  For example, if a Rotator Schedule file contains three ads with impressions set to 2, 3, and 5, the first advertisement is displayed 20 percent of the time, the second 30 percent of the time, and the third 50 percent of the time.

The *redirection file* can be anything that can read the `Request.QueryString` collection value and redirect an HTTP request. In general, it could be a CGI script, an ISAPI component, an ASP page, a Java servlet, or a WebItem in your WebClass.

The Ad Rotator Component has one method and three properties. Descriptions of the method and the properties are provided in the following sections.

Method

The `GetAdvertisement` method gets the specifications for the next scheduled advertisement from the data file and formats it as HTML.

Properties

The properties of the Ad Rotator object are as follows:

- `Border`: Enables you to specify whether to display the advertisements with a surrounding border. If present, it specifies the size of the border around the advertisement.

- `Clickable`: Specifies whether the advertisement is a hyperlink.

- `TargetFrame`: Specifies the name of the frame in which to display the advertisement.

The next example illustrates the use of the Ad Rotator component. To use the following code, you must first create a custom WebItem called Redirect as a substitute of the redirection file. You must also create a schedule file called Schedule.txt as in Listing 11-1. The code for the WebClass is given in Listing 11-2.

Listing 11-1

```
REDIRECT WebClass1.asp?WCI=Redirect&
WIDTH 600
HEIGHT 70
BORDER 2
*
Images/Arcadia.gif
http://www.labsale.com
Go Arcadia
1
Images/Funbus.gif
http://localhost/asp.asp
A message from your local store
1
```

Listing 11-2

```
Private Sub WebClass_Start()

  Dim objAdRot As Object
  Set objAdRot = Server.CreateObject("MSWC.AdRotator")

  objAdRot.Clickable = True
  Response.Write objAdRot.GetAdvertisement("Schedule.txt")
  Set objAdRot = Nothing

End Sub


Private Sub Redirect_Respond()

  Response.Redirect Request.QueryString("?url")

End Sub
```

When you call the `GetAdvertisement` method, the string that is returned look
like this:

```
<A HREF="WebClass1.asp?WCI=Redirect&?url=http://www.labsale.com&
image=Images/Arcadia.gif">
<IMG SRC="Images/Arcadia.gif" ALT="Go Arcadia" WIDTH=600
HEIGHT=70 BORDER=1></A>
```

The code in Listing 11-2 applies only when the `Clickable` property is True,
which is true in most cases.

However, a problem exists with the code in Listing 11-2. When the user clicks
on the image, instead of going directly to the advertiser's Web site, the request
goes to your Web site. This results in an unnecessary workload for your Web site,
not to mention that it will take longer because with the `Redirect` method, the
browser has to make a new connection, this time to the correct site.

The WebClass can simplify this process. You can remove the redirection file
(in the previous example, the custom WebItem), and then send the advertiser's
URL directly. When the image is clicked, the request goes directly to the advertiser's site. The code is given in Listing 11-3.

Listing 11-3

```
Private Sub WebClass_Start()

  Dim objAdRot As Object
  Dim str As String
```

```
Dim strHyperlink As String
Dim strImage As String
Dim intStarting As Integer
Dim intEnding As Integer

Set objAdRot = Server.CreateObject("MSWC.AdRotator")
objAdRot.Clickable = True
str = objAdRot.GetAdvertisement("Schedule.txt")

intStarting = InStr(str, "url=") + 4
intEnding = InStrRev(str, "&") - 1
strHyperlink = Mid$(str, intStarting, intEnding - intStarting + 1)

intStarting = InStr(str, "<IMG")
intEnding = InStrRev(str, "</A>") - 1
strImage = Mid$(str, intStarting, intEnding - intStarting + 1)

Response.Write "<a href=""" & strHyperlink & """>" & strImage & "</A>"

Set objAdRot = Nothing

End Sub
```

The Content Linking Component

The Content Linking component creates a NextLink object that manages a list of URLs, so that you can treat the pages in your Web site like the pages in a book. You can use the Content Linking component to automatically generate and update tables of contents and navigational links to previous and subsequent Web pages. This is ideal for applications, such as online newspapers and forum message listings.

The Content Linking component references a Content Linking List file that contains the list of the linked Web pages. This list is stored on the Web server.

To use the Content Linking component, you must have the Nextlink.dll file installed in your computer.

Methods

The methods of the Content Linking object are as follows:

- GetListCount(listURL): Returns an integer value specifying the total number of Web pages listed in the Content Linking List file. The listURL parameter is the location of the Content Linking List file.

- GetListIndex(listURL): Returns an integer value specifying the index number of the current item in the Content Linking List file. The listURL parameter is the location of the Content Linking List file.

- GetNextDescription(listURL): Returns a string describing the next item in the Content Linking List file. If the current page is not found in the list file, this method returns the string description of the last page on the list. The listURL parameter is the location of the Content Linking List file.

- GetNextURL(listURL): Returns the URL of the next item in the Content Linking List file. If the current page is not found in the list file, this method returns the URL of the last page on the list. The listURL parameter is the location of the Content Linking List file.

- GetNthDescription(listURL, i): Returns a string describing the Nth item in the Content Linking List file. The listURL parameter is the location of the Content Linking List file, and the i parameter is the index number of an item in the Content Linking List file.

- GetNthURL(listURL, i): Returns the URL of the Nth item in the Content Linking List file. The listURL parameter is the location of the Content Linking List file, and the i parameter is the index number of an item in the Content Linking List file.

- GetPreviousDescription(listURL): Returns a string describing the previous item in the Content Linking List file. If the current page is not found in the list file, this method returns the string description of the first page on the list. The listURL parameter is the location of the Content Linking List file.

- GetPreviousURL(listURL): Returns the URL of the previous item in the Content Linking List file. If the current page is not found in the list file, this method returns the URL of the first page on the list. The listURL parameter is the location of the Content Linking List file.

To demonstrate the use of this component, you must have a NextLink.txt file, given in Listing 11-4, as the Content Linking List file. The example demonstration is in Listing 11-5. This example displays all the URLs and descriptions of each item in the Content Linking List file.

In this example, the NextLink.txt file must be in the same directory as your WebClass, that is, in the virtual root. You can, however, store this file in any directory under the virtual root if you make adjustments to the argument passed to the methods that refer to this file.

Listing 11-4

```
bulbul.asp?WCI=HealthCare HealthCare report
bulbul.asp?WCI=GST The introduction of the new tax system
bulbul.asp?WCI=Emergency What you should do when you see an accident
bulbul.asp?WCI=Eye New eye hospital to open
```

Listing 11-5

```
Dim Count As Integer
Dim I As Integer

Dim objNextLink As Object
Set objNextLink = Server.CreateObject("MSWC.NextLink")

Count = objNextLink.GetListCount("NextLink.txt")
I = 1
Do While (I <= Count)
  Response.Write "<li><a href=""" & _
    objNextLink.GetNthURL("nextlink.txt", I) & """>"
  Response.Write objNextLink.GetNthDescription("nextlink.txt", I) & "</a>"
  I = I + 1
Loop

Set objNextLink = Nothing
```

The Content Rotator Component

The Content Rotator component is similar to the Ad Rotator component, except instead of rotating an advertisement, the Content Rotator component creates a ContentRotator object that automatically rotates HTML content strings on a Web page. Each time a user requests the Web page, the object displays a new HTML content string based upon information that you specify in a Content Schedule file.

Because the content strings can contain HTML tags, you can display any type of content that HTML can represent: text, images, or hyperlinks. For example, you can use this component to rotate through a list of daily quotations or hyperlinks, or use it to change text and background colors each time the Web page is opened.

Before using the Content Rotator component, you must have the ContRot.dll file installed. If you are using IIS 4.0, this file can be found in the CD that comes with the IIS Resource Kit. You must also have the ContentSchedule file installed. This file contains information that is used by the ContentRotator object to manage and display the specified content.

In this file, you include any number of HTML content string entries. Each entry consists of two parts: The first part is a line that begins with double percent symbols (%%) and contains both the relative weight and any comments; the second part contains the HTML content string itself.

The Content Schedule file has the following syntax:

```
%% [#Weight] [//Comments]
ContentString
```

The following list describes each syntax component in more detail:

- Weight: This optional parameter specifies a number between 0 and 65,535, which indicates the relative weight of the HTML content string. The probability of a particular content string being displayed by the ContentRotator object can be expressed as the Weight of that content string divided by the sum of Weight values for all entries in the Content Schedule file.

  For example, if a Content Schedule file contains three content strings with respective weights of 1, 3, and 4, the Content Rotator displays the first content string one-eighth of the time, the second string three-eighths of the time, and the third string half of the time.

  A Weight of 0 causes a content entry to be ignored.

  If Weight is not specified, the default value is 1.

- Comments: This optional parameter contains comments about the entry. These comments are for development use only and are not displayed to the user. If you require more than one line of comments, you must start each additional comment line with a line delimiter (%%) followed by a comment delimiter (//).

- ContentString: This is the HTML content that the ContentRotator object displays. For example, you can present a line of text, an image, or a sound. ContentString may include one or more lines. The ContentRotator object treats characters between blocks of double percent symbols (%%) as a single HTML content string.

Methods

The methods of the ContentRotator object are as follows:

- ChooseContent(content-schedule-path): This method retrieves an HTML content string from the Content Schedule file and displays it on the current page. It retrieves a new content string each time the script is run, such as when a user opens or reloads a page. The content-schedule-path parameter specifies the location of the Content Schedule file. This parameter can be specified as either a relative or virtual path.

- GetAllContent(content-schedule-path): This method retrieves all the HTML content strings from the Content Schedule file and writes them directly to the Web page as a list with an <HR> tag after each entry. The content-schedule-path parameter specifies the location of the Content Schedule file. This parameter can be specified either as a relative or virtual path.

The examples in Listing 11-6 and 11-7 demonstrate how to use the Content Rotator component in the WebClass. The Content Schedule file name is ContentSchedule.txt and is given in Listing 11-6. The code that you need to paste into the WebClass is given in Listing 11-7.

Listing 11-6

```
%% // No value is set for Weight, the default value is 1.
Welcome to Spotty website.
%% #2
<IMG SRC="images/Key.gif">
Please click this <A HREF="MembersOnly.asp">secret link</A> to enter
```

Listing 11-7

```
    Dim objContentRotator As Object
    Set objContentRotator = Server.CreateObject("MSWC.ContentRotator")
    Response.Write objContentRotator.choosecontent("ContentSchedule.txt")
    Set objContentRotator = Nothing
```

The Counters Component

You can use the Counter component to create a Counters object that can create, store, increment, and retrieve any number of individual counters. A *counter* is a persistent value that contains an integer. Once you create the counter, it persists until you remove it.

Counters do not automatically increment on an event like a page hit. You must manually set or increment counters using the Set and Increment methods. Counters are not limited in scope. Once you create a counter, you can manipulate its value from any part of your WebClass. For example, if you increment and display a counter named MemberCount in a WebItem called Login and you increment MemberCount in another WebItem called Members, both WebItems will increment the same counter.

To use the Counters component, you must have the Counters.dll file installed on your computer. If you are using IIS 4.0, this file can be found in the CD included with the IIS Resource Kit.

All counters are stored in a single text file called counters.txt, which is located in the same directory as the counters.dll file. The Counters component provides four methods that you can use to maintain the value of each counter you create.

Methods

The methods of the Counters object are as follows:

- Get (counter_name): Returns the current value of the specified counter. If the counter has not been previously created, the counter is created and set to zero. The counter_name parameter is a string containing the name of the counter.

- Increment(counter_name): Increments the current value of the specified counter. If the counter has not been previously created, the counter is created and set to one. The counter_name parameter is a string containing the name of the counter.

- Remove(counter_name): Removes the counter from the counters.txt file. The counter_name parameter is a string containing the name of the counter.

- Set(counter_name, value): Sets the value of the counter to a specific integer. If the counter has not been previously created, the counter is created first. The counter_name parameter is a string containing the name of the counter, and the value parameter is the new integer value for the counter_name parameter.

The Counters component is very easy to use. The code in Listing 11-8 demonstrates the use of this component.

Listing 11-8

```
Dim objCounters As New COUNTERLib.CounterCtl
objCounters.Increment ("VisitorCount")
Response.Write objCounters.Get("VisitorCount")
  Set objCounters = Nothing
```

The File Access Component

The File Access component exposes methods and properties you can use to access a computer's file system. You can use this component to create a FileSystemObject object, which provides methods, properties, and collections to access the file system.

Even though you can use VB built-in functions to read and write to a file, you might find some of this component's functionality very useful. For further information on the FileSystemObject, see the VBScript reference at `http://msdn.microsoft.com/scripting/`.

The Log Component

The IIS Log component is used to create an IISLog object, which enables your applications to read from the IIS log. This component allows you to quickly create, for example, scripts in ASP pages or code in a WebClass that programmatically walks through daily log files, so that certain types of information can be extracted.

When using this component, the user accessing the IIS application must be authenticated as an Administrator or Operator on the server on which IIS 5.0 is running. If the user is no more than Anonymous, the IIS Log component will not function properly.

Methods

The methods of the Logging Utility object are as follows:

- `AtEndOfLog`: Indicates whether any more records are available in the log file. It only returns true after an attempt to read past the end of the file.

- `CloseLogFiles( IOMode )`: Causes the IIS Log component to close particular open log files. The `IOMode` parameter indicates which log file or files should be closed. It can take one of the values shown in the following table:

CONSTANT	VALUE	DESCRIPTION
ForReading	1	Closes log files that have been opened for reading.
ForWriting	2	Closes log files that have been opened for writing.
AllOpenFiles	32	Closes all open log files.

- OpenLogFile(FileName, [IOMode], [ServiceName], [ServiceInstance], [OutputLogFileFormat]): Opens a log file for reading or writing. The parameters for this method are

  - FileName: Name of the log file to open.

  - IOMode: Optional parameter indicating whether the log file is opened for reading or writing. This parameter can take one of the values shown in the following table:

CONSTANT	VALUE	DESCRIPTION
ForReading	1	Opens the specified log file for reading.
ForWriting	2	Opens the specified log file for writing.

  - ServiceName: Optional parameter indicating that the logging module should only return records matching this service.

  - ServiceInstance: Optional parameter indicating that the logging modules should only return records matching this server instance.

- ReadFilter([startDateTime], [endDateTime]): Allows you to read log records between a date and time range. The startDateTime optional parameter indicates the date and time after which log records are to be read. The endDateTime optional parameter indicates the date and time before which log records are to be read.

- ReadLogRecord: Allows you to read the next available log record.

- WriteLogRecord(IISLog): Allows you to write new log records that have been read from another IISLog object.

Properties

The properties of the LoggingUtility object are as follows:

- `BytesReceived`: Indicates the bytes received during the operation from the current log record.

- `BytesSent`: Indicates the bytes sent during the operation referred to by the current log record.

- `ClientIP`: Indicates the client's IP address for the operation referred to by the current log record.

- `Cookie`: Indicates the client's cookie.

- `CustomFields`: Indicates an array of custom headers. This property allows you to retrieve any extra HTTP headers that were included in the HTTP operation referred to by the current log record. The extra headers returned are contained within a two-dimensional array consisting of key-value pairs.

- `DateTime`: Indicates the date and time in GMT for the current log record.

- `Method`: Enables you to extract the HTTP operation type from the current log record.

- `ProtocolStatus`: Indicates the HTTP protocol status code for the HTTP operation referred to by the current log record.

- `ProtocolVersion`: Indicates the protocol version string from the current log record.

- `Referer`: Indicates the referrer URL.

- `ServerIP`: Indicates the server's IP address for the operation referred to by the current log record.

- `ServerName`: Indicates the server name.

- `ServerPort`: Indicates the server port number.

- `ServiceName`: Indicates the service name and server instance.

- `TimeTaken`: Indicates the total processing time required for the operation referred to by the current log record.

- URIQuery: Indicates any parameters passed with the request. This property enables you to extract any HTTP request parameters that were passed during the HTTP operation referred to by the current log record.

- URIStem: Indicates the target URL.

- UserAgent: Indicates the browser user agent string.

- UserName: Indicates the user's name. This property enables you to discover the username for non-anonymous clients that participated in the operation referred to by the current log record.

- Win32Status: Indicates the Win32 status code.

The MyInfo Component

The MyInfo component creates a MyInfo object that keeps track of personal information, such as the site administrator's name, address, and display choices. Typically, the administrator types this information directly into the Web server interface. However, you can set the values of the properties directly from the WebClass.

Each property of a MyInfo object returns a string. If a MyInfo property has no value set, the property returns an empty string. You can create new MyInfo properties by simply assigning a string value to them.

To use the MyInfo component, you need the MyInfo.dll file.

The values of MyInfo properties are stored in a single text file, myinfo.xml. This file is installed to the \winnt\system32 directory on Windows NT and to the root directory on Windows 95. In Windows 98, it can be found under the Windows\System\Inetsvr directory.

The example given in Listing 11-9 shows a simple usage of the MyInfo component.

Listing 11-9

```
Dim objMyInfo As New MYINFOLib.MyInfoCtl

objMyInfo.ProductID = "AW23"
objMyInfo.ProductName = "CC Candy"
objMyInfo.Manufacturer = "Love Kidz Ltd."

Set objMyInfo = Nothing
```

If you open the myInfo.xml file, the content of the file will look similar to the following:

```
<XML>
<theme></>
<ProductID>AW23</>
<ProductName>CC Candy</>
<Manufacturer>Love Kidz Ltd.</>
</XML>
```

You can read the values back using the code in Listing 11-10.

Listing 11-10

```
Dim objMyInfo As New MYINFOLib.MyInfoCtl
Dim strProductID As String
Dim strProductName As String
Dim strManufacturer As String

strProductID = objMyInfo.ProductID
strProductName = objMyInfo.ProductName
strManufacturer = objMyInfo.Manufacturer

Set objMyInfo = Nothing
```

The Page Counter Component

The Page Counter component creates a PageCounter object that counts and displays the number of times a Web page has been opened. At regular intervals, the object writes the number of hits to a text file, so that in the event of a server shutdown, the data is not lost. The Page Counter component uses an internal Central Management object to record how many times each page in the application has been opened.

When an instance of the PageCounter object is created on a page, the object retrieves the current hit count for the specified Web page from the Central Management object. The object can then be manipulated with the methods it exposes.

To use the Page Counter component, you need the Pagecnt.dll file.

Methods

The methods of the PageCounter object are as follows:

- Hits([pathInfo]): Returns a long value specifying the number of times that a specified Web page has been opened. The pathInfo optional parameter specifies the PATH_INFO of the Web page using the format /virtualdirectoryname/filename.asp. If this parameter is not specified, the hit count for the current page is displayed.

- PageHit: Increments the hit count for the current Web page.

- Reset: Sets the hit count for a specified Web page to 0.

In an IIS application, because you normally only have one ASP page that is not to be modified, you can use this component in your WebClass. However, because each procedure in your WebClass is called through the same ASP page, you can only have one page counter for the whole WebClass.

You normally increment the page counter from the Webclass_Start event procedure, that is, when someone first goes to the first page of your application. If you want to have a different page counter for each HTML template or WebItem, you have to write your own code, as in Listing 11-11.

Listing 11-11

```
Dim objPageCounter As Object
Set objPageCounter = Server.CreateObject("MSWC.PageCounter")
objPageCounter.PageHit
Response.Write "You are visitor #" & objPageCounter.Hits
Set objPageCounter = Nothing
```

The Permission Checker Component

The Permission Checker component is used to check whether a user has permission to access another page on your site. By using this component, you can first check whether the user who is currently accessing your page has the Read permission to the page whose hyperlink you want to display. It is especially useful if the other page is in another virtual directory that does not allow anonymous access.

If the user does not have permission to access a page, there is no point in displaying the hyperlink. In fact, it is advisable to *not* display a hyperlink for which a user does not have permission to avoid tempting the user to try to hack into it.

You can use this component only if your Web server is installed on an NTFS partition. For more information on the Windows NT security system, see Chapter 10.

The Permission Checker component only has one method: HasAccess.

Method

The *HasAccess*(*FilePath*) method returns a boolean value that indicates whether the Web user has access to the specified file. This method returns True if the current user has permission to read the page passed as the argument; otherwise it returns False. If the file does not exist, the PermissionChecker object returns false. The FilePath parameter is a string that specifies the path and name of the file; it can be either a physical or virtual path.

The code in Listing 11-12 displays the hyperlink to a page in another virtual directory if the current user has permission to read it.

Listing 11-12

```
Dim objPC As Object
Set objPC = Server.CreateObject("MSWC.PermissionChecker")
If objPC.HasAccess("/AnotherVirtualDirectory/restricted.html") Then
Response.Write "<a href=""/AnotherVirtualDirectory/restricted.html"">" &_
  "Restricted Area</a>"
End If

Set objPC = Nothing
```

The Tools Component

The Tools component provides helpful methods that can be used to check for the existence of a file, generate a random integer, or process an HTML form. For Personal Web Server for Macintosh, there are also methods for checking for the existence of a server plug-in and for checking whether the current user is the site owner.

Although this component is quite useful in an ASP application, the Tools component is not significant in an IIS application. The Tools component's methods can easily be replaced by more efficient functions in VB.

To use the Tools component, you need to have the Tools.dll file. If you are using IIS 4.0, this file can be obtained from the CD included with the IIS Resource Kit.

The Tools component has five methods, two of which work only on the Macintosh Personal Web Server.

Methods

The methods of the Tools object are as follows:

- FileExists (relative_url): Checks the existence of a file. It returns −1 if the specified URL exists within a published directory. If the file does not exist, it returns 0. The `relative_url` parameter specifies the relative URL of the file you are checking.

- Random: Returns an integer between –32768 to 32767.

- `ProcessForm ( output_url, template_url, [insertion_point] )`: Processes an HTML form by taking the file specified in `template_url` and inserting into it the values from a form that has been submitted to the current page. The result is written to the file specified in `output_url`. If the optional `insertion_point` (string) parameter is specified, the component finds this string in the existing output file and inserts the new content at that point. If the `insertion_point` parameter is not specified, any existing `output_url` file is replaced with the new output.

- `Owner`: Works only in Personal Web Server for Macintosh. This method checks whether the current user is the site administrator. It returns –1 if the name and password submitted in the request header match the Administrator name and password set in the Personal Web Server interface. It returns 0 if there is no match.

- `PluginExists ( plugin_name )`: Works only in Personal Web Server for Macintosh. This method checks whether the specified Macintosh server plug-in exists. It returns –1 if the specified Macintosh server plug-in name is currently registered. It returns 0 if the plug-in is not registered. The `plugin_name` parameter specifies the name of the server plug-in.

The example in Listing 11-13 demonstrates the use of the `FileExists` method.

Listing 11-13

```
Dim objTools As New TOOLSLib.ToolsCtl
If Tools.FileExists("theFile.gif") Then
  'Display the image file here.

End If
Set objTools = Nothing
```

In IIS applications, you can also check for the existence of a file using the `Dir$` function. This function provides a more efficient way to check for the existence of a file because there is no processing time spent on instantiating the Tools component.

The example in Listing 11-14 demonstrates the use of the `Random` method to produce a random integer.

Listing 11-14

```
Dim objTools As New TOOLSLib.ToolsCtl
Response.Write "Here is a random integer:" & objTools.Random
Set objTools = Nothing
```

You can accomplish a similar result using the Rnd function in Visual Basic. For example, the code in Listing 11-15 generates a random integer between 1 and 6.

Listing 11-15

```
Dim intRandomValue as Integer
intRandomValue = Int((6 * Rnd) + 1)
```

The ProcessForm method is the most complex method in the Tools component. In an ASP application, the template files can contain ASP scripts. A script between the <% and %> delimiters is treated just like other text in the template and copied into the output file. If the output file is an ASP document, the script will run when the output file is accessed.

Scripts in template files can also be placed between special <%% and %%> delimiters, which cause the script to execute while Tools.ProcessForm is executing. Because these scripts are executed before the template data is saved in the output file, the results get saved in the output file, usually as standard text. If the specified output file does not exist, the server creates it.

If the InsertionPoint parameter does not exist, Tools.ProcessForm replaces the entire output file. If the InsertionPoint parameter does exist and does not begin with an asterisk (*), Tools.ProcessForm finds the InsertionPoint string in the output file and inserts the data immediately after it. If the InsertionPoint string does begin with an asterisk (*), Tools.ProcessForm finds the InsertionPoint string in the output file and inserts the data immediately before it. If the InsertionPoint string exists, but is not found in the output file, the data is appended to the end of the file.

In a WebClass, you can use the ProcessTag event procedure of an HTML Template Web Item to get the same result.

CHAPTER 12

Deploying Your IIS Application

AFTER YOU FINISH DEVELOPING YOUR IIS APPLICATION, you need to port it to the production server. If you are not the person who will install the application in the real server, you need to package your application in a way that can be distributed easily.

Unlike the early MS-DOS era, when most applications consisted of only one file, Windows programs normally use ActiveX components whose files not only need to be copied but also need to be registered. More often than not, developers include components without bothering with whatever files constitute those components. Sometimes, developers don't realize that a component often depends on seemingly unrelated files that also need to be included in the distribution. A successful installation on a new machine therefore requires two separate steps.

1. The packaging of all programs and related files onto distribution media. The media used is a vehicle to transfer those files and could include diskettes, CDs, networks, or be in the form of Internet or intranet downloads.

2. The movement of your packaged application to the location from which users can install it. In Microsoft terminology, this is called *deployment*.

The first step must guarantee that *all* files are copied onto the deployment media. In addition, information on which files to copy to which directory and which files need to be registered must also be provided on the media chosen. The second step, on the other hand, must assure that *all* files in the package are copied to the correct directory and any file that must be registered is properly registered.

With version 6 of Visual Studio, Microsoft provides the Package and Deployment Wizard as an add-in in Visual Basic IDE. As its name indicates, this wizard helps you with two procedures: packaging and deployment. The wizard is new to version 6. In previous versions of Visual Basic, a similar tool was called the Setup Wizard. This chapter focuses on using the Package and Deployment Wizard to package your IIS application and deploy it on the production server.

Checking for the Package and Deployment Wizard

Before you can start using the Package and Deployment Wizard, you need to make sure that the add-in is available. If your Visual Basic installation went smoothly, you should be able to see the list of all add-ins in the Add-In Manager. Select Add-In Manager from the Add-Ins menu to display the Add-In Manager window. See Figure 12-1.

Select the Package and Deployment Wizard, and make sure that the Load on Startup in the Load Behavior frame is selected. This ensures that the Package and Deployment Wizard is loaded when you start Visual Basic. After you select the Load on Startup option, click OK and close VB. The next time you open VB, you will find the Package and Deployment Wizard menu item under the Add-Ins menu. When you select the wizard from the Add-Ins menu, Visual Basic assumes that you want to work with the project you currently have open. If you want to work with another project, you must open that project before starting the add-in (see Figure 12-2).

You can also use the wizard as a stand-alone component. When you do this, the last project used with the wizard is selected as the default. However, there is a Browse button to the right of the Active project text box that enables you to select another project. To start the Package and Deployment wizard as a stand-alone

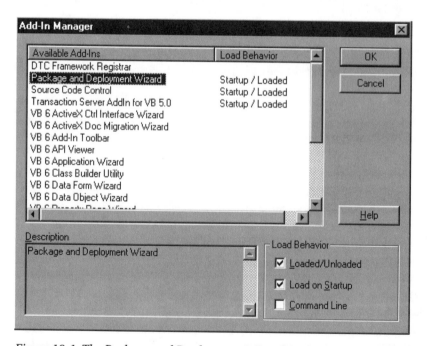

Figure 12-1. The Package and Deployment Wizard in the Add-in Manager window

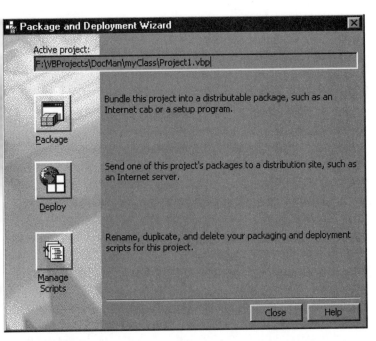

Figure 12-2. The Package and Deployment Wizard displaying the Active project

component, select Start → Programs → Microsoft Visual Studio → Microsoft Visual Studio Tools → Package and Deployment Wizard.

If you need to perform packaging and deployment on a regular basis, you can also automate this process by using scripts to run the wizard in silent mode. In silent mode, the wizard runs without user intervention. Instead, it packages and deploys your project using the settings contained in the script.

Silent mode is especially useful if you are packaging and deploying as part of a batch process. For example, early in the development of your project, you may use the Package and Deployment Wizard to package your project and deploy it to a test location. You can later create a batch file to perform the same packaging and deployment steps periodically as you update your project.

There are three main tasks you can perform using the Package and Deployment Wizard: package, deploy, and manage scripts. Package and deploy should be self-explanatory. The third task, manage scripts, helps you manipulate the scripts you have saved from previous packaging and deployment sessions in the wizard. Each time you use the wizard, you save a script that contains all the choices that were made. You can reuse these scripts in later sessions if you want to use similar settings and make the same choices as you did previously.

Packaging Your Application

The main objective of packaging your application is to produce an installation package that works well when it is run on a different machine. However, it is also important to guarantee that your installation package is as compact as possible. You want to make sure that you don't include unnecessary files that get installed and just waste disk space. The following steps provide the necessary preparations you should perform prior to using the Package and Deployment Wizard to package your application.

1. Remove all unneeded references to class libraries or data access libraries.

2. Make sure that the option Remove Information About Unused ActiveX Controls is selected on the Make tab of the Project Properties dialog box. You can display this dialog box by selecting the ProjectName Properties from the Project menu.

3. Save your project and all updated files. You should also compile your application prior to packaging. If you don't, the Package and Deployment Wizard forces you to perform this task by displaying a dialog box like the one in the Figure 12-3.

The Package and Deployment Wizard allows you to choose from three types of packages:

1. *Standard Setup Package*: This option should be chosen when you want to package and deploy an IIS application. This option is described in detail in the next section.

2. *Internet Package*: This option creates cabinet files (compressed files) and other files necessary to install your package as a download over the Internet or an intranet. (This option is not discussed in this book.) Note that this option is not available when you are using the Package and Deployment Wizard for a standard .exe project.

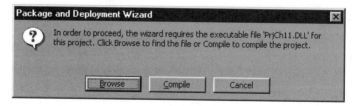

Figure 12-3. You must compile your application before packaging it.

3. *Dependency File*: This option creates a single .dep (DEP) file that can be used to show your project's dependencies or the other files that your project needs to run correctly on a computer. This option is explained later in the section "Creating a Dependency File."

Creating the Standard Setup Package

Choose the Standard Setup Package when you want to package and deploy an IIS application. With this option, the Package and Deployment Wizard creates an application called setup.exe, which you can run to install your application at deployment. It also compresses the application and all related files into .cab files. Cab is an abbreviation for cabinet. Cabinet files are the standard archive file that Microsoft uses for distribution.

With an IIS application, the following files must be included in the package you create for installation:

- The .dll files for the project including the WebClass object and the Visual Basic runtime as well as the .dsr and .dsx files for the project. These are automatically packaged into the .cab file when you run the Package and Deployment Wizard.

- The .asp and/or .htm files associated with the project. According to the documentation from Microsoft, the Package and Deployment Wizard does not package these into the .cab file, but instead copies them to the indicated location on the Web site when you deploy the .cab file. Because the Package and Deployment Wizard does not package these files, you must include these files yourself.

- Any files referenced by the .htm files, such as images. The Package and Deployment Wizard does not automatically recognize these dependencies, but you can add them to the list of dependency files the wizard displays.

To start the Package and Deployment Wizard, perform the following steps:

1. If you run the Package and Deployment Wizard as a stand-alone component, select the project you want to package.

2. Click the Package icon from the Package and Deployment Wizard's first dialog box. The wizard displays the dialog box shown in Figure 12-4, which prompts you to select the Package Type.

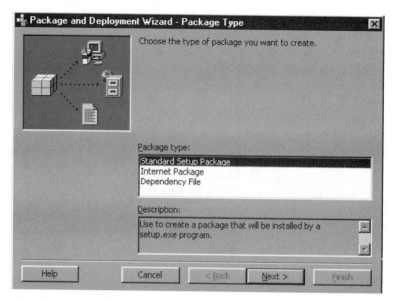

Figure 12-4. Use the Standard Setup Package for an IIS application.

3. Select Standard Setup Package, and click Next. The dialog box in Figure 12-5 appears.

4. On this screen, you must choose a directory where the Package and Deployment Wizard will assemble your package. By default, the wizard

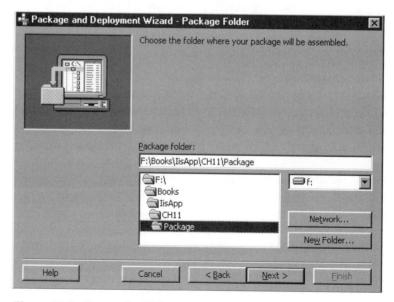

Figure 12-5. Choose the folder where your package will be assembled.

points to the folder where the project's .vbp file resides. However, it is recommended that you create a new folder (just call it Package), so that the package files don't mingle with other files. To create a new folder, click New Folder and name the folder. Click Next to continue.

5. The Package and Deployment Wizard then displays all the files that it determines are needed in the distribution package. You can use this screen to exclude files that you know are not needed. To exclude a file, clear the checkbox to the left of the file name (see Figure 12-6).

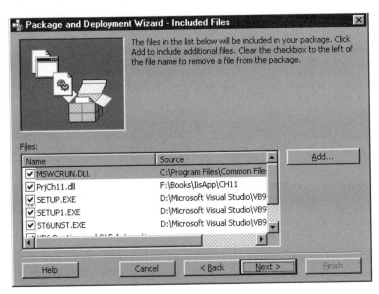

Figure 12-6. You can add necessary files or remove unnecessary ones from the package.

Realizing that it is not very intelligent, the Package and Deployment Wizard provides you with an Add button to include files that you know are needed but are not shown on the list. If you click this button, the wizard displays the common dialog window, which allows you to browse the hard drive and select a file.

You should add your .asp files and/or .htm files that are used by your IIS Application. If you use a global.asa file, it must also be added. Also, include all the data files that are referenced by the project, such as the image files.

6. Continue clicking the Add button and selecting files until all the needed files are included.

After you have selected all the files to include in the package, you may see the Missing Dependency Information dialog box, which is shown in Figure 12-7.

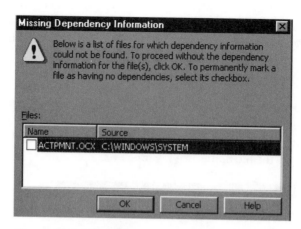

Figure 12-7. Missing Dependency Information dialog box

This screen warns you that the Package and Deployment Wizard could not find a .dep file for an included file. If you select the checkbox next to the file name on this screen, the wizard will not ask you again for this file's dependencies. If you leave the file name checkbox cleared, you should create a dependency file for this file and include the dependency file in the distribution package for this project. Creating a dependency file is explained in the next section.

7. When you are confident that you've included all the needed files, click Next to proceed to the subsequent dialog box shown in Figure 12-8.

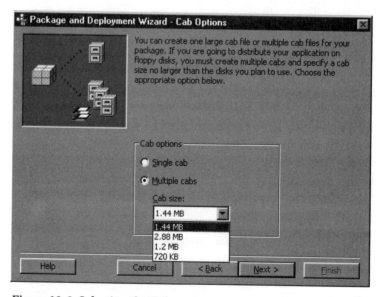

Figure 12-8. Selecting the Cab options

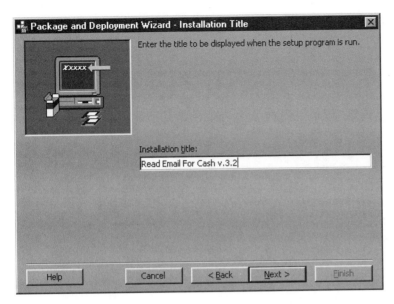

Figure 12-9. Installation Title dialog box

8. The Cab options dialog box politely asks you to select a Cab option. You can either select the Single cab option or the Multiple cabs option. Choose the Single cab option if you can write the package to a CD or copy it to a network directory. Otherwise, select Multiple cabs. If you choose the latter, select the Cab size that fits your media from the Cab size drop-down list.

9. Click Next. The Installation Title dialog box shown in Figure 12-9 appears. The text you type in the Installation Title text box appears on the Setup screen when the Setup program is run. Click Next to proceed.

10. In this dialog box, you can determine which menu groups and items will be created by the installation process. Because an IIS application is not a stand-alone program, skip this screen by clicking Next. The dialog box shown in Figure 12-10 appears.

    In the Install Locations dialog box, you can modify the install location for each of the files listed. By default, your .dll file, global.asa file, .asp and .htm files are installed in the $(AppPath) directory, which in this case, is a virtual directory on the Web server. For files that should reside in a sub-directory under the virtual directory, you should edit the Install Location of those files.

    In Figure 12-10, two .gif files are to be installed in the Images sub-directory, so the value of the Install Location for the two files is $(AppPath)\Images. You can modify the Install Location for each file by

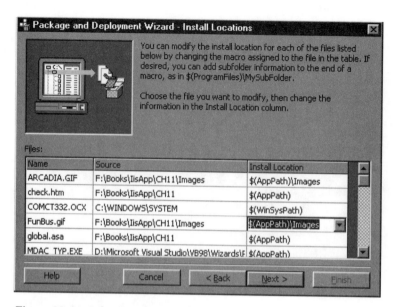

Figure 12-10. Selecting the Install Locations

clicking the drop-down arrow of the list box, which appears once you click the Install Location box of a particular file. Click Next when you have finished.

11. The Shared Files dialog box offers to make a file shareable and to install it in a shared folder. See Figure 12-11. Shared files may be used by more

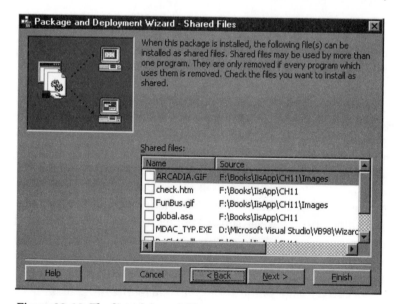

Figure 12-11. The list of shared files

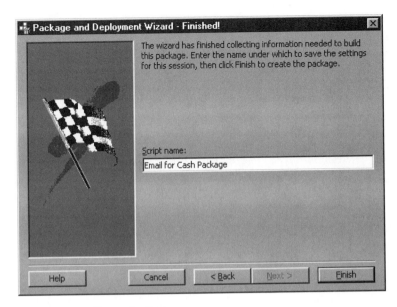

Figure 12-12. Enter the Script name.

than one program. These files are removed only if every program that uses them is removed. The dialog box lists all files that can be shared. To make a file shareable, select the checkbox beside the file name.

12. Click Next. The Finished! dialog box is the last screen in the series. See Figure 12-12.

13. Enter a Script name to save the settings for this session. This name is important if you plan to use the values you entered in the previous dialog boxes for subsequent packaging.

14. Click Finish to start the packaging process. When it has finished, the Package and Deployment Wizard displays a report about the location of the newly created package. It also reports the location of a batch file that you can use to re-create the project's .cab file or files if you need to change any files that make up the package and redistribute it.

Once the packaging process is complete, you may want to examine the package directory to familiarize yourself with the files that have been created. Understanding the function of each file helps you resolve any packaging and deployment problem should the process not go smoothly.

In the Package folder, there is one or more .cab files, depending on whether you selected the Single cab or Multiple cabs option as your Cab option. You will also find the setup.exe and the setup.lst files. There is also a folder called Support. This subfolder contains the following files:

- The files that are distributed in the .cab file (including setup1.exe, setup.exe, setup.lst files, and the st6unst.exe, which is the VB Application Removal Utility).

- A batch file with the same name as the IIS application. This file is used to run the MakeCab utility to re-create the project's .cab files. This file is especially useful if you update one of the distribution files and need to re-create the deployment package quickly. You can just copy the new version of the updated file into the Support folder, and then run the batch file, thus updating the .cab files. If you open the batch file using a text editor, it looks like the following script:

```
@echo off
ECHO Use this batch file to make a new cab file. Press CTRL-C to cancel, or↵
pause↵
"D:\MICROSOFT VISUAL STUDIO\VB98\WIZARDS\PDWIZARD\MAKECAB.EXE" /↵
f "Project1.DDF"↵
```

- A .ddf file with the same name as your IIS application. This file is a text file that is read by the MakeCab utility to determine how to build the .cab files and also to determine which source files to use.

All the files in the Support directory are not included with the setup package when you distribute it on your media. However, the compressed versions of most of these files are packed into the .cab file(s).

Note that the same setup.exe and setup.lst files appear twice, once in the Package directory and once in the Support subdirectory. These files are not compressed into one of the .cab files. The setup.exe cannot be present in a compressed form because it is the first file that must be run by the user who installs the application. The setup.lst file could be included in a .cab file, however, doing so would eliminate the modifiability of this file. This file is a text file that looks like an .ini file. If you open the file with a text editor, it looks like Listing 12-1.

Listing 12-1

```
[Bootstrap]
SetupTitle=Install
SetupText=Copying Files, please stand by.
CabFile=PrjCh11.CAB
Spawn=Setup1.exe
Uninstal=st6unst.exe
```

```
TmpDir=msftqws.pdw
Cabs=2
```

[Bootstrap Files]
```
File1=@VB6STKIT.DLL,$(WinSysPathSysFile),,,6/18/98 12:00:00 AM,102912,6.0.81.69
File2=@COMCAT.DLL,$(WinSysPathSysFile),$(DLLSelfRegister),,5/31/98 12:00:00
AM,22288,4.71.1460.1
File3=@STDOLE2.TLB,$(WinSysPathSysFile),$(TLBRegister),,10/27/98 11:28:38
AM,16896,2.40.4267.1
File4=@ASYCFILT.DLL,$(WinSysPathSysFile),,,10/27/98 2:55:58 PM,147728,2.40.4267.1
File5=@OLEPRO32.DLL,$(WinSysPathSysFile),$(DLLSelfRegister),,10/27/98 2:56:00
PM,164112,5.0.4267.1
File6=@OLEAUT32.DLL,$(WinSysPathSysFile),$(DLLSelfRegister),,10/27/98 2:55:56
PM,606480,2.40.4267.1
File7=@msvbvm60.dll,$(WinSysPathSysFile),$(DLLSelfRegister),,10/20/98 11:19:54
PM,1409024,6.0.82.44
```

[Setup]
```
Title=Email For Cash v.3.2
DefaultDir=$(ProgramFiles)\Project1
AppExe=PrjCh11.dll
AppToUninstall=PrjCh11.dll
```

[Setup1 Files]
```
File1=@ARCADIA.GIF,$(AppPath)\Images,,,6/1/98 12:00:00 AM,1913,0.0.0.0
File2=@FunBus.gif,$(AppPath)\Images,,,5/11/98 7:01:00 PM,2813,0.0.0.0
File3=@check.htm,$(AppPath),,,4/22/00 11:29:40 AM,801,0.0.0.0
File4=@WebClass1.ASP,$(AppPath),,,4/23/00 10:25:26 AM,565,0.0.0.0
File5=@global.asa,$(AppPath),,,4/22/00 12:41:30 PM,124,0.0.0.0
File6=@COMCT332.OCX,$(WinSysPath),$(DLLSelfRegister),$(Shared),6/24/98 12:00:00
AM,369696,6.0.0.8169
File7=@MDAC_TYP.EXE,$(AppPath),,,6/26/98 12:00:00 AM,8124720,4.71.1015.0
File8=@MSADO20.TLB,$(WinSysPath),$(TLBRegister),$(Shared),11/20/98 12:00:00
AM,48528,0.0.0.0
File9=@RDOCURS.DLL,$(WinSysPath),,$(Shared),6/18/98 12:00:00 AM,151552,5.0.81.69
File10=@msrdo20.dll,$(WinSysPath),$(DLLSelfRegister),$(Shared),6/18/98 12:00:00
AM,393216,6.0.81.69
File11=@MSCDRUN.DLL,$(CommonFiles)\Designer,$(DLLSelfRegister),$(Shared),6/18/98
12:00:00 AM,49152,6.0.81.69
File12=@MSWCRUN.DLL,$(CommonFiles)\designer,$(DLLSelfRegister),$(Shared),6/18/98
12:00:00 AM,253952,6.0.81.69
File13=@PrjCh11.dll,$(AppPath),$(DLLSelfRegister),,3/31/00 10:20:20
PM,24576,1.0.0.0
```

```
; The following lines may be deleted in order to obtain extra
; space for customizing this file on a full installation diskette.
;
; XXXXXXXXXXXXXXXXXXXXXXXXXXXXXXXXXXXXXXXXXXXXXXXXXXXXXXXXXXX
; XXXXXXXXXXXXXXXXXXXXXXXXXXXXXXXXXXXXXXXXXXXXXXXXXXXXXXXXXXX
; XXXXXXXXXXXXXXXXXXXXXXXXXXXXXXXXXXXXXXXXXXXXXXXXXXXXXXXXXXX
; XXXXXXXXXXXXXXXXXXXXXXXXXXXXXXXXXXXXXXXXXXXXXXXXXXXXXXXXXXX
; XXXXXXXXXXXXXXXXXXXXXXXXXXXXXXXXXXXXXXXXXXXXXXXXXXXXXXXXXXX
; XXXXXXXXXXXXXXXXXXXXXXXXXXXXXXXXXXXXXXXXXXXXXXXXXXXXXXXXXXX
; XXXXXXXXXXXXXXXXXXXXXXXXXXXXXXXXXXXXXXXXXXXXXXXXXXXXXXXXXXX
; XXXXXXXXXXXXXXXXXXXXXXXXXXXXXXXXXXXXXXXXXXXXXXXXXXXXXXXXXXX
; XXXXXXXXXXXXXXXXXXXXXXXXXXXXXXXXXXXXXXXXXXXXXXXXXXXXXXXXXXX
; XXXXXXXXXXXXXXXXXXXXXXXXXXXXXXXXXXXXXXXXXXXXXXXXXXXXXXXXXXX
; XXXXXXXXXXXXXXXXXXXXXXXXXXXXXXXXXXXXXXXXXXXXXXXXXXXXXXXXXXX
; XXXXXXXXXXXXXXXXXXXXXXXXXXXXXXXXXXXXXXXXXXXXXXXXXXXXXXXXXXX
; XXXXXXXXXXXXXXXXXXXXXXXXXXXXXXXXXXXXXXXXXXXXXXXXXXXXXXXXXXX
; XXXXXXXXXXXXXXXXXXXXXXXXXXXXXXXXXXXXXXXXXXXXXXXXXXXXXXXXXXX
; XXXXXXXXXXXXXXXXXXXXXXXXXXXXXXXXXXXXXXXXXXXXXXXXXXXXXXXXXXX
; XXXXXXXXXXXXXXXXXXXXXXXXXXXXXXXXXXXXXXXXXXXXXXXXXXXXXXXXXXX
; XXXXXXXXXXXXXXXXXXXXXXXXXXXXXXXXXXXXXXXXXXXXXXXXXXXXXXXXXXX
; XXXXXXXXXXXXXXXXXXXXXXXXXXXXXXXXXXXXXXXXXXXXXXXXXXXXXXXXXXX
; XXXXXXXXXXXXXXXXXXXXXXXXXXXXXXXXXXXXXXXXXXXXXXXXXXXXXXXXXXX
; XXXXXXXXXXXXXXXXXXXXXXXXXXXXXXXXXXXXXXXXXXXXXXXXXXXXXXXXXXX
; XXXXXXXXXXXXXXXXXXXXXXXXXXXXXXXXXXXXXXXXXXXXXXXXXXXXXXXXXXX
; XXXXXXXXXXXXXXXXXXXXXXXXXXXXXXXXXXXXXXXXXXXXXXXXXXXXXXXXXXX
; XXXXXXXXXXXXXXXXXXXXXXXXXXXXXXXXXXXXXXXXXXXXXXXXXXXXXXXXXXX
; XXXXXXXXXXXXXXXXXXXXXXXXXXXXXXXXXXXXXXXXXXXXXXXXXXXXXXXXXXX
; XXXXXXXXXXXXXXXXXXXXXXXXXXXXXXXXXXXXXXXXXXXXXXXXXXXXXXXXXXX
; XXXXXXXXXXXXXXXXXXXXXXXXXXXXXXXXXXXXXXXXXXXXXXXXXXXXXXXXXXX
; XXXXXXXXXXXXXXXXXXXXXXXXXXXXXXXXXXXXXXXXXXXXXXXXXXXXXXXXXXX
; XXXXXXXXXXXXXXXXXXXXXXXXXXXXXXXXXXXXXXXXXXXXXXXXXXXXXXXXXXX
; XXXXXXXXXXXXXXXXXXXXXXXXXXXXXXXXXXXXXXXXXXXXXXXXXXXXXXXXXXX
; XXXXXXXXXXXXXXXXXXXXXXXXXXXXXXXXXXXXXXXXXXXXXXXXXXXXXXXXXXX
; XXXXXXXXXXXXXXXXXXXXXXXXXXXXXXXXXXXXXXXXXXXXXXXXXXXXXXXXXXX
; XXXXXXXXXXXXXXXXXXXXXXXXXXXXXXXXXXXXXXXXXXXXXXXXXXXXXXXXXXX
; XXXXXXXXXXXXXXXXXXXXXXXXXXXXXXXXXXXXXXXXXXXXXXXXXXXXXXXXXXX
```

The setup.lst file has named sections with headers surrounded by brackets. The headers look like this:

```
[Bootstrap]
```

Each section contains entries of this form:

```
ItemName=value
```

The content of the setup.lst file describes all the files that must be installed on the user's machine for your application and contains crucial information for the setup process. For example, the setup.lst file tells the system the name of each file, where to install it, and how it should be registered. There are five sections to the setup.lst file.

- *The BootStrap section*: Lists the core information about the application, such as the name of the main program for the application, the temporary directory to use during the installation process, and the text in the startup window that appears during installation.

- *The BootStrap Files section*: Lists all files required by the main installation file. Normally, this includes just the Visual Basic runtime files.

- *The Setup1 Files section*: Lists all other files required by your application, such as .exe files, data, and text.

- *The Setup section*: Contains information needed by other files in the application.

- *The Icon Groups section*: Contains information about the groups your installation process will create. Each member of this section has a correlating section containing the icons to be created in that group.

Creating a Dependency File

When the Package and Deployment Wizard includes a file in the project's setup, especially if the file is a COM component, that file might require that other supporting files also be included. The Package and Deployment Wizard is smart enough to include these additional files in the setup if each component that it needs to distribute has an accompanying .dep file.

When you package your application, the Package and Deployment Wizard scans all available dependency information for the application to build a comprehensive list of information about the runtime files the application needs; it then builds installation information from that list. For a standard package, the information from the .dep files is written to a setup.lst file that is stored outside the packaged .cab file. It is recommended that you package and deploy your component before you package and deploy your dependency file, so that the packaging portion of the wizard knows the source location of the component that the dependency file references.

You can create a dependency file by running the Package and Deployment Wizard and selecting the Package option on the first screen. The sequence is described in the following steps:

1. After clicking the Package icon, a second window appears.

2. Select Dependency File, and then click Next.

3. Choose the folder where you want the Package and Deployment wizard to create your .dep file. Click Next.

4. If the folder you choose is not the same as the folder where your application's .dll or .exe files reside, you will be asked to confirm this folder.

5. The next screen lists all files that will be included. This screen is the same as the one in the standard setup of the Package and Deployment Wizard. Click Next.

6. The Cab Information Screen shown in Figure 12-13 appears. Click Next.

7. The Install Locations screen, which is the same as the standard setup package's Install Locations screen appears. Click Next.

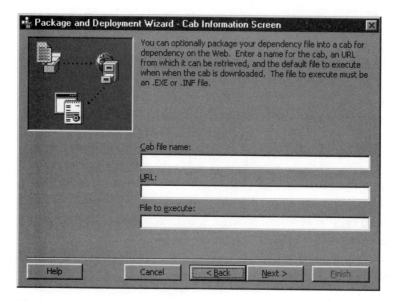

Figure 12-13. Cab Information Screen

8. Type in a name for your script, and click Finish.

9. If the wizard can finish its job without any problem, it should display a window that reports where the dependency file has been created.

A dependency file is a text file with the same name but a different extension as the file whose dependencies it describes. The contents of a dependency file looks like an .ini file. Open it with a text editor, and you'll see something like Listing 12-2.

Listing 12-2
```
[Version]
Version=1.0.0.0

[PrjCh11.dll <0009>]
Dest=$(AppPath)
Date=31/03/00
Time=22:20
Version=1.0.0.0
CABFilename=PrjCh11.CAB
CABINFFile=PrjCh11.INF
Uses1=msvbvm60.dll
Uses2=OLEAUT32.DLL
Uses3=OLEPRO32.DLL
Uses4=ASYCFILT.DLL
Uses5=STDOLE2.TLB
Uses6=COMCAT.DLL
Uses7=MSWCRUN.DLL
Uses8=IETIMER.OCX

[IETIMER.OCX <0009>]
Dest=$(WinSysPath)
Date=11/05/98
Time=19:01
Version=4.72.3110.0
```

If a component of your setup has an accompanying .dep file, the Package and Deployment Wizard can include the other files that the component needs in the final setup. If the wizard can't find a component's .dep file, it will warn you. You can still continue to create the setup, but the distributed version of your application might not run on a user's system if the component requires other files to run or if these files are missing from the user's system.

Microsoft recommends that you always create a dependency file for an application that you are distributing, especially if the application is a COM component.

Deploying Your Application

After you create the setup package, you then need to copy it onto the selected media. You can use diskettes, CDs, or a network. You use the Package and Deployment Wizard to deploy your application. However, using the Package and Deployment Wizard for deployment is only the first of many steps required for the entire process. This wizard only helps you transfer the package to the distribution media. Once the package has been transferred, there are still a few steps you need to perform to complete the deployment process.

1. Start the Package and Deployment Wizard, and select the project if you start the wizard as a stand-alone program.

2. Click the Deploy icon. The wizard displays the Package to Deploy screen. See Figure 12-14.

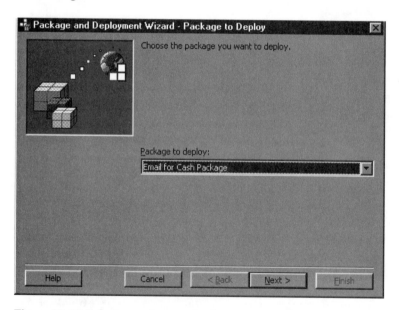

Figure 12-14. Select a package to deploy.

3. Select the package to deploy from the drop-down list box. Click Next. The screen in Figure 12-15 appears.

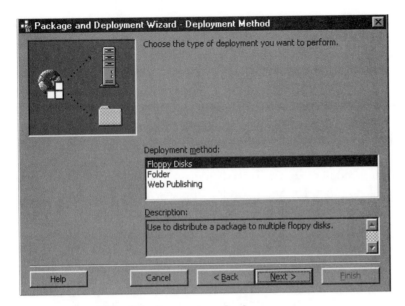

Figure 12-15. A list of deployment methods

4. Select a deployment method. If you select Floppy Disks, the .cab files will be distributed on diskettes, and you will be prompted to insert a diskette, one at a time, until all the .cab files are copied. If you choose Folder, you will have to select the folder where the .cab files should be copied to. If you choose Web Publishing, you can automatically publish your package to the Internet/intranet. In this example, diskettes are used as the media, so click Floppy Disks, and click Next.

5. Click Next again.

6. Type in a Script name, and click Finish.

7. Insert all the diskettes needed.

Installing Your Application

After copying your package to the media, you can transport, and then install your IIS application. Perform the following steps to install the IIS application:

1. Log on to the Web server as an Administrator or as a user with Administrator privileges.

2. Create a virtual directory for your IIS application on your Web server. You don't need to create the subdirectories for data files included in the package. The installation process automatically creates them.

3. Stop the IIS service to make sure that the old system files that are being used by IIS, if any, can be overwritten.

4. Insert the CD or diskette where the package resides.

5. Using Windows Explorer, browse to the setup.exe file and double-click the file to run it. The Setup window appears, as shown in Figure 12-16.

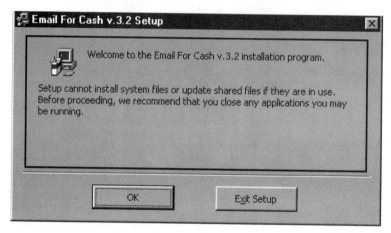

Figure 12-16. Installing the IIS application

6. Click OK.

7. Select the directory where you want to install your IIS application. Naturally, this is the virtual directory you created in Step 2.

8. Click the button on the top left of the dialog box to start the installation.

If everything goes well, a dialog box appears at the end of the process telling you that the application has been successfully installed. You can now restart the IIS service.

The following is a checklist containing tasks you need to perform after the installation.

1. Make sure that the .asp and/or .htm files are copied to the correct directory.

2. Make sure that the data files are copied to the correct directory.

3. Assign the correct permissions to the virtual directory and each subdirectory under it. For example, if your IIS application will be accessible by anyone on the Internet, you may want to give Read permission to all files in the virtual directory. You may also want to use anonymous access and disable the other types of access.

4. Convert the virtual directory into an application, if necessary. As an application, it will isolate your IIS application in its address space. If your IIS application fails, it won't bring down other applications. Converting the virtual directory into an application also allows your IIS application to have its own global.asa file.

> **NOTE:** *If the directory where your IIS application resides is just a normal virtual directory, your IIS application cannot have its own global.asa file. All applications (ASP and IIS) in virtual directories on the Web server will share the same global.asa file, the one in the home directory of IIS.*

   Converting a virtual directory into an application does not change the URL used to access your IIS application. To convert a virtual directory into an application, open the Properties page of your IIS application in the Internet Service Manager or IIS snap-in, and then click Create.

5. Test your IIS application before it goes live. Make sure all functions work properly. For example, make sure that database access works and the access time is as expected.

HTML 4.01 Basics

THIS APPENDIX PROVIDES A SHORT COURSE on Hypertext Markup Language (HTML) for those new to HTML, plus a reference on HTML 4.01, which became a specification in December 1999. HTML 4.01 makes obsolete version 4.0 that was published in December 1997 and revised in April 1998. Versions of HTML, nevertheless, change very quickly.

At the time of this writing, the World Wide Web Consortium (W3C), the body that produces HTML specifications, has released XHTML 1.0 as the latest major change to HTML. XHTML 1.0 is a reformulation of HTML 4.01 in XML, and combines the strength of HTML 4 with the power of XML. However, XHTML 1.0 requires understanding of XML, which is beyond the scope of this book.

This appendix is divided into two parts: an introduction to HTML and a group of tables that serve as a handy reference on HTML 4.01 tags. It is intended only as a quick reference; a complete reference on HTML 4.01 can be found at the W3C Web site at http://www.w3.org.

> **NOTE:** *Due to the rapid growth of the Internet-related industry, Web browser makers often implement their own extensions to the HTML standard in their products before W3C comes up with a standard that specifies those extensions. As a result, modern Web browsers don't fully comply with the standards that came later. Worse still, extensions are almost always different in different browsers, sometimes resulting in confusion for those who plan to implement HTML in their systems or applications. Several tags in HTML 4.01, for example, are not supported in Netscape and Microsoft browsers, even though this may change in the future.*

A Crash Course on HTML

The following is a short but invaluable primer on HTML. It is intended as a quick tour of the basics of HTML, which you should be able to breeze though here. However, feel free to go back for a refresher later on.

Document Structure

An HTML file consists of HTML elements represented by tags. A standard HTML file consists of three parts: a line containing HTML version information, the head section, and the body section. The skeleton of an HTML file is as follows:

```
<!DOCTYPE . . . >
<HTML>
<HEAD>
    . . . the head section
</HEAD>

<BODY>
    . . . the body section
</BODY>
</HTML>
```

The `<!DOCTYPE>` tag specifies the version of the HTML in the document; for example:

```
<!DOCTYPE HTML PUBLIC "-//W3C//DTD HTML 4.0 Transitional//EN" "html4.dtd">
```

This tag is useful for Web browsers and other HTML parsers to correctly interpret the HTML coding.

Web browsers are lenient, though. For example, they seem quite happy to accept an HTML file in which the `<!DOCTYPE>` tag has been left out.

The head section is the HTML document header. It contains generic information about the document, including the title, the base URL, the style, and such.

The body section contains the text you want the Web browser to display.

Note that elements are not the same as tags. Tags are the *representation* of elements in the file. For instance, the HEAD element is always present, even though the HEAD tags may not be.

Tags are always enclosed by angled brackets (for example, `<HEAD>`), and case-insensitive. Normally, they are written in uppercase letters to make them stand out.

There are two types of tags: the start tag and the end tag. End tags are the same as start tags, except that they are preceded by a forward slash (for example, `</HEAD>`). Some elements, such as the HEAD element, are represented by both the start tag and the end tag. Some, such as `<BR>`, are represented by start tags only.

Most elements can be nested. However, you should always pay attention to the order. For instance, the following is a valid code line:

```
<B>This is printed in bold. <I>And this is in bold and italic</I></B>
```

The following is illegal, even though most browsers will still render it:

```
<B>This is printed in bold. <I>And this is in bold and italic</B></I>
```

An element can also have one or more properties, which are called attributes, that extend its capabilities. Each attribute may have a default value, and an attribute's value can be set by scripts or the HTML author. The attribute/value pair must appear before the final ">" of an element's start tag. Because an element can have more than one attribute, these attribute/value pairs are separated by spaces. The attribute/value pairs may appear in any order.

According to the HTML Recommendations, all attribute values must be delimited using either double quotation marks (ASCII decimal 34) or single quotation marks (ASCII decimal 38). Again, Web browsers are not fussy if you don't use these marks. If you don't use single or double quotation marks, however, the value may contain only letters (a-z and A-Z), digits (0-9), underscore characters, and colons. The following is the syntax for attributes:

```
<TagName Attribute=value>
```

Text Formatting

You can format text using the tags listed on the section "A Quick Reference to HTML Tags" later in this appendix. For example, to display a piece of text in bold, you can enclose it with the `<B>` and `</B>` pair:

```
This is <b>bold</b>
```

You can also use the `<I>` ... `</I>` tags to italicize text and `<U>` ... `</U>` tags to underline it.

On top of that, you can use the `<FONT>` ... `</FONT>` tags to display text using certain fonts. The `<FONT>` tag has attributes such as COLOR and SIZE to let you control the text appearance.

Special Characters

Some characters, such as "<", ">" and "&", have special meanings in HTML. Upon encountering these characters in text, the HTML parser may interpret these characters incorrectly. To include these characters in text, you can use character references, which are numeric equivalents of symbolic names for these special characters.

Character references are also useful for referring to characters that cannot be entered directly from the keyboard, such as å or Æ. Character references always begin with a "&" sign and end with a semicolon. Some examples include:

-   for space, because you can only have one space between words or non-space characters

- < for the < sign.

- > for the > sign.

- " for the double quotation mark.

- & for the ampersand & character.

- À for ASCII character number 192 decimal.

Images

You use the `<IMG>` tag to include an image in an HTML document. There are two types of image files that can be rendered by Web browsers: .gif and .jpg (or .jpeg). You must use the SRC attribute of the `<IMG>` tag to specify the file you use as the source of the inclusion. For instance, to display the butterfly.gif image file that resides in the images directory of your Web site, you can write the following:

```
<IMG SRC=http://www.yourdomain.com/images/butterfly.gif>
```

Colors

Some tags have the attributes that accept color values. For example, the `<FONT>` tag has the COLOR attribute that determines the color of the text enclosed by the `<FONT>` and `</FONT>` tags.

A color value is represented as a six-digit hexadecimal value. The first two digits represent the red component, the next two the green component, and the last two digits represent the blue component. Each component can have values in the range 00 to FF inclusively. For example, pure green is represented by 00FF00. The value 00EE00 is also green, only less intense. By changing the three components values, you can produce more than 24 million different colors. The following example displays text in red:

```
<FONT COLOR=FF0000>This is red.</FONT>
```

Hyperlinks

Hyperlinks are what you use to enable your users to navigate to other documents or URLs by a single click of mouse. To include a hyperlink in your HTML document, you use the anchor element which is represented by the <A> tag. In order for the hyperlink to reference the correct document or URL, you must use the HREF attribute. An example is

```
<A HREF=www.MyDomain.com/AnotherPage.htm>Click here to see another page.</A>
```

If the base part of the URL is not present, the Web browser will search the page in the same URL base as the current HTML document.

Tables

You can use tables to display a set of data structured in rows and columns. The individual cell can contain not only text, but other HTML elements such as images. A table is enclosed by the <TABLE> and </TABLE> tags. When using a table, chances are you will also be using the <TR> and <TD> elements. The <TR> tag defines the start of the table row and the <TD> tag defines the start of the table cell. An example of a simple table is given here. The table has three rows and two columns.

```
<TABLE>
  <TR>
    <TD>
      <B>Country</B>
    </TD>
    <TD>
      <B>Capital</B>
    </TD>
  </TR>
  <TR>
    <TD>
      Australia
    </TD>
    <TD>
      Canberra
    </TD>
  </TR>
  <TR>
    <TD>
      Malaysia
    </TD>
```

```
    <TD>
      Kuala Lumpur
    </TD>
  </TR>
</TABLE>
```

This will be displayed like a normal table in the Web browser. It should look like the following table:

COUNTRY	CAPITAL
Australia	Canberra
Malaysia	Kuala Lumpur

Forms

You can use forms to prompt users for information, and then carry out actions based on that input. You use the <FORM> and </FORM> tags to create a FORM element in your HTML document. The <FORM> and </FORM> tags enclose one or more other elements, especially INPUT elements.

An INPUT element can have the following types: TEXT, PASSWORD, HIDDEN, CHECKBOX, RADIO, RESET, SUBMIT, IMAGE, BUTTON and FILE. In addition to INPUT elements, you can also insert TEXTAREA and SELECT elements into a FORM element.

An important attribute of the FORM element is the METHOD attribute. This attribute defines the method used to send the data to the server and can have one of these values: POST and GET. When the METHOD attribute is not present, the Web browser will use the GET method to submit the form. Another important attribute is the ACTION attribute. It is used to specify the URL that will receive the data when the form is submitted.

You can have more than one FORM element in your HTML document, but you can't nest the elements. Following is an example of a form:

```
<FORM METHOD=POST ACTION="Processor.asp">
Last name: <INPUT NAME=LastName TYPE=TEXT>
<BR>First name: <INPUT NAME=FirstName TYPE=TEXT>
<BR>Password: <INPUT NAME=Password TYPE=PASSWORD>
<BR><INPUT TYPE=SUBMIT>
</FORM>
```

Quick Reference to HTML Tags

Tables A-1 through A-8 in this section list commonly used HTML tags and descriptions of how they are used.

Table A-1. Document Structure

TAG	DESCRIPTION
<!-- -->	Denotes a comment that is ignored by Web browsers.
<!DOCTYPE>	Declares the type and content format of the document.
<BDO>	Turns off the bidirectional rendering algorithm for selected fragments of text.
<BODY>	Defines the beginning and the end of the body section of the page.
<COMMENT>	Denotes a comment that will not be displayed.
<DEL>	Indicates a section of the document that has been deleted since a previous version.
<DIV>	Defines a container section within the page that can hold other elements.
<HEAD>	Contains tags holding unviewed information about the document.
<HTML>	The outer tag for the page, identifying the document as an HTML page.
<INS>	Indicates a section of the document that has been inserted since a previous version.
<ISINDEX>	Indicates the presence of a searchable index.
<META>	Provides various types of unviewed information or instructions to the browser.
<NOSCRIPT>	Defines the HTML to be displayed in browsers that do not support scripting.
<SCRIPT>	Specifies a script for the page that will be interpreted by a script engine.
<SPAN>	Used with a style sheet to define nonstandard attributes for text on the page.

Table A-2. Text Formatting

TAG	DESCRIPTION
<ABBR>	Indicates a sequence of characters that compose an acronym.
<ACRONYM>	Indicates a sequence of characters that compose an acronym.
<ADDRESS>	Specifies information such as address, signature, and authorship.
<B>	Renders text in boldface.
<BIG>	Renders text in a relatively larger font than the current font.
<BLOCKQUOTE>	Denotes a quotation in text, usually a paragraph or more.
 	Inserts a line break.
<CENTER>	Causes the enclosed text and other elements to be displayed on the center of the page.
<CITE>	Cites text by rendering it in italics.
<CODE>	Renders text as a code sample in a fixed-width font.
<EM>	Renders text as emphasized, usually in italics.
<FONT>	Deprecated in HTML 4.0. This tag specifies the font face, size, and color for rendering the text.
<H*n*>	The six elements <H1> to <H6> render text as a range of heading styles.
<HR>	Places a horizontal rule in the page.
<I>	Renders text in an italic font where available.
<KBD>	Renders text in fixed-width font.
<P>	Denotes a paragraph. The end tag is optional.
<PRE>	Renders text in fixed-width type.
<SAMP>	Renders text as a code sample listing.
<SMALL>	Specifies that text be displayed with a smaller font than the current font.
<STRONG>	Renders text in bold face.
<STYLE>	Specifies the style sheet properties for the page.
<SUB>	Renders text as a subscript using a smaller font than the current font.
<SUP>	Renders text as a superscript using a smaller font than the current font.
<TT>	Renders text in fixed-width type.
<U>	Renders text underlined.
<VAR>	Renders text as a small fixed-width font.

Table A-3. Lists and Definitions

TAG	DESCRIPTION
<DD>	The definition of an item in a definition list, usually indented from other text.
<DL>	Denotes a definition list.
<DFN>	The defining instance of a term.
<DT>	Denotes a definition term within a definition list.
<LI>	Denotes one item within an ordered or unordered list.
<OL>	Renders lines of text that have <LI> tags as an ordered list.
<UL>	Renders lines of text that have <LI> tags as a bulleted list.

Table A-4. Links to Other Documents and Resources

TAG	DESCRIPTION
<A>	Defines a hypertext link. The HREF or the NAME attribute must be specified.
<AREA>	Specifies the shape of a "hot spot" in a client-side image map.
<BASE>	Specifies the document's base URL.
<LINK>	Defines a hyperlink between the document and some other resource.
<MAP>	Specifies a collection of hot spots for a client-side image map.
<Q>	The URL of the source document or message used as a quotation in the page.

Table A-5. Forms and Form Elements

TAG	DESCRIPTION
<BUTTON>	Renders an HTML button; the enclosed text is used as the button's caption.
<FIELDSET>	Draws a box around the contained elements to indicate related items.
<FORM>	Denotes a form containing elements, whose values can be sent to a server.
<INPUT>	Specifies a form input element, such as text or check box.
<LABEL>	Defines the text of a label for a label control like element.
<LEGEND>	Defines the title text to place in the 'box' created by a <FIELDSET> tag.
<OPTION>	Denotes one choice in a <SELECT> drop-down or list element.
<OPTGROUP>	Allows authors to group choices into a hierarchy.
<SELECT>	Defines a list box or drop-down list.
<TEXTAREA>	Specifies a multi-line text input element.

Table A-6. Tables

TAG	DESCRIPTION
<CAPTION>	Specifies a caption to be placed next to a table.
<COL>	Used to specify column based defaults for a table.
<COLGROUP>	Used as a container for a group of columns.
<TABLE>	Denotes a table.
<TBODY>	Denotes the body of a table.
<TD>	Specifies a cell in a table.
<TFOOT>	Denotes a set of rows to be used as the footer of a table.
<TH>	Denotes a set of rows to be used as the header of a table.
<THEAD>	Denotes a set of rows to be used as the header of a table.
<TITLE>	Denotes the title of the document, and used in the browser's window title bar.
<TR>	Specifies a row in a table.

Table A-7. Frames and Layers

TAG	DESCRIPTION
<FRAME>	Specifies an individual frame within a frameset.
<FRAMESET>	Specifies a frameset containing multiple frames and other nested framesets.
<IFRAME>	Used to create in-line floating frames within the page.
<NOFRAMES>	Defines the HTML to be displayed in browsers that do not support frames.

Table A-8. Graphics and Other Objects

TAG	DESCRIPTION
<APPLET>	Deprecated in HTML 4.0. Places a Java applet or other executable content in the page.
<IMG>	Embeds an image or a video clip in the document.
<OBJECT>	Inserts an object or other non-intrinsic HTML element into the page.
<PARAM>	Used in an <OBJECT> or <APPLET> tag to set the object's properties.

ASP 2.0 and ASP 3.0 Built-in Objects

THIS APPENDIX COVERS ASP 2.0 AND ASP 3.0 objects that are included with the installation of IIS 4.0 and IIS 5.0. It provides a reference on the methods, properties, collections, and syntax for each object. I've also made note of any ASP 3.0-only objects, properties, or methods.

Application Object

You can use the Application object to share information among all users of your IIS application. Note that the Lock and Unlock methods can ensure that multiple users do not try to alter a property simultaneously.

Syntax

Application.*method*

Collections

The Application object's collections include:

COLLECTION	DESCRIPTION
Contents	Contains all of the items that have been added to the Application through script commands.
StaticObjects	Contains all of the objects added to the session with the <OBJECT> tag.

Methods

The Application object's methods include:

METHOD	DESCRIPTION
Contents.Remove (ASP 3.0 only)	Deletes an item from the Application object's Contents collection.
Contents.RemoveAll (ASP 3.0 only)	Deletes all items from the Application object's Contents collection.
Lock	Prevents other clients from modifying Application object properties.
Unlock	Allows other clients to modify Application object properties.

Events

Scripts for the following events are declared in the Global.asa file:

```
Application_OnEnd
Application_OnStart
```

ASPError Object (ASP 3.0 only)

You can use the ASPError object to obtain information about an error condition that has occurred within a script in an ASP page. The ASPError object is returned by the Server.GetLastError method

Syntax

```
ASPError.property
```

Properties

The ASPError object exposes the following read-only properties:

PROPERTY	DESCRIPTION
ASPCode	Returns an error code generated by IIS 5.0.
Number	Returns the standard COM error code.
Source	Returns the actual source code, when available, of the line that caused the error.

Category	Indicates if the source of the error was internal to ASP, the scripting language, or an object.
File	Indicates the name of the .asp file that was being processed when the error occurred.
Line	Indicates the line within the .asp file that generated the error.
Column	Indicates the column position within the .asp file that generated the error.
Description	Returns a short description of the error.
ASPDescription	Returns a more detailed description of the error if it is an ASP-related error.

Request Object

The Request object retrieves the values that the client browser passed to the server during an HTTP request.

Syntax

```
Request[.collection|property|method](variable)
```

The *variable* parameters are strings that specify the item to be retrieved from a collection or to be used as input for a method or property.

Collections

The Request object's collections include:

COLLECTION	DESCRIPTION
ClientCertificate	The values of fields stored in the client certificate that is sent in the HTTP request.
Cookies	The values of cookies sent in the HTTP request.
Form	The values of form elements in the HTTP request body.
QueryString	The values of variables in the HTTP query string.
ServerVariables	The values of predetermined environment variables. The server environment variables are summarized in Table B-1.

Table B-1 Server Environment Variables

VARIABLE	DESCRIPTION
ALL_HTTP	All HTTP headers sent by the client.
ALL_RAW	Retrieves all headers in the raw-form. ALL_HTTP place an HTTP_ prefix before the header name and the header-name is always capitalized, whereas in ALL_RAW the header name and values appear as they are sent by the client.
APPL_MD_PATH	Retrieves the metabase path for the Application for the ISAPI DLL.
APPL_PHYSICAL_PATH	Retrieves the physical path corresponding to the metabase path. IIS converts the APPL_MD_PATH to the physical (directory) path to return this value.
AUTH_PASSWORD	The value entered in the client's authentication dialog. This variable is only available if Basic authentication is used.
AUTH_TYPE	The authentication method that the server uses to validate users when they attempt to access a protected script.
AUTH_USER	Raw authenticated user name.
CERT_COOKIE	Unique ID for client certificate, Returned as a string. Can be used as a signature for the whole client certificate.
CERT_FLAGS	bit0 is set to 1 if the client certificate is present. bit1 is set to 1 if the Certifying Authority of the client certificate is invalid (not in the list of recognized CA on the server).
CERT_ISSUER	Issuer field of the client certificate (O=MS, OU=IAS, CN=user name, C=USA).
CERT_KEYSIZE	Number of bits in Secure Sockets Layer connection key size; for example, 128.
CERT_SECRETKEYSIZE	Number of bits in server certificate private key; for example, 1024.
CERT_SERIALNUMBER	Serial number field of the client certificate.
CERT_SERVER_ISSUER	Issuer field of the server certificate.
CERT_SERVER_SUBJECT	Subject field of the server certificate.
CERT_SUBJECT	Subject field of the client certificate.
CONTENT_LENGTH	The length of the content as given by the client.
CONTENT_TYPE	The data type of the content. Used with queries that have attached information, such as the HTTP queries GET, POST, and PUT.

RIABLE	DESCRIPTION
ATEWAY_INTERFACE	The revision of the CGI specification used by the server. The format is CGI/revision.
TTP_*<HeaderName>*	The value stored in the header *HeaderName*. Any header other than those listed in this table must be prefixed by HTTP_ in order for the ServerVariables collection to retrieve its value. **Note:** The server interprets any underscore (_) characters in *HeaderName* as dashes in the actual header. For example if you specify HTTP_MY_HEADER, the server searches for a header sent as MY-HEADER.
TTP_ACCEPT	Returns the value of the Accept header.
TTP_ACCEPT_LANGUAGE	Returns a string describing the language to use for displaying content.
TTP_USER_AGENT	Returns a string describing the browser that sent the request.
TTP_COOKIE	Returns the cookie string that was included with the request.
TTP_REFERER	Returns a string containing the URL of the original request when a redirect has occurred.
TTPS	Returns ON if the request came in through secure channel (SSL) or it returns OFF if the request is for a nonsecure channel.
TTPS_KEYSIZE	Number of bits in Secure Sockets Layer connection key size; for example, 128.
TTPS_SECRETKEYSIZE	Number of bits in server certificate private key; for example, 1024.
TTPS_SERVER_ISSUER	Issuer field of the server certificate.
TTPS_SERVER_SUBJECT	Subject field of the server certificate.
NSTANCE_ID	The ID for the IIS instance in textual format. If the instance ID is 1, it appears as a string. You can use this variable to retrieve the ID of the Web-server instance (in the metabase) to which the request belongs.
NSTANCE_META_PATH	The metabase path for the instance of IIS that responds to the request.
OCAL_ADDR	Returns the Server Address on which the request came in. This is important on multi-homed machines where there can be multiple IP addresses bound to a machine and you want to find out which address the request used.
OGON_USER	The Windows NT account that the user is logged into.

Table B-1 Continued

VARIABLE	DESCRIPTION
PATH_INFO	Extra path information as given by the client. You can access scripts by using their virtual path and the PATH_INFO server variable. If this information comes from a URL, it is decoded by the server before it is passed to the CGI script.
PATH_TRANSLATED	A translated version of PATH_INFO that takes the path and performs any necessary virtual-to-physical mapping.
QUERY_STRING	Query information stored in the string following the question mark (?) in the HTTP request.
REMOTE_ADDR	The IP address of the remote host making the request.
REMOTE_HOST	The name of the host making the request. If the server does not have this information, it will set REMOTE_ADDR and leave this empty.
REMOTE_USER	Unmapped user-name string sent in by the User. This is the name that is really sent by the user as opposed to the names that are modified by any authentication filter installed on the server.
REQUEST_METHOD	The method used to make the request. For HTTP, this is GET, HEAD, POST, and so on.
SCRIPT_NAME	A virtual path to the script being executed. This is used for self-referencing URLs.
SERVER_NAME	The server's host name, DNS alias, or IP address as it would appear in self-referencing URLs.
SERVER_PORT	The port number to which the request was sent.
SERVER_PORT_SECURE	A string that contains either 0 or 1. If the request is being handled on the secure port, then this will be 1. Otherwise, it will be 0.
SERVER_PROTOCOL	The name and revision of the request information protocol. The format is *protocol/revision.*
SERVER_SOFTWARE	The name and version of the server software that answers the request and runs the gateway. The format is *name/version.*
URL	Gives the base portion of the URL.

Property

The Request object has one read-only property, TotalBytes, which specifies the total number of bytes the client is sending in the body of the request.

Method

The Request object has a BinaryRead method, which retrieves data sent to the server from the client as part of a POST request.

Response Object

The Response object is used to send output to the client.

Syntax

Response [.collection|property|method](variable)

Collections

The Response object has a Cookies collection, which specifies cookie values. Using this collection, you can set cookie values.

Properties

The properties of the Response object include:

PROPERTY	DESCRIPTION
Buffer	Indicates whether page output is buffered.
CacheControl	Determines whether proxy servers are able to cache the output generated by ASP.
Charset	Appends the name of the character set to the content-type header.
ContentType	Specifies the HTTP content type for the response.
Expires	Specifies the length of time before a page cached on a browser expires.
ExpiresAbsolute	Specifies the date and time on which a page cached on a browser expires.
IsClientConnected	Indicates whether the client has disconnected from the server.
Pics	Adds the value of a PICS label to the pics-label field of the response header.
Status	The value of the status line returned by the server.

Methods

The Response object has the following methods:

METHOD	DESCRIPTION
AddHeader	Sets the HTML header *name* to *value*.
AppendToLog	Adds a string to the end of the Web server log entry for this request
BinaryWrite	Writes the given information to the current HTTP output without any character-set conversion.
Clear	Erases any buffered HTML output.
End	Stops processing the .asp file and returns the current result.
Flush	Sends buffered output immediately.
Redirect	Sends a redirect message to the browser, causing it to attempt to connect to a different URL.
Write	Writes a variable to the current HTTP output as a string.

Server Object

The Server object provides access to methods and properties on the server. Most of these methods and properties serve as utility functions.

Syntax

Server.*property*|*method*

Property

The Server object has a ScriptTimeout property which indicates the amount of time that a script can run before it times out.

Methods

The Server object has the following methods:

METHOD	DESCRIPTION
CreateObject	Creates an instance of a server component.
Execute (ASP 3.0 only)	Executes an .asp file.
GetLastError (ASP 3.0 only)	Returns an ASPError object that describes the error condition.
HTMLEncode	Applies HTML encoding to the specified string.

ETHOD	DESCRIPTION
MapPath	Maps the specified virtual path, either the absolute path on the current server or the path relative to the current page, into a physical path.
ransfer (ASP 3.0 only)	Sends all of the current state information to another .asp file for processing.
RLEncode	Applies URL encoding rules, including escape characters, to the string.

ession Object

ou can use the Session object to store information needed for a particular user ession. Variables stored in the Session object are not discarded when the user imps between pages in the application; instead, these variables persist for the ntire user session.

The Web server automatically creates a Session object when a Web page from he application is requested by a user who does not already have a session in rogress. The server destroys the Session object when the session expires or is bandoned.

yntax

ession.collection|property|method

ollections

he Session object's collections include:

OLLECTION	DESCRIPTION
Contents	Contains the items that you have added to the session with script commands.
taticObjects	Contains the objects created with the <OBJECT> tag and given session scope.

roperties

he properties of the Session object include:

PROPERTY	DESCRIPTION
CodePage	The codepage that will be used for symbol mapping.
LCID	The locale identifier.
SessionID	Returns the session identification for this user.
Timeout	The timeout period for the session state for this application, in minutes.

Methods

The methods of the Session object include:

METHOD	DESCRIPTION
Abandon	Destroys a Session object and releases its resources.
Contents.Remove (ASP 3.0 only)	Deletes an item from the Contents collection.
Contents.RemoveAll (ASP 3.0 only)	Deletes all items from the Contents collection.

Events

Scripts for the following events are declared in the global.asa file:

```
Session_OnEnd
Session_OnStart
```

APPENDIX C

ADO 2.5 Objects and Collections at a Glance

Due to space limitations, a complete reference for all ADO 2.5 objects and collections cannot be included here. Nevertheless, you can obtain a comprehensive version of this brief appendix by heading to the Apress Web site (http://www.apress.com) and looking up this title's page.

At the Web site, you will find a complete reference on the methods, properties, and events of the objects and collections, and enumerated constants for parameter values of the methods, all in a downloadable PDF file. The concise version, presented in the following table, summarizes all the ADO 2.5 objects and collections.

Table C-1. ADO 2.5 Objects and Collections

OBJECT/COLLECTION	DESCRIPTION
Command	A Command object is a definition of a specific command that you intend to execute against a data source.
Connection	A Connection object represents an open connection to a data source.
Error	An Error object contains details about data access errors pertaining to a single operation involving the provider.
Errors	The Errors collection contains all the Error objects created in response to a single failure involving the provider.
Field	A Field object represents a column of data within a common data type.
Fields	A Fields collection contains all of the Field objects of a Recordset object.
Parameter	A Parameter object represents a parameter or argument associated with a Command object based on a parameterized query or stored procedure.
Parameters	A Parameters collection contains all the Parameter objects of a Command object.
Properties	A Properties collection contains all the Property objects for a specific instance of an object.
Property	A Property object represents a dynamic characteristic of an ADO object that is defined by the provider.

Table C-1. ADO 2.5 Objects and Collections (continued)

OBJECT/COLLECTION	DESCRIPTION
Record	A Record object represents a row in a recordset, or a file or directory in a file system or Web resource.
Recordset	A Recordset object represents the entire set of records from a base table or the results of an executed command. At any time, the Recordset object only refers to a single record within the set as the current record.
Stream	A Stream object represents a stream of text or binary data.

APPENDIX D

Structured Query Language (SQL)

THIS APPENDIX SERVES AS A GUIDE TO WRITING SQL statements most commonly used with the SQL2-compliant RDBMS products. The SQL statements and examples described in this appendix should work in any RDBMS. However, implementations are slightly different from one vendor to another, in which each RDBMS vendor usually adds its own functions to the standard SQL2.

In a RDBMS, SQL can be used for

- Data manipulation, such as retrieving data, inserting new rows of data, updating rows of data, and deleting rows of data

- Data definition; for example, creating and deleting a table, an index, or a view

- Access control; that is, granting and revoking access to a certain user

- Transaction control

SQL is the language for retrieving, managing and organizing data stored in a relational database management system (RDBMS). The official standard for SQL was published by the American National Standards Institute (ANSI) and the International Standards Organization (ISO) in 1986 and was expanded in 1989. This first version of SQL is also known as SQL1. SQL1 was then expanded as SQL2 in October 1992. SQL2 is also known as SQL-92.

> **NOTE:** *In this appendix, the words "columns" and "fields" are used interchangeably, as are the words "rows" and "records."*

Table Data Types

Each column or field in a table has a data type and only data of this type can be inserted into the column. For example, if a column data type is numeric, you can only store numbers in that column, not text or dates. A list of data types specified in SQL2 is provided in Table D-1.

Table D-1. SQL2 Data Types

DATA TYPE	DESCRIPTION
CHAR (length) CHARACTER (length)	Fixed-length character strings
VARCHAR (length) CHAR VARYING (length) CHARACTER VARYING (length)	Variable-length character strings
NCHAR (length) NATIONAL CHAR (length) NATIONAL CHARACTER (length)	Fixed-length national character strings
NCHAR VARYING (length) NATIONAL CHAR VARYING (length) NATIONAL CHARACTER VARYING (length)	Variable-length national character strings
INTEGER INT	Integer numbers
SMALLINT	Small integer numbers
BIT (length)	Fixed-length bit string
BIT VARYING (length)	Variable-length bit string
NUMERICAL (precision, scale) DECIMAL (precision, scale) DEC (precision, scale)	Decimal numbers
FLOAT (precision)	Floating point numbers
REAL	Low-precision floating point numbers
DOUBLE PRECISION	High-precision floating point numbers
DATE	Calendar date
TIME (precision)	Clock time
TIMESTAMP (precision)	Date and Time
INTERVAL	Time interval

Again, different database system vendors use different data types in their products, introducing one of the practical barriers to the portability of SQL-based applications.

Determining Nullability

In addition to data types, when designing a database, you also need to determine the *nullability* of each column and whether or not a column is indexed and can contain duplicate values. A *nullable* column, by the way, can contain nulls. Nullability is often a source of confusion and is best explained with an example.

Consider a table called Friends that has two columns, Name and Phone Number. Suppose that when designing the database, you specify that the Name column is not nullable but the Phone Number column is nullable. This means that if you know someone named John Spring but do not know his telephone number, you can still store his name in the Name column without any value in the Phone Number column.

In the database jargon, you are allowed to enter a Null into the Phone Number column because the column is nullable.

In other words, you are permitted to *not* enter a value in the Phone Number column. However, if you have a telephone number but don't remember whom that number belongs to, you can't store the number without a name, because the Name column in not nullable. Note that a Null is not the same as a blank string.

Retrieving Data from a Single Table

You use a SELECT statement to retrieve data from a single table. A SELECT statement has the following syntax:

```
SELECT clause
FROM clause
[WHERE clause]
[GROUP BY clause]
[HAVING clause]
[ORDER BY clause]
```

The SELECT clause lists all the data items to be retrieved by the SELECT statement. The data items may be fields from a table, expressions to be calculated as the database engine performs the query, or constants specifying the same values to appear in every row of the query result. The list of fields can be replaced by an asterisk to include all fields in the table. The SELECT clause may contain the keyword DISTINCT to eliminate duplicate values in a column.

The FROM clause lists the tables that contain the data to be retrieved by the query.

The WHERE clause specifies a condition that must be met by data in the tables in the FROM clause for the data to be included in the query result. If the WHERE clause is not present, the query result includes all the rows from the tables.

The GROUP BY clause specifies a summary query. A summary query groups together similar rows and produces one summary row for each group.

The HAVING clause specifies a condition for the GROUP BY clause.

The ORDER BY clause sorts the query result based on data in one or more table columns. If not present, the query result presents the data in their natural order, that is, in the order the data are inserted. Data can be sorted in an ascending order or a descending order. The keyword ASC indicates sorting in an ascending order whereas the keyword DESC indicates sorting in a descending order. If neither the keyword ASC nor DESC is present, ASC is assumed.

Examples

All the examples in this section are based on Table D-2.

Table D-2. Employee Information

EMPLOYEEID	LASTNAME	FIRSTNAME	NATIONALITY	BIRTHDATE
1	Sawaki	Tomoko	Japanese	18-Dec-49
2	Burke	Michael	American	02-Mar-58
3	Callahan	Laura	American	30-Sep-63
4	Lindsay	Margaret	British	19-Oct-37
5	Buchanan	Steven	Australian	04-Oct-55
6	Lee	Keunho	Korean	02-Jun-63
7	Ramanlal	Prakash	Indian	19-Dec-60
8	Wong	Suzie	Taiwanese	09-Jun-58
9	Gomez	Andrez	Mexican	

Note that there is a Null value in the BirthDate column for Andrez Gomez in Table D-2.

The following SQL statement returns all the data in Table D-2:

```
SELECT *
FROM Employees
```

The query result looks the same as Table D-2.

The following SQL statement returns the LastName, FirstName, and Nationality columns in the table:

```
SELECT LastName, FirstName, Nationality
FROM Employees
```

The query results are given in Table D-3.

Table D-3. Query Results for LastName, FirstName, and Nationality

LASTNAME	FIRSTNAME	NATIONALITY
Sawaki	Tomoko	Japanese
Burke	Michael	American
Callahan	Laura	American
Lindsay	Margaret	British
Buchanan	Steven	Australian
Lee	Keunho	Korean
Ramanlal	Prakash	Indian
Wong	Suzie	Taiwanese
Gomez	Andrez	Mexican

The following SQL statement sorts the data by the nationality in ascending alphabetical order:

```
SELECT LastName, FirstName, Nationality
FROM Employees
ORDER BY Nationality ASC
```

The query results are displayed in Table D-4.

Table D-4. Query Results by Nationality in Ascending Order

LASTNAME	FIRSTNAME	NATIONALITY
Callahan	Laura	American
Burke	Michael	American
Buchanan	Steven	Australian
Lindsay	Margaret	British
Ramanlal	Prakash	Indian
Sawaki	Tomoko	Japanese
Lee	Keunho	Korean
Gomez	Andrez	Mexican
Wong	Suzie	Taiwanese

The following SQL statement sorts the data on the nationality and the last name. The data will first be sorted on the nationality in descending alphabetical order, and all records that have the same value in the Nationality column will be sorted on the LastName column in a ascending alphabetical order. The results are shown in Table D-5.

```
SELECT LastName, FirstName, Nationality
FROM Employees
ORDER BY Nationality DESC, LastName ASC
```

Table D-5. Query Results Based on Nationality in Descending Order, and Last Name in Ascending Order

LASTNAME	FIRSTNAME	NATIONALITY
Wong	Suzie	Taiwanese
Gomez	Andrez	Mexican
Lee	Keunho	Korean
Sawaki	Tomoko	Japanese
Ramanlal	Prakash	Indian
Lindsay	Margaret	British
Buchanan	Steven	Australian
Burke	Michael	American
Callahan	Laura	American

The following SQL statement uses the keyword DISTINCT to eliminate duplicates in nationality:

```
SELECT DISTINCT Nationality
FROM Employees
```

The previous SQL statement results in the list shown in Table D-6.

Table D-6. Query Results When Eliminating Duplications in Nationality

NATIONALITY
American
Australian
British
Indian
Japanese
Korean
Mexican
Taiwanese

The following SQL statement uses the WHERE clause to select employees whose nationality is American:

```
SELECT *
FROM Employees
WHERE Nationality = 'American'
```

The query results of the previous SQL statement are presented in Table D-7.

Table D-7. Query Results of American Nationality-Only Search

EMPLOYEEID	LASTNAME	FIRSTNAME	NATIONALITY	BIRTHDATE
2	Burke	Michael	American	02-Mar-58
3	Callahan	Laura	American	30-Sep-63

The following SQL statement selects all records whose BirthDate values are Null. It uses the IS NULL phrase to test nullability:

```
SELECT *
FROM Employees
WHERE BirthDate IS NULL
```

The query results are given in Table D-8.

Table D-8. Query Results of Null Birthdate Values

EMPLOYEEID	LASTNAME	FIRSTNAME	NATIONALITY	BIRTHDATE
9	Gomez	Andrez	Mexican	

The following SQL statement selects all records whose BirthDate values are not Null. It uses the IS NOT NULL phrase to test non-nullability:

```
SELECT *
FROM Employees
WHERE BirthDate IS NOT NULL
```

The query results are given in Table D-9.

Table D-9. Query Results for Non-Null Birthdates

EMPLOYEEID	LASTNAME	FIRSTNAME	NATIONALITY	BIRTHDATE
1	Sawaki	Tomoko	Japanese	18-Dec-49
2	Burke	Michael	American	02-Mar-58
3	Callahan	Laura	American	30-Sep-63
4	Lindsay	Margaret	British	19-Oct-37
5	Buchanan	Steven	Australian	04-Oct-55
6	Lee	Keunho	Korean	02-Jun-63
7	Ramanlal	Prakash	Indian	19-Dec-60
8	Wong	Suzie	Taiwanese	09-Jun-58

The following SQL statement selects all records whose BirthDate values are Null and whose Nationality is Japanese:

```
SELECT *
FROM Employees
WHERE BirthDate IS NULL AND Nationality = 'Japanese'
```

The previous SQL statement returns no records.

The following SQL statement selects all employees whose Employee ID is greater than 5 and sorts the resulting records by last name alphabetically in ascending order:

```
SELECT *
FROM Employees
WHERE EmployeeID > 5
ORDER BY LastName
```

The query results are provided in Table D-10.

Table D-10. Query Results of Employee ID Greater Than 5, Sorted by Last Name

EMPLOYEEID	LASTNAME	FIRSTNAME	NATIONALITY	BIRTHDATE
9	Gomez	Andrez	Mexican	
6	Lee	Keunho	Korean	02-Jun-63
7	Ramanlal	Prakash	Indian	19-Dec-60
8	Wong	Suzie	Taiwanese	09-Jun-58

The following SQL statement selects all employees whose employee ID number is not 6. It uses the <> sign to indicate inequality.

```
SELECT *
FROM Employees
WHERE EmployeeID <> 6
```

The query results are given in Table D-11.

Table D-11. Query Results of Employee ID Numbers That Are Not 6

EMPLOYEEID	LASTNAME	FIRSTNAME	NATIONALITY	BIRTHDATE
1	Sawaki	Tomoko	Japanese	18-Dec-49
2	Burke	Michael	American	02-Mar-58
3	Callahan	Laura	American	30-Sep-63
4	Lindsay	Margaret	British	19-Oct-37
5	Buchanan	Steven	Australian	04-Oct-55
7	Ramanlal	Prakash	Indian	19-Dec-60
8	Wong	Suzie	Taiwanese	09-Jun-58
9	Gomez	Andrez	Mexican	

Note that the complete list of comparison tests includes =, <>, <, <=, >, and >=.

The following SQL statement uses BETWEEN ... AND to select all employees whose employee ID number is within the range of 3 and 6, inclusive:

```
SELECT *
FROM Employees
WHERE EmployeeID BETWEEN 3 AND 6
```

The query results are provided in Table D-12.

Table D-12. Query Results of All Employee ID Numbers within 3 and 6

EMPLOYEEID	LASTNAME	FIRSTNAME	NATIONALITY	BIRTHDATE
3	Callahan	Laura	American	30-Sep-63
4	Lindsay	Margaret	British	19-Oct-37
5	Buchanan	Steven	Australian	04-Oct-55
6	Lee	Keunho	Korean	02-Jun-63

The following SQL statement uses the keyword IN to test whether an employee ID value matches one of a list of values:

```
SELECT *
FROM Employees
WHERE EmployeeID IN (1, 3, 5)
```

The query results are given in Table D-13.

Table D-13. Query Results of Employee ID Number Matching One of a List of Values

EMPLOYEEID	LASTNAME	FIRSTNAME	NATIONALITY	BIRTHDATE
1	Sawaki	Tomoko	Japanese	18-Dec-49
3	Callahan	Laura	American	30-Sep-63
5	Buchanan	Steven	Australian	04-Oct-55

Note that the following SQL statement returns the same query result as the previous SQL statement:

```
SELECT *
FROM Employees
WHERE EmployeeID = 1
OR EmployeeID = 3
OR EmployeeID = 5
```

The following SQL statement uses the keyword `LIKE` to perform pattern matching on the LastName column. It selects all employees whose last name starts with a B:

```
SELECT *
FROM Employees
WHERE LastName LIKE 'B%'
```

The query results are given in Table D-14.

Table D-14. Query Results of All Employees with Last Names Starting with B

EMPLOYEEID	LASTNAME	FIRSTNAME	NATIONALITY	BIRTHDATE
5	Buchanan	Steven	Australian	04-Oct-55
2	Burke	Michael	American	02-Mar-58

Note that in some implementations the percentage sign (%) represents the wildcard character that matches any sequence of zero or more characters and the underscore character (_) represents the wildcard character that matches any single character. However, in other implementations, the percentage sign represents the wildcard that matches any single character and the asterisk (*) represents the wildcard character that matches any sequence of zero or more characters. You should consult the documentation of the SQL product you are using.

Inserting New Rows of Data into a Table

You can insert one row of data or multiple rows of data into a table. The information in this section shows you how.

Inserting Single Row

To insert a single row of data into a table, use the following syntax:

```
INSERT INTO table [(field1[, field2[, ...]])]
VALUES (value1[, value2[, ...])
```

For example, the following SQL statement inserts a row into Table D-2, the original employee data table shown earlier:

```
INSERT INTO Employees
(EmployeeID, LastName, FirstName, Nationality)
VALUES
(10, 'Mustafa', 'Ali', 'Iranian')
```

The database engine automatically assigns a NULL value to any column whose name is missing from the column list in the INSERT statement. Consequently, all non-nullable fields must be present in the field list.

You may also omit the field list from the INSERT statement. When the field list is not present, the database engine generates a field list consisting of all fields in the table, in left-to-right sequence. Therefore, the order of values in the value list must be correct and all field values must be present.

Inserting Multiple Rows

To insert multiple rows into a table, use the following syntax. The new rows come from a different table:

```
INSERT INTO table (field1[, field2[, ...]])
SELECT clause
FROM clause
WHERE clause
```

For example, the following SQL statements insert a query result from a table called NewEmployees to the Employees table (Table D-2):

```
INSERT INTO Employees (LastName, FirstName, Nationality, BirthDate)
SELECT (Surname, FirstName, Nationality, BirthDate)
FROM NewEmployees
WHERE EmployeeID IS NOT NULL
```

Note that the corresponding field names from the source table and the target table may be different, but the data types must be the same. In the previous SQL statement, the first field of the target table is LastName and the first field of the source table is Surname.

Updating Data

You can update the values of one or more columns in selected rows of a table. To update one or more records, use the following syntax:

```
UPDATE table
SET newvalue
[WHERE clause]
```

For example, the following SQL statement changes the value of the Nationality field of the employee with the ID number of 5 in Table D-2:

```
UPDATE Employees
SET Nationality = 'American'
WHERE EmployeeID = 5
```

If the WHERE clause is not present, the UPDATE statement modifies all records in the table. For example, the following SQL statement increases the price by 10 percent for all records in the Products table, Table D-15:

```
UPDATE Products
SET UnitPrice = UnitPrice * 1.1
```

Table D-15. Products Information

PRODUCTID	PRODUCTNAME	QUANTITYPERUNIT	UNITPRICE	UNITSINSTOCK	UNITSONORDER
1	Tibani	10 boxes x 20 bags	$11.00	34	0
2	Astea	24 - 12 oz bottles	$9.00	17	40
3	Ranjabee	12 - 550 ml bottles	$12.00	13	70
4	Pakistani Sweet	48 - 6 oz jars	$22.00	34	0
5	Chef Mix	36 boxes	$21.35	0	10
6	Equippt	12 - 8 oz jars	$25.00	120	0

Deleting Rows of Data

To delete rows of data from a table, use the following syntax:

```
DELETE
FROM table
[WHERE clause]
```

For example, the following SQL statement deletes records in the Employees table whose nationality is Fijian:

```
DELETE
FROM Employees
WHERE Nationality = 'Fijian'
```

If the WHERE clause is not present, all records in the table will be deleted.

Summary Queries

With SQL you can summarize data from the database through a set of column functions. A column function takes an entire column of data as its argument and produces a single data item that summarizes the column. The six column functions are

- SUM():Calculates the total of a column of type numeric.

- AVG(): Computes the average value in a column of type numeric.

- MIN(): Finds the smallest value in a column of type numeric.

- MAX(): Finds the largest value in a column of type numeric.

- COUNT(): Counts the number of values in a column.

- COUNT(*): Counts the number of rows of the query result.

According to the ANSI/ISO SQL standard, NULL values in a column are ignored by the SUM(), AVG(), MIN(), MAX(), and COUNT() functions. However, implementations by RDBMS vendors might be different from the standard.

Examples

The following SQL statement computes the sum of the order value, the average of the order value, the minimum order value, the maximum order value, and the number of values in the OrderValue column in the Orders table, Table D-16:

```
SELECT SUM(OrderValue), AVG(OrderValue), MIN(OrderValue), MAX(OrderValue),
COUNT(OrderValue)
FROM Orders
```

Table D-16. Orders Information

ORDERID	CUSTOMERID	PRODUCTID	QUANTITY	ORDERDATE
1	1	2	3	01/01/00
2	1	3	5	02/02/00
3	2	4	4	03/03/00
4	2	3	5	04/04/00
5	2	6	66	05/05/00

The following SQL statement returns the number of rows in the Table D-2:

```
SELECT COUNT(*)
FROM Employees
```

Summary of a Group

The previous examples compute summaries of data in the whole table. It is also possible to obtain summaries of a group of rows using the GROUP BY clause and column functions.

For example, the following SQL statement groups orders by customers and gives the summaries of each group:

```
SELECT CustomerID, Sum(OrderValue) AS Sum, Avg(OrderValue) AS Average,
Min(OrderValue) AS Minimum, Max(OrderValue) AS Maximum, Count(OrderValue) AS Count
FROM Orders
GROUP BY CustomerID
```

The query results look similar to Table D-17.

Table D-17. Query Results of Grouping Orders by Customer

CUSTOMERID	SUM	AVERAGE	MINIMUM	MAXIMUM	COUNT
1	2,235.00	1,117.50	890.00	1,345.00	2
2	23,990.00	7,996.67	890.00	22,000.00	3

Retrieving Data from Multiple Tables

To retrieve data from more than one table, you can either use the keyword UNION or create a join between two tables.

UNION

The keyword UNION can be used to retrieve data from more than one table. Data from the second or next table are appended to the query result from the first table. Each table must return the same number of fields and each corresponding field from the source tables must have the same data type. If you retrieve data from two tables and the first field from the first table is an Integer, the first field from the second table must also be an Integer.

The following example retrieves data from the Employees table (Table D-2) and another table called NewEmployees, and orders the query result by last name:

```
SELECT LastName, FirstName, BirthDate
FROM Employees
UNION
SELECT Surname, FirstName, BirthDate
FROM NewEmployees
WHERE Hired = True
ORDER BY LastName ASC
```

Joins

A *join* is the query result containing data from two or more tables in which each table in the join has a matching column. When using joins, there is a possibility that tables in a join have fields with the same name. To avoid confusion as to which table a field comes from, each field in the field list of the SELECT clause is prefixed by its table name and a period, such as *tablename.fieldname*.

Because repeating the table name for each field can make the statement unnecessarily long, you are allowed to use an alias for a table name. Table name aliases are defined in the FROM clause. For instance, this following SQL statement uses table name aliases:

```
SELECT A.LastName, A.FirstName, P.Publisher
FROM Authors A, Publishers P
```

There are several types of joins, including a(n):

- inner join or equi-join

- outer join

- self join

The examples in this section use the information in Tables D-15, D-16, and D-18.

Inner Join

An inner join is a join in which the values in the columns being joined are compared using a comparison operator. In the SQL2 standard, inner joins can be specified in either the FROM or WHERE clause. This is the only type of join that SQL2 supports in the WHERE clause. Inner joins specified in the WHERE clause are known as old-style inner joins.

Inner joins return rows only when there is at least one row from both tables that matches the join condition. Inner joins eliminate the rows that do not match with a row from the other table.

The following SQL statement retrieves orders information from Table D-16. and the customer details for each order from Table D-18:

```
SELECT O.OrderID, O.OrderDate, C.CompanyName, C.Address, C.City, C.Country
FROM Orders O INNER JOIN Customers C
ON O.CustomerID = C.CustomerID
```

The query results from the previous SQL statement are shown in Table D-19.

The previous SQL statement returns the same results as the following SQL statement:

```
SELECT O.OrderID, O.OrderDate, C.CompanyName, C.Address, C.City, C.Country
FROM Orders O, Customers C
WHERE O.CustomerID = C.CustomerID
```

The SQL statement that creates the join can be filtered further, such as with the following statement to retrieve orders from U.K. customers only:

```
SELECT O.OrderID, O.OrderDate, C.CompanyName, C.Address, C.City, C.Country
FROM Orders O INNER JOIN Customers C
ON O.CustomerID = C.CustomerID
WHERE C.Country = 'UK'
```

Or, the following statement can be used to perform the same task:

```
SELECT O.OrderID, O.OrderDate, C.CompanyName, C.Address, C.City, C.Country
FROM Orders O, Customers C
WHERE O.CustomerID = C.CustomerID
AND C.Country = 'UK'
```

The following SQL statement retrieves data from Tables D-15, D-16, and D-18:

```
SELECT O.OrderID, P.ProductName, C.CompanyName, C.Address, C.City, C.Country
FROM (Orders O INNER JOIN Customers C ON O.CustomerID = C.CustomerID)
INNER JOIN Products P ON
O.ProductID = P.ProductID
```

The query results are provided in Table D-20.

Table D-18. Customer Information

CUSTOMERID	COMPANY NAME	ADDRESS	CITY	POSTAL CODE	COUNTRY	PHONE	FAX
1	Kedai Ikan Masin Lian Hin	23 Jalan Gong Kapas	Kuala Lumpur	58102	Malaysia	60-3-6265431	60-3-6265433
2	Muriels Supermarket	890 Cromwell Rd	London	SW7 2EH	UK	(171) 555-7908	(171) 555-3750
3	Crownland warehouse	377 Langley Street	Vancouver	V6T 2E7	Canada	604-2216869	604-2216769

Table D-19. Query Results of Retrieving Orders Information from One Table and Customer Information from Another Table

ORDERID	ORDERDATE	COMPANY NAME	ADDRESS	CITY	COUNTRY
1	01/01/00	Kedai Ikan Masin Lian Hin	23 Jalan Gong Kapas	Kuala Lumpur	Malaysia
2	02/02/00	Kedai Ikan Masin Lian Hin	23 Jalan Gong Kapas	Kuala Lumpur	Malaysia
3	03/03/00	Muriels Supermarket	890 Cromwell Rd	London	UK
4	04/04/00	Muriels Supermarket	890 Cromwell Rd	London	UK
5	05/05/00	Muriels Supermarket	890 Cromwell Rd	London	UK

Table D-20. Query Results of Retrieving Data from Three Tables

ORDERID	PRODUCTNAME	COMPANY NAME	ADDRESS	CITY	COUNTRY
1	Astea	Kedai Ikan Masin Lian Hin	23 Jalan Gong Kapas	Kuala Lumpur	Malaysia
2	Ranjabee	Kedai Ikan Masin Lian Hin	23 Jalan Gong Kapas	Kuala Lumpur	Malaysia
4	Ranjabee	Muriels Supermarket	890 Cromwell Rd	London	UK
3	Pakistani Sweet	Muriels Supermarket	890 Cromwell Rd	London	UK
5	Equippt	Muriels Supermarket	890 Cromwell Rd	London	UK

Outer Joins

Outer joins return all rows from at least one of the tables or views mentioned in the FROM clause, as long as those rows meet any WHERE or HAVING search conditions.

You can have a left outer join or a right outer join. In a left outer join, all rows are retrieved from the left table referenced with a left outer join. In a right outer join, all rows from the right table referenced in a right outer join.

The following SQL statement retrieves all customers and their orders from Table D-16 and D-18. Customers who don't have orders are still included in the query result, but their orders will have NULL values:

```
SELECT C.CompanyName, O.OrderID, O.OrderDate
FROM Customers C LEFT OUTER JOIN Orders O
ON C.CustomerID = O.CustomerID
```

The query results are given in Table D-21.

Table D-21. Results of Retrieving All Customers and Their Orders

COMPANY NAME	ORDERID	ORDERDATE
Kedai Ikan Masin Lian Hin	1	01/01/00
Kedai Ikan Masin Lian Hin	2	02/02/00
Muriels Supermarket	3	03/03/00
Muriels Supermarket	4	04/04/00
Muriels Supermarket	5	05/05/00
Crownland warehouse		

Note that the previous SQL statement returns the same results as the following SQL statement:

```
SELECT C.CompanyName, O.OrderID, O.OrderDate
FROM Orders O RIGHT OUTER JOIN Customers C
ON C.CustomerID = O.CustomerID
```

Self Joins

Self joins refer to relationships that a table has with itself. This type of join, for example, occurs in the Table D-22, which has a ReportTo field as well as an EmployeeID field. The ReportTo field is for storing the ID of each employee's manager. Because managers are also employees, retrieving the list of employees and their managers involves a relationship of the Employees table with itself. As an example, consider Table D-22.

Table D-22. Employee Information Requiring Self Joins

EMPLOYEEID	LASTNAME	FIRSTNAME	NATIONALITY	BIRTHDATE	REPORTTO
1	Sawaki	Tomoko	Japanese	18-Dec-49	
2	Burke	Michael	American	02-Mar-58	1
3	Callahan	Laura	American	30-Sep-63	2
4	Lindsay	Margaret	British	19-Oct-37	1
5	Buchanan	Steven	Australian	04-Oct-55	2
6	Lee	Keunho	Korean	02-Jun-63	2
7	Ramanlal	Prakash	Indian	19-Dec-60	4
8	Wong	Suzie	Taiwanese	09-Jun-58	4
9	Gomez	Andrez	Mexican		2

In Table D-22, there are two managers, Michael Burke and Margaret Lindsay. Both report to the director, Tomoko Sawaki.

The following SQL statement returns the list of employees and their immediate boss and sorts the records by employee last name:

```
SELECT A.LastName AS EmployeeLastName, A.FirstName AS EmployeeFirstName,
B.LastName AS BossLastName, B.FirstName AS BossFirstName
FROM Employees A LEFT OUTER JOIN Employees B
ON A.ReportTo = B.EmployeeID
ORDER BY A.LastName ASC
```

The query results are given in Table D-23.

Table D-23. Query Results of Returning a List of Employees and Their Immediate Boss

EMPLOYEELASTNAME	EMPLOYEEFIRSTNAME	BOSSLASTNAME	BOSSFIRSTNAME
Buchanan	Steven	Burke	Michael
Burke	Michael	Sawaki	Tomoko
Callahan	Laura	Burke	Michael
Gomez	Andrez	Burke	Michael
Lee	Keunho	Burke	Michael
Lindsay	Margaret	Sawaki	Tomoko
Ramanlal	Prakash	Lindsay	Margaret
Sawaki	Tomoko		
Wong	Suzie	Lindsay	Margaret

Data Definition

Data definition is concerned with changes to the structure of a database. This section shows you how to use SQL statements to change the structure of a database object.

Creating a Table

You can use the following syntax to create a table:

```
CREATE TABLE table
    (field1 type [(size)] [NOT NULL] [index1]
    [, field2 type [(size)] [NOT NULL] [index2]
    [, ...]]
    [, CONSTRAINT multifieldindex [, ...]])
```

Every RDBMS has its own data types, so you should consult your RDBMS documentation for the supported data types.

The following example creates a table called Products in a Microsoft SQL Server 7.0 database with the following four fields:

- ProductID (primary key, integer, non-nullable)

- ProductName (not indexed, varchar(25), non-nullable)

- UnitPrice (not indexed, small money, non-nullable)

- Description (not indexed, varchar(50), nullable)

  Here's the syntax:

```
CREATE TABLE Products
(ProductID INTEGER PRIMARY KEY,
ProductName VARCHAR(25) NOT NULL,
UnitPrice SMALLMONEY NOT NULL,
Description VARCHAR(50) NULL)
```

Dropping a Table

You can drop a table using the following syntax:

```
DROP TABLE tablename
```

For example, the following SQL statement deletes the Products table:

```
DROP TABLE Products
```

Altering a Table

You can alter the structure of a table by adding or dropping a column, for example.

To add a column, use the following syntax:

```
ALTER TABLE tablename ADD column-definition
```

For example, the following SQL statement adds a new nullable column of type integer called SupplierID to the Products table:

```
ALTER TABLE Products
ADD SupplierID Integer NULL
```

To drop a column, use the following syntax:

```
ALTER TABLE tablename DROP column-name
```

The following SQL statement drops the SupplierID column from the Products table:

```
ALTER TABLE Products DROP SupplierID
```

However, in Microsoft SQL Server you must use the word COLUMN to drop a column. Therefore, the previous SQL statement must be written like this:

```
ALTER TABLE Products DROP COLUMN SupplierID
```

CDO for NTS Objects

THIS APPENDIX CONTAINS INFORMATION ON the properties and methods for the Collaboration Data Objects for Windows NT Server (CDO for NTS) Library objects. Table E-1 summarizes each object's properties and methods.

Table E-1. CDO Properties and Methods

OBJECT	PROPERTIES	METHODS
AddressEntry	Address, Application, Class, Name, Parent, Session, Type	(none)
Attachment	Application, Class, ContentBase, ContentID, ContentLocation, Name, Parent, Session, Source, Type	Delete, ReadFromFile, WriteToFile
Attachments collection	Application, Class, Count, Item, Parent, Session	Add, Delete
Folder	Application, Class, Messages, Name, Parent, Session	(none)
Message	Application, Attachments, Class, ContentBase, ContentID, ContentLocation, HTMLText, Importance, MessageFormat, Parent, Recipients, Sender, Session, Size, Subject, Text, TimeReceived, TimeSent	Delete, Send
Messages collection	Application, Class, Count, Item, Parent, Session	Add, Delete, GetFirst, GetLast, GetNext, GetPrevious
NewMail	Bcc, Body, BodyFormat, Cc, ContentBase, ContentLocation, From, Importance, MailFormat, Subject, To, Value, Version	AttachFile, AttachURL, Send, SetLocaleIDs
Recipient	Address, Application, Class, Name, Parent, Session, Type	Delete
Recipients collection	Application, Class, Count, Item, Parent, Session	Add, Delete

Table E-1. Continued

OBJECT	PROPERTIES	METHODS
Session	Application, Class, Inbox, MessageFormat, Name, Outbox, Parent, Session, Version	GetDefaultFolder, Logoff, LogonSMTP, SetLocaleIDs

This appendix is organized by object, with the objects listed alphabetically. For each object a reference documentation for each property or method that belongs to the object is listed. The properties and methods are also organized alphabetically.

Properties Common to All CDO for NTS Library Objects

All CDO for NTS Library objects except the NewMail object expose the properties Application, Class, Parent, and Session. The Application and Session properties have the same values for all objects within a given session. The Parent property indicates the immediate parent of the object, and the Class property is an integer value that identifies the CDO for NTS Library object.

The NewMail object is self-contained and does not expose any of these properties.

All four of these common properties have read-only access in all objects. Note that for the Session object, the Parent and Session properties are assigned the value Nothing. The Session object represents the highest level in the CDO for NTS Library object hierarchy and has no parent.

Properties

Application

The read-only Application property returns the name of the active application, namely the CDO for NTS Library.

Syntax

object.Application

Data Type

String

Remarks

The Application property always contains the string Collaboration Data Objects for NTS version 1.2.

The version number of the CDO for NTS Library is available through the Session object's Version property.

Class

The read-only Class property returns the object class of the object.

Syntax

object.Class

Data Type

Long

Remarks

The Class property contains a numeric constant that identifies the CDO for NTS Library object. The possible values for the Class property are defined in Table E-2.

Table E-2. Class Property Values

CDO FOR NTS LIBRARY OBJECT	CLASS VALUE	TYPE LIBRARY CONSTANT
AddressEntry	8	CdoAddressEntry
Attachment	5	CdoAttachment
Attachments collection	18	CdoAttachments
Folder	2	CdoFolder
Message	3	CdoMsg
Messages collection	16	CdoMessages
Recipient	4	CdoRecipient
Recipients collection	17	CdoRecipients
Session	0	CdoSession

Parent

The read-only Parent property returns the parent of the object.

Syntax

```
Set objParent = object.Parent
```

Data Type

Object

Remarks

The Parent property in the CDO for NTS Library returns the *immediate* parent of an object. The immediate parent for each object is shown in Table E-3.

Table E-3. Immediate Parent for Each NTS Library Object

CDO FOR NTS LIBRARY OBJECT	IMMEDIATE PARENT IN OBJECT HIERARCHY
AddressEntry	Message
Attachment	Attachments collection
Attachments collection	Message
Folder	Session
Message	Messages collection
Messages collection	Folder, including Inbox or Outbox
Recipient	Recipients collection
Recipients collection	Message
Session	Set to Nothing

The Parent property represents the *immediate* parent of the object, rather than the *logical* parent. For example, a folder contains a Messages collection, which contains Message objects. The Parent property for a message is the immediate parent, the Messages collection, rather than the logical parent, the Folder object.

The Session object represents the highest level in the hierarchy of CDO for NTS Library objects and its Parent property is set to Nothing. The AddressEntry object does not have a true hierarchical parent but can only be obtained through the Sender property of a Message object. Its Parent property returns the Message object.

Session

The read-only Session property returns the top-level Session object associated with the specified CDO for NTS Library object.

Syntax

et objSession = object.**Session**

Data Type

)bject (Session)

Remarks

The Session object represents the highest level in the CDO for NTS Library object 1ierarchy. If you invoke the Session property of a Session object, it returns the :ame Session object.

AddressEntry Object

The AddressEntry object defines addressing information that is valid for a given messaging system.

Properties

Address

The Address property specifies the messaging address of an address entry. Read-only.

Syntax

objAddressEntry.**Address**

Data Type

String

Remarks

The AddressEntry object's Address property contains a unique string that identifies a messaging user and provides routing information for messaging systems. The format of the address string is specific to each messaging system.

Name

The Name property returns the display name or alias of the AddressEntry object as a string. Read-only.

Syntax

objAddressEntry.Name

The Name property is the default property of an AddressEntry object, meaning that *objAddressEntry* is syntactically equivalent to *objAddressEntry*.Name in Microsoft Visual Basic code.

Data Type

String

Type

The Type property specifies the address type, such as SMTP. Read-only.

Syntax

objAddressEntry.Type

Data Type

String

Remarks

The address type is usually a tag referring to the messaging system that routes messages to this address, such as SMTP. The Type property always returns SMTP in the current version of CDO for NTS.

Attachment Object

The Attachment object represents a file or message that is an attachment of a message.

Properties

ContentBase

The ContentBase property returns the Content-Base header of a MIME (Multipurpose Internet Mail Extensions) message attachment. Read-only.

Syntax

objAttach.**ContentBase**

Data Type

String

Remarks

The ContentBase property is used for MHTML (MIME HTML) support. It represents the Content-Base header for the appropriate MIME body part.

ContentID

The ContentID property returns the Content-ID header of a MIME (Multipurpose Internet Mail Extensions) message attachment. Read-only.

Syntax

objAttach.**ContentID**

Data Type

String

Remarks

The ContentID property is used for MHTML (MIME HTML) support. It represents the Content-ID header for the appropriate MIME body part.

The CDO for NTS Library does not generate Content-ID headers for outgoing messages or attachments. This property is provided to inspect an incoming message for Content-ID headers.

ContentLocation

The ContentLocation property returns the Content-Location header of a MIME (Multipurpose Internet Mail Extensions) message attachment. Read-only.

Syntax

objAttach.ContentLocation

Data Type

String

Remarks

The ContentLocation property is used for MHTML (MIME HTML) support. It represents the Content-Location header for the appropriate MIME body part.

Name

The Name property returns or sets the display name of the Attachment object as a string. Read/write (read-only for an attachment on a message in the Inbox).

Syntax

objAttach.Name

Data Type

String

Source

The Source property returns or sets information specifying the location of the data for the attachment. Read/write (read-only for an attachment on a message in the Inbox).

Syntax

objAttach.Source

Data Type

String or Object (Message)

Remarks

The Source property is not used for `CdoFileData` attachments. For `CdoEmbeddedMessage` attachments, the Source property returns or sets the `Message` object to be embedded. An embedded message is copied into the attachment at creation time.

> **NOTE:** *The* Source *property is a string except when it returns the source of a* CdoEmbeddedMessage *attachment.*

The return value or setting of the Source property depends on the value of the Type property, as described in the Table E-4.

Table E-4. Source Property Given the Type Property Value

TYPE PROPERTY	SOURCE PROPERTY
CdoFileData	Not used; contains an empty string. The source for this type of attachment must be specified in the call to the Add method.
CdoEmbeddedMessage	Specifies the Message object to be embedded.

Type

The Type property describes the attachment type. Read/write (read-only for an attachment on a message in the Inbox).

Syntax

objAttach.**Type**

Data Type

Long

Remarks

The attachment types supported by the Type property are shown in Table E-5.

Table E-5. Type Property Attachment Types

TYPE PROPERTY	VALUE	DESCRIPTION
CdoFileData	1	Attachment is the contents of a file. (Default value.)
CdoEmbeddedMessage	4	Attachment is an embedded message.

The value of the Type property determines the valid values for the Source property. Consequently, you must set Type before setting Source in order for the ReadFromFile and WriteToFile methods to work correctly.

Methods

Delete

The Delete method removes the Attachment object from the Attachments collection.

Syntax

objAttach.**Delete**

ReadFromFile

The ReadFromFile method loads the contents of an attachment from a file.

Syntax

objAttach.**ReadFromFile(***fileName***)**

Parameter

fileName (required) String: The full path and file name to read from, for example: C:\DOCUMENT\BUDGET.XLS.

WriteToFile

The WriteToFile method saves the attachment to a file in the file system.

Syntax

objAttach.**WriteToFile(** *fileName* **)**

Parameter

fileName (required) String: The full path and file name for the saved attachment, for example: C:\DOCUMENT\BUDGET.XLS.

Attachments Collection

The Attachments collection contains zero or more Attachment objects.

Properties

Count

The Count property returns the number of Attachment objects in the collection. Read-only.

Syntax

collAttachments.**Count**

Data Type

Long

Item

The Item property returns a single Attachment object from the Attachments collection. Read-only.

Syntax

collAttachments.**Item(** *index* **)**

Parameter

index Long. An integer ranging from 1 to *collAttachments*.Count.

Data Type

Object (Attachment)

Methods

Add

The `Add` method creates and returns a new `Attachment` object in the `Attachments` collection.

Syntax

```
Set objAttach = collAttachments.Add( [name] [, type] [, source] [, Content
Location] [, ContentBase] )
```

Parameters

> `collAttachments` (required): The Attachments collection object.
> `name` (optional) String: The display name of the attachment. The default value is an empty string. To allow a user to click the attachment that appears in the message and activate an associated application, supply the full file name, including the file extension.
> `type` (optional) Long: The type of attachment; either CdoFileData or CdoEmbeddedMessage. The default value is CdoFileData.
> `source` (optional) String or Object: The path and file name of the file containing the data for the attachment, or the `Message` object to be embedded. The path and file name must be in the appropriate format for the attachment type, specified by the `type` parameter. The default value is an empty string.
> `ContentLocation` (optional) String: The content location header for the appropriate body part of a MIME message attachment.
> `ContentBase` (optional) String: The content base header for the appropriate body part of a MIME message attachment.

Delete

The `Delete` method removes all the `Attachment` objects from the `Attachments` collection.

Syntax

```
ollAttachments.Delete
```

Folder Object

The Folder object represents a folder or container in a message store.

Properties

Messages

The Messages property returns a Messages collection object within the folder. Read-only.

Syntax

```
bjFolder.Messages
```

Data Type

Object (Messages collection).

Name

The Name property returns the name of the Folder object as a string. Read-only.

Syntax

```
bjFolder.Name
```

Data Type

String

Message Object

The Message object represents a single message, item, document, or form in a folder.

Properties

Attachments

The `Attachments` property returns a single Attachment object or an Attachments collection object. Read-only.

Syntax

```
Set collAttachments = objMessage.Attachments
Set objAttach = objMessage.Attachments(index)
```

Parameter

index Long: Specifies the number of the attachment within the Attachments collection. Ranges from 1 to the value specified by the Attachments collection's Coun property.

Return Values

collAttachments Object: An Attachments collection object.
objAttach: On successful return, contains the new Attachment object.

Data Type

Object (`Attachment` or `Attachments` collection)

ContentBase

The `ContentBase` property returns or sets the Content-Base header of a MIME (Multipurpose Internet Mail Extensions) message body. Read/write (read-only for a message in the Inbox).

Syntax

objMessage.`ContentBase`

Data Type

String

ontentID

he ContentID property returns or sets the Content-ID header of a MIME
Multipurpose Internet Mail Extensions) message body. Read-only.

yntax

bjAttach.**ContentID**

Data Type

tring

ontentLocation

he ContentLocation property returns or sets the Content-Location header of a
MIME (Multipurpose Internet Mail Extensions) message body. Read/write (read-
nly for a message in the Inbox).

yntax

bjMessage.**ContentLocation**

Data Type

tring

TMLText

he HTMLText property returns or sets the Hypertext Markup Language (HTML)
epresentation of the message's text. Read/write (read-only for a message in the
nbox).

yntax

bjMessage.**HTMLText**

Data Type

Object (IStream) or String

Importance

The Importance property returns or sets the importance of the message. Read/write (read-only for a message in the Inbox).

Syntax

objMessage.**Importance**

Data Type

Long

Remarks

The possible values for the Importance property are are listed in Table E-6.

Table E-6. Important Property Values for Message Object

CONSTANT	VALUE	DESCRIPTION
CdoLow	0	Low importance
CdoNormal	1	Normal importance (default)
CdoHigh	2	High importance

MessageFormat

The write-only MessageFormat property sets the encoding format of the message.

Syntax

objMessage.**MessageFormat**

Data Type

Long

Remarks

The MessageFormat property determines how a message is encoded. The possible values for the MessageFormat property are shown in Table E-7.

Table E-7. MessageFormat Property Values for the Message Object

MESSAGEFORMAT SETTING	VALUE	DESCRIPTION
CdoMime	0	The message is in MIME format.
CdoText	1	The message is in uninterrupted plain text.

The MessageFormat property is not used on incoming messages in the Inbox.

Recipients

The Recipients property returns a single Recipient object or a Recipients collection object. Read-only.

Syntax

Set *collRecips* = *objMessage*.**Recipients**
Set *objRecip* = objMessage.**Recipients(**index**)**

Parameters

collRecips Object: A Recipients collection object.
objMessage Object: The Message object.
objRecip Object: A single Recipient object.
index Long: Specifies the number of the recipient within the Recipients collection. Ranges from 1 to the value specified by the Recipients collection's Count property.

Data Type

Object (Recipient or Recipients collection)

Sender

The Sender property returns the sender of a message as an AddressEntry object. Read-only.

Syntax

Set *objAddrEntry* = *objMessage*.**Sender**

Return Value

objAddrEntry Object: The returned AddressEntry object that represents the messaging user that sent the message.

Data Type

Object (AddressEntry)

Size

The Size property returns the approximate size in bytes of the message. Read-only.

Syntax

objMessage.Size

Data Type

Long

Subject

The Subject property returns or sets the subject of the message as a string. Read/write (read-only for a message in the Inbox).

Syntax

objMessage.Subject

The Subject property is the default property of a Message object, meaning that *objMessage* is syntactically equivalent to *objMessage*.Subject in Microsoft Visual Basic code.

Data Type

String

Text

The Text property returns or sets the plain text representation of the message's text. Read/write (read-only for a message in the Inbox).

Syntax

objMessage.**Text**

Data Type

Object (IStream) or String

TimeReceived

The TimeReceived property sets or returns the date and time a message is received as a vbDate variant data type. Read-only.

Syntax

objMessage.**TimeReceived**

Data Type

Variant (vbDate format)

TimeSent

The TimeSent property sets or returns the date and time the message was sent as a vbDate variant data type. Read-only.

Syntax

objMessage.**TimeSent**

Data Type

Variant (vbDate format)

Methods

Delete

The Delete method removes the Message object from the Messages collection.

Syntax

objMessage.**Delete**

Send

The Send method sends the message to the recipients through the messaging system.

Syntax

objMessage.**Send**

Messages Collection

The Messages collection contains zero or more Message objects.

Properties

Count

The Count property returns the number of Message objects in the collection, or a very large number if the exact count is not available. Read-only.

Syntax

collMessages.**Count**

Data Type

Long

Item

The Item property returns a single Message object from the Messages collection. Read-only.

Syntax

collMessages.**Item(***index***)**

Parameter

index: A long integer ranging from 1 to the size of the Messages collection.

Data Type

Object (Message)

Methods

Add

The Add method creates and returns a new Message object in the Messages collection.

Syntax

Set objMessage = collMessages.**Add(** [subject] [, text] [, importance] **)**

Parameters

collMessages (required): The Messages collection object.
subject (optional) String: The subject line for the message.
text (optional) IStream object or String: The text of the message.
importance (optional) Long: The importance associated with the message.

Return Value

objMessage: On successful return, represents the new Message object added to the collection.

Delete

The Delete method removes all the Message objects from the Messages collection.

Syntax

`collMessages.Delete`

GetFirst

The GetFirst method returns the first Message object in the Messages collection. It returns Nothing if no first object exists.

Syntax

`Set objMessage = collMessages.GetFirst`

Return Value

objMessage: On successful return, represents the first Message object in the collection.

GetLast

The GetLast method returns the last Message object in the Messages collection. It returns Nothing if no last object exists.

Syntax

`Set objMessage = collMessages.GetLast`

Return Value

objMessage: On successful return, represents the last Message object in the collection.

GetNext

The GetNext method returns the next Message object in the Messages collection. It returns Nothing if no next object exists, for example if already positioned at the end of the collection.

Set *objMessage* = *collMessages*.**GetNext**

Return Value

objMessage: On successful return, represents the next Message object in the collection.

GetPrevious

The GetPrevious method returns the previous Message object in the Messages collection. It returns Nothing if no previous object exists, for example, if the pointer is already positioned at the beginning of the collection.

Set *objMessage* = *collMessages*.**GetPrevious**

Return Value

objMessage: Upon successful return, represents the previous Message object in the collection.

NewMail Object

The NewMail object provides for sending a message with very few lines of code.

Properties

Bcc

The Bcc property adds to the list of blind copy (Bcc) recipients for the NewMail object. Write-only.

Syntax

objNewMail.**Bcc**

Data Type

String

Body

The Body property sets the text of the NewMail object. Write-only.

Syntax

objNewMail.**Body**

Data Type

Object (IStream) or String

BodyFormat

The BodyFormat property sets the text format of the NewMail object. Write-only.

Syntax

objNewMail.**BodyFormat**

Data Type

Long

Remarks

BodyFormat can contain exactly one of the values listed in Table E-8.

Table E-8. BodyFormat Values for the NewMail Object

BODYFORMAT SETTING	VALUE	DESCRIPTION
CdoBodyFormatHTML	0	The Body property is to include Hypertext Markup Language (HTML).
CdoBodyFormatText	1	The Body property is to be exclusively in plain text (default value).

Cc

The Cc property adds to the list of copy (Cc) recipients for the NewMail object. Write-only.

`objNewMail`.`Cc`

String

ContentBase

The `ContentBase` property sets a base for all URLs relating to the `NewMail` object's message body. Write-only.

Syntax

`objNewMail`.`ContentBase`

Data Type

String

ContentLocation

The `ContentLocation` property sets an absolute or relative path for all URLs relating to the `NewMail` object's message body. Write-only.

Syntax

`objNewMail`.`ContentLocation`

Data Type

String

From

The `From` property sets the full messaging address to be used for the sender of the `NewMail` object. Write-only.

Syntax

objNewMail.**From**

Data Type

String

Importance

The Importance property sets the importance associated with the NewMail object. Write-only.

Syntax

objNewMail.**Importance**

Data Type

Long

Remarks

The possible values for the Importance property are listed in Table E-9.

Table E-9. Importance property values for NewMail object

CONSTANT	VALUE	DESCRIPTION
CdoLow	0	Low importance
CdoNormal	1	Normal importance (default)
CdoHigh	2	High importance

MailFormat

The MailFormat property sets the encoding for the NewMail object. Write-only.

Syntax

objNewMail.**MailFormat**

Data Type

Long

Remarks

`MailFormat` can contain exactly one of the values shown in Table E-10.

Table E-10. MailFormat Values for the NewMail Object

MAILFORMAT SETTING	VALUE	DESCRIPTION
CdoMailFormatMime	0	The NewMail object is to be in MIME format.
CdoMailFormatText	1	The NewMail object is to be in uninterrupted plain text (default value).

Subject

The `Subject` property sets the subject of the `NewMail` object as a string. Write-only.

Syntax

objNewMail.`Subject`

Data Type

String

To

The `To` property adds to the list of principal (To) recipients for the `NewMail` object. Write-only.

Syntax

objNewMail.`To`

Data Type

String

Value

The Value property sets the value and contents of an additional header for the NewMail object. Write-only.

Syntax

objNewMail.**Value**(*header*) = *strHdrValue*

Parameter

header: A character string containing the name of the header to be added.

Setting

strHdrValue: A character string containing the value of the header to be added.

Data Type

String

Version

The Version property returns the version of the CDO for NTS Library. Read-only.

Syntax

objNewMail.**Version**

Data Type

String

Methods

AttachFile

The AttachFile method adds an attachment to the message by reading a file.

Syntax

objNewMail.**AttachFile**(*Source* [, *FileName*] [, *EncodingMethod*])

Parameters

Source (required) IStream object or String: The full path and file name of the file
to be attached to the message, or a pointer to an IStream object containing the
file data.

FileName (optional) String: The file name to appear in the attachment's placeholder in the message. If *FileName* is not supplied, the file name from the *Source*
parameter is used.

EncodingMethod (optional) Long: The manner of encoding the attachment. The
possible values are shown in Table E-11.

Table E-11. EncodingMethod Values for AttachFile

ENCODINGMETHOD SETTING	VALUE	DESCRIPTION
doEncodingUUencode	0	The attachment is to be in UUEncode format (default).
doEncodingBase64	1	The attachment is to be in base 64 format.

AttachURL

The AttachURL method adds an attachment to the message and associates a
Uniform Resource Locator (URL) with the attachment.

Syntax

objNewMail.**AttachURL**(*Source*, *ContentLocation* [, *ContentBase*] [, *EncodingMethod*])

Parameters

Source (required) IStream object or String: The full path and file name of the resource to be attached to the message, or a pointer to an IStream object containing
the file data.

ContentLocation (required) String: The absolute or relative prefix for the URL that
the rendering client can use to reference this attachment.

ContentBase (optional) String: A base for the URL used to reference this attachment.

EncodingMethod (optional) Long: The manner of encoding the attachment. The
possible values are shown in Table E-12.

Table E-12. EncodingMethod Values for AttachURL

ENCODINGMETHOD SETTING	VALUE	DESCRIPTION
CdoEncodingUUencode	0	The attachment is to be in UUEncode format (default).
CdoEncodingBase64	1	The attachment is to be in base 64 format.

Send

The Send method sends the NewMail object to the specified recipients.

Syntax

objNewMail.**Send(** [*From*] [, *To*] [, *Subject*] [, *Body*] [, *Importance*] **)**

Parameters

From (optional) String: The full messaging address to be identified as the sender.
To (optional) String: A list of full messaging addresses of recipients. The individual recipient addresses are separated by semicolons.
Subject (optional) String: The subject line for the message.
Body (optional) IStream object or String: The text of the message.
Importance (optional) Long: The importance associated with the message.

SetLocaleIDs

The SetLocaleIDs method sets identifiers that define a messaging user's locale.

Syntax

objNewMail.**SetLocaleIDs(***CodePageID***)**

Parameter

CodePageID (required) Long: The code page identifier to be used for this messaging user.

Recipient Object

The Recipient object represents a recipient of a message.

Properties

Address

The Address property specifies the full messaging address for the recipient. Read/write (read-only for a recipient on a message in the Inbox).

Syntax

objRecip.**Address**

Data Type

String

Name

The Name property returns or sets the name of the Recipient object as a string. Read/write (read-only for a recipient on a message in the Inbox).

Syntax

objRecip.**Name**

Data Type

String

Type

The Type property specifies the recipient type of the Recipient object, that is, whether it is a To, Cc, or Bcc recipient. Read/write (read-only for a recipient on a message in the Inbox).

Syntax

objRecip.**Type**

Data Type

Long

Remarks

The Type property has the defined values shown in Table E-13.

Table E-13. Type Property Values for Recipient Object

RECIPIENT TYPE	VALUE	DESCRIPTION
CdoTo	1	The recipient is on the To line (default).
CdoCc	2	The recipient is on the Cc line.
CdoBcc	3	The recipient is on the Bcc line.

Method

Delete

The Delete method removes the Recipient object from the Recipients collection.

Syntax

*objRecip.*Delete

Recipients Collection

The Recipients collection object contains zero or more Recipient objects and specifies the recipients of a message.

Properties

Count

The Count property returns the number of Recipient objects in the collection. Read-only.

Syntax

*collRecips.*Count

Data Type

Long

Item

The Item property returns a single Recipient object from the Recipients collection. Read-only.

Syntax

collRecips.**Item(***index***)**

Parameter

index: A long integer ranging from 1 to *collRecips*.Count, or a string that specifies the name of the object.

Data Type

Object (Recipient)

Methods

Add

The Add method creates and returns a new Recipient object in the Recipients collection.

Syntax

Set *objRecip* = *collRecips*.**Add(** [*name*] [, *address*] [, *type*]**)**

Parameters

name (optional) String: The display name of the recipient. When this parameter is not present, the new Recipient object's Name property is set to an empty string.
address (optional). String: The full messaging address of the recipient. When this parameter is not present, the new Recipient object's Address property is set to an empty string.
type (optional) Long: The recipient type; the initial value for the new recipient's Type property. The values shown in Table E-14 are valid.

Table E-14. *Recipient Type Values*

RECIPIENT TYPE	VALUE	DESCRIPTION
CdoTo	1	The recipient is on the To line (default).
CdoCc	2	The recipient is on the Cc line.
CdoBcc	3	The recipient is on the Bcc line.

Return Value

objRecip: On successful return, represents the new Recipient object added to the collection.

Delete

The Delete method removes all the Recipient objects from the Recipients collection.

Syntax

collRecips.**Delete**

Session Object

The Session object contains session-wide settings and options.

Properties

Inbox

The Inbox property returns a Folder object representing the current messaging user's Inbox folder. Read-only.

Syntax

objSession.**Inbox**

Data Type

Object (Folder)

essageFormat

he MessageFormat property returns or sets the default message encoding.
ead/write.

yntax

jSession.MessageFormat

ata Type

ong

emarks

he MessageFormat property has the defined values shown in Table E-15.

able E-15. MessageFormat Values for Session Object

ESSAGEFORMAT SETTING	VALUE	DESCRIPTION
doMime	0	The message is in MIME format.
doText	1	The message is in uninterrupted plain text (default value).

he MessageFormat property defaults to CdoMime. It serves as the default value for
ne MessageFormat property of the Message object.

ame

he Name property returns the display name used to log on to this session.
ead-only.

yntax

bjSession.Name

Data Type

tring

Outbox

The Outbox property returns a Folder object representing the current messaging user's Outbox folder. Read-only.

Syntax

objSession.**Outbox**

Data Type

Object (Folder)

Version

The Version property returns the version of the CDO for NTS Library. Read-only.

Syntax

objSession.**Version**

Data Type

String

Methods

GetDefaultFolder

The GetDefaultFolder method returns a Folder object from a message store.

Syntax

Set *objFolder* = *objSession*.**GetDefaultFolder(***folderType***)**

Parameter

FolderType (required) Long: The folder type. This parameter can have exactly one of the values shown in Table E-16.

Table E-16. FolderType Values for Session object

FOLDERTYPE STTING	DECIMAL VALUE	MEANING
CdoDefaultFolderInbox	1	The CDO for NTS Library's Inbox.
CdoDefaultFolderOutbox	2	The CDO for NTS Library's Outbox.

Return Value

objFolder: On successful return, contains the store's default Folder object of the specified type. When the folder does not exist, GetDefaultFolder returns Nothing.

Logoff

The Logoff method uninitializes the Session object.

Syntax

objSession.**Logoff( )**

LogonSMTP

The LogonSMTP method initializes the Session object.

Syntax

objSession.**LogonSMTP(**DisplayName, Address**)**

Parameters

DisplayName (required) String: The display name to use for the messaging user logging on, such as John Q. Doe.
Address (required) String: The full e-mail address to use for the messaging user logging on, such as \jdoe@company.com.

SetLocaleID

The SetLocaleIDs method sets identifiers that define a messaging user's locale.

Syntax

*objSession.***SetLocaleIDs***(CodePageID)*

Parameter

CodePageID (required) Long: The code page identifier to be used for this messaging user.

IIS Applications Performance Benchmarking

IIS APPLICATIONS CONSTITUTE A RELATIVELY NEW technology and can be considered an enhancement to the ever popular Active Server Pages (ASP). But, what performance advantages do you get with an IIS application as compared with an ASP application?

To answer that question, three benchmark test results are presented in this appendix. All tests were done on an AMD 350Mhz machine with 64MB RAM running Personal Web Server on a Windows 98 operating system. These tests included Server Variables 1, Server Variables 2, and Database Access.

For each type of test, an ASP application and an IIS application were written, and the code for both the ASP application and the WebClass was basically the same. In all of the ASP applications, no COM component was used.

Each operation category was performed five times for each application, and the results were averaged. The Visual Basic Timer function was used to measure performance in both types of applications. The Timer function returns a number representing the number of seconds elapsed since midnight, precise to hundredths of a second.

The function was invoked twice, once at the beginning of the process and once at the end. By subtracting the first number from the second, the result indicates how long (in hundredths of a second) it takes the Web server to complete the process. The results of the three tests are provided at the end of this appendix.

Server Variables 1

In this test, both the IIS application and ASP application read 16 server variables and sent them to the browser. The code of the ASP application is given in Listing F-1 and the code for the IIS application is given in Listings F-2 and F-3.

Listing F-2 is the ASP file of the IIS application and Listing F-3 is the code in the WebClass. Note that in Listing F-2 the code generated by Visual Basic has been modified to include the Timer function at the beginning and end of the code to measure the elapsed time for the operation.

Listing F-1

```
<%
  Application("t1") = timer

  Response.Write "ALL_HTTP:" & _
    Request.ServerVariables("ALL_HTTP") & "<br>"
  Response.Write "ALL_RAW:" & _
    Request.ServerVariables("ALL_RAW") & "<br>"
  Response.Write "APPL_MD_PATH:" & _
    Request.ServerVariables("APPL_MD_PATH") & "<br>"
  Response.Write "APPL_PHYSICAL_PATH:" & _
    Request.ServerVariables("APPL_PHYSICAL_PATH") & "<br>"
  Response.Write "LOCAL_ADDR:" & _
    Request.ServerVariables("LOCAL_ADDR") & "<br>"
  Response.Write "PATH_INFO:" & _
    Request.ServerVariables("PATH_INFO") & "<br>"
  Response.Write "PATH_TRANSLATED" & _
    Request.ServerVariables("PATH_TRANSLATED") & "<br>"
  Response.Write "REMOTE_ADDR" & _
    Request.ServerVariables("REMOTE_ADDR") & "<br>"
  Response.Write "REMOTE_HOST" & _
    Request.ServerVariables("REMOTE_HOST") & "<br>"
  Response.Write "REQUEST_METHOD:" & _
    Request.ServerVariables("REQUEST_METHOD") & "<br>"
  Response.Write "SCRIPT_NAME" & _
    Request.ServerVariables("SCRIPT_NAME") & "<br>"
  Response.Write "SERVER_NAME:" & _
    Request.ServerVariables("SERVER_NAME") & "<br>"
  Response.Write "SERVER_PORT:" & _
    Request.ServerVariables("SERVER_PORT") & "<br>"
  Response.Write "SERVER_PROTOCOL:" & _
    Request.ServerVariables("SERVER_PROTOCOL") & "<br>"
  Response.Write "SERVER_SOFTWARE:" & _
    Request.ServerVariables("SERVER_SOFTWARE") & "<br>"
  Response.Write "URL:" & Request.ServerVariables("URL") & "<br>"

Application("t2") = timer
%>
```

Listing F-2

```
Application("t1") = timer
Server.ScriptTimeout=600
Response.Buffer=True
Response.Expires=0

If (VarType(Application("~WC~WebClassManager")) = 0) Then
    Application.Lock
    If (VarType(Application("~WC~WebClassManager")) = 0) Then
            Set Application("~WC~WebClassManager") = _
                Server.CreateObject("WebClassRuntime.WebClassManager")
    End If
    Application.UnLock
End If
Application("~WC~WebClassManager").ProcessNoStateWebClass _
            "Test1.WebClass1", _
            Server, _
            Application, _
            Session, _
            Request, _
            Response
Application("t2") = timer
%>
```

Listing F-3

```
Private Sub WebClass_Start()
Response.Write "ALL_HTTP:" & Request.ServerVariables("ALL_HTTP") & "<br>"
 Response.Write "ALL_RAW:" & Request.ServerVariables("ALL_RAW") & "<br>"
 Response.Write "APPL_MD_PATH:" & _
   Request.ServerVariables("APPL_MD_PATH") & "<br>"
Response.Write "APPL_PHYSICAL_PATH:" & _
   Request.ServerVariables("APPL_PHYSICAL_PATH") & "<br>"
Response.Write "LOCAL_ADDR:" & _
   Request.ServerVariables("LOCAL_ADDR") & "<br>"
Response.Write "PATH_INFO:" & _
   Request.ServerVariables("PATH_INFO") & "<br>"
Response.Write "PATH_TRANSLATED" & _
   Request.ServerVariables("PATH_TRANSLATED") & "<br>"
Response.Write "REMOTE_ADDR" & _
   Request.ServerVariables("REMOTE_ADDR") & "<br>"
```

```
    Response.Write "REMOTE_HOST" & _
      Request.ServerVariables("REMOTE_HOST") & "<br>"
    Response.Write "REQUEST_METHOD:" & _
      Request.ServerVariables("REQUEST_METHOD") & "<br>"
    Response.Write "SCRIPT_NAME" & _
      Request.ServerVariables("SCRIPT_NAME") & "<br>"
    Response.Write "SERVER_NAME:" & _
      Request.ServerVariables("SERVER_NAME") & "<br>"
    Response.Write "SERVER_PORT:" & _
      Request.ServerVariables("SERVER_PORT") & "<br>"
    Response.Write "SERVER_PROTOCOL:" & _
      Request.ServerVariables("SERVER_PROTOCOL") & "<br>"
    Response.Write "SERVER_SOFTWARE:" & _
      Request.ServerVariables("SERVER_SOFTWARE") & "<br>"
    Response.Write "URL:" & Request.ServerVariables("URL") & "<br>"

End Sub
```

The code that is used to read the starting and end times of each test is given in Listing F-4. The same code is also used for the second and third tests.

Listing F-4

```
<%
  Response.Write "End:" & Application("t2") & "<br>"
  Response.Write "Start:" & Application("t1")
%>
```

Server Variables 2

The Server Variables 2 test was that same as Server Variables 1, except that the process was repeated 100 times with a loop such as

```
For I = 1 to 100
  <the code from previous test>
Next
```

Server Variables 2 was conducted because the Server Variables 1 proved too easy for the IIS application.

In Server Variables 1, the two Timer function invocations resulted in the same number, which provides no useful information other than the assurance that the process took less than 10 milliseconds.

atabase Access

ne third test, Database Access, performed three database operations: Insert, elect, and Delete. It first inserted three hundred records into an empty Access atabase table, and then selected all the records and displayed them in an HTML age before deleting all the records.

The code for the ASP application in this test is given in Listing F-5. Listings -6 and F-7 provide the code for the IIS application. Listing F-6 provides the code r the ASP file and Listing F-7 provides the code in the IIS application's WebClass.

sting F-5

```
 @Language="VBScript"%>

Application("t1") = timer
strConnectionString = "DRIVER={Microsoft Access Driver (*.mdb)};" & _
   "DBQ=" & Server.MapPath("dbs\db01.mdb")
strSQL = "INSERT INTO Products" & _
   " (Category, Manufacturer, ProductName)" & _
   " VALUES (4, 'Universal Teeth', 'Kidz.Toothbrush')"
Set cn = Server.CreateObject("ADODB.Connection")
cn.Open strConnectionString

'Insert records
For i = 1 to 300
   cn.Execute strSQL
Next

strSQL = "SELECT * FROM Products"
Set rs = Server.CreateObject("ADODB.Recordset")
rs.Open strSQL, cn

Do Until rs.EOF
   Response.Write "ProductID:" & rs("ProductID") & "<br>" & _
     "Manufacturer:" & rs("Manufacturer") & "<br>" & _
     "ProductName:" & rs("ProductName")
   rs.MoveNext
Loop
rs.Close
Set rs = Nothing
strSQL = "DELETE FROM Products"
cn.Execute strSQL
cn.Close
```

```
      Set cn = Nothing
      Application("t2") = timer


%>
```

Listing F-6

```
<%
Application("t1") = timer
Server.ScriptTimeout=600
Response.Buffer=True
Response.Expires=0

If (VarType(Application("~WC~WebClassManager")) = 0) Then
      Application.Lock
      If (VarType(Application("~WC~WebClassManager")) = 0) Then
            Set Application("~WC~WebClassManager") =
Server.CreateObject("WebClassRuntime.WebClassManager")
      End If
      Application.UnLock
End If

Application("~WC~WebClassManager").ProcessNoStateWebClass _
            "Project1.WebClass1", _
            Server, _
            Application, _
            Session, _
            Request, _
            Response
Application("t2") = timer

%>
```

Listing F-7

```
Private Sub WebClass_Start()
  Dim strConnectionString As String
  Dim strSQL As String
  Dim i As Integer
  Dim cn As ADODB.Connection
  Dim rs As ADODB.Recordset
```

```
strConnectionString = "DRIVER={Microsoft Access Driver (*.mdb)}; " & _
   "DBQ=" & Server.MapPath("dbs\db01.mdb")
strSQL = "INSERT INTO Products" & _
   " (Category, Manufacturer, ProductName)" & _
   " VALUES (4, 'Universal Teeth', 'Kidz.Toothbrush')"
Set cn = New ADODB.Connection
cn.Open strConnectionString

'Insert records
For i = 1 To 300
   cn.Execute strSQL
Next i

strSQL = "SELECT * FROM Products"
Set rs = New ADODB.Recordset
rs.Open strSQL, cn

Do Until rs.EOF
   Response.Write "ProductID:" & rs("ProductID") & "<br>" & _
      "Manufacturer:" & rs("Manufacturer") & "<br>" & _
      "ProductName:" & rs("ProductName")
   rs.MoveNext
Loop
rs.Close
Set rs = Nothing

strSQL = "DELETE FROM Products"
cn.Execute strSQL
cn.Close
Set cn = Nothing

End Sub
```

Test Results

The results of the ASP applications are given in Table F-1 and those of the IIS applications are in Table F-2.

Table F-1. Test Results for ASP Applications

	TEST 1	TEST 2	TEST 3	TEST 4	TEST 5	AVERAGE
Server Variables 1	0.06s	0.06s	0.06s	0.00s	0.05s	**0.046s**
Server Variables 2	5.05s	4.28s	3.85s	4.01s	4.07s	**4.252s**
Database Access	4.33s	4.45s	4.77s	4.72s	4.78s	**4.61s**

Table F-2. Test Results for IIS Applications

	TEST 1	TEST 2	TEST 3	TEST 4	TEST 5	AVERAGE
Server Variables 1	0.00s	0.00s	0.00s	0.00s	0.00s	**0.00s**
Server Variables 2	0.16s	0.16s	0.16s	0.16s	0.16s	**0.16s**
Database Access	4.01s	3.57s	3.35s	3.39s	3.68s	**3.60s**

Index

C